Nightmares
& Fairy Tales

Once Upon a Time...

Nightmares & Fairy Tales

Volume One: Once upon a Time...

written by
Serena Valentino

art by
FSc

lettering by
Joshua Archer & FSc

introduction by
Tommy Kovac

pin-ups by
Eric Jones
Jhonen Vasquez
Roman Dirge

editrix
Julia Dvorin

Published by SLG Publishing

PRESIDENT & PUBLISHER
Dan Vado

EDITOR-IN-CHIEF
Jennifer de Guzman

DIRECTOR OF SALES
Deb Moskyok

PRODUCTION ASSISTANT
Eleanor Lawson

SLG Publishing
P.O. Box 26427
San Jose, CA 95159-6427

Nightmares & Fairytales Volume One: Once Upon a Time... collects issues 1-6 of the SLG Publishing series *Nightmares and Fairy Tales*.

www.slavelabor.com
www.serenavalentino.com
www.fscwasteland.com

Second Printing: July 2004
ISBN 0-943151-87-2

Lovingly
dedicated to
My Husband Eric
&
My Sister Jesse
·· Serena

Once upon a time, a
bratty little princess named
Serena heard wondrous tales, then
placed them on her be-spelled loom
and wove the darkest tapestries
from them. She knew how to spin
them, and twist and entwine them
into dangerous NEW shapes that
thrill and enchant those who read
them.   Was she a witch princess?
or was she influenced by the strange
little rag doll that slumped on a stool
beside her loom, staring and staring? The
doll's name is Annabelle, and you shall soon
fall under her spell within the pages of this
book.

I have heard tell that soon after these stories
were written, they and the mysterious doll named
Annabelle somehow came to be in a faraway place
and fell into the possession of another talented
princess called FSc. Under Annabelle's watchful
eyes FSc took up pen and paper and unspooled the
most wondrous images to accompany the Princess
Serena's darkly hypnotic stories. There was
a spark of lightning, and a great, ominous
BARROOM of thunder as the words and
the pictures met and fused.

The art of storytelling is
a powerful magic.

Nightmares and Fairytales, by Serena Valentino and FSc
's an exciting witch's brew of vengeful demons, sad ghosts,
esbian vampires, evil nuns and more. Serena creates the most
perfectly clever plot twists that make me say, Why didn't
 think of that? There is a deceptive simplicity to Serena's
writing, but it has a scorpion's tail. She knows what she's
doing, and you are in good hands.

 I have to rein myself in from gushing about Serena, since
she is a personal friend. Let me just say that one of the
things I like most about her is that she is genuinely sweet,
yet also has a wicked sense of humor, and a keen intellect.
She is ladylike, cultured, well-mannered and can cuss like a
sailor.

 Serena lives and breathes her own spooky, rarified world
of beneficent darkness, and welcomes everyone to join her
there for tea. She is the real thing, a natural born gloom
cookie. You should see the way her fans' faces light up at
conventions, as she calls them Sweetie, and shows genuine
interest in them and their lives. It's all very squishy, as
Serena would say.

 Serena has worked with several different artists, and
when she started working with FSc, she told me how
grateful she was to be working with an artist who just
seemed to know intuitively how to translate Serena's words
into images, with minimal art direction. And I think it's just
cool to have a comic book both written and illustrated by
talented ladies.

 As an artist, I greatly admire FSc's work, and wasn't
at all surprised to hear other artists and creators buzzing
excitedly about her. Everybody loves FSc. There's so much
movement and momentum in her drawings, a sort of wild
grace that pulls you in with vertiginous perspectives and
playfully strange details. Then sudden, slashing violence!

 FSc is an artist with a vision. She creates a surprising,
cute world I'd love to live in, if it weren't so dangerous and
lined with sharp teeth.

 Curl up in a big chair with this book, and if it's not
raining outside, pretend that it is.

Tommy Kovac
Creator of Stitch,
Skelebunnies, and Autumn,
published by SLG
www.tommykovac.com

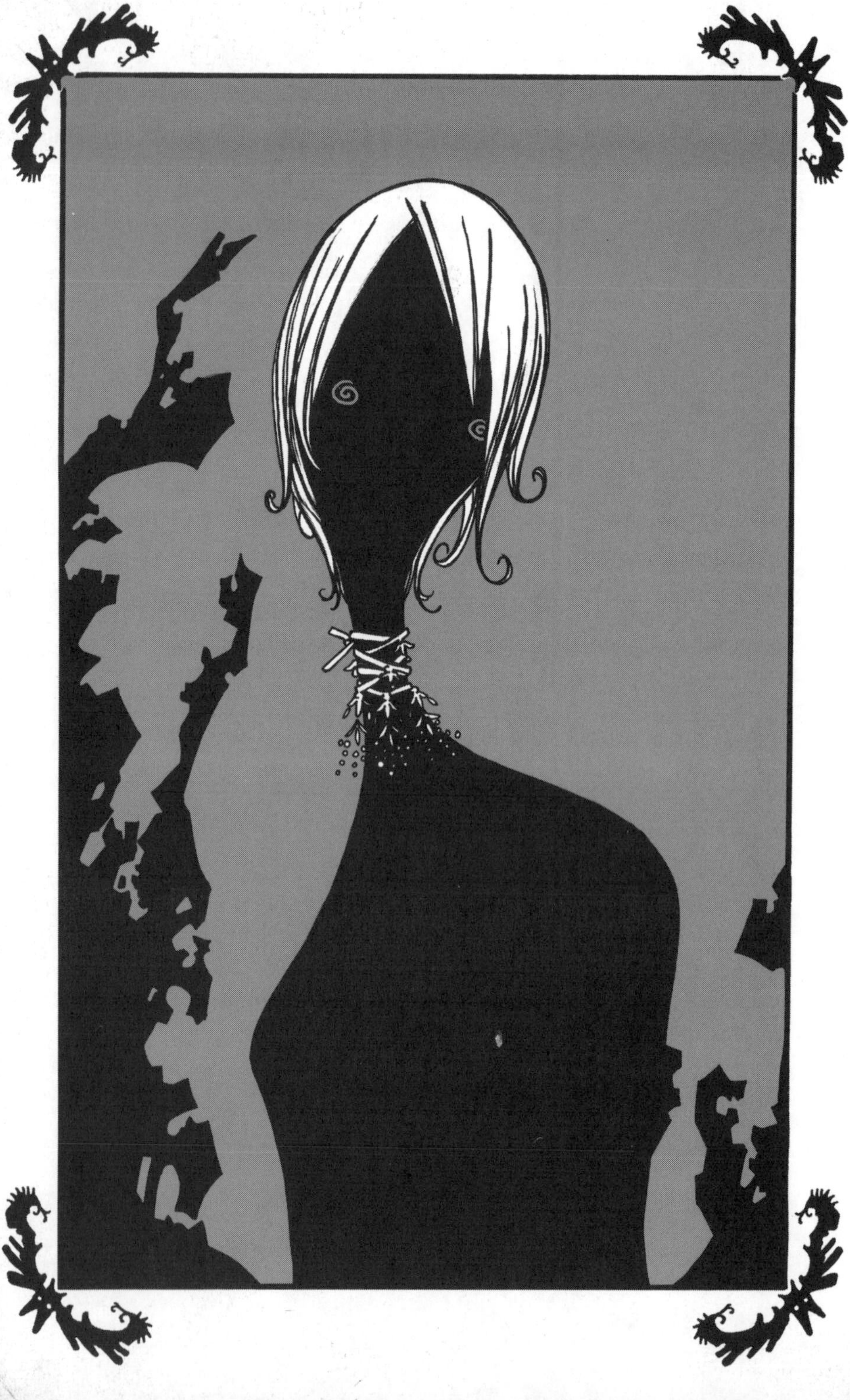

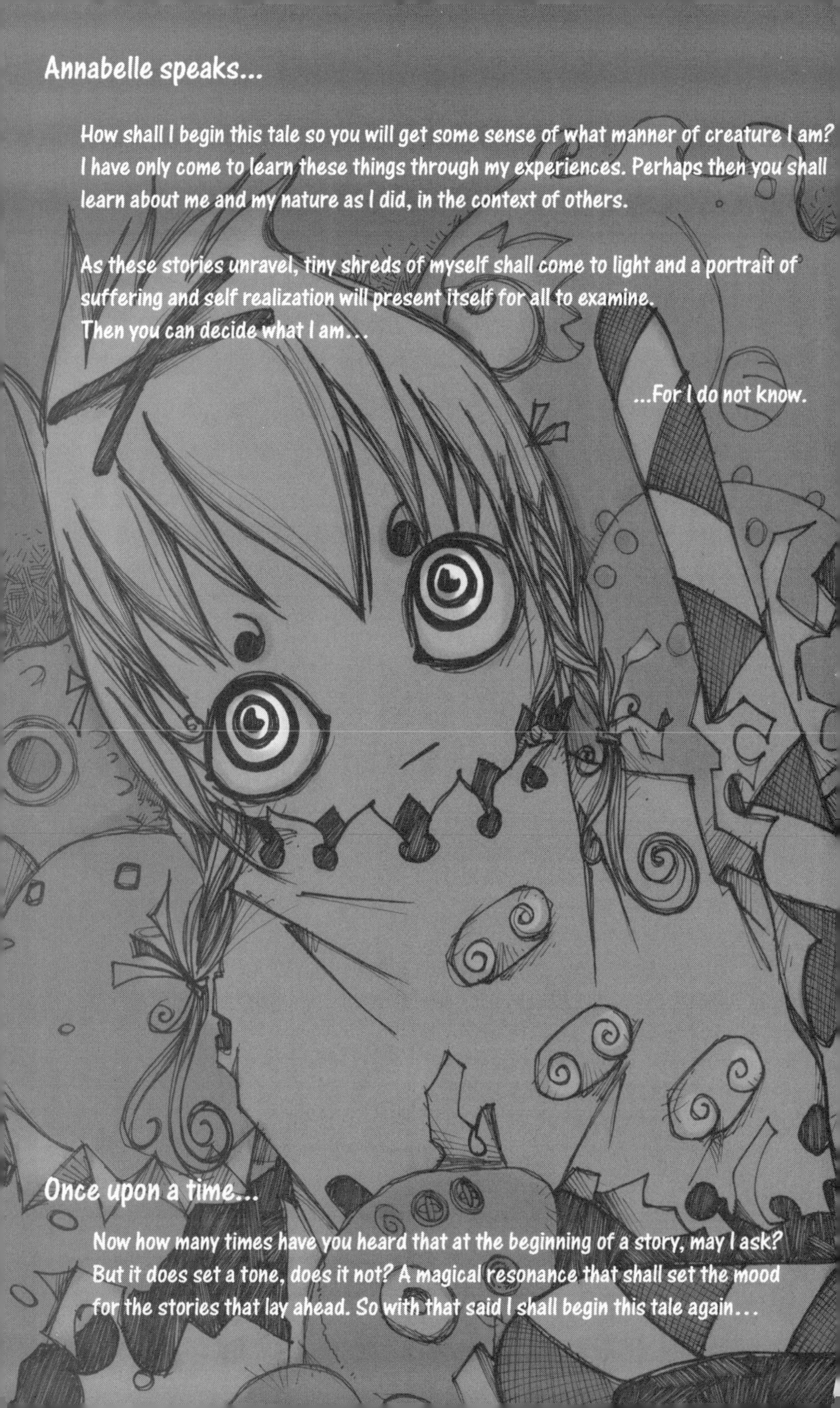

Annabelle speaks...

How shall I begin this tale so you will get some sense of what manner of creature I am? I have only come to learn these things through my experiences. Perhaps then you shall learn about me and my nature as I did, in the context of others.

As these stories unravel, tiny shreds of myself shall come to light and a portrait of suffering and self realization will present itself for all to examine.
Then you can decide what I am...

...For I do not know.

Once upon a time...

Now how many times have you heard that at the beginning of a story, may I ask? But it does set a tone, does it not? A magical resonance that shall set the mood for the stories that lay ahead. So with that said I shall begin this tale again...

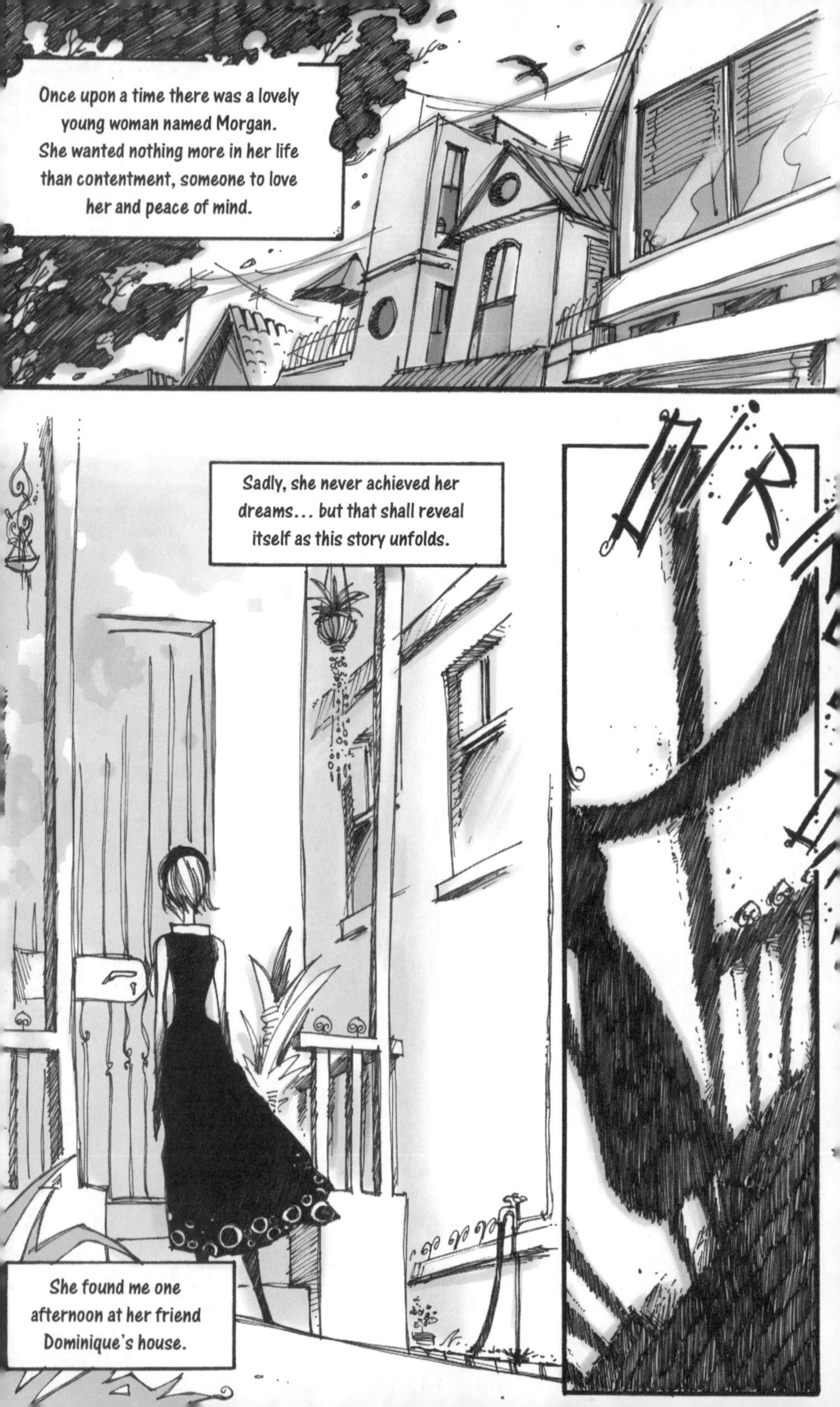
Once upon a time there was a lovely young woman named Morgan. She wanted nothing more in her life than contentment, someone to love her and peace of mind.
Sadly, she never achieved her dreams... but that shall reveal itself as this story unfolds.
She found me one afternoon at her friend Dominique's house.

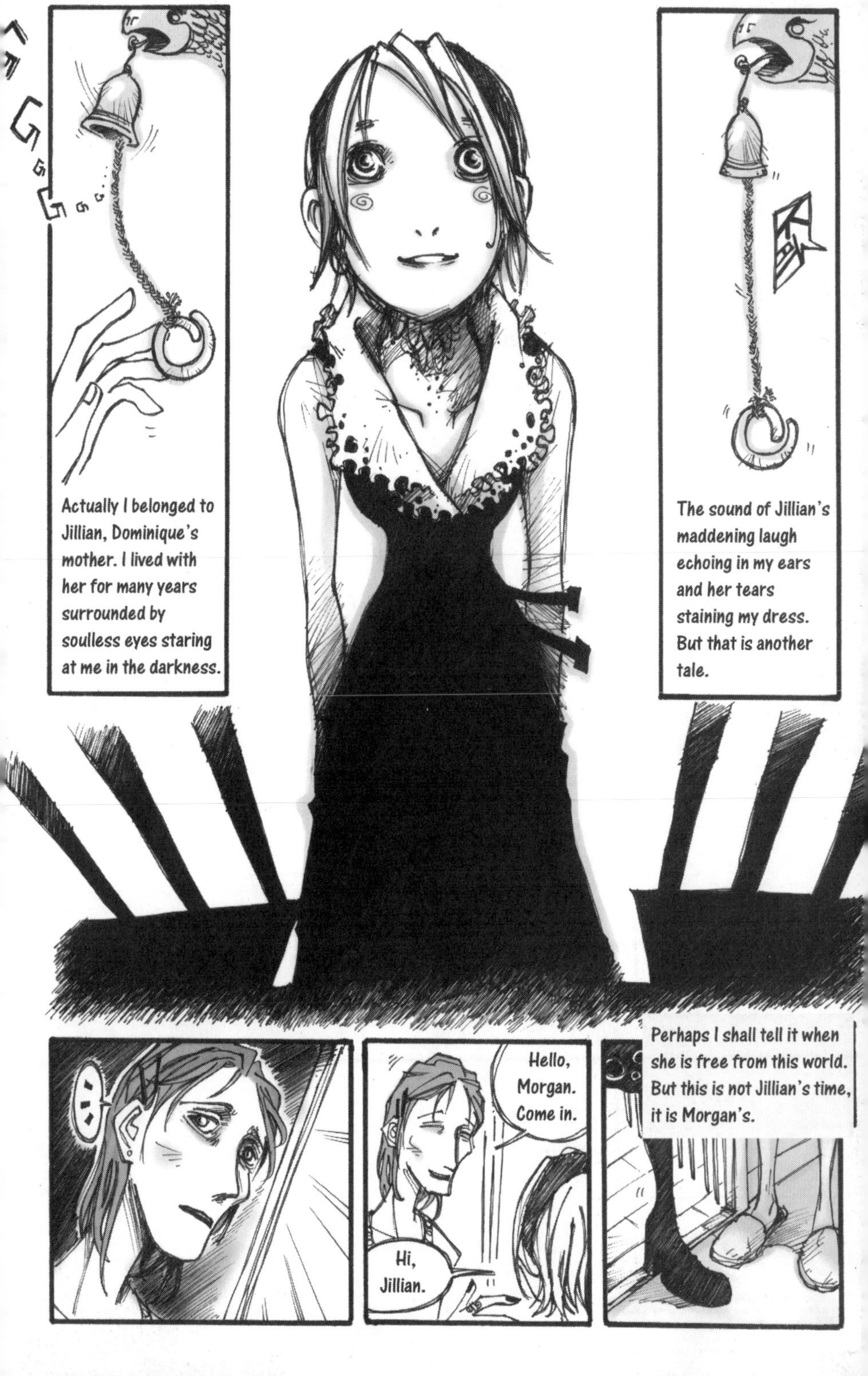
Actually I belonged to Jillian, Dominique's mother. I lived with her for many years surrounded by soulless eyes staring at me in the darkness.
The sound of Jillian's maddening laugh echoing in my ears and her tears staining my dress. But that is another tale.
Hello, Morgan. Come in.
Hi, Jillian.
Perhaps I shall tell it when she is free from this world. But this is not Jillian's time, it is Morgan's.

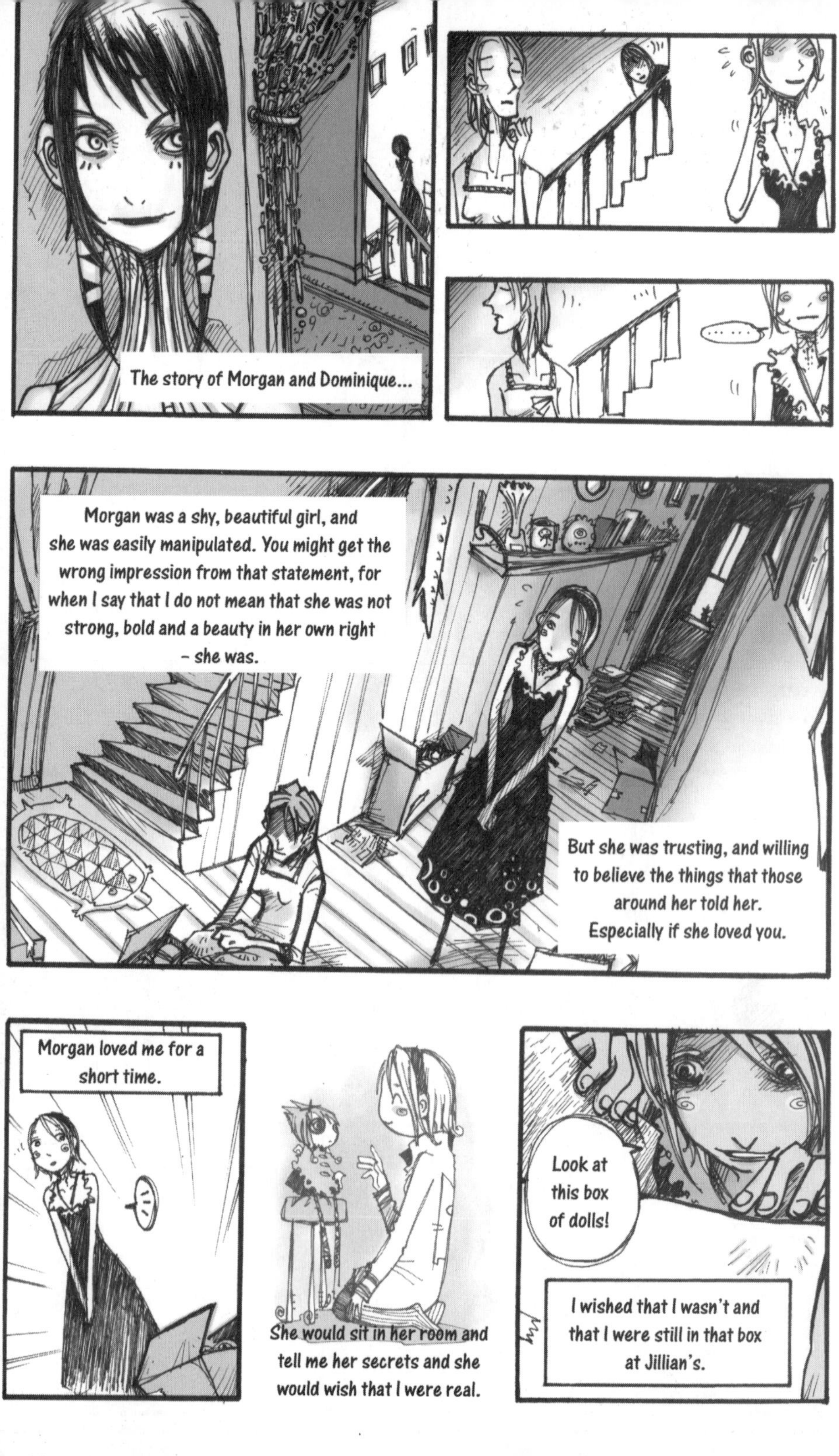
The story of Morgan and Dominique...
......
Morgan was a shy, beautiful girl, and she was easily manipulated. You might get the wrong impression from that statement, for when I say that I do not mean that she was not strong, bold and a beauty in her own right – she was.
But she was trusting, and willing to believe the things that those around her told her. Especially if she loved you.
Morgan loved me for a short time.
She would sit in her room and tell me her secrets and she would wish that I were real.
Look at this box of dolls!
I wished that I wasn't and that I were still in that box at Jillian's.

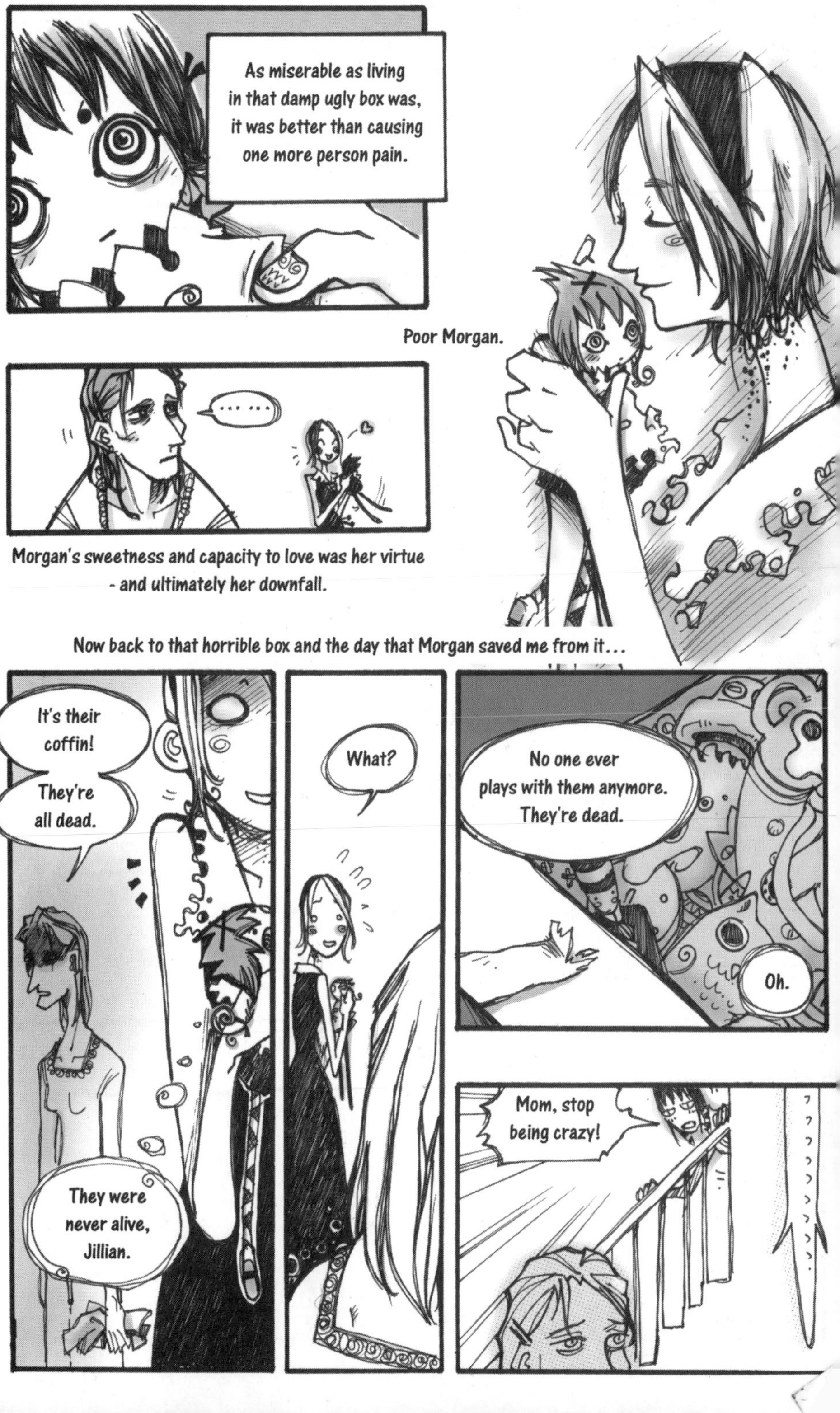

As miserable as living in that damp ugly box was, it was better than causing one more person pain.
Poor Morgan.
... ...
Morgan's sweetness and capacity to love was her virtue - and ultimately her downfall.
Now back to that horrible box and the day that Morgan saved me from it...
It's their coffin!
They're all dead.
They were never alive, Jillian.
What?
No one ever plays with them anymore. They're dead.
Oh.
Mom, stop being crazy!

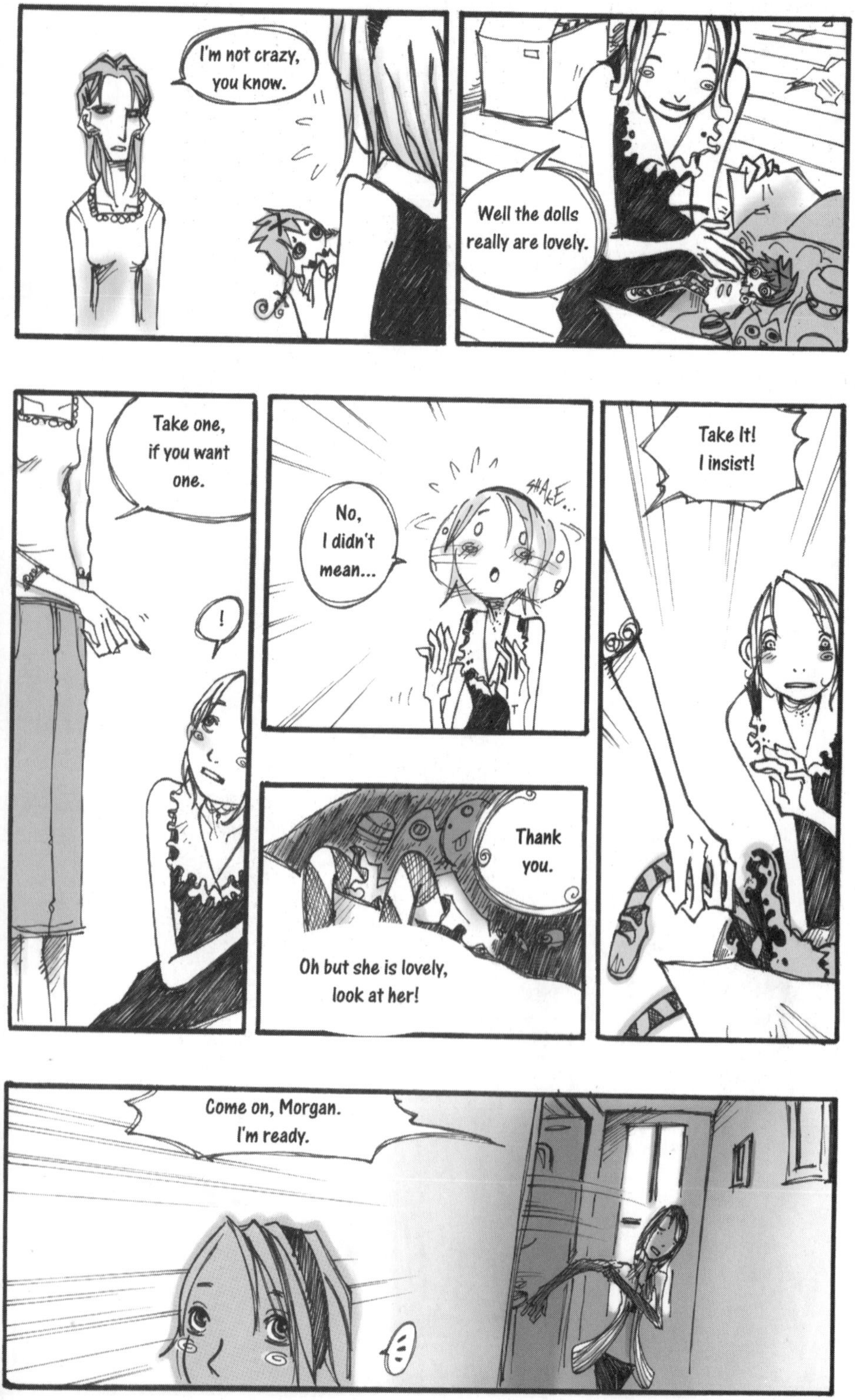
I'm not crazy, you know.
Well the dolls really are lovely.
Take one, if you want one.
!
No, I didn't mean...
SHAKE...
Take It! I insist!
Thank you.
Oh but she is lovely, look at her!
Come on, Morgan. I'm ready.

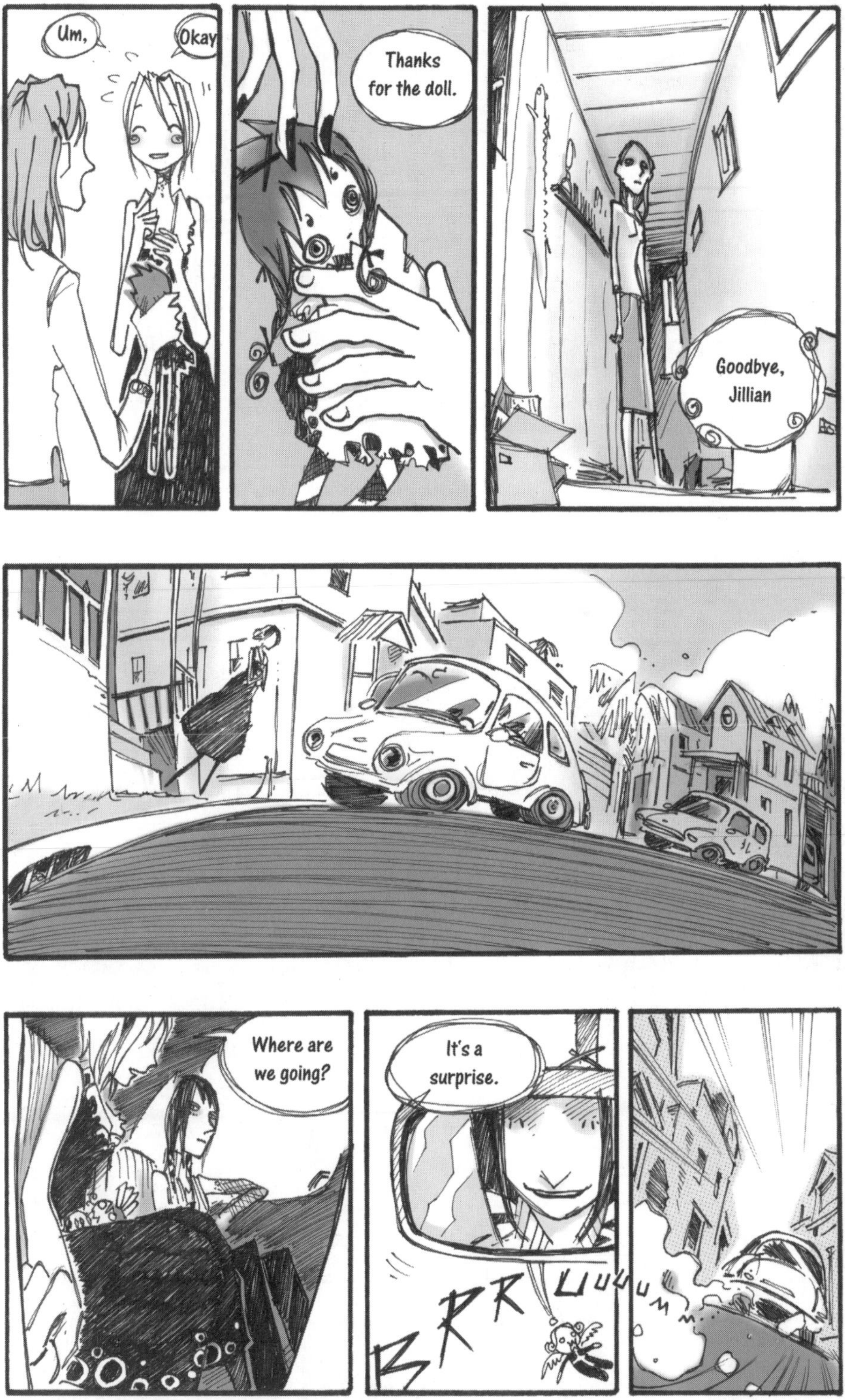
Um,
Okay
Thanks for the doll.
Goodbye, Jillian
Where are we going?
It's a surprise.
BRRUuuumm

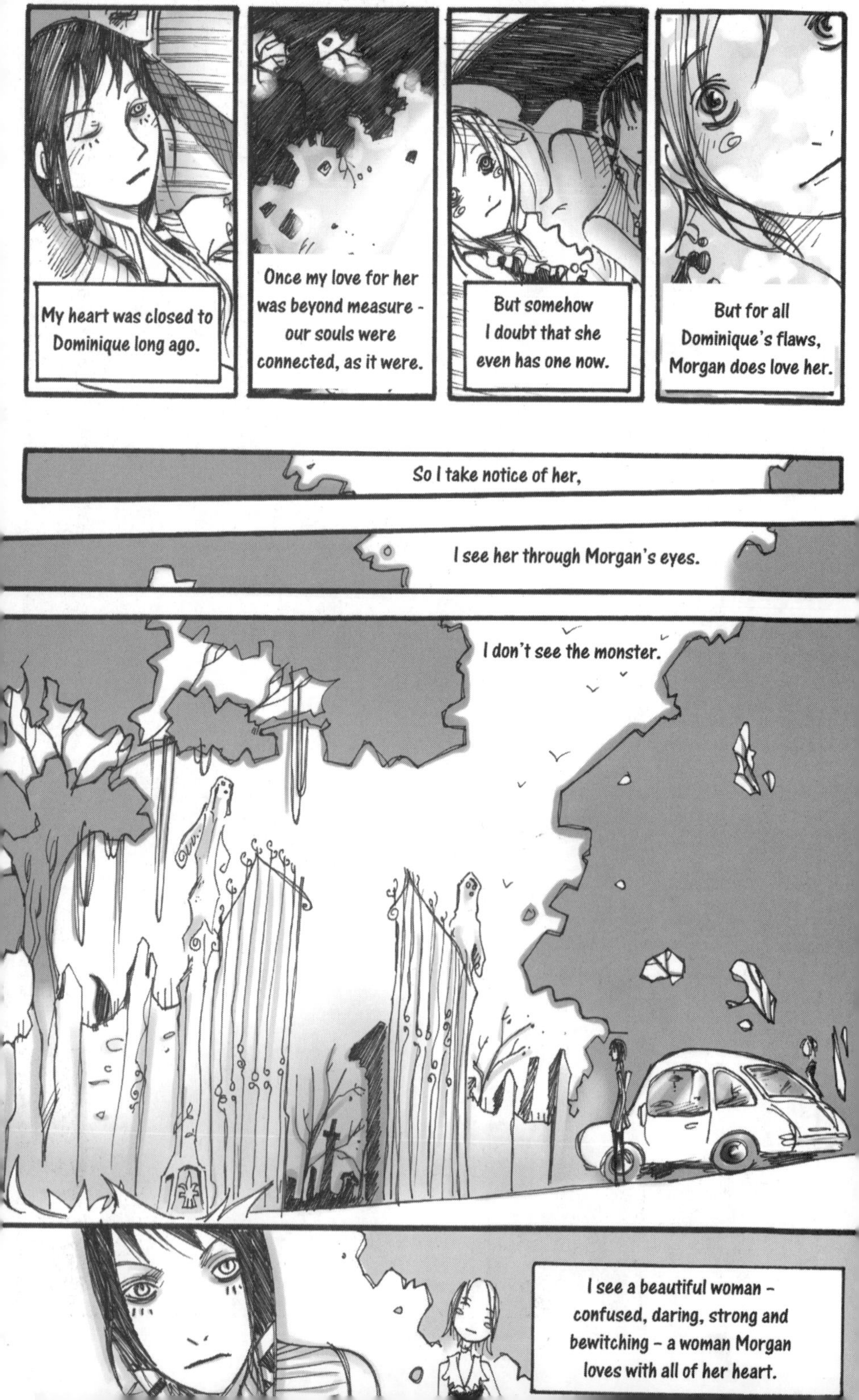
My heart was closed to Dominique long ago.
Once my love for her was beyond measure - our souls were connected, as it were.
But somehow I doubt that she even has one now.
But for all Dominique's flaws, Morgan does love her.
So I take notice of her,
I see her through Morgan's eyes.
I don't see the monster.
I see a beautiful woman - confused, daring, strong and bewitching - a woman Morgan loves with all of her heart.

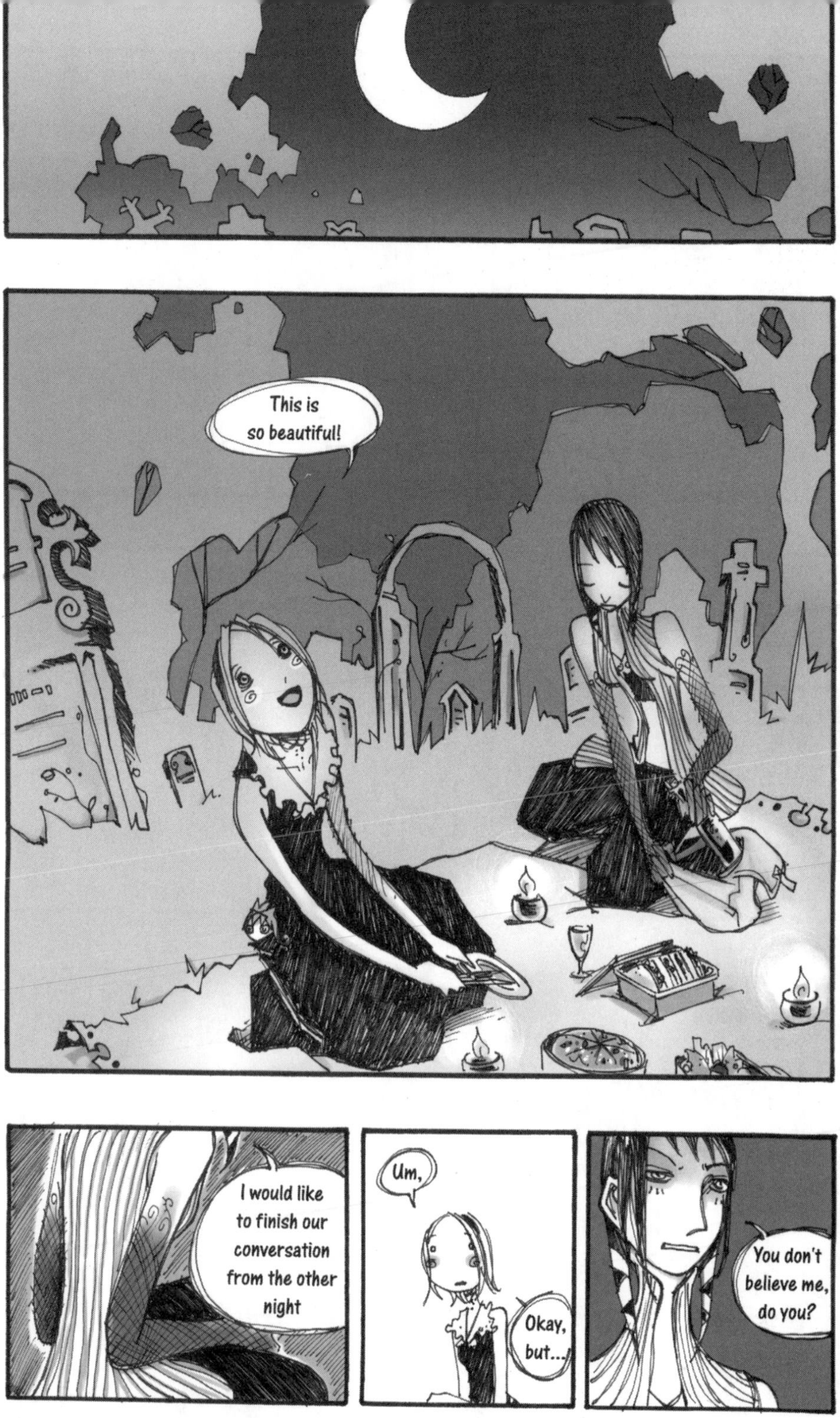
This is so beautiful!
I would like to finish our conversation from the other night
Um,
Okay, but...
You don't believe me, do you?

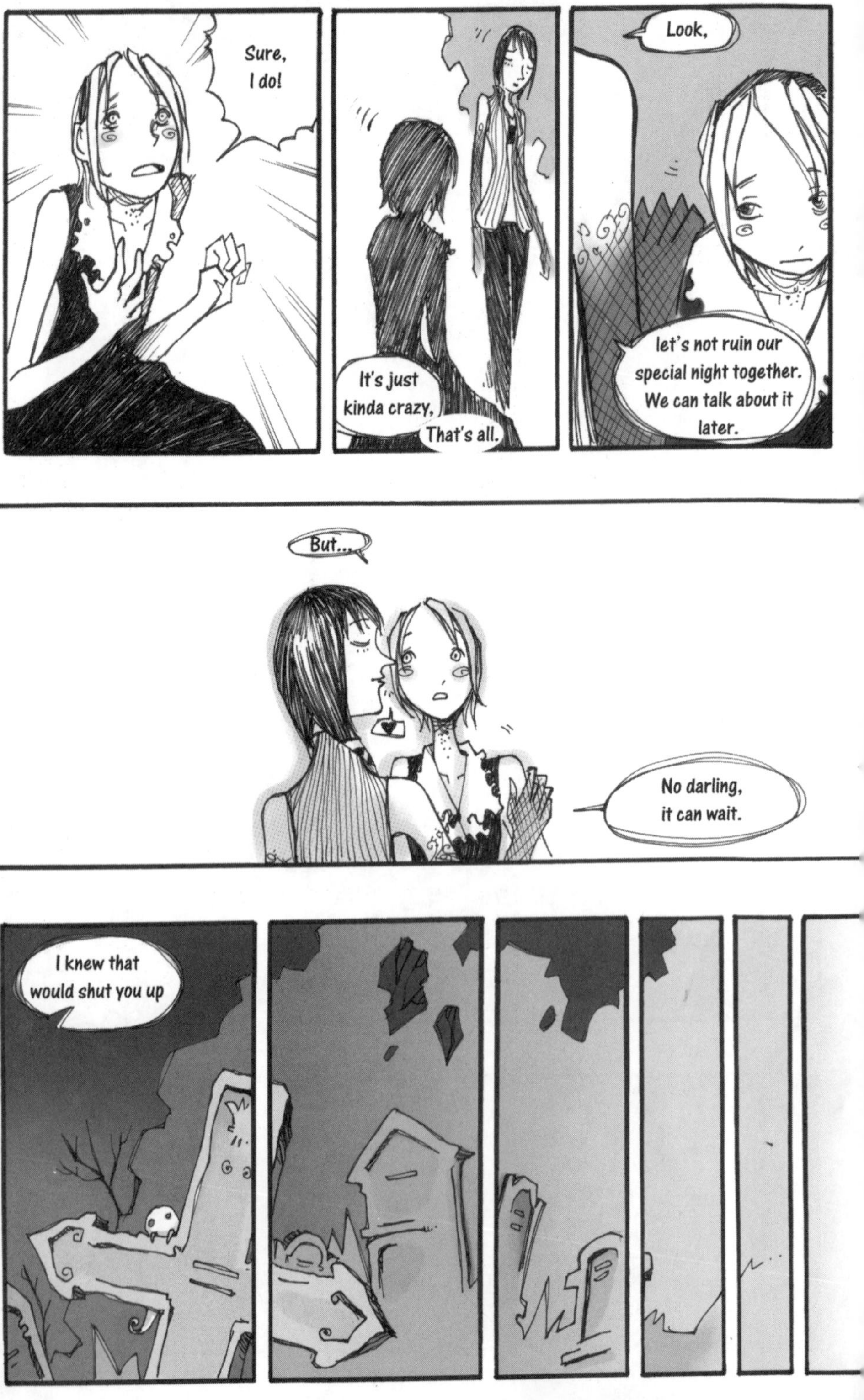
Sure, I do!
It's just kinda crazy,
That's all.
Look,
let's not ruin our special night together. We can talk about it later.
But...
No darling, it can wait.
I knew that would shut you up

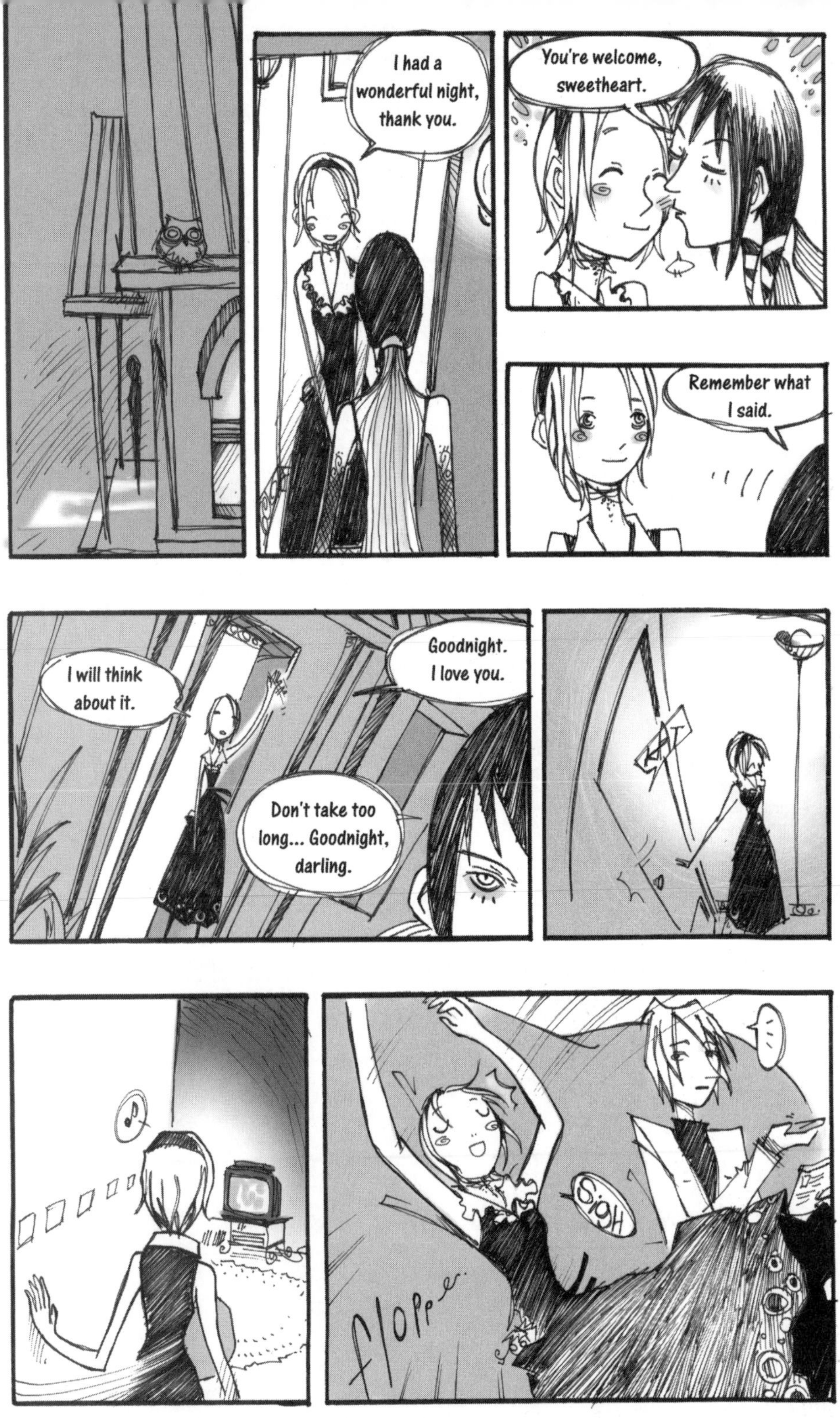
I had a wonderful night, thank you.
You're welcome, sweetheart.
Remember what I said.
I will think about it.
Goodnight. I love you.
Don't take too long... Goodnight, darling.
Sigh
flopp

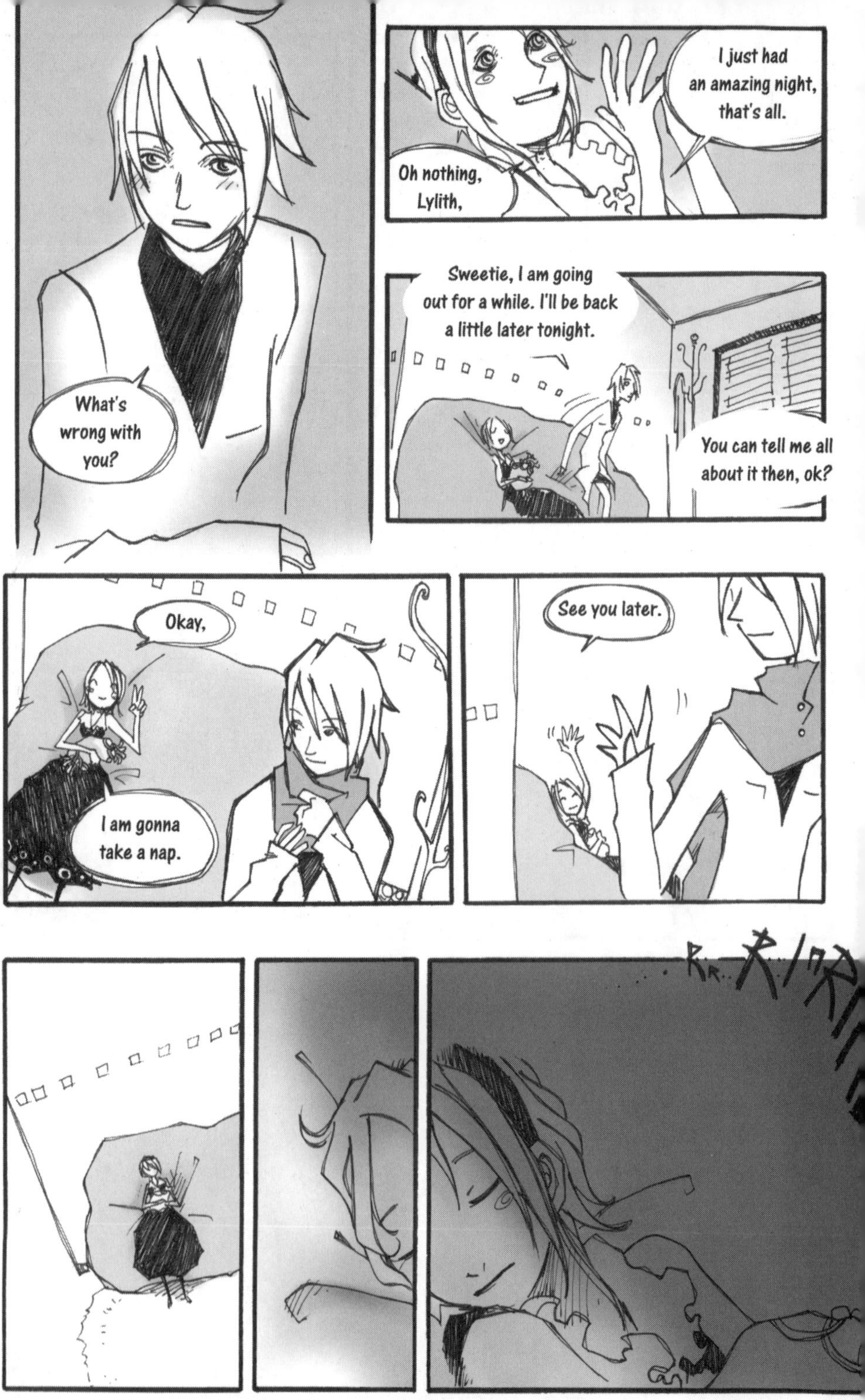
What's wrong with you?
Oh nothing, Lylith,
I just had an amazing night, that's all.
Sweetie, I am going out for a while. I'll be back a little later tonight.
You can tell me all about it then, ok?
Okay,
I am gonna take a nap.
See you later.

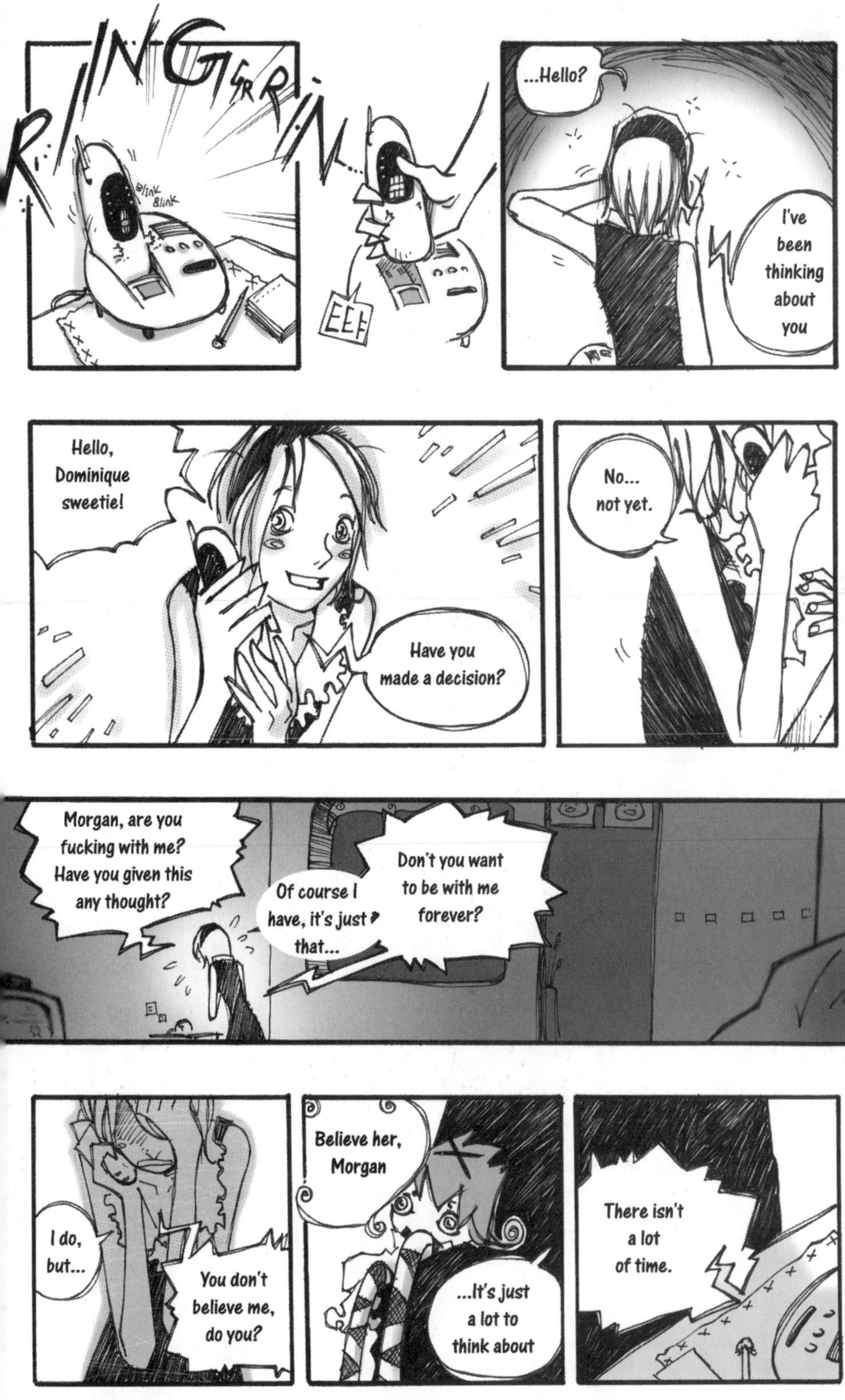
RIING
GRRIN
Blink Blink
EEF
...Hello?
I've been thinking about you
Hello, Dominique sweetie!
Have you made a decision?
No... not yet.
Morgan, are you fucking with me? Have you given this any thought?
Of course I have, it's just that...
Don't you want to be with me forever?
I do, but...
You don't believe me, do you?
Believe her, Morgan
...It's just a lot to think about
There isn't a lot of time.

You better make up your mind soon.

Okay...

I'll call you soon.

Bye.

... ...

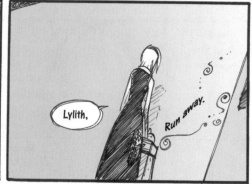
Lylith,

Run away.

I made some screwdrivers earlier. They're in the fridge

Thank you, sweetheart.

Let's have some.

Okay.

Here you go, honey.

What's wrong?

Um...

Do you mind answering the phone tonight? I don't feel like talking to Dominique right now.

Is she being crazy again?

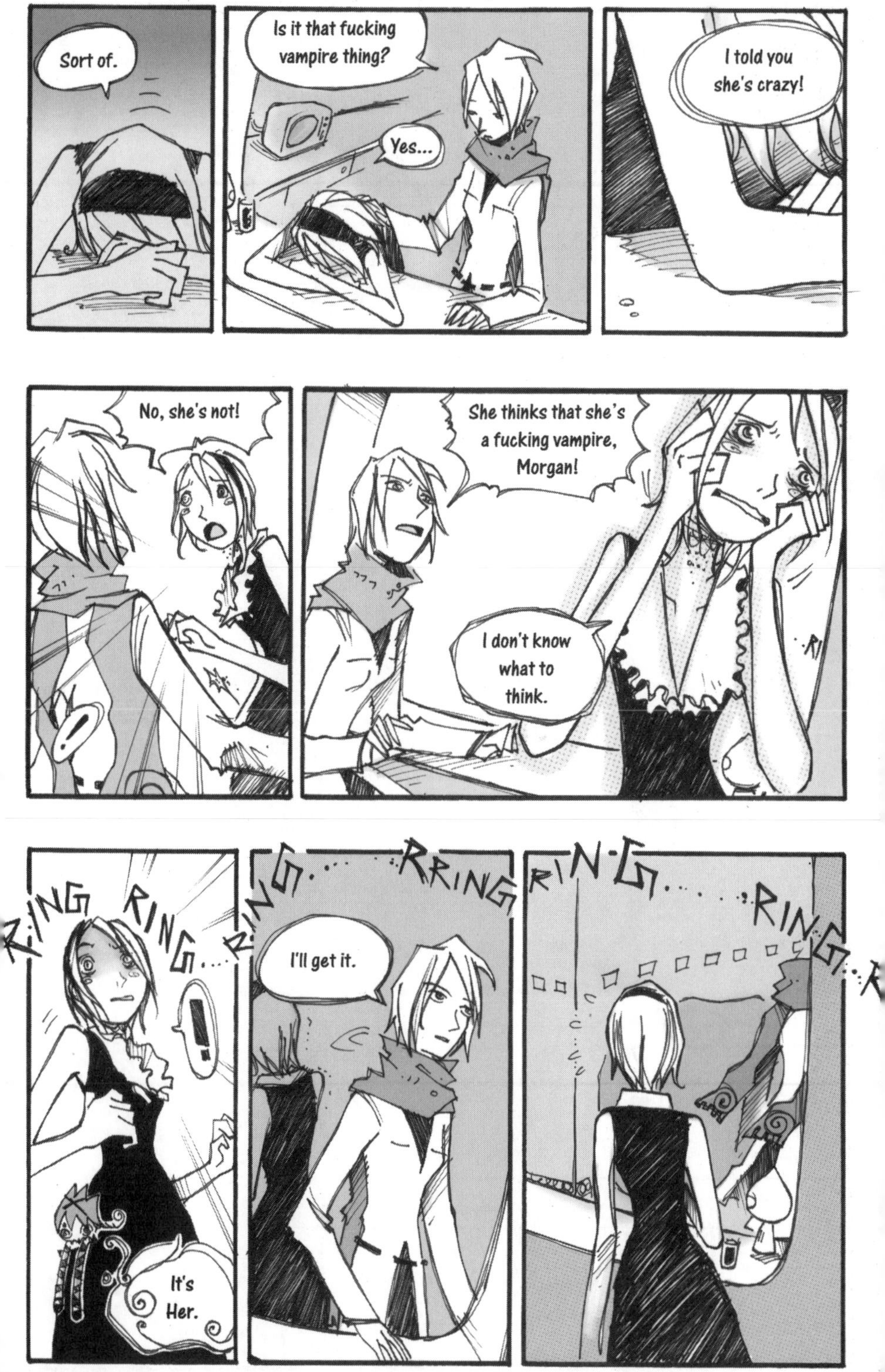
Sort of.
Is it that fucking vampire thing?
Yes...
I told you she's crazy!
No, she's not!
She thinks that she's a fucking vampire, Morgan!
I don't know what to think.
RING RING...RING
It's Her.
RRING RING...
I'll get it.
RING...RING...R

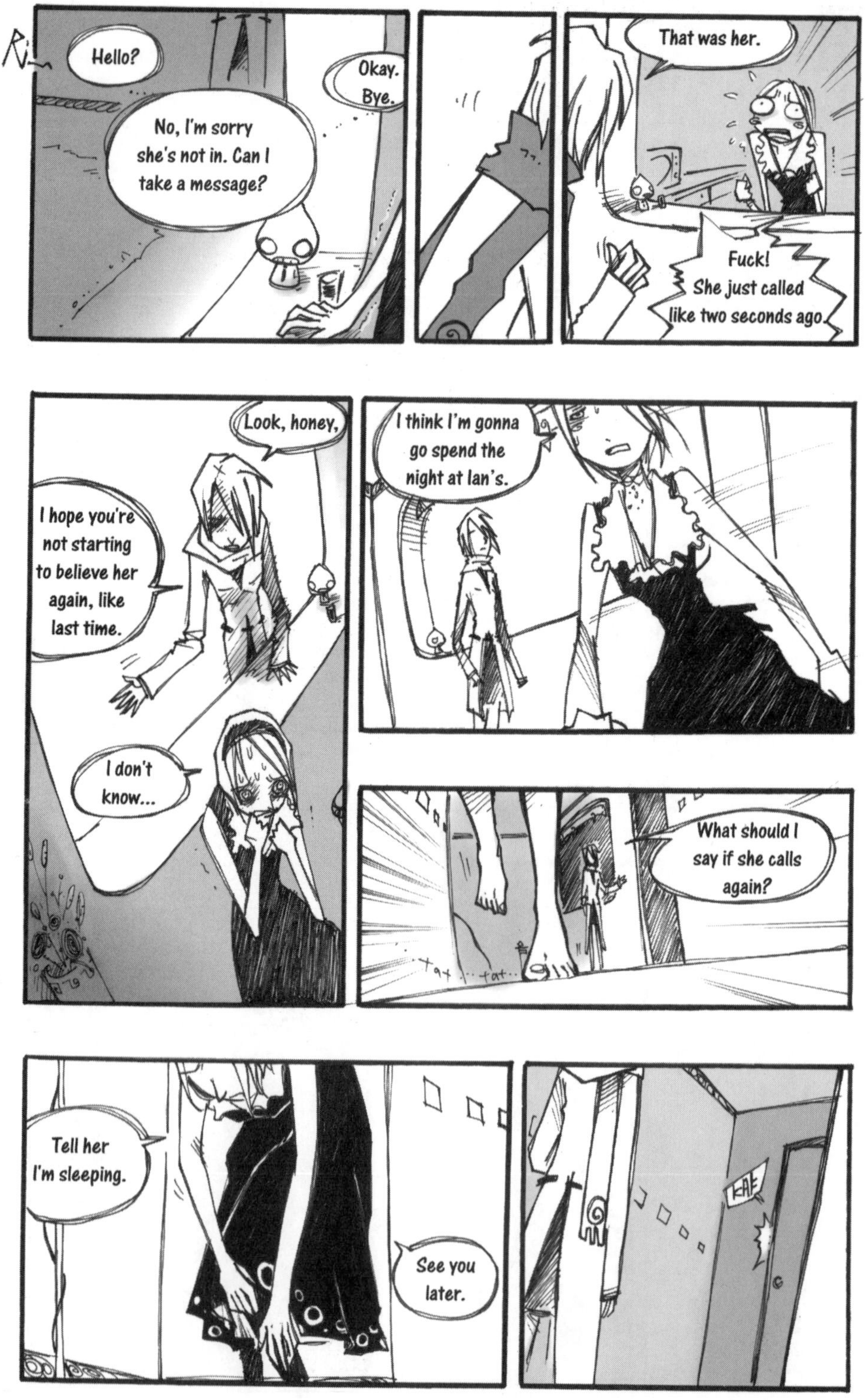
Ri
Hello?
No, I'm sorry she's not in. Can I take a message?
Okay. Bye.
That was her.
Fuck! She just called like two seconds ago.
Look, honey,
I hope you're not starting to believe her again, like last time.
I don't know...
I think I'm gonna go spend the night at Ian's.
What should I say if she calls again?
tat tat
Tell her I'm sleeping.
See you later.

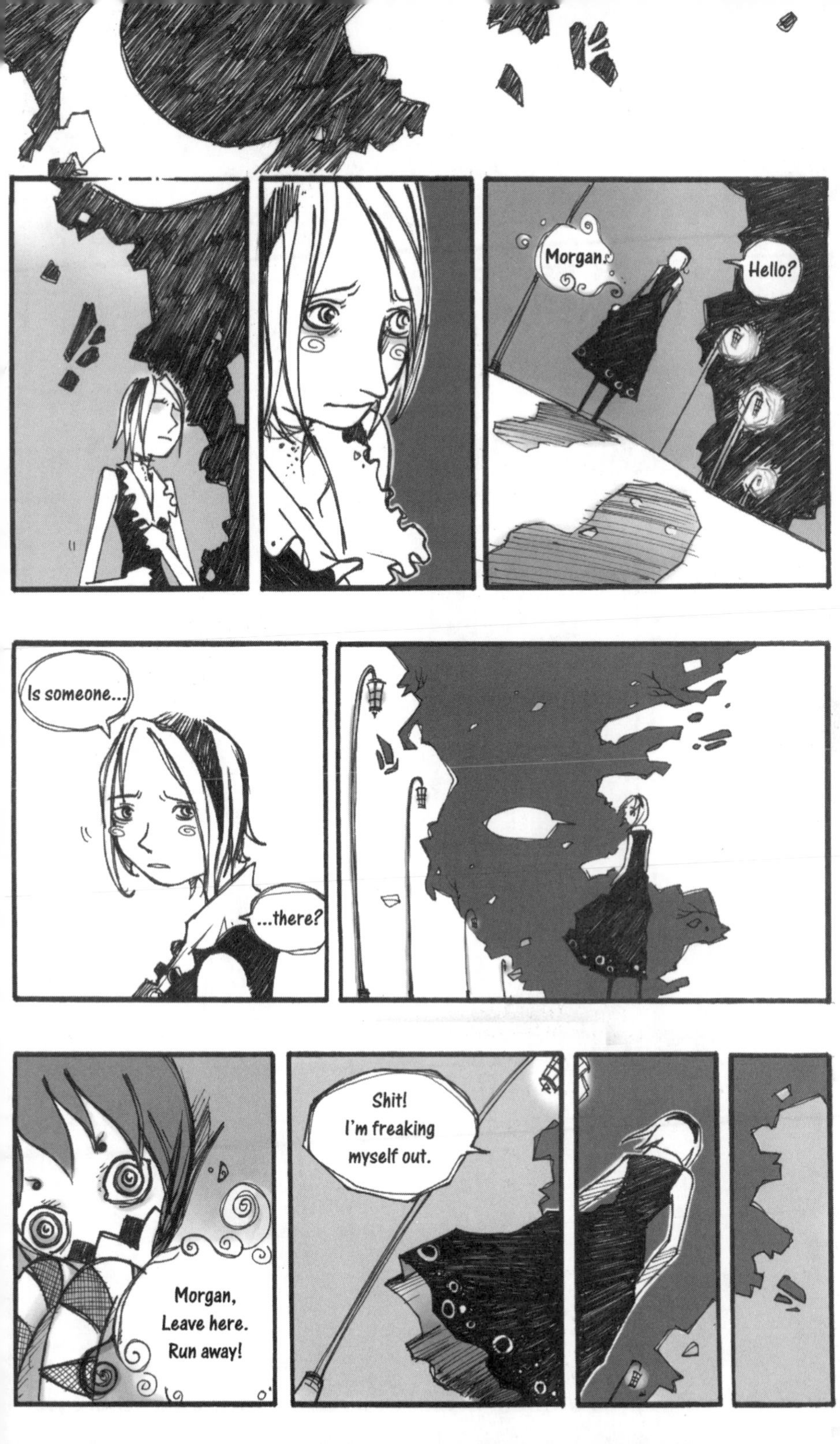
Morgan?
Hello?
Is someone...
...there?
Morgan,
Leave here.
Run away!
Shit!
I'm freaking
myself out.

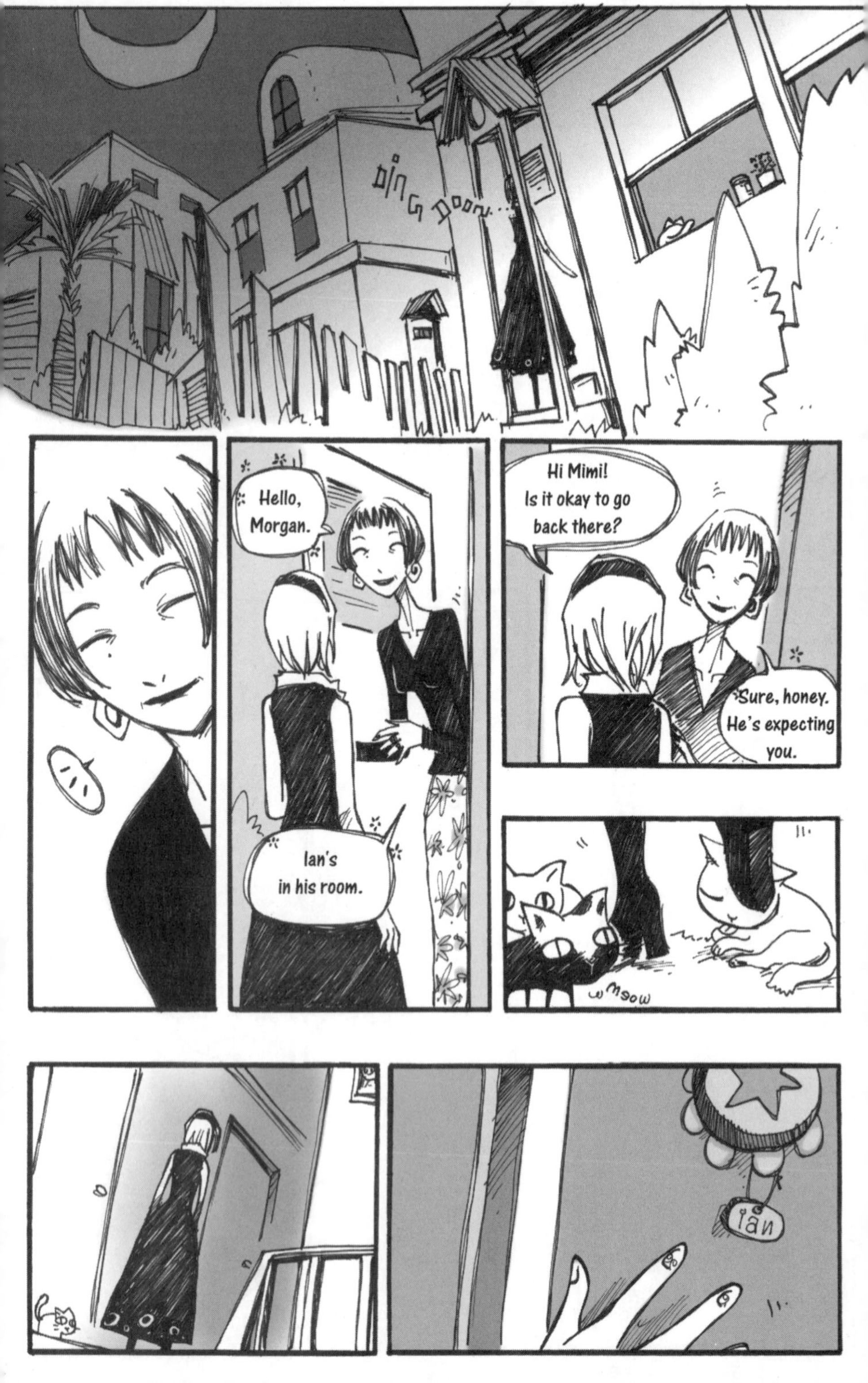

DING DONG...
...
Hello, Morgan.
Ian's in his room.
Hi Mimi! Is it okay to go back there?
Sure, honey. He's expecting you.
meow
Ian

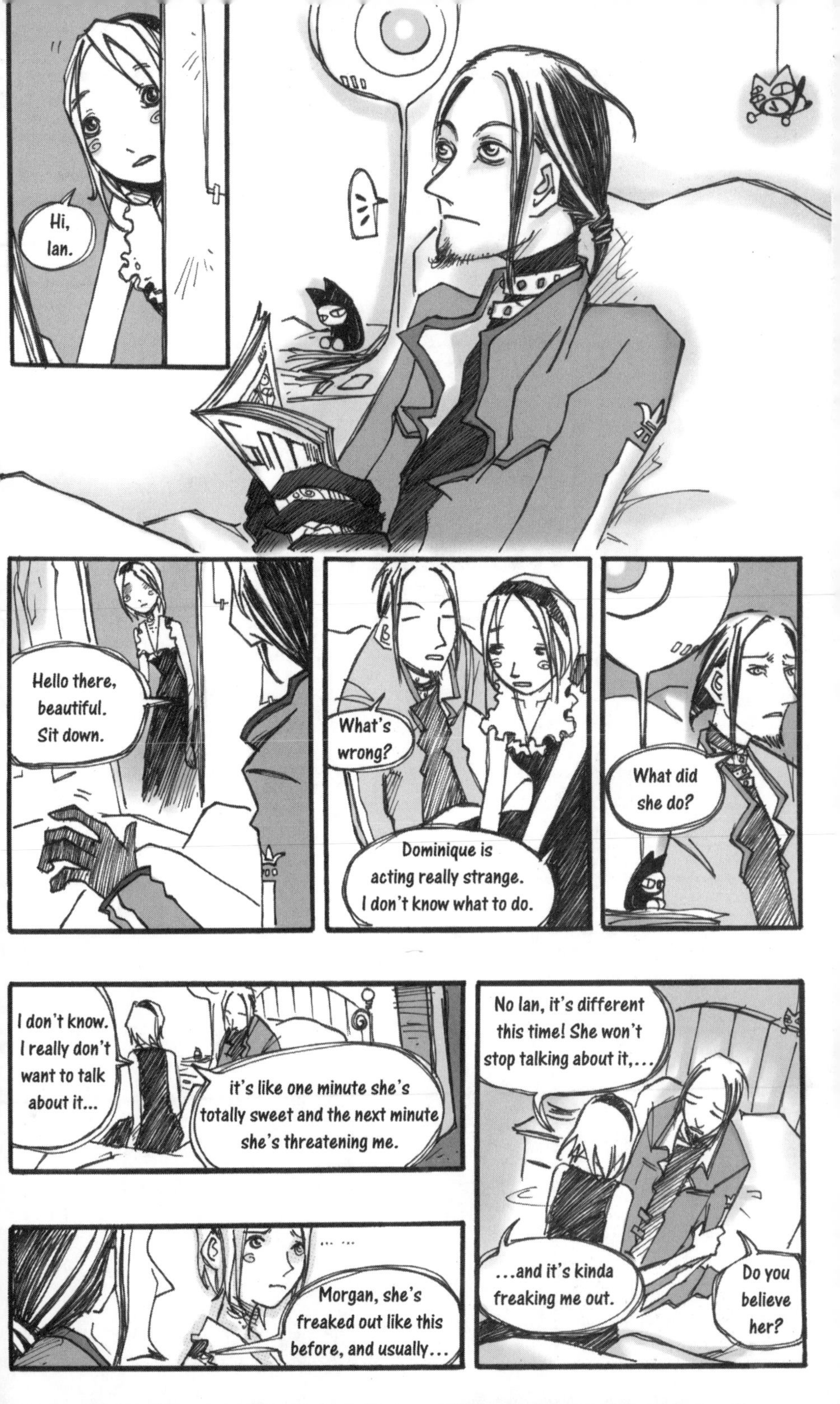
Hi, Ian.
Hello there, beautiful. Sit down.
What's wrong?
Dominique is acting really strange. I don't know what to do.
What did she do?
I don't know. I really don't want to talk about it...
it's like one minute she's totally sweet and the next minute she's threatening me.
Morgan, she's freaked out like this before, and usually...
No Ian, it's different this time! She won't stop talking about it,...
...and it's kinda freaking me out.
Do you believe her?

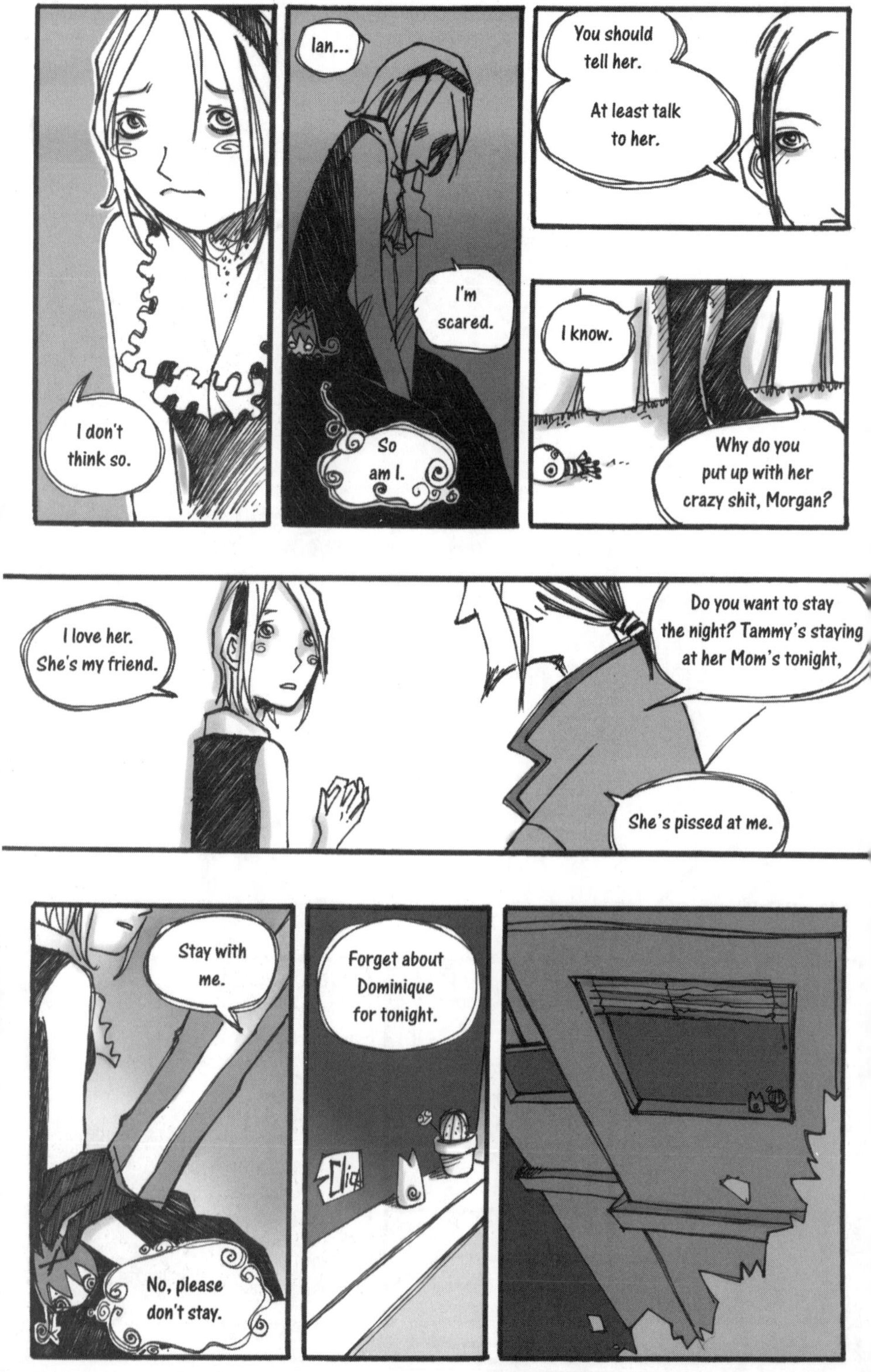
Ian...
I'm scared.
So am I.
I don't think so.
You should tell her.
At least talk to her.
I know.
Why do you put up with her crazy shit, Morgan?
I love her. She's my friend.
Do you want to stay the night? Tammy's staying at her Mom's tonight,
She's pissed at me.
Stay with me.
No, please don't stay.
Forget about Dominique for tonight.
Click

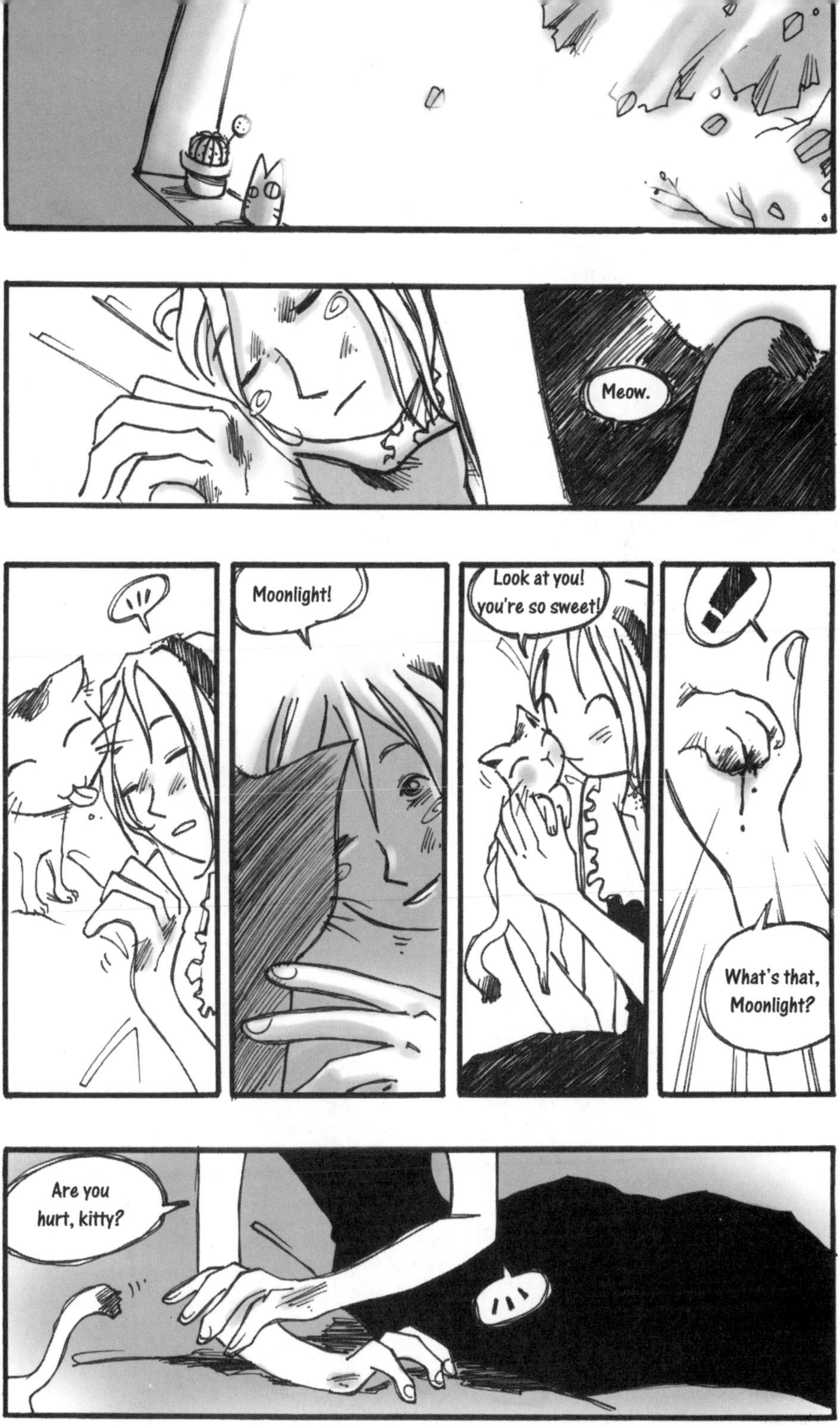
Meow.
Moonlight!
Look at you! you're so sweet!
What's that, Moonlight?
Are you hurt, kitty?

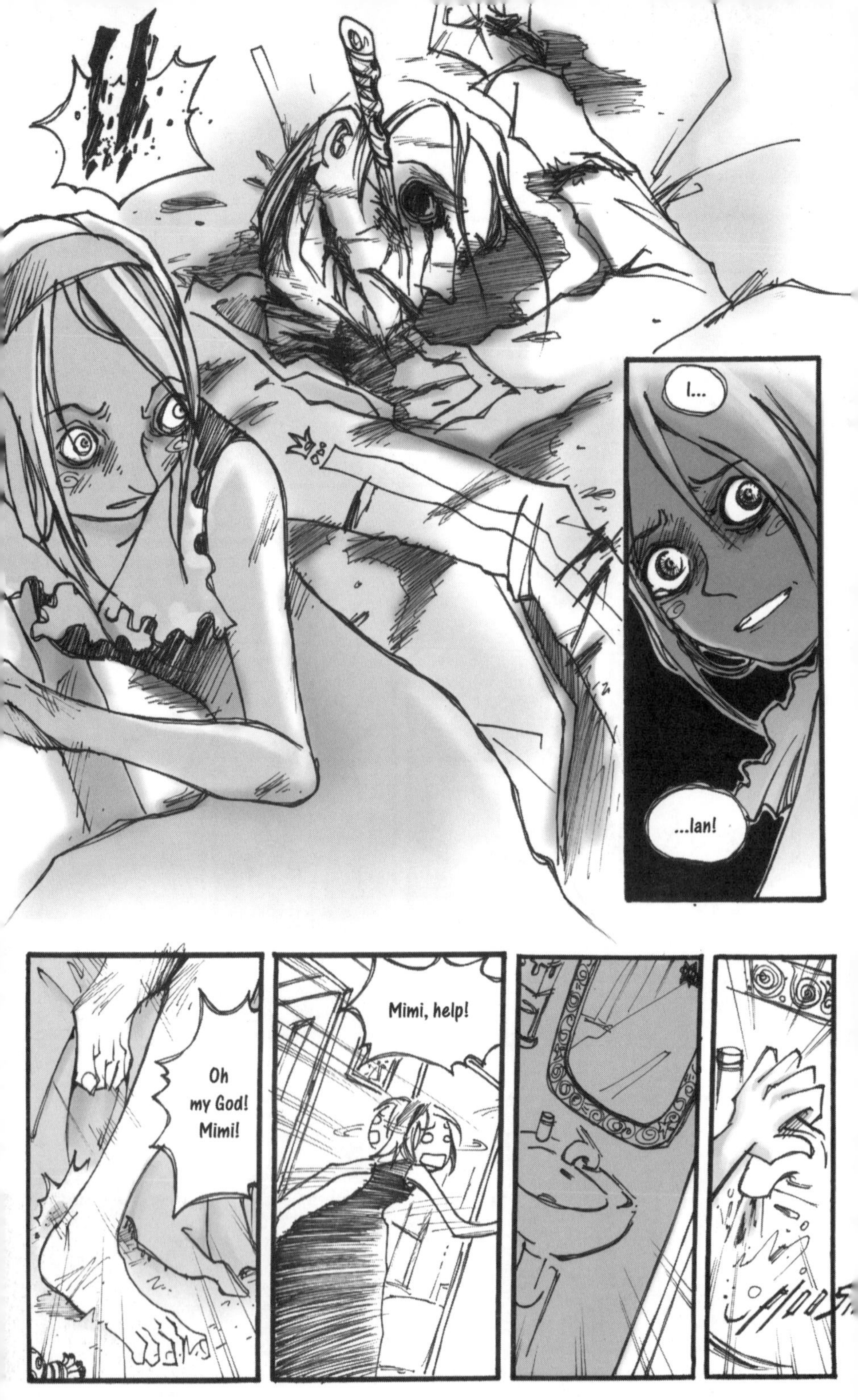
I...
...Ian!
Oh my God! Mimi!
Mimi, help!

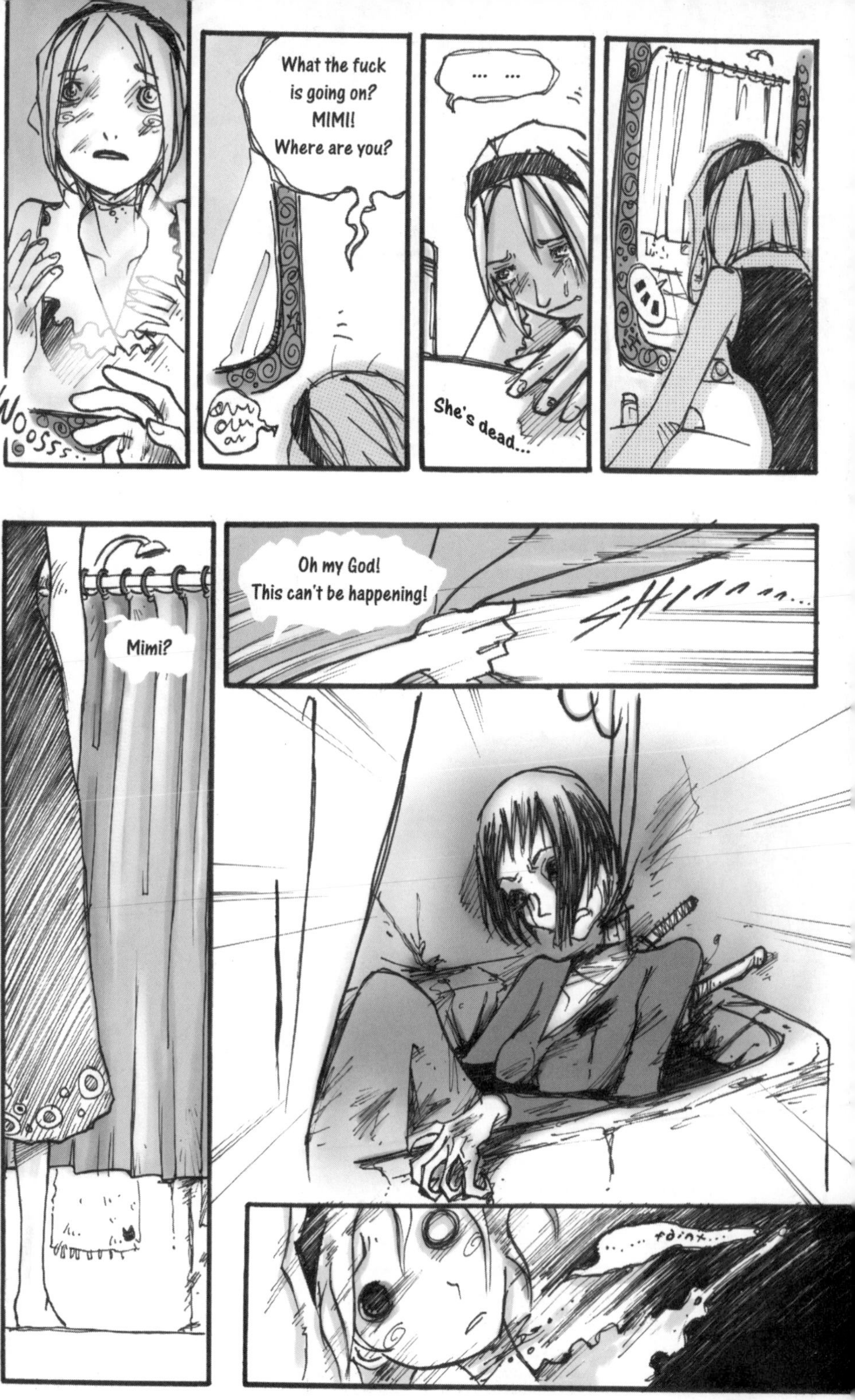

WOOSSS...
What the fuck is going on? MIMI! Where are you?
... ...
She's dead...
Mimi?
Oh my God! This can't be happening!
SHLAAAAA...
..... faint...

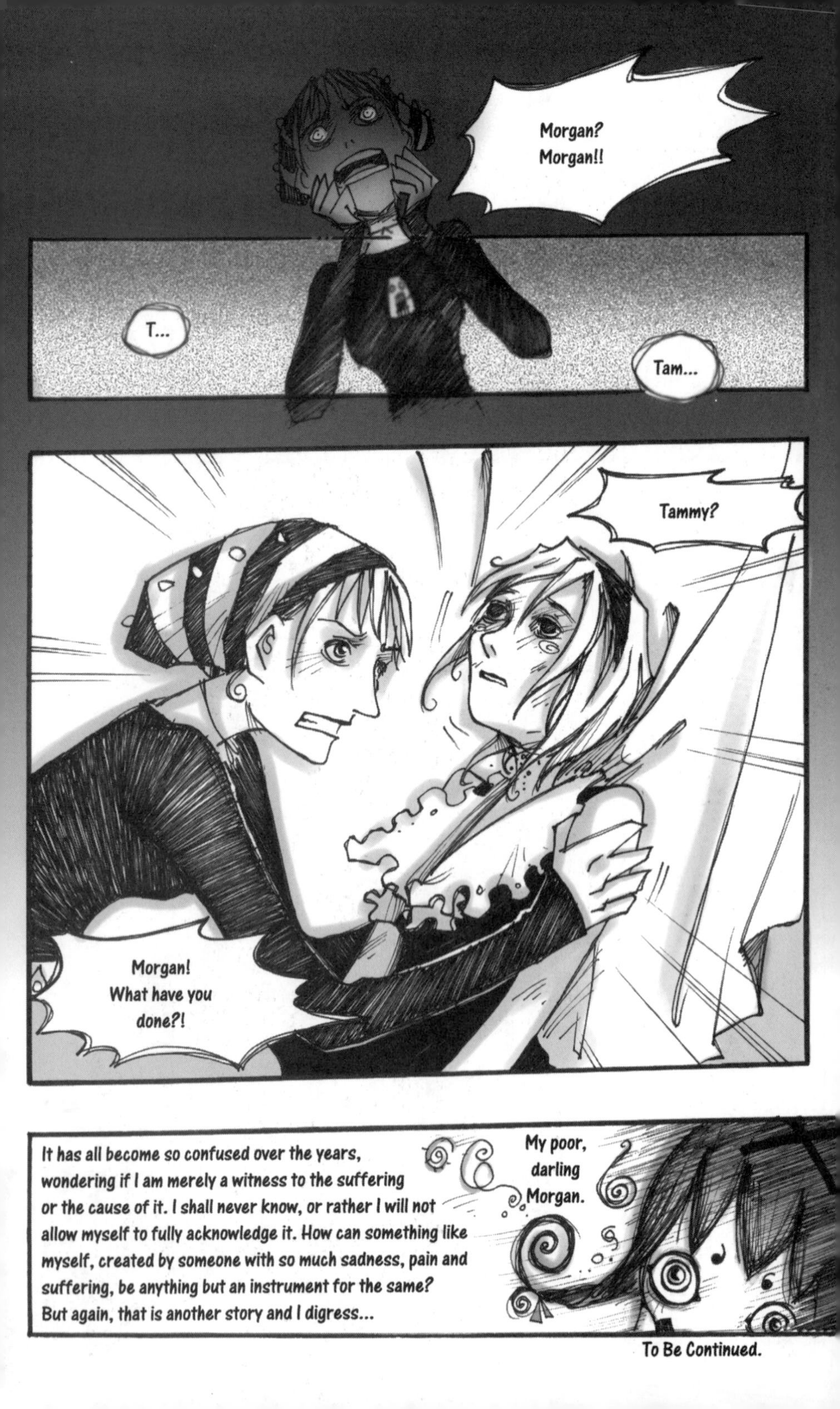
Morgan?
Morgan!!
T...
Tam...
Tammy?
Morgan! What have you done?!
It has all become so confused over the years, wondering if I am merely a witness to the suffering or the cause of it. I shall never know, or rather I will not allow myself to fully acknowledge it. How can something like myself, created by someone with so much sadness, pain and suffering, be anything but an instrument for the same? But again, that is another story and I digress...
My poor, darling Morgan.
To Be Continued.

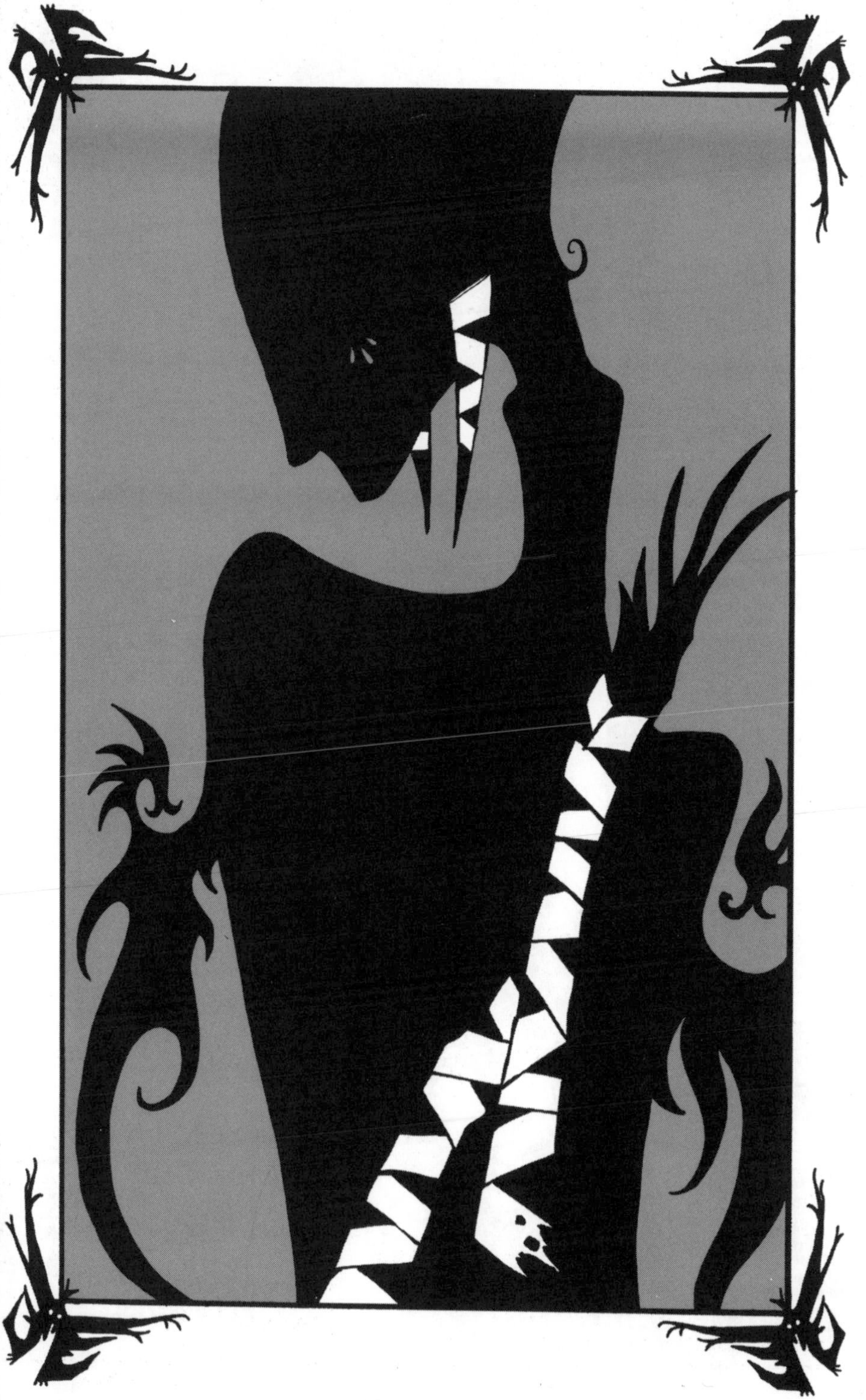

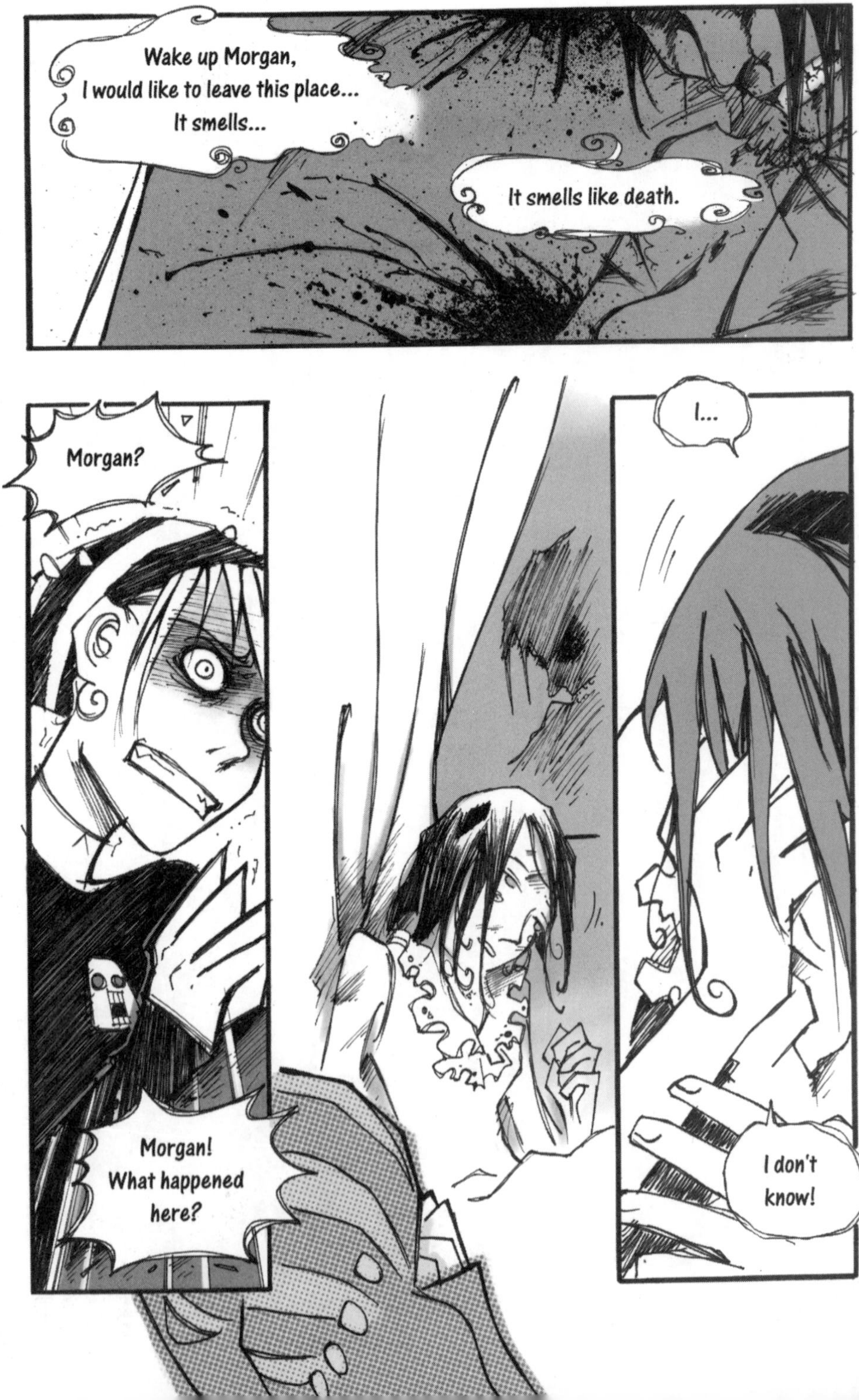
Wake up Morgan,
I would like to leave this place...
It smells...
It smells like death.
Morgan?
I...
Morgan!
What happened
here?
I don't
know!

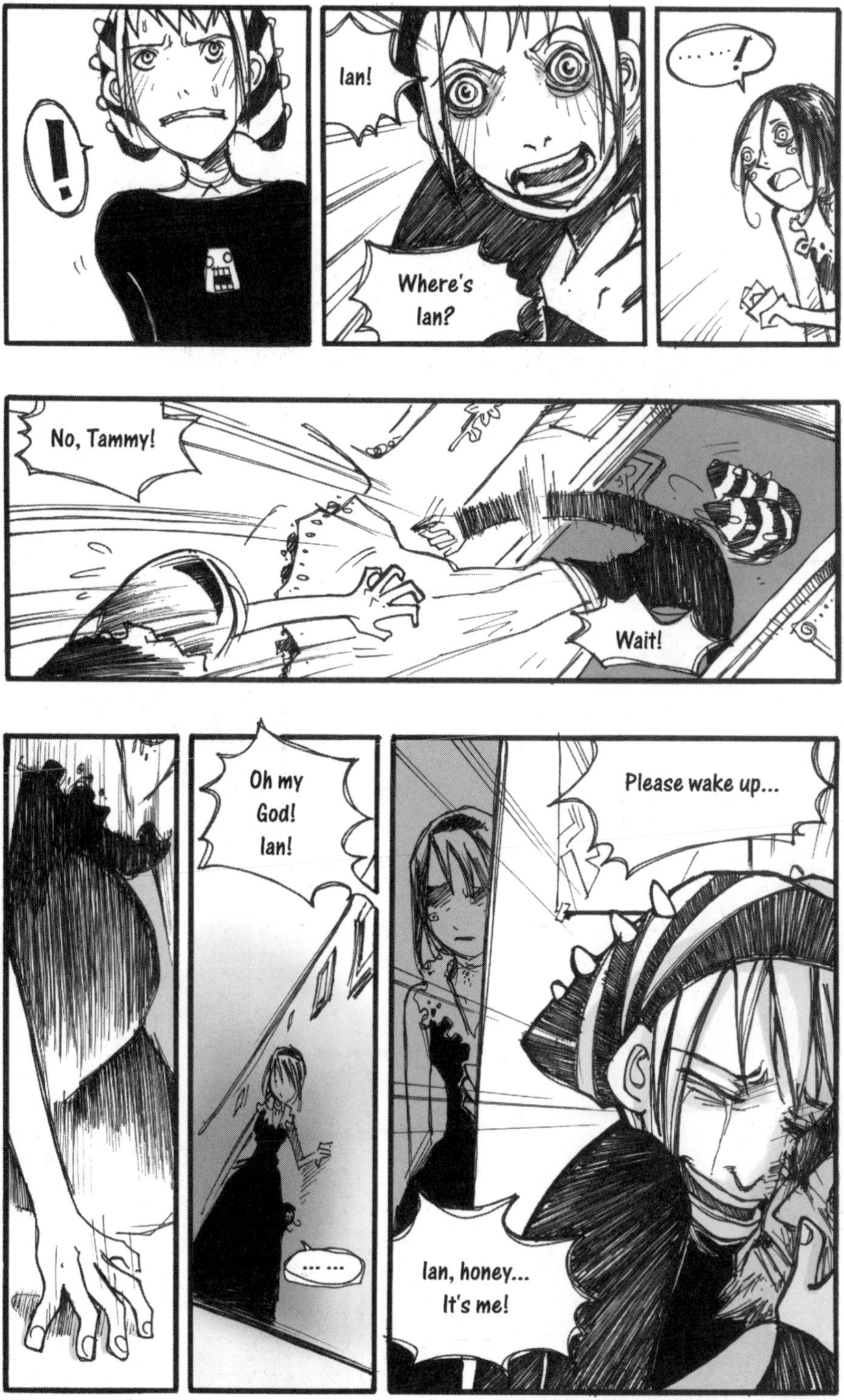
!
Ian!
Where's Ian?
……!
No, Tammy!
Wait!
Oh my God! Ian!
… …
Please wake up...
Ian, honey... It's me!

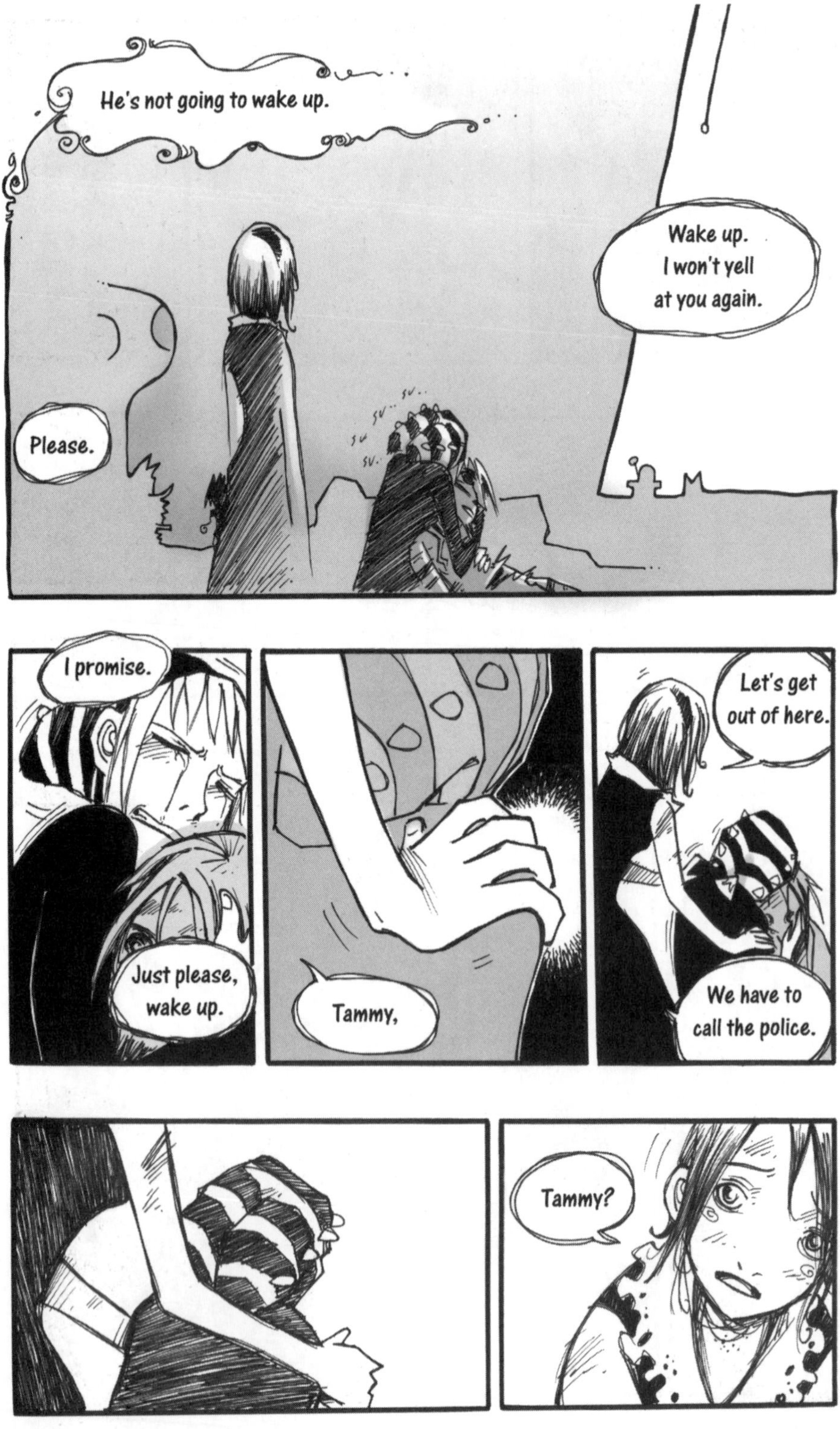
He's not going to wake up.
Wake up. I won't yell at you again.
Please.
SU.. SU.. SU.. SU..
I promise.
Just please, wake up.
Tammy,
Let's get out of here.
We have to call the police.
Tammy?

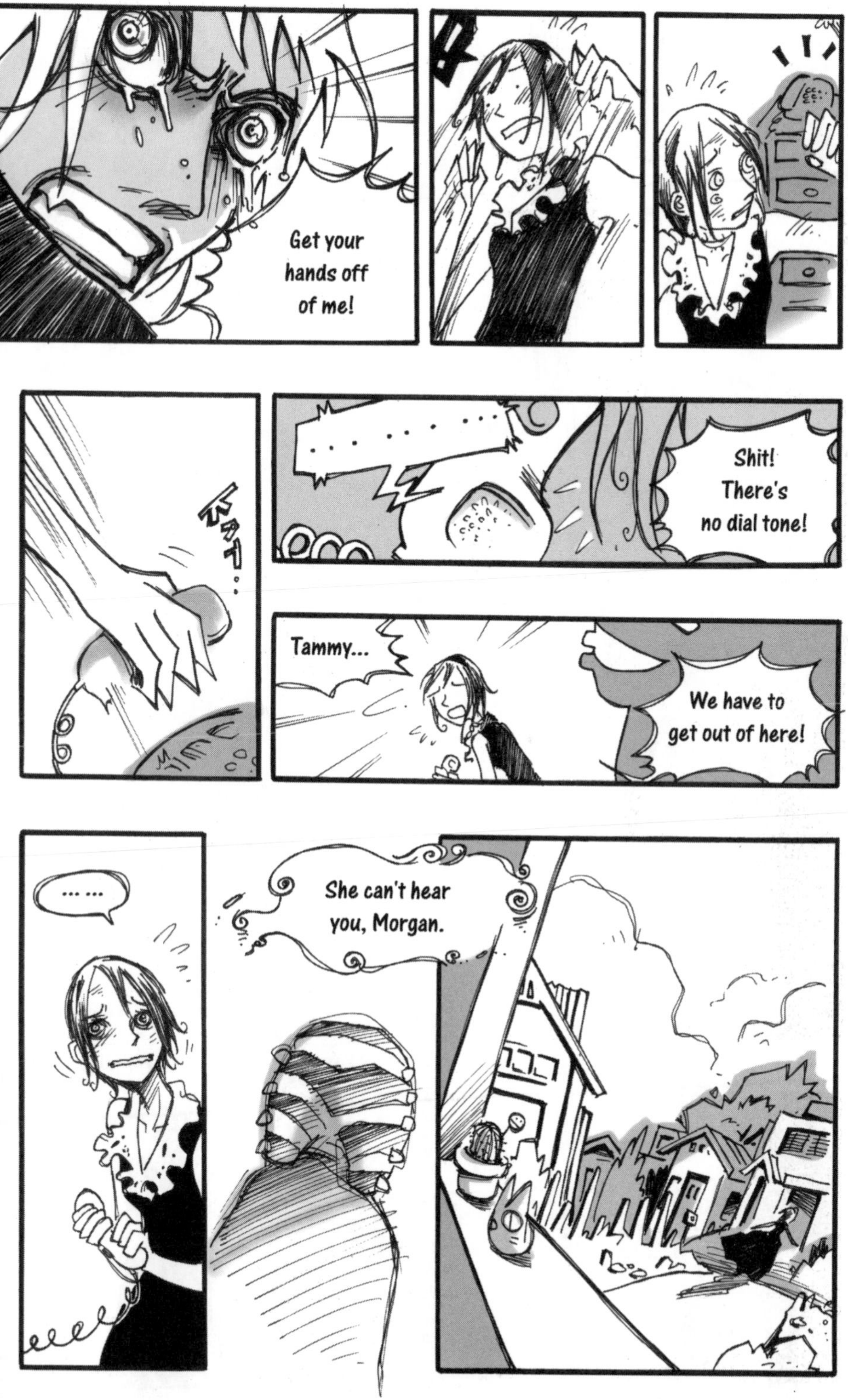
Get your hands off of me!
. . . .
Shit! There's no dial tone!
Tammy...
We have to get out of here!
... ...
She can't hear you, Morgan.

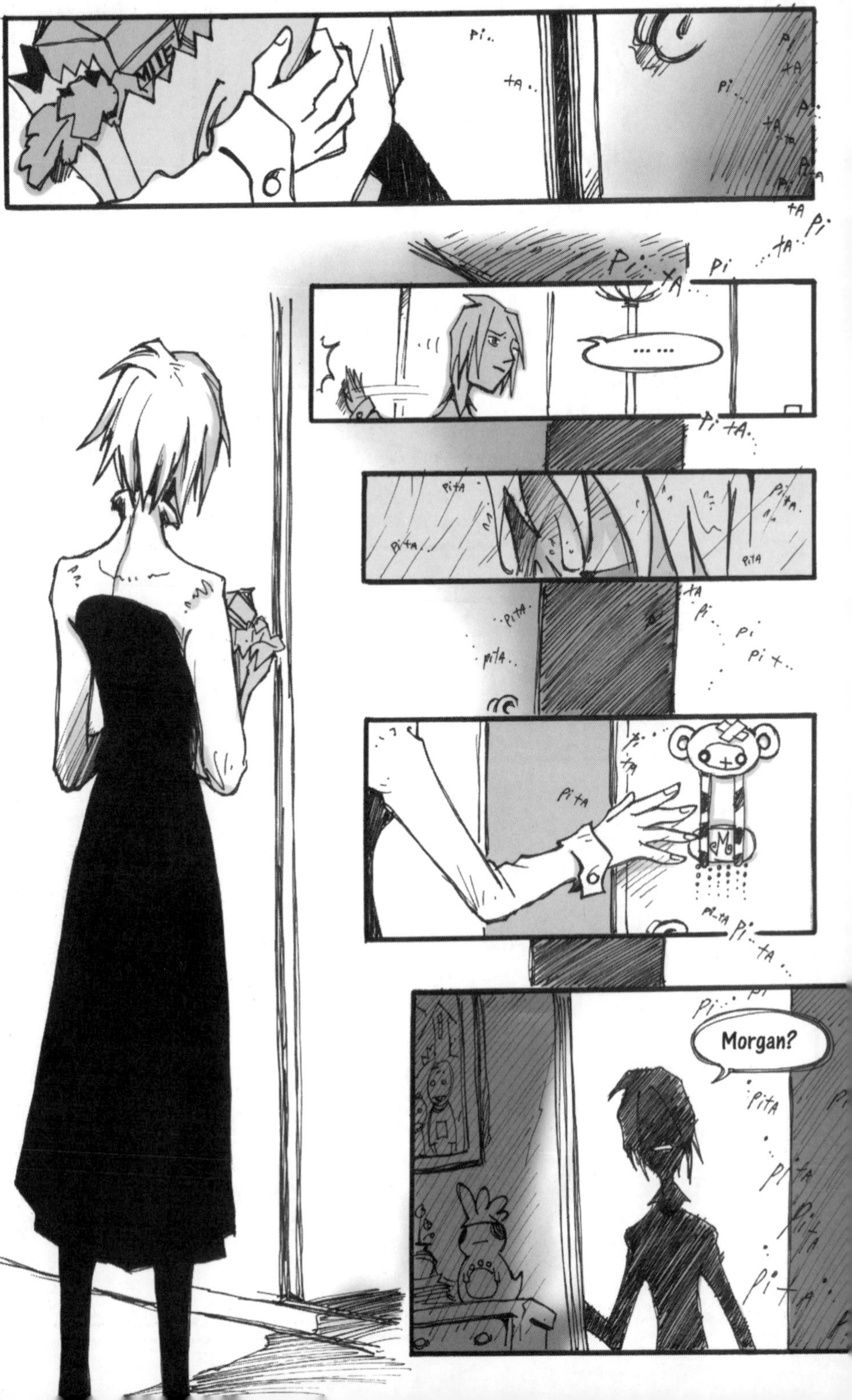
pi..
ta..
....
pita
Morgan?

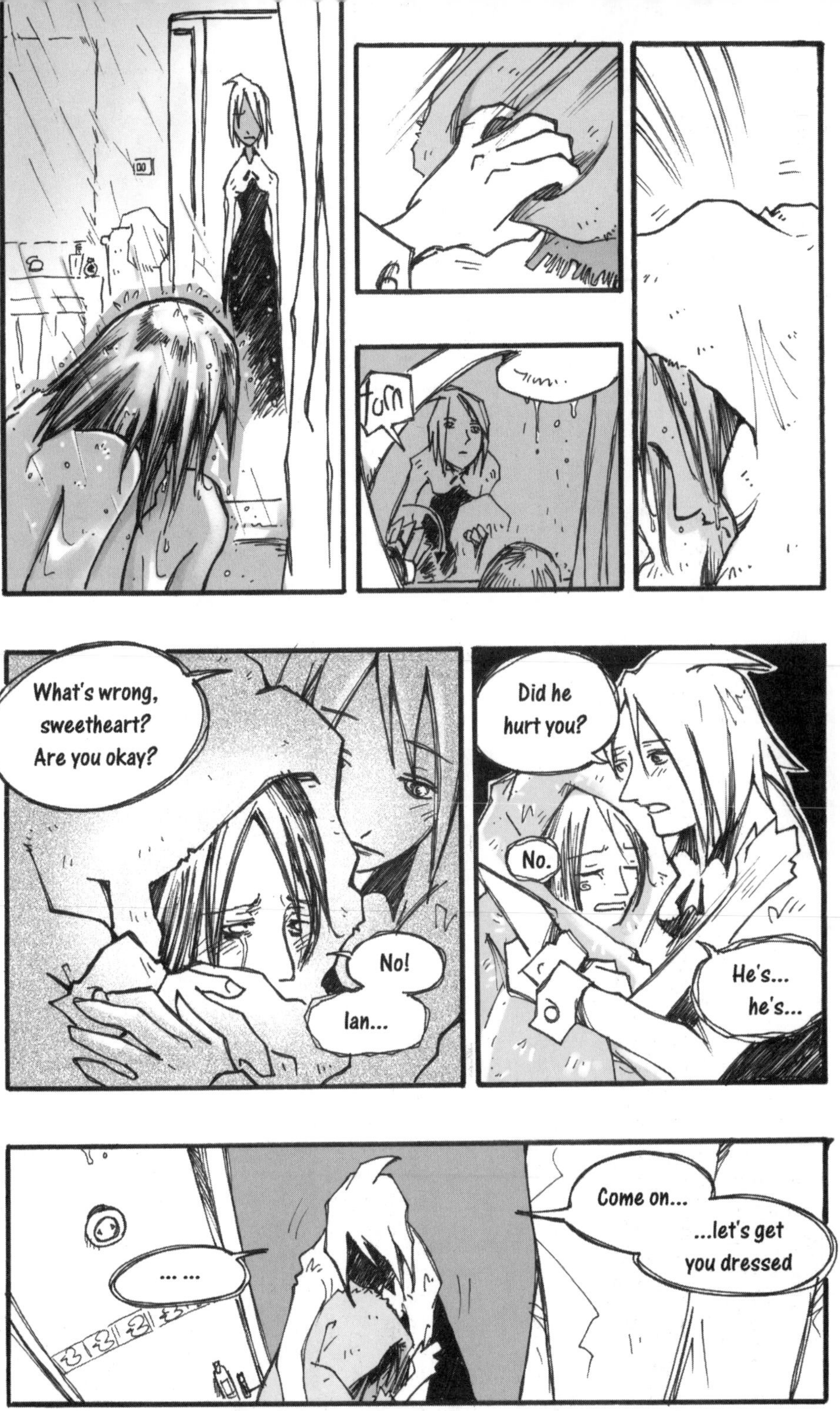
turn
What's wrong, sweetheart? Are you okay?
No!
Ian...
Did he hurt you?
No.
He's... he's...
... ...
Come on...
...let's get you dressed

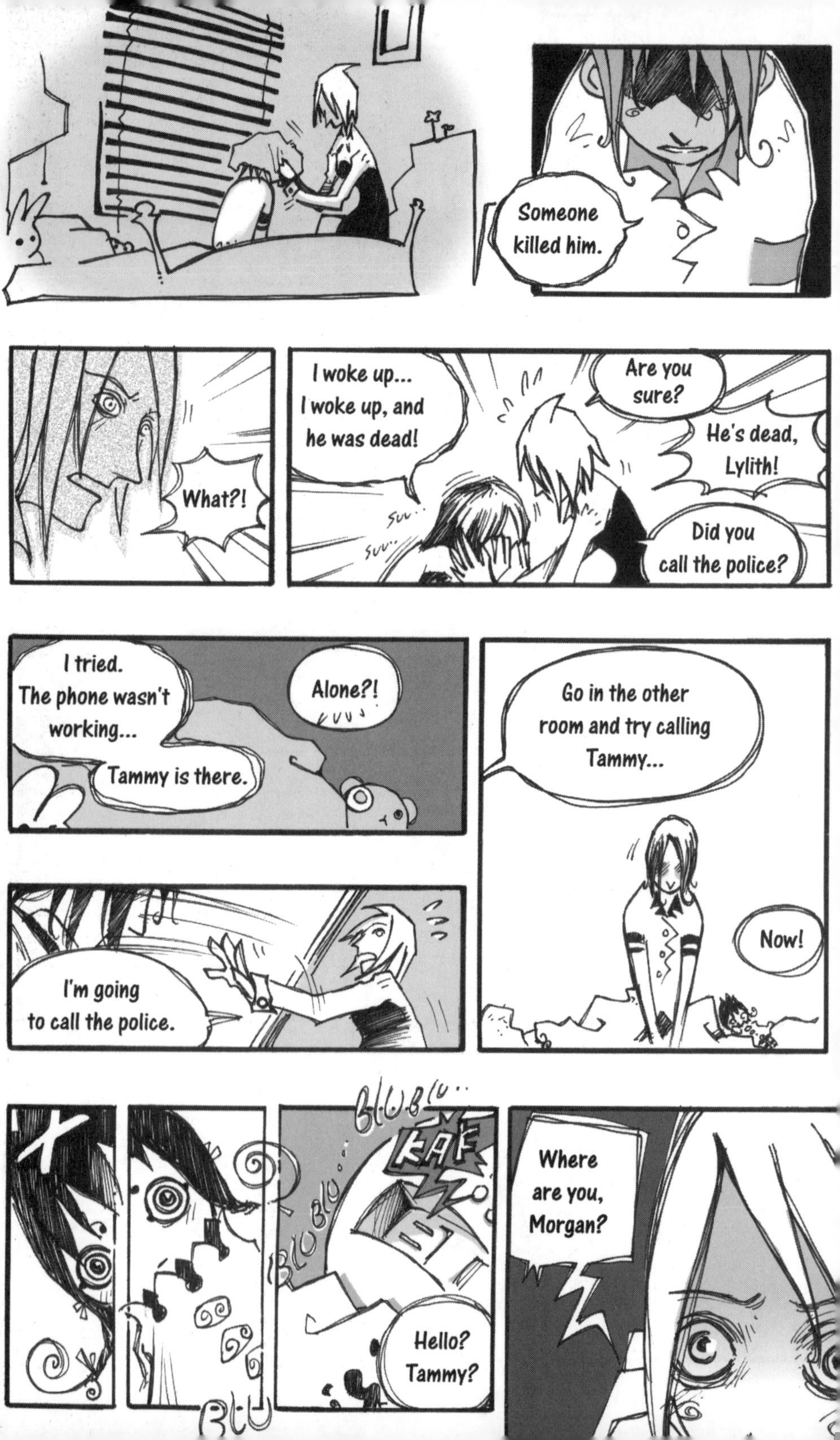
Someone killed him.
What?!
I woke up... I woke up, and he was dead!
Are you sure?
He's dead, Lylith!
Did you call the police?
I tried. The phone wasn't working...
Tammy is there.
Alone?!
Go in the other room and try calling Tammy...
Now!
I'm going to call the police.
KAF
Hello? Tammy?
Where are you, Morgan?

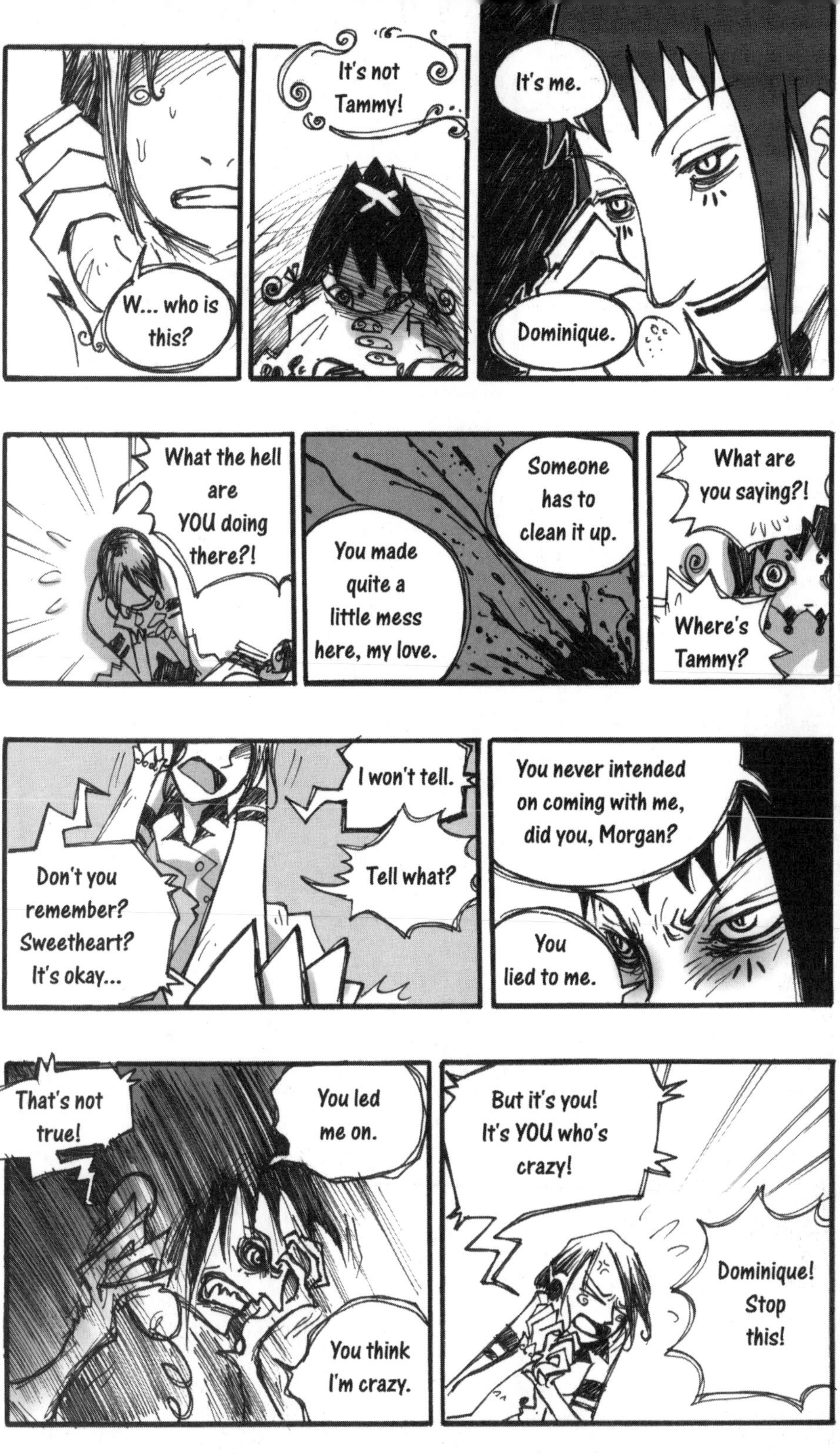
W... who is this?
It's not Tammy!
It's me.
Dominique.
What the hell are YOU doing there?!
Someone has to clean it up.
You made quite a little mess here, my love.
What are you saying?!
Where's Tammy?
I won't tell.
Tell what?
Don't you remember? Sweetheart? It's okay...
You never intended on coming with me, did you, Morgan?
You lied to me.
That's not true!
You led me on.
You think I'm crazy.
But it's you! It's YOU who's crazy!
Dominique! Stop this!

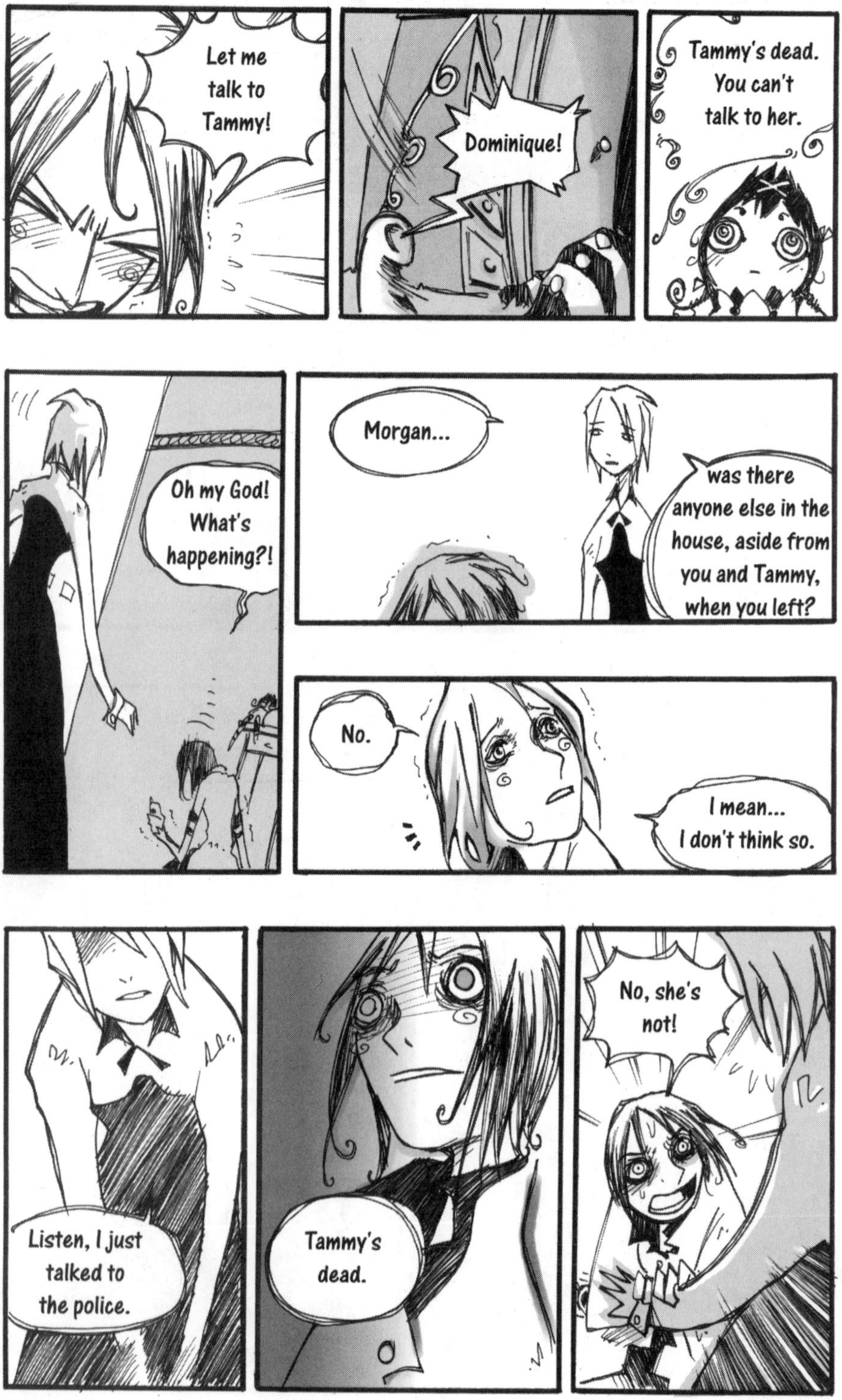
Let me talk to Tammy!
Dominique!
Tammy's dead. You can't talk to her.
Oh my God! What's happening?!
Morgan...
was there anyone else in the house, aside from you and Tammy, when you left?
No.
I mean... I don't think so.
Listen, I just talked to the police.
Tammy's dead.
No, she's not!

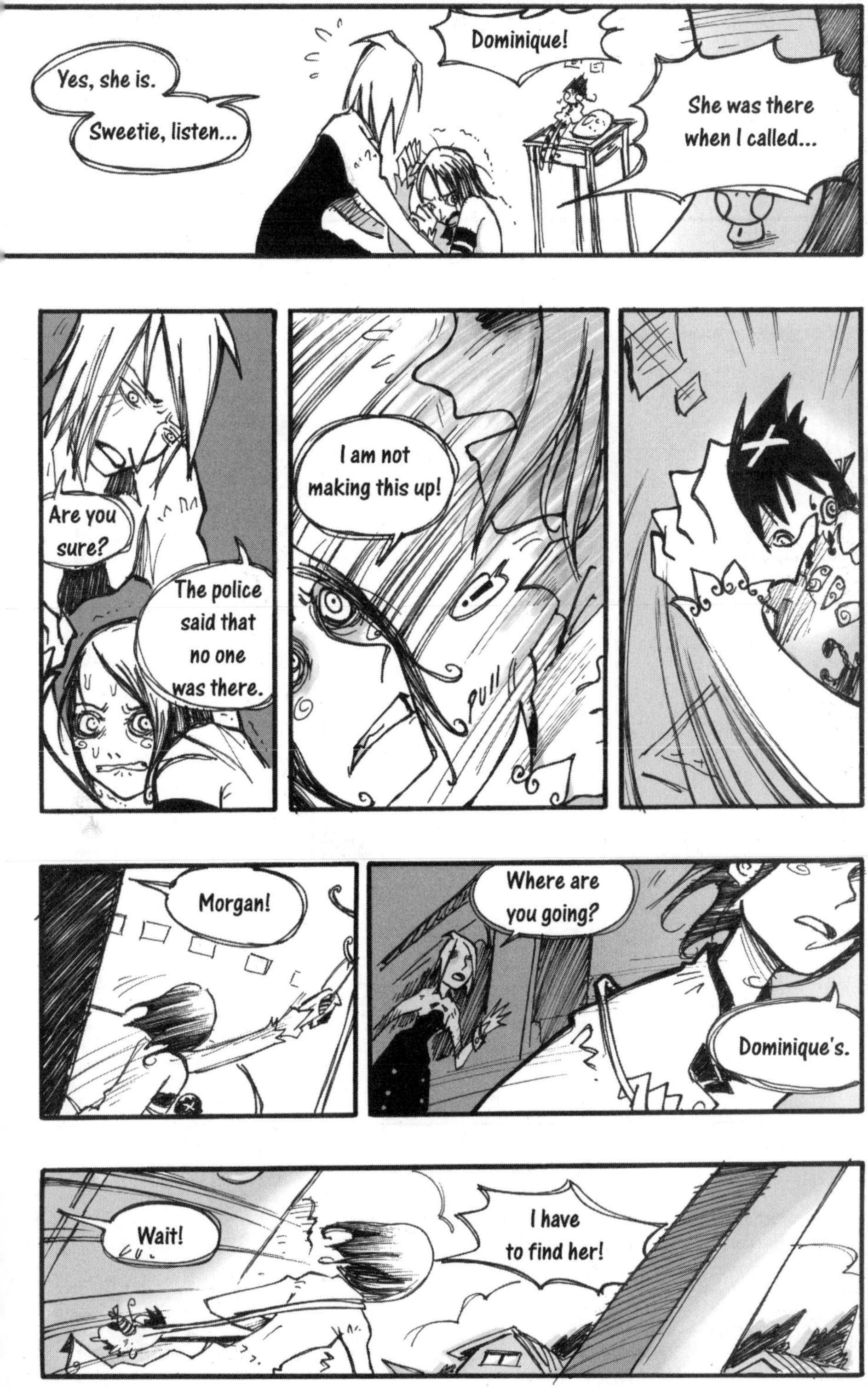
Yes, she is.
Sweetie, listen...
Dominique!
She was there when I called...
Are you sure?
The police said that no one was there.
I am not making this up!
PULL
Morgan!
Where are you going?
Dominique's.
Wait!
I have to find her!

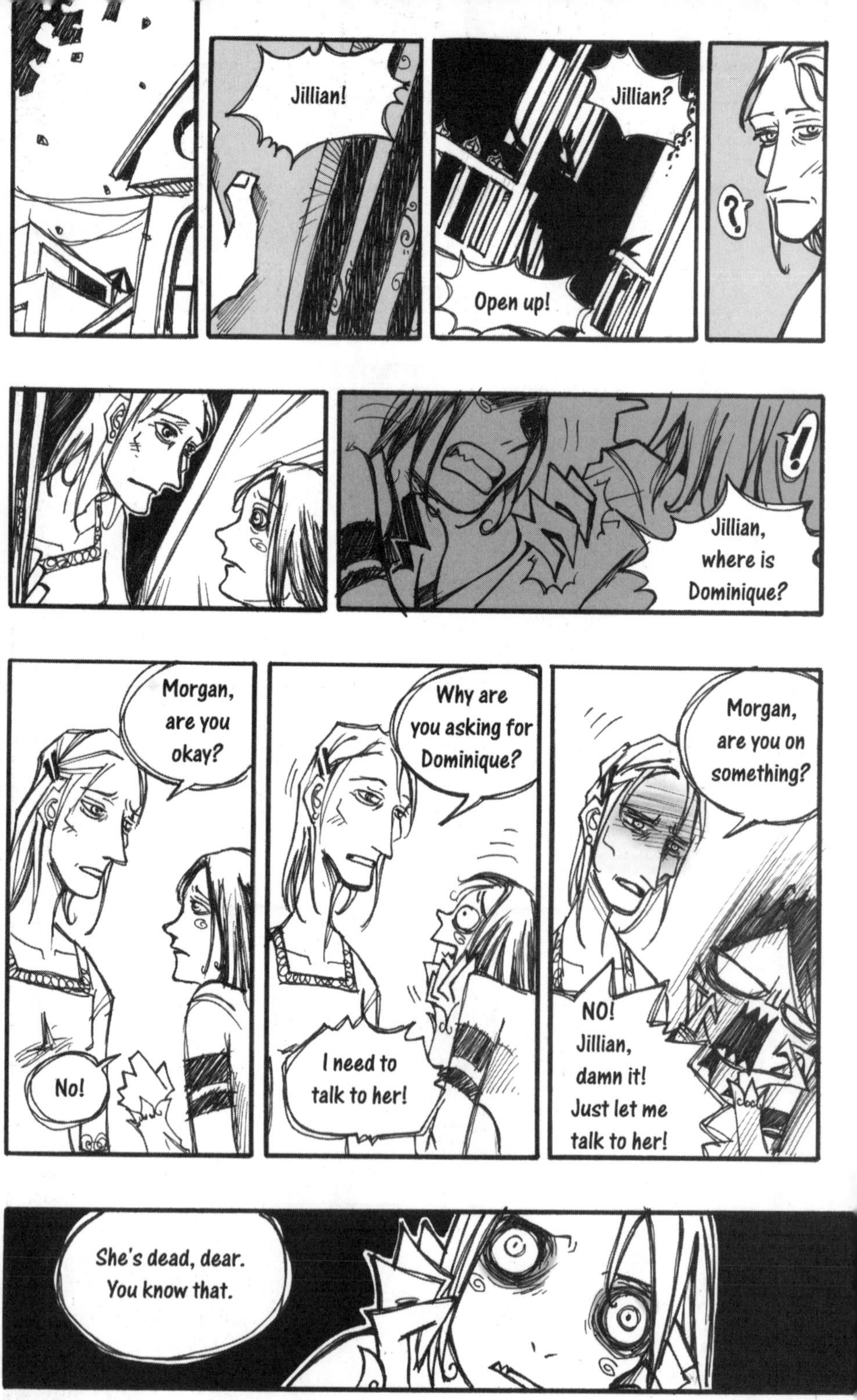

Jillian!
Jillian?
Open up!
?
!
Jillian, where is Dominique?
Morgan, are you okay?
No!
Why are you asking for Dominique?
I need to talk to her!
Morgan, are you on something?
NO! Jillian, damn it! Just let me talk to her!
She's dead, dear. You know that.

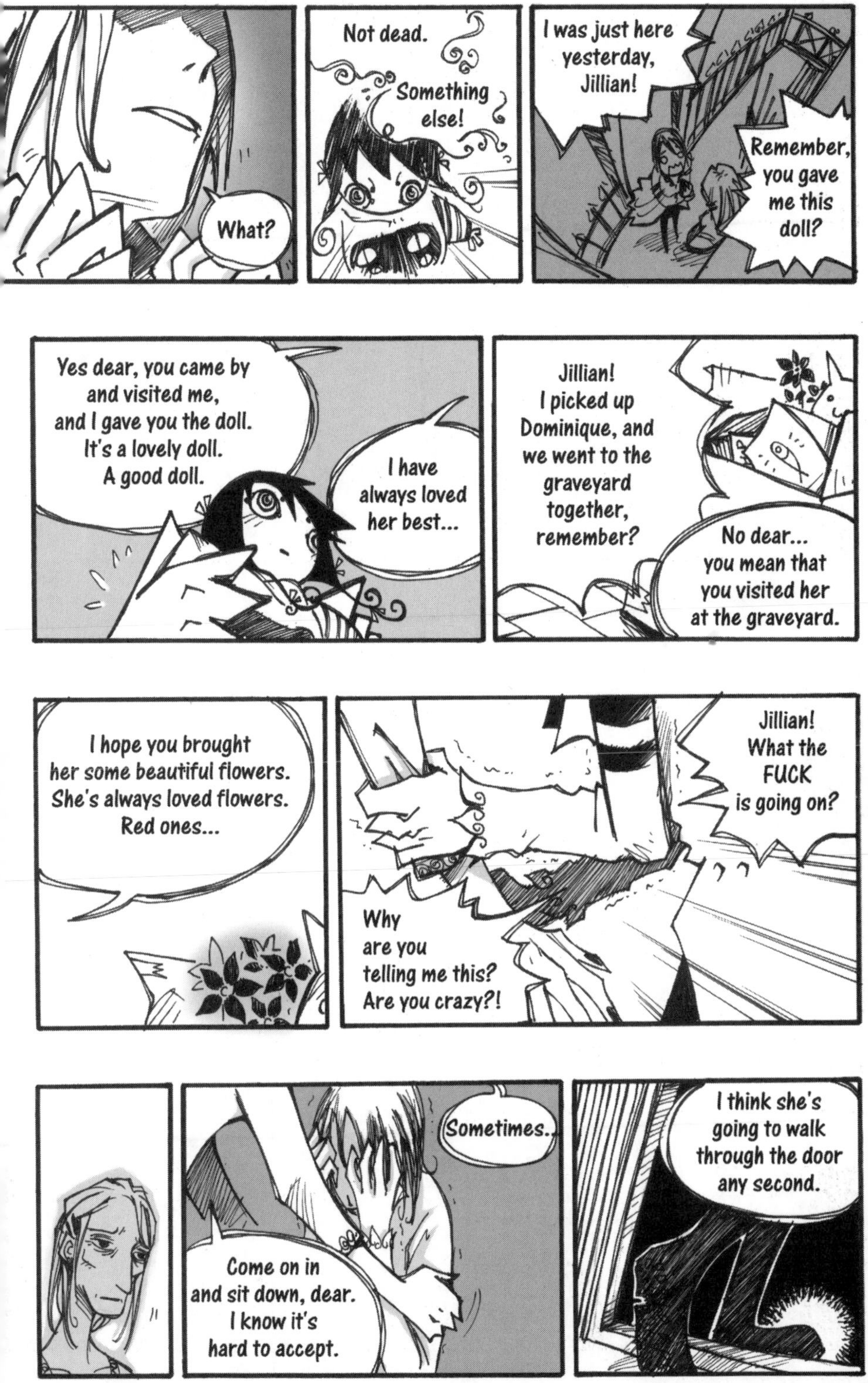
What?
Not dead.
Something else!
I was just here yesterday, Jillian!
Remember, you gave me this doll?
Yes dear, you came by and visited me, and I gave you the doll. It's a lovely doll. A good doll.
I have always loved her best...
Jillian! I picked up Dominique, and we went to the graveyard together, remember?
No dear... you mean that you visited her at the graveyard.
I hope you brought her some beautiful flowers. She's always loved flowers. Red ones...
Jillian! What the FUCK is going on?
Why are you telling me this? Are you crazy?!
Sometimes...
Come on in and sit down, dear. I know it's hard to accept.
I think she's going to walk through the door any second.

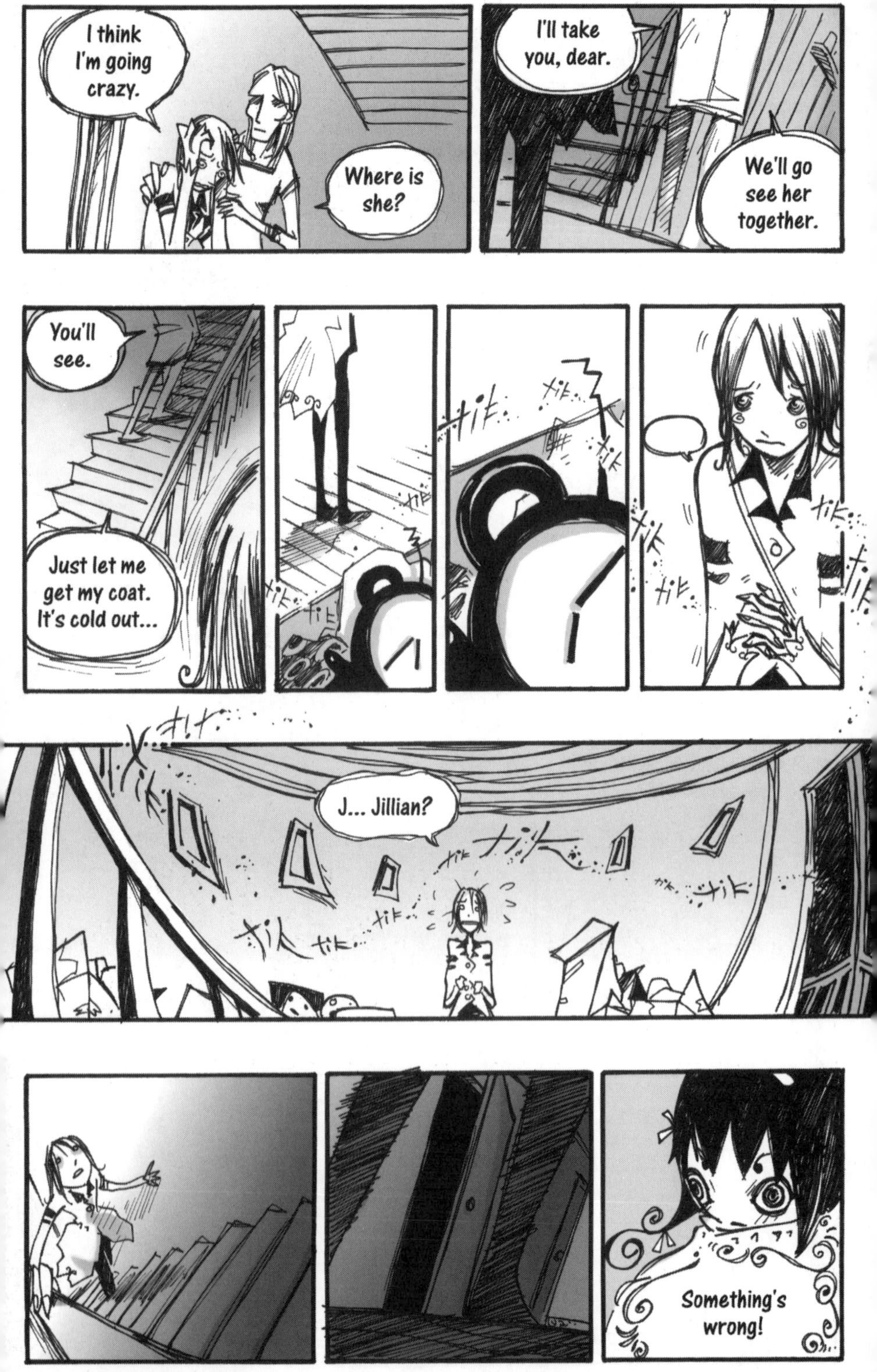
I think I'm going crazy.
Where is she?
I'll take you, dear.
We'll go see her together.
You'll see.
Just let me get my coat. It's cold out...
J... Jillian?
Something's wrong!

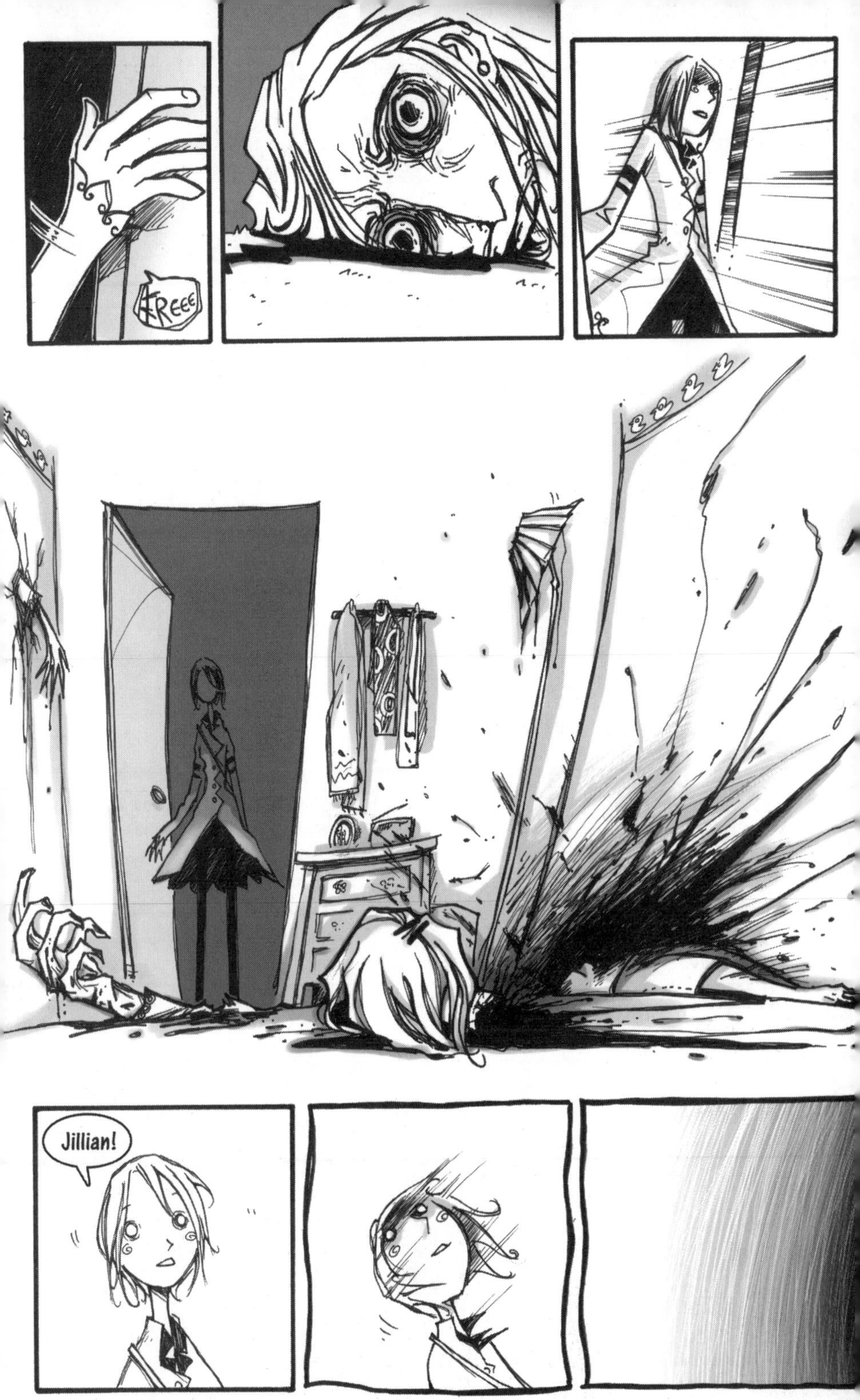
KREEE
Jillian!

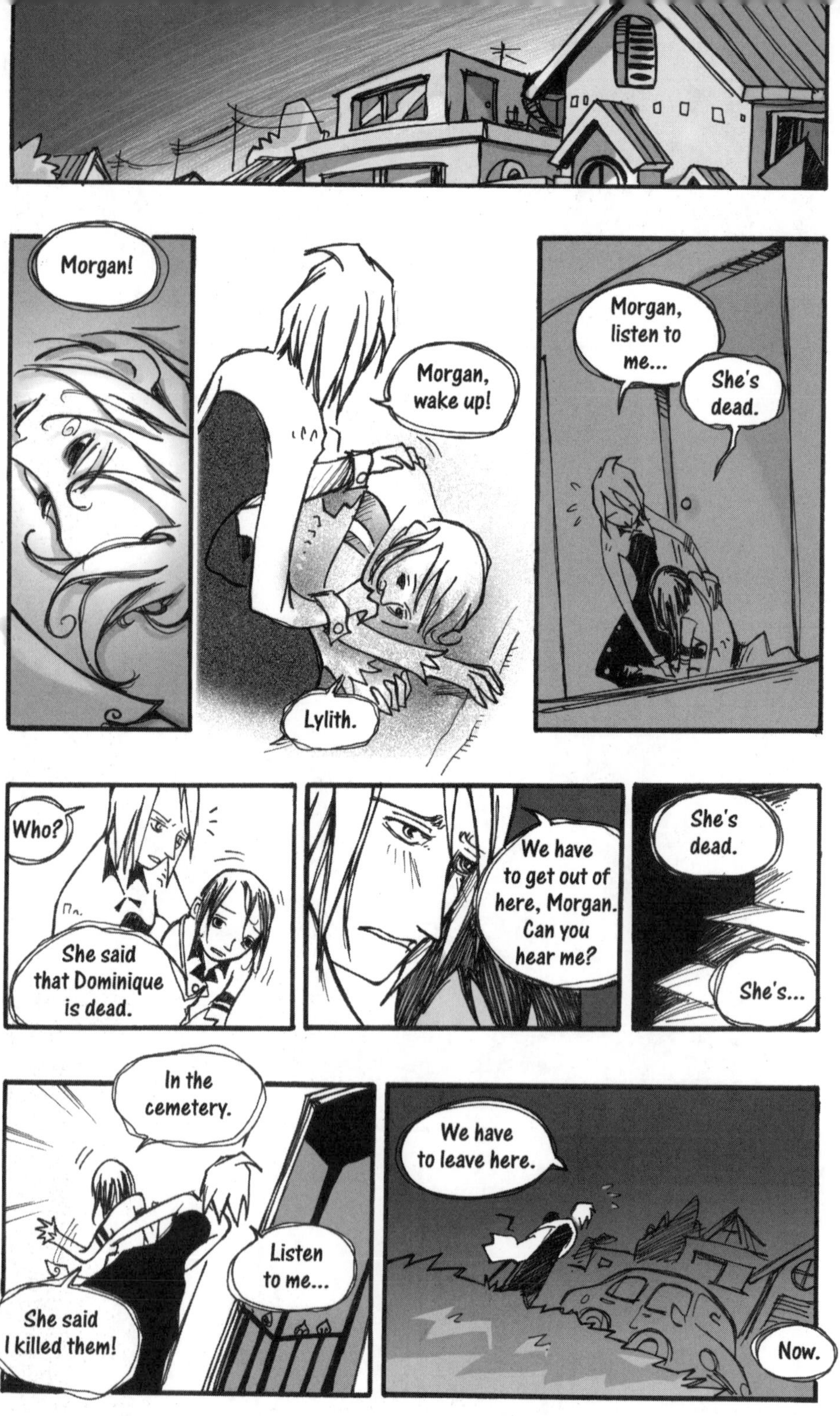

Morgan!
Morgan, wake up!
Lylith.
Morgan, listen to me...
She's dead.
Who?
She said that Dominique is dead.
We have to get out of here, Morgan. Can you hear me?
She's dead.
She's...
In the cemetery.
Listen to me...
She said I killed them!
We have to leave here.
Now.

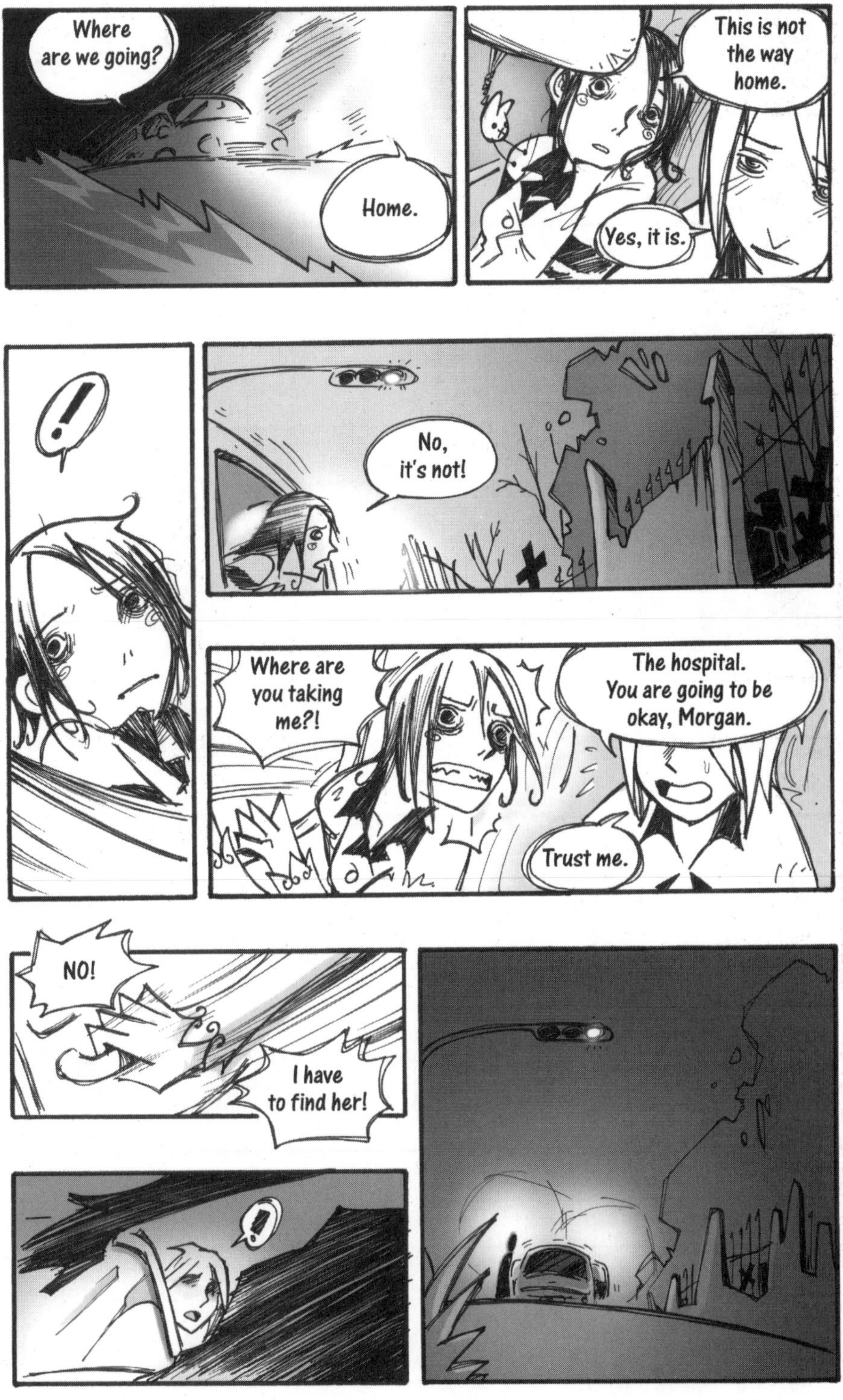
Where are we going?
Home.
This is not the way home.
Yes, it is.
!
No, it's not!
Where are you taking me?!
The hospital. You are going to be okay, Morgan.
Trust me.
NO!
I have to find her!
!

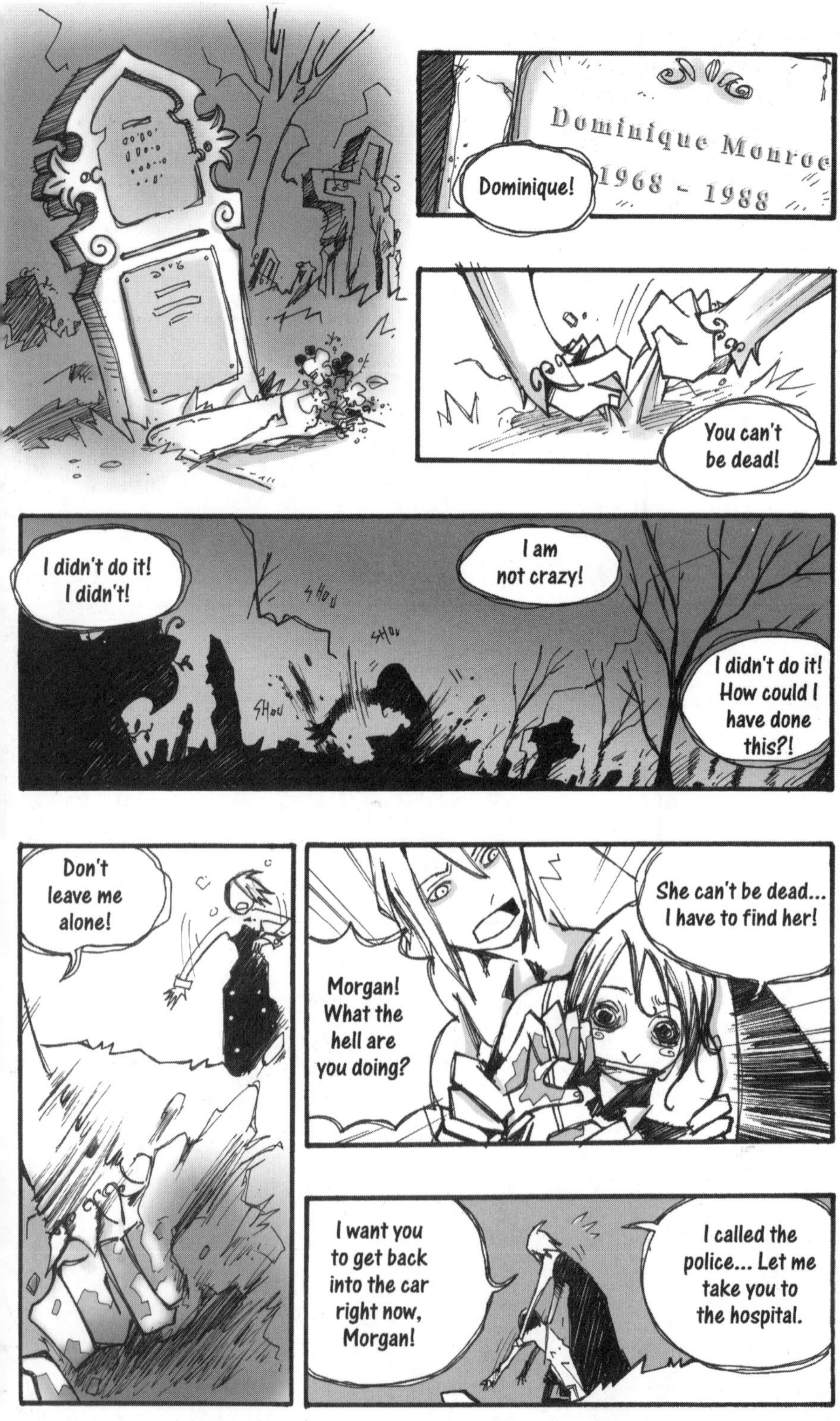

Dominique Monroe
1968 - 1988
Dominique!
You can't be dead!
I didn't do it! I didn't!
I am not crazy!
SHOU
SHOU
SHOU
I didn't do it! How could I have done this?!
Don't leave me alone!
She can't be dead... I have to find her!
Morgan! What the hell are you doing?
I called the police... Let me take you to the hospital.
I want you to get back into the car right now, Morgan!

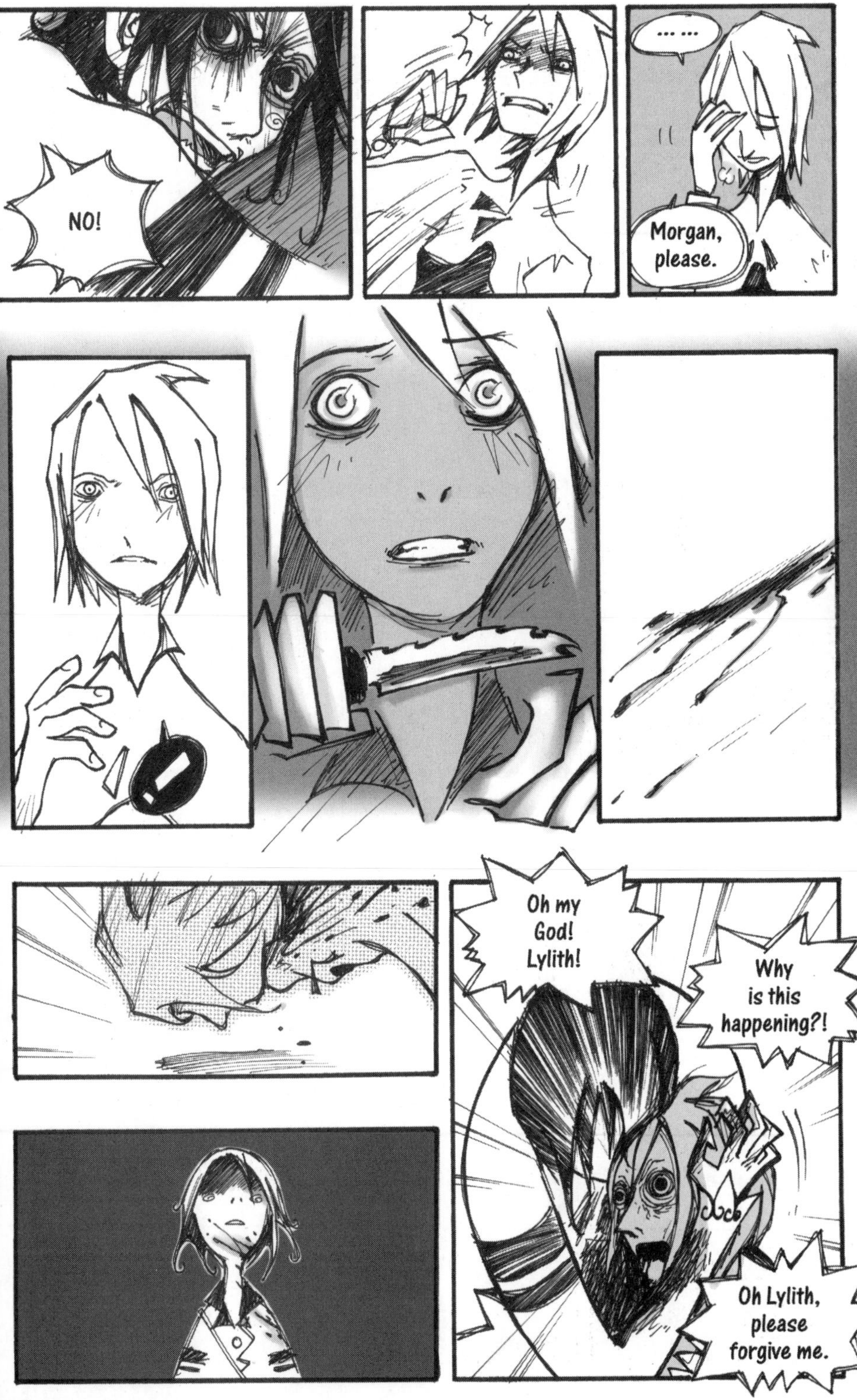
NO!
... ...
Morgan, please.
Oh my God! Lylith!
Why is this happening?!
Oh Lylith, please forgive me.

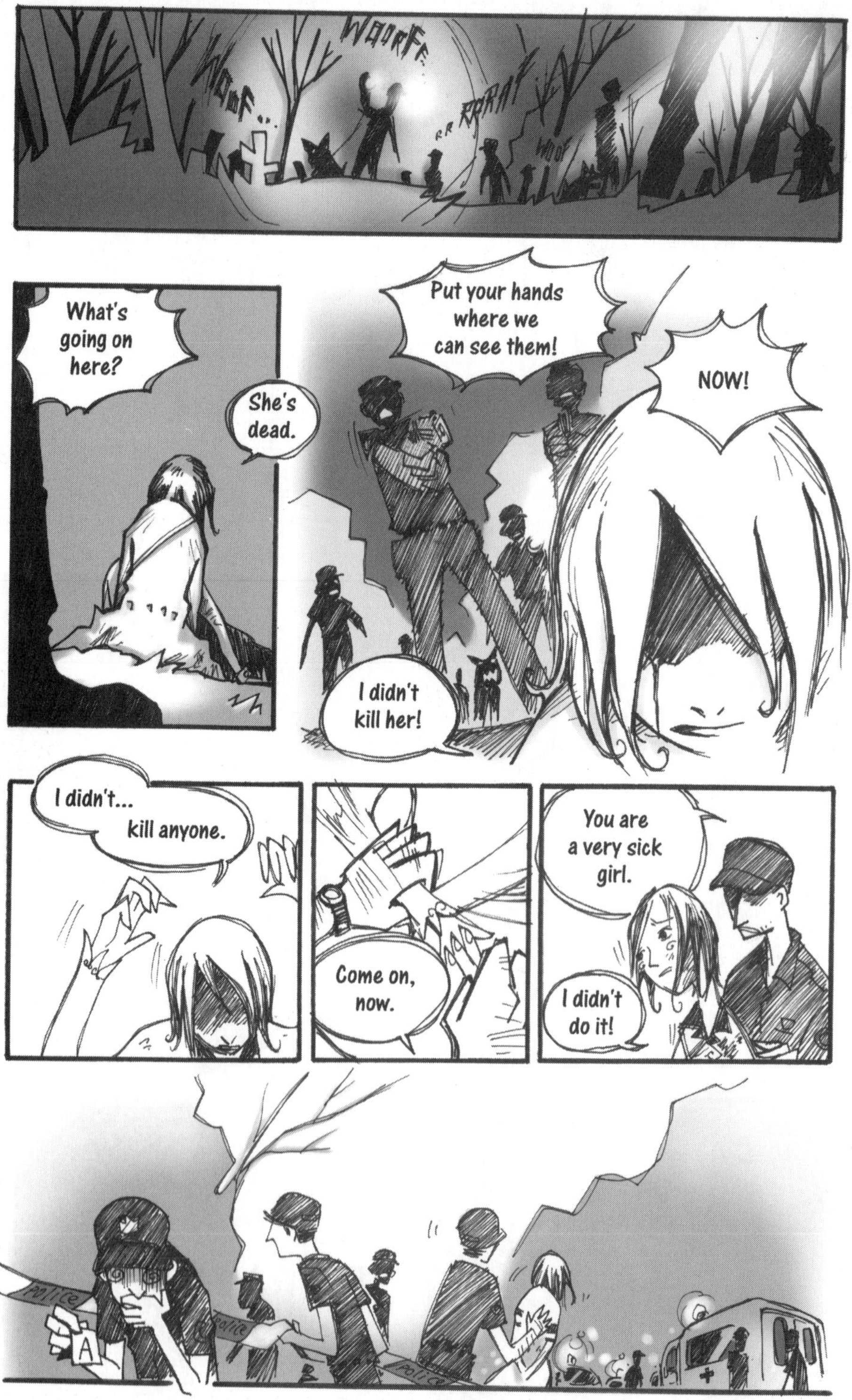
What's going on here?
She's dead.
Put your hands where we can see them!
NOW!
I didn't kill her!
I didn't... kill anyone.
Come on, now.
You are a very sick girl.
I didn't do it!

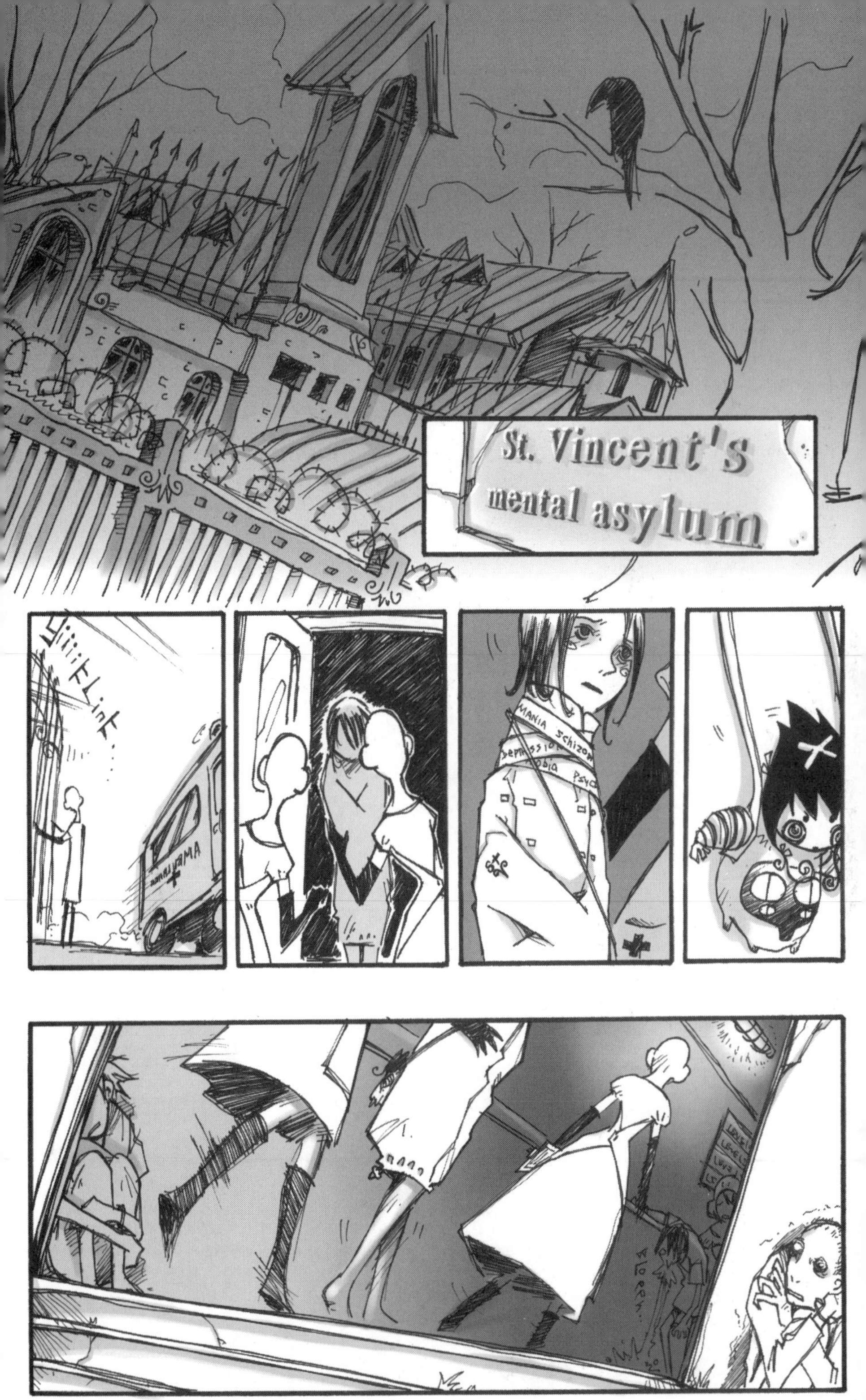
St. Vincent's
mental asylum
MANIA

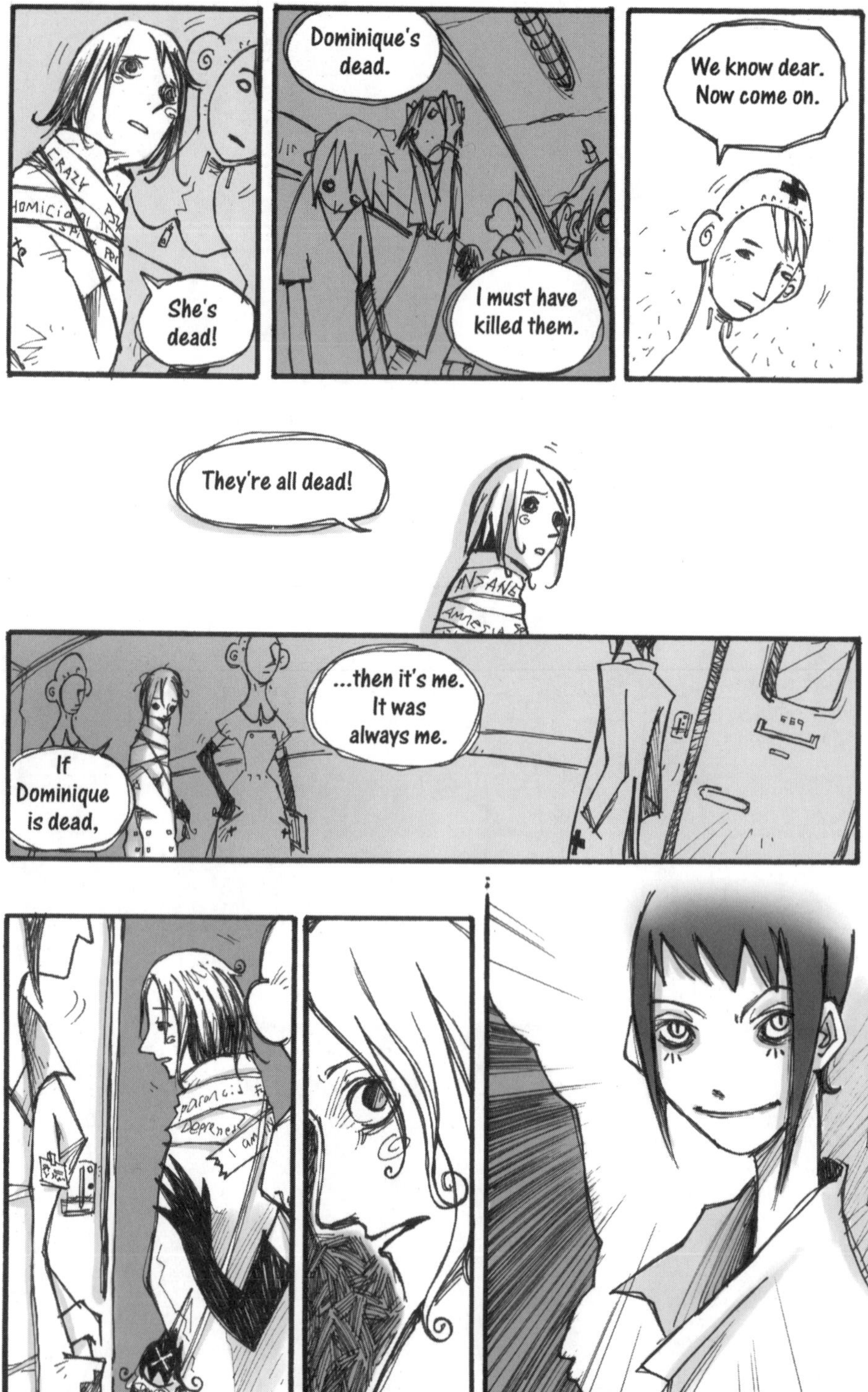
She's dead!
Dominique's dead.
I must have killed them.
We know dear. Now come on.
They're all dead!
If Dominique is dead,
...then it's me. It was always me.

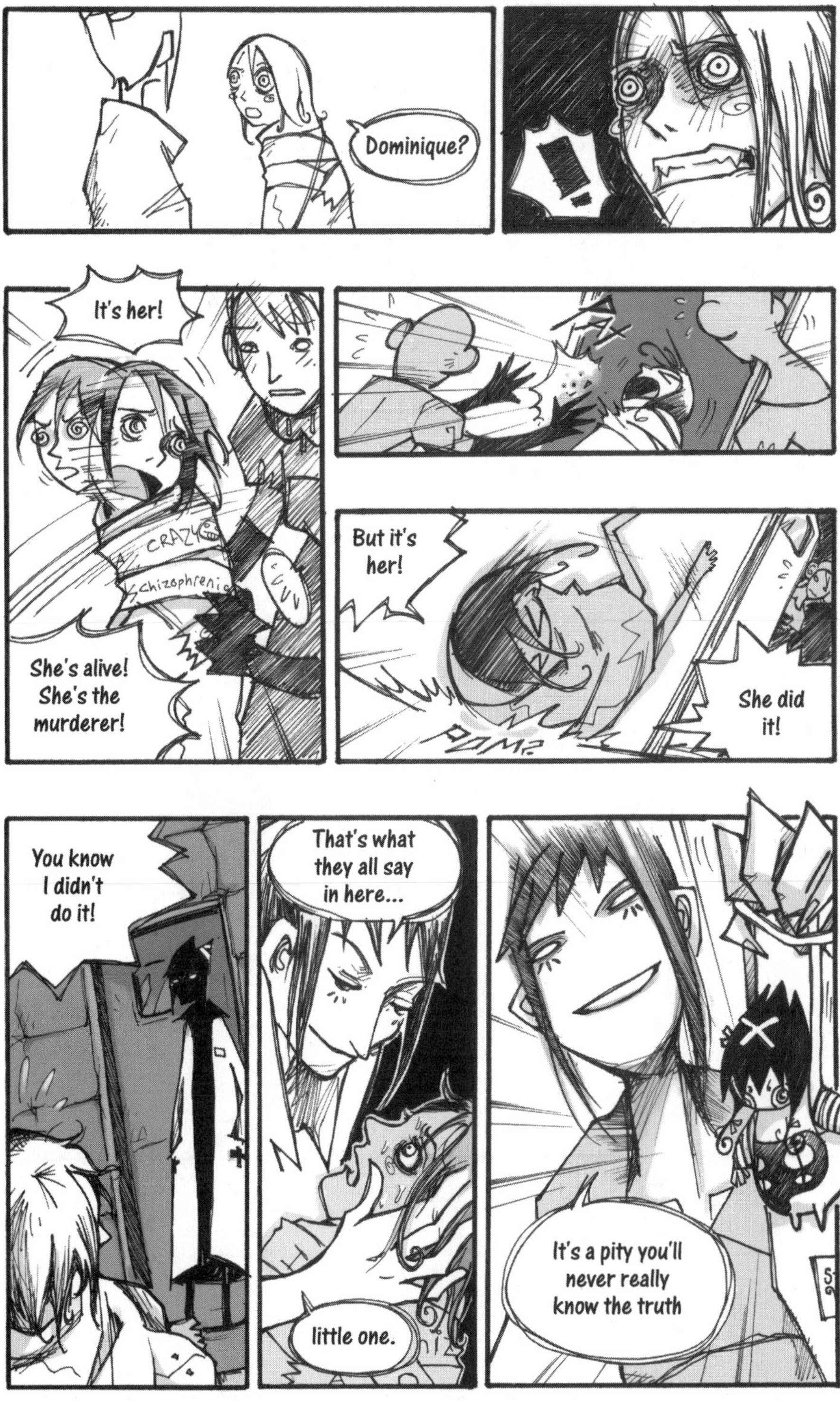
Dominique?
!
It's her!
CRAZY
schizophrenic
She's alive! She's the murderer!
But it's her!
POM?
She did it!
You know I didn't do it!
That's what they all say in here...
little one.
It's a pity you'll never really know the truth

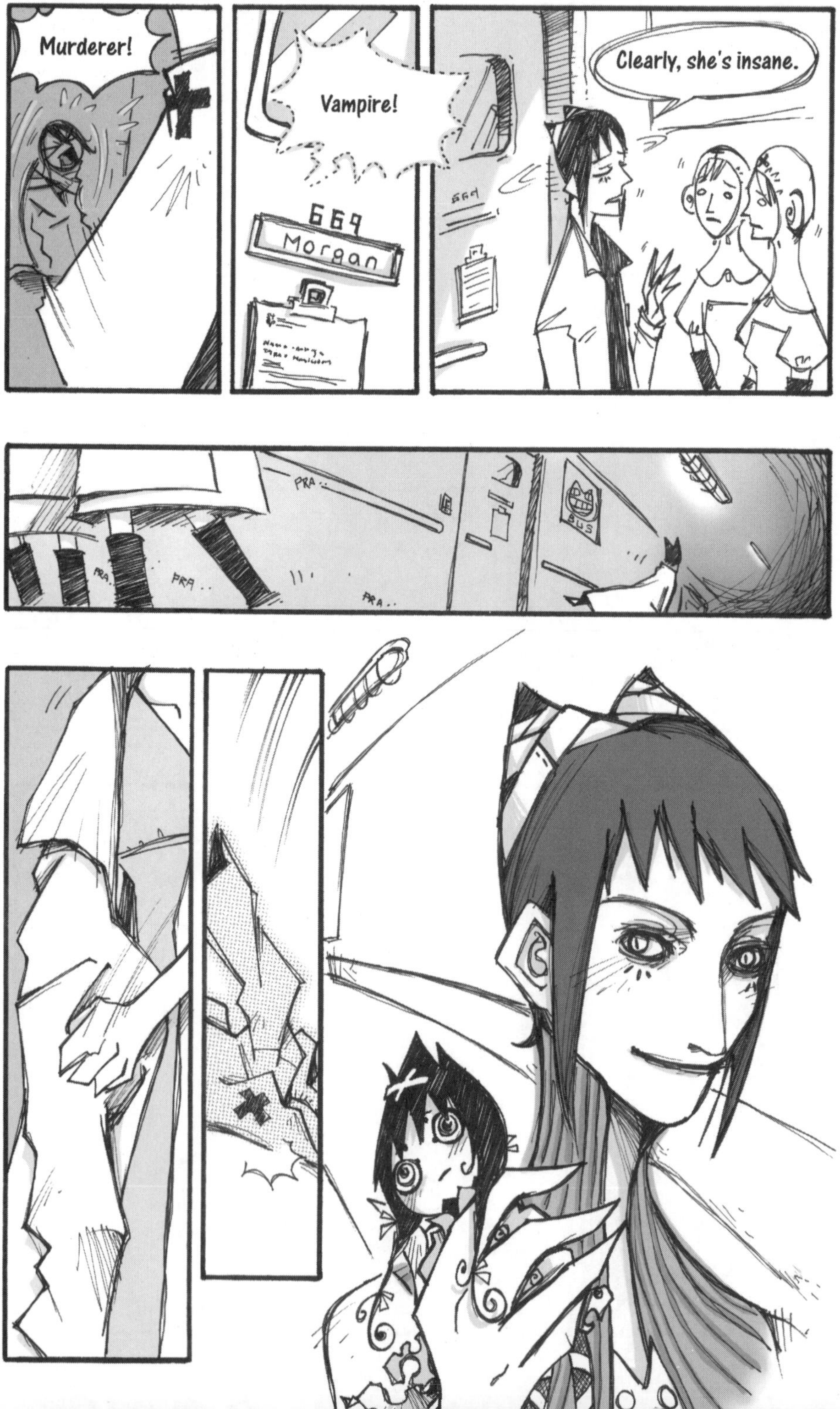

Murderer!
Vampire!
669
Morgan
Clearly, she's insane.
669
PRA..
PRA..
PRA..
PRA..
BUS

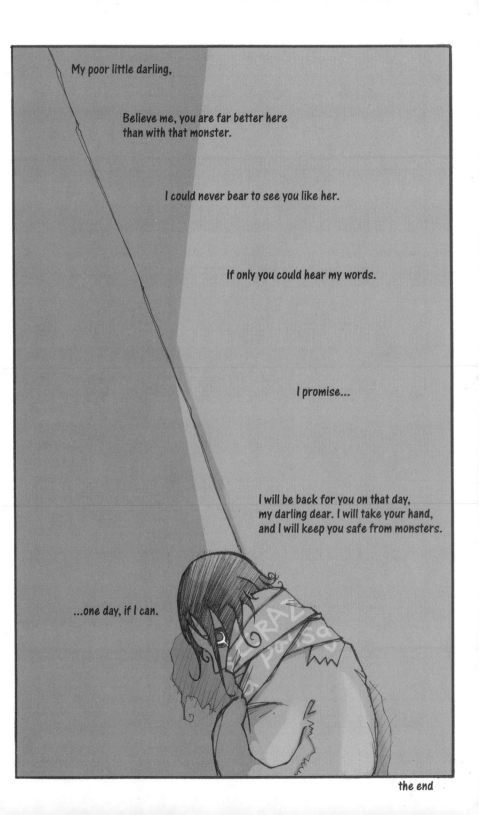

My poor little darling,

Believe me, you are far better here
than with that monster.

I could never bear to see you like her.

If only you could hear my words.

I promise...

I will be back for you on that day,
my darling dear. I will take your hand,
and I will keep you safe from monsters.

...one day, if I can.

the end

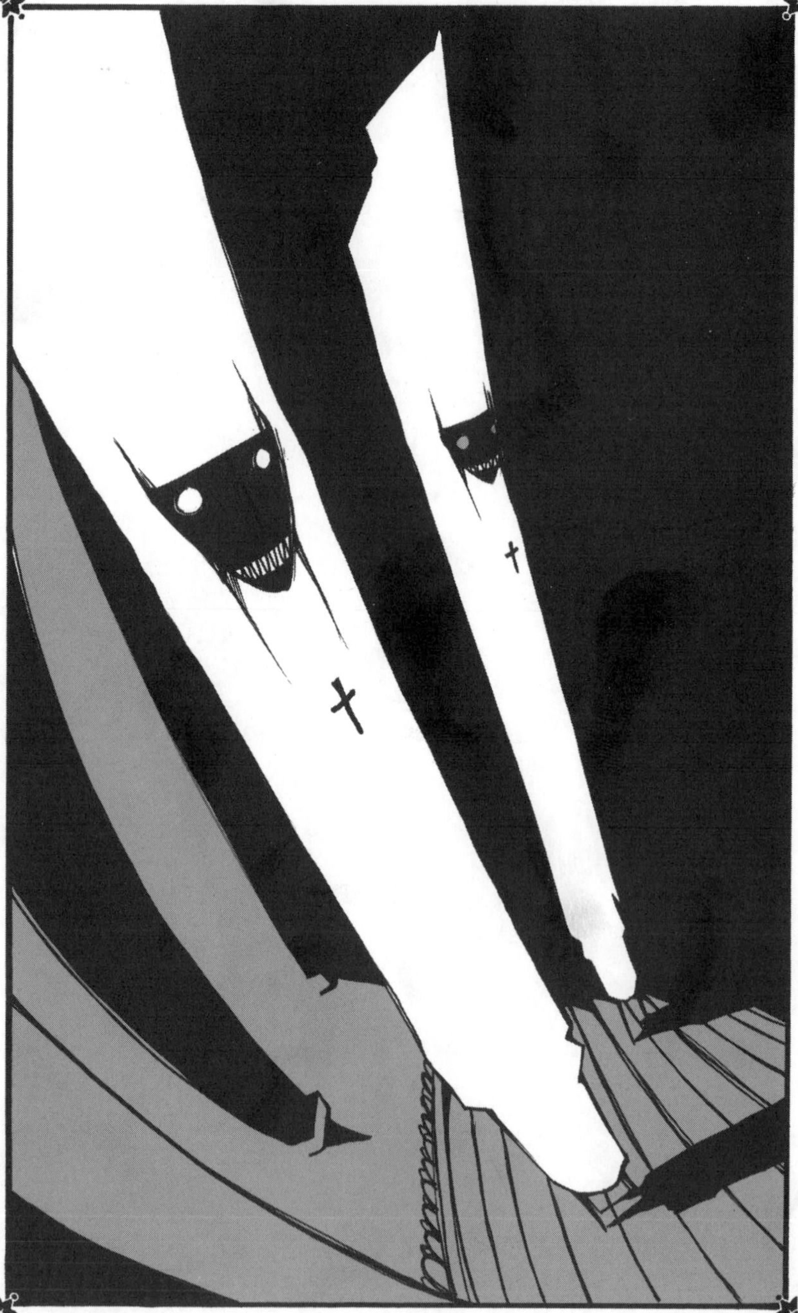

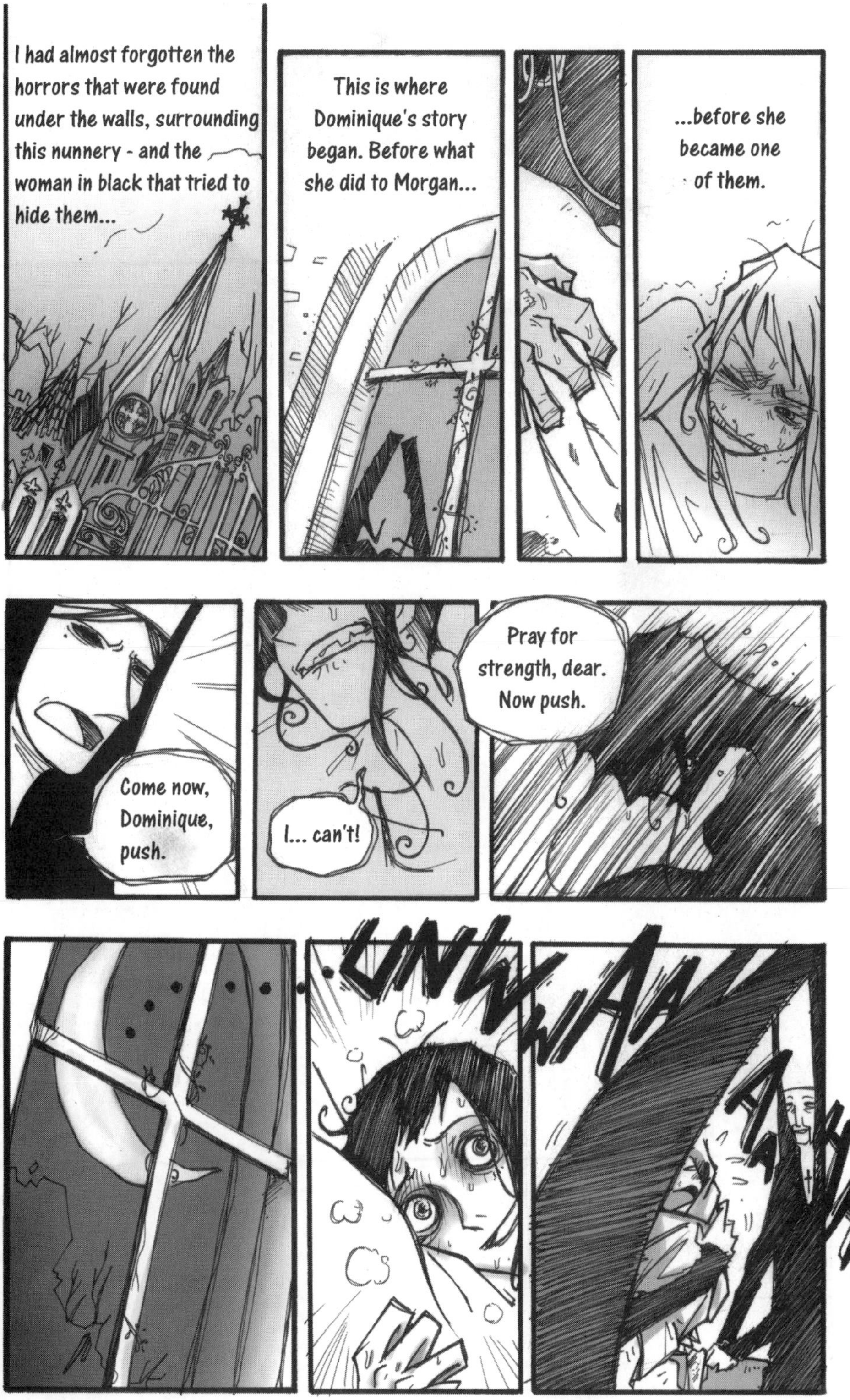
I had almost forgotten the horrors that were found under the walls, surrounding this nunnery - and the woman in black that tried to hide them...
This is where Dominique's story began. Before what she did to Morgan...
...before she became one of them.
Come now, Dominique, push.
I... can't!
Pray for strength, dear. Now push.
UNWAAAAAH

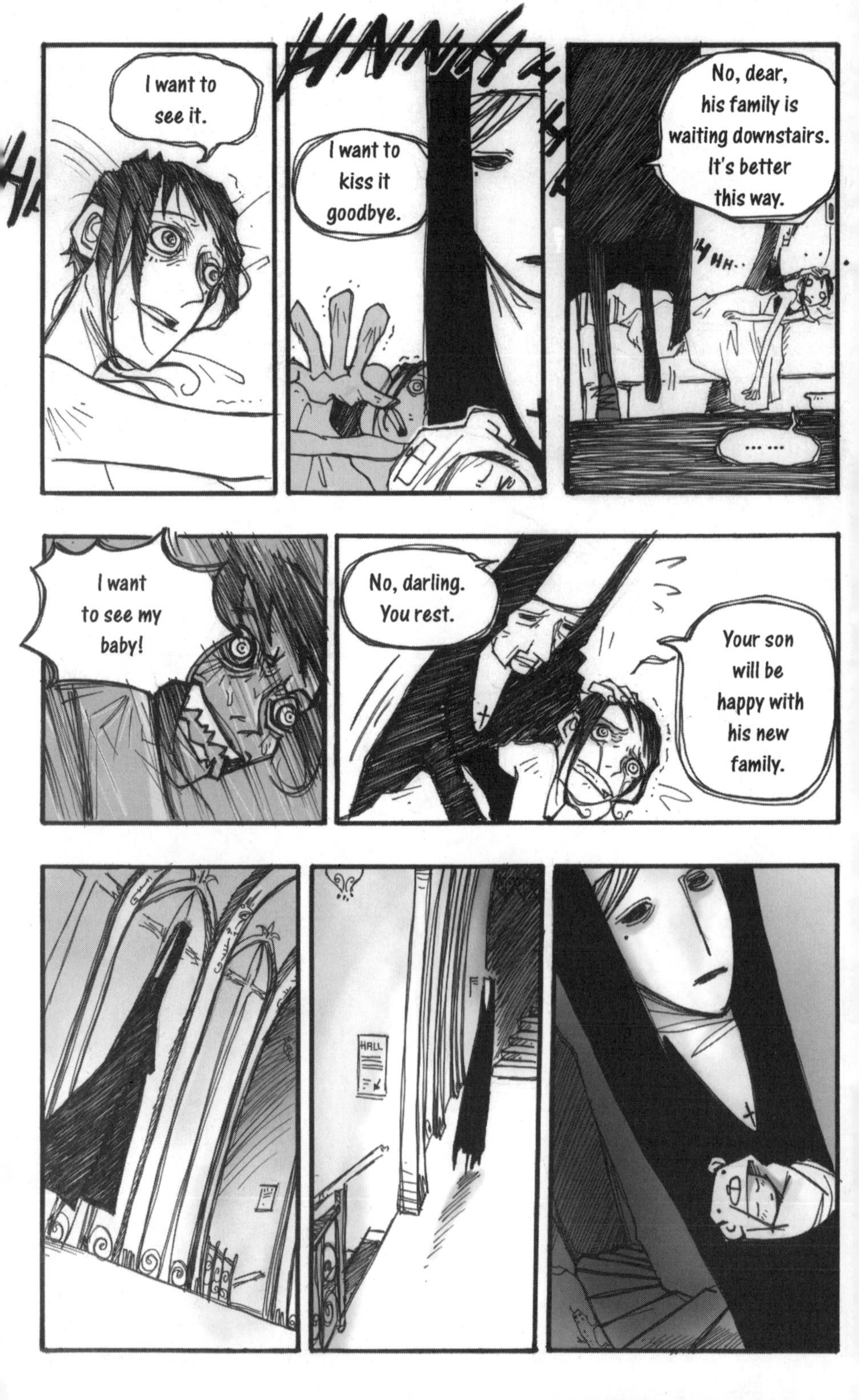
I want to see it.
I want to kiss it goodbye.
No, dear, his family is waiting downstairs. It's better this way.
... ...
I want to see my baby!
No, darling. You rest.
Your son will be happy with his new family.
HALL

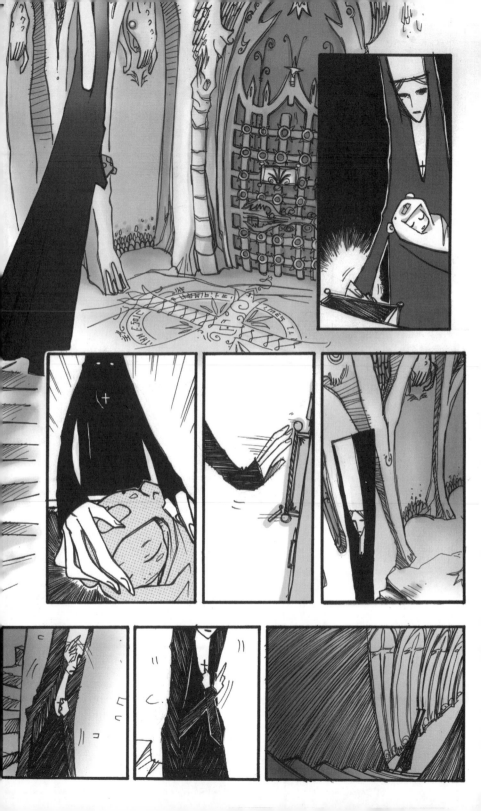

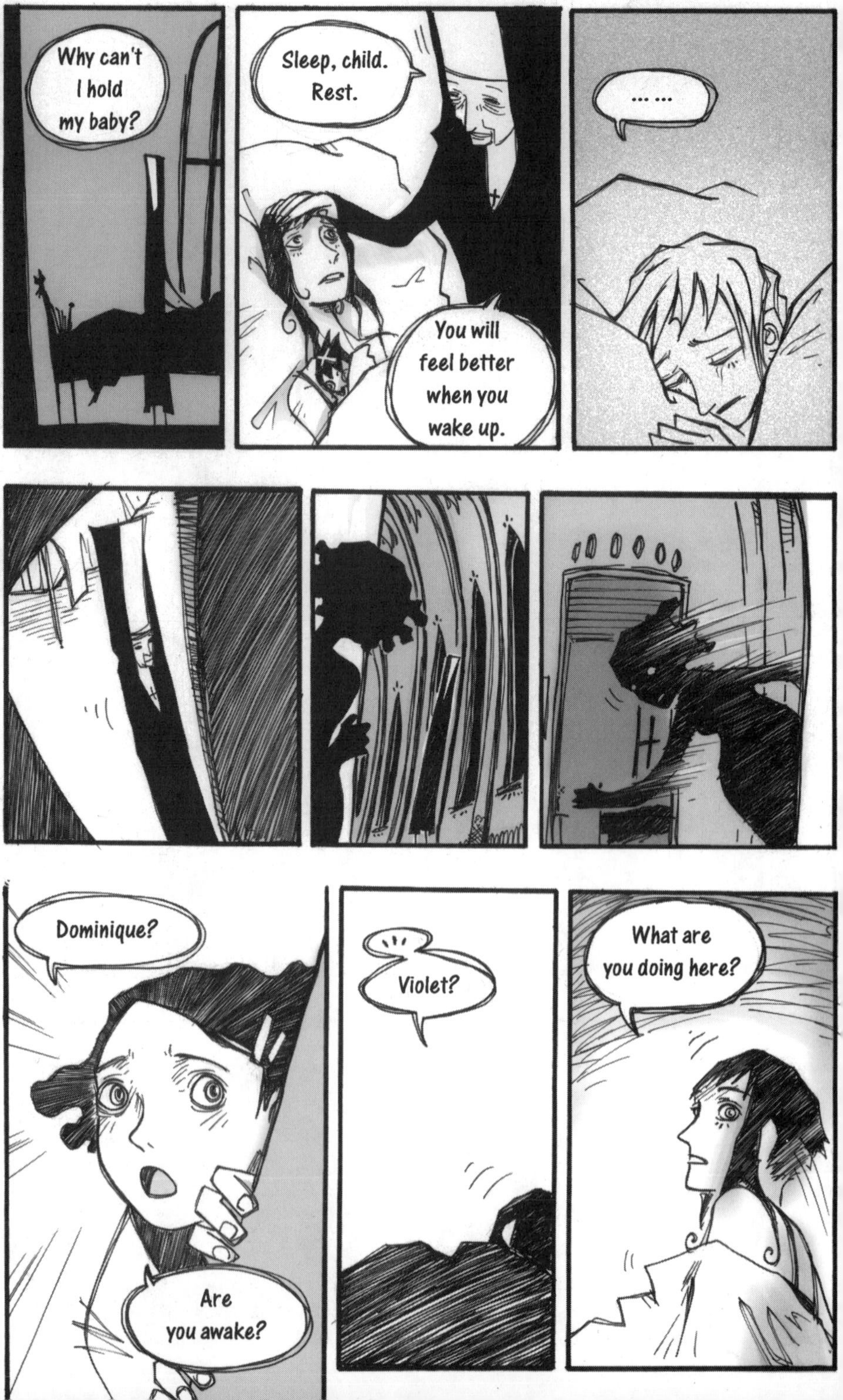
Why can't I hold my baby?
Sleep, child. Rest.
You will feel better when you wake up.
... ...
Dominique?
Are you awake?
Violet?
What are you doing here?

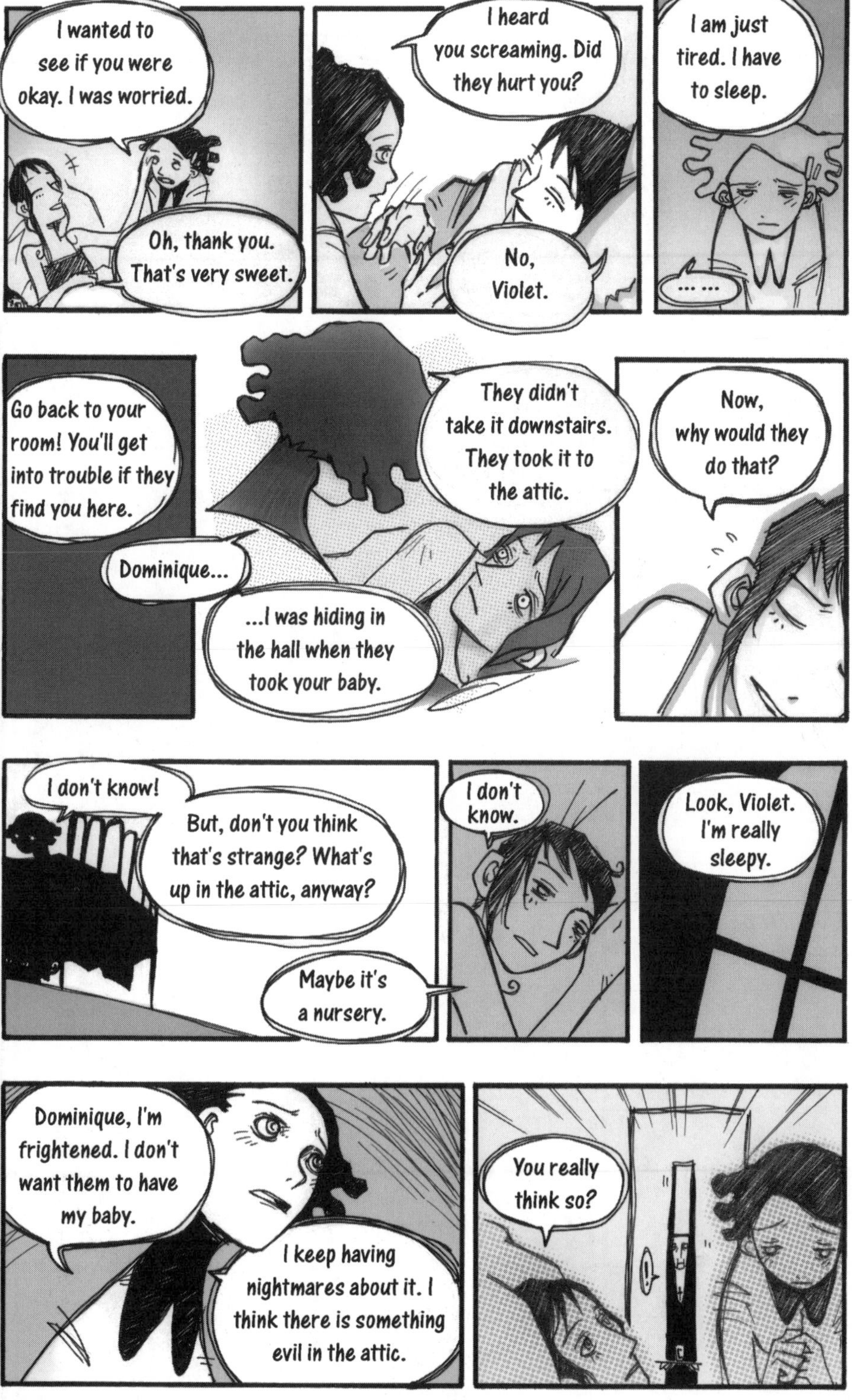
I wanted to see if you were okay. I was worried.
Oh, thank you. That's very sweet.
I heard you screaming. Did they hurt you?
No, Violet.
I am just tired. I have to sleep.
... ...
Go back to your room! You'll get into trouble if they find you here.
Dominique...
...I was hiding in the hall when they took your baby.
They didn't take it downstairs. They took it to the attic.
Now, why would they do that?
I don't know!
But, don't you think that's strange? What's up in the attic, anyway?
Maybe it's a nursery.
I don't know.
Look, Violet. I'm really sleepy.
Dominique, I'm frightened. I don't want them to have my baby.
I keep having nightmares about it. I think there is something evil in the attic.
You really think so?

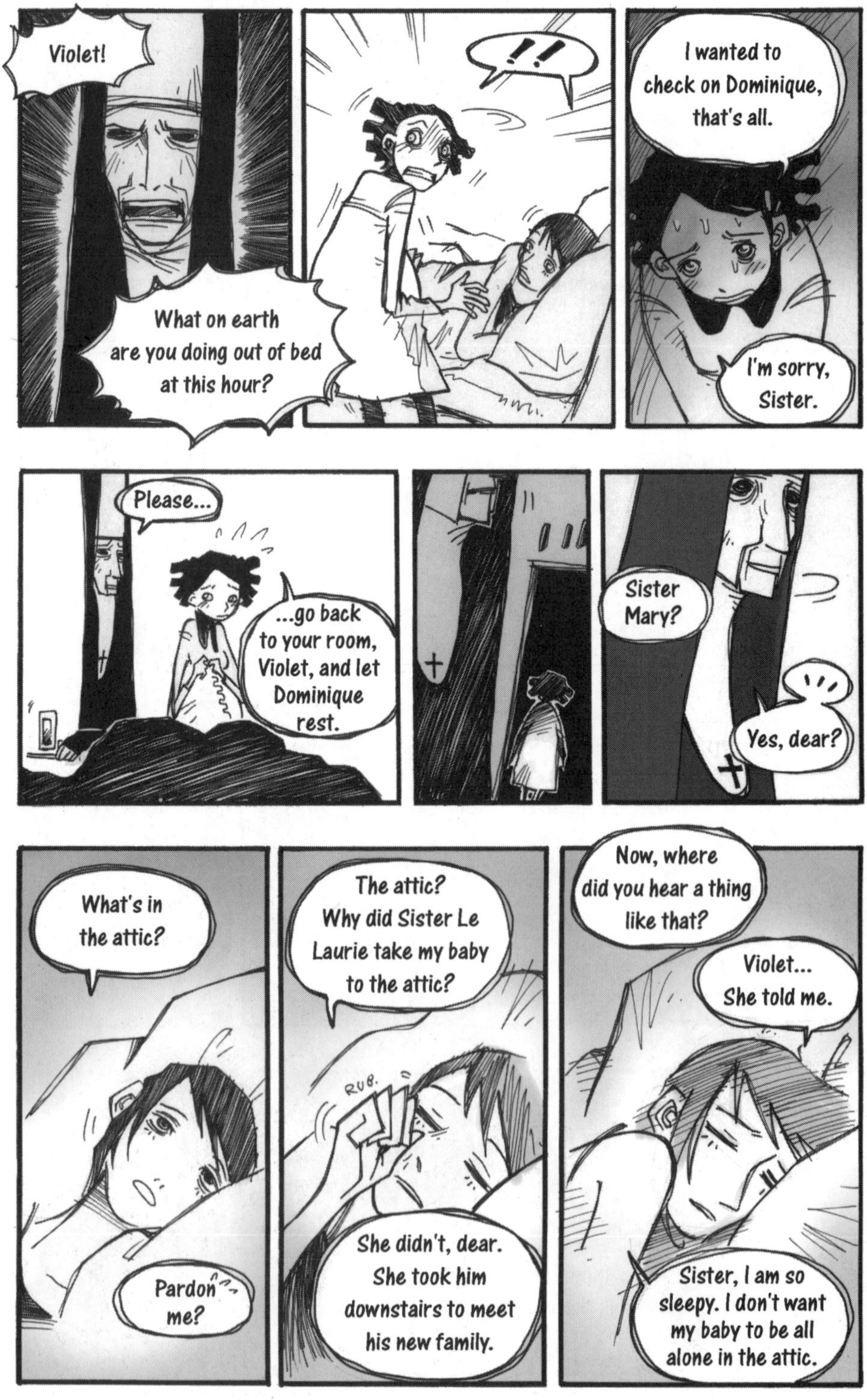
Violet!
What on earth are you doing out of bed at this hour?
!!
I wanted to check on Dominique, that's all.
I'm sorry, Sister.
Please...
...go back to your room, Violet, and let Dominique rest.
Sister Mary?
Yes, dear?
What's in the attic?
Pardon me?
The attic? Why did Sister Le Laurie take my baby to the attic?
RUB.
She didn't, dear. She took him downstairs to meet his new family.
Now, where did you hear a thing like that?
Violet... She told me.
Sister, I am so sleepy. I don't want my baby to be all alone in the attic.

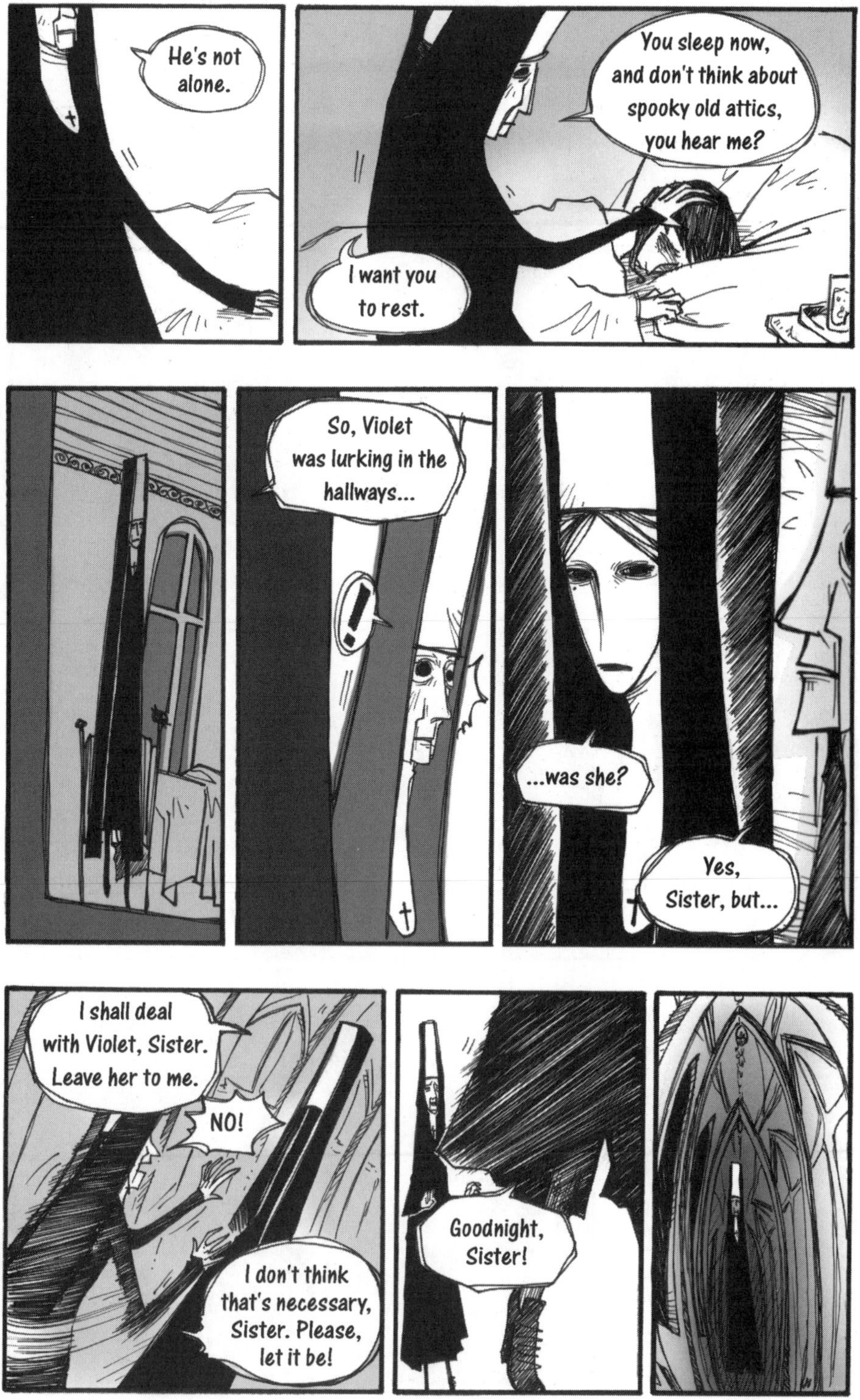
He's not alone.
You sleep now, and don't think about spooky old attics, you hear me?
I want you to rest.
So, Violet was lurking in the hallways...
!
...was she?
Yes, Sister, but...
I shall deal with Violet, Sister. Leave her to me.
NO!
I don't think that's necessary, Sister. Please, let it be!
Goodnight, Sister!

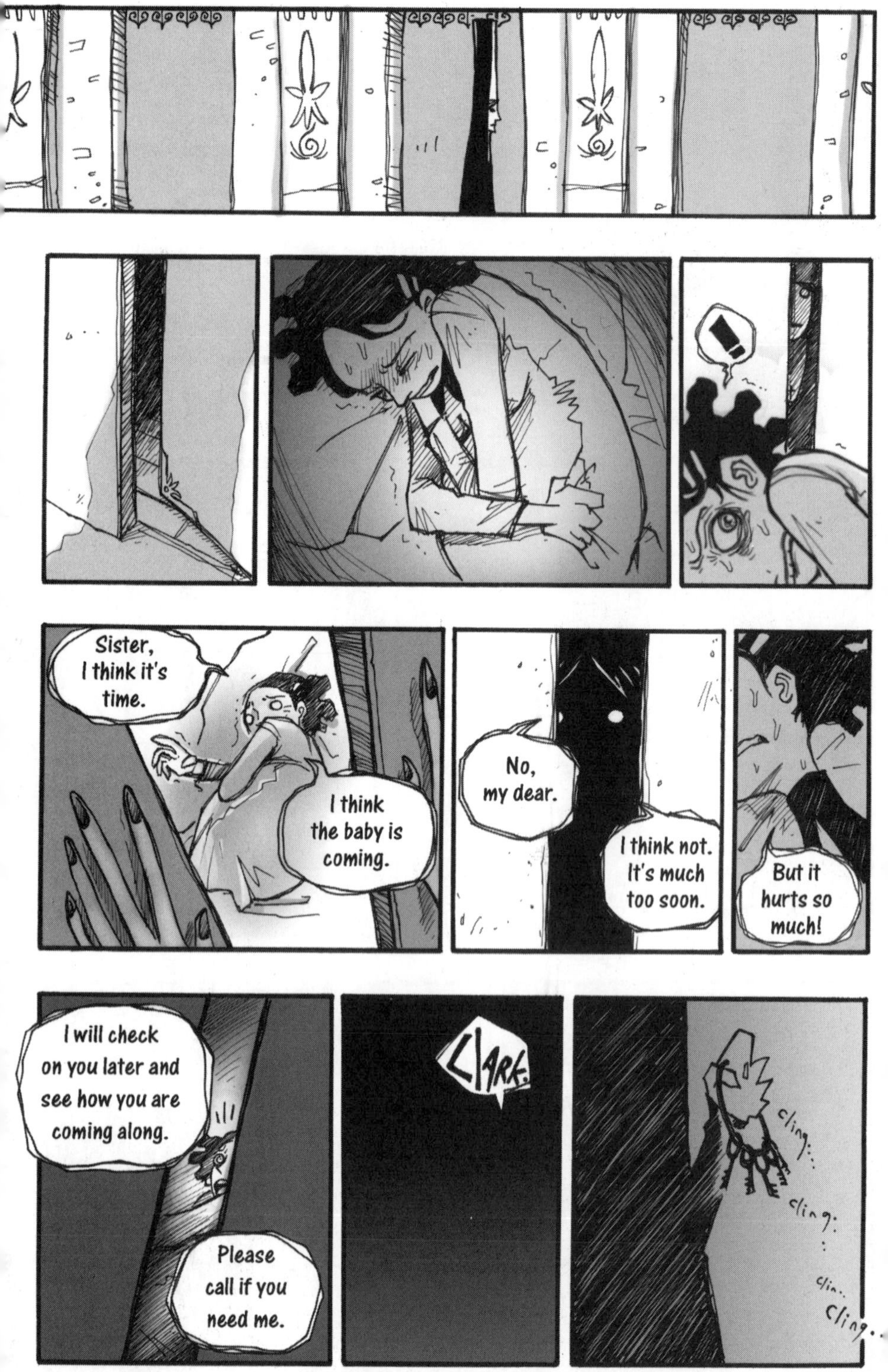
Sister, I think it's time.
I think the baby is coming.
No, my dear.
I think not. It's much too soon.
But it hurts so much!
I will check on you later and see how you are coming along.
Please call if you need me.
CLARK.
cling...
cling.
clin..
cling..

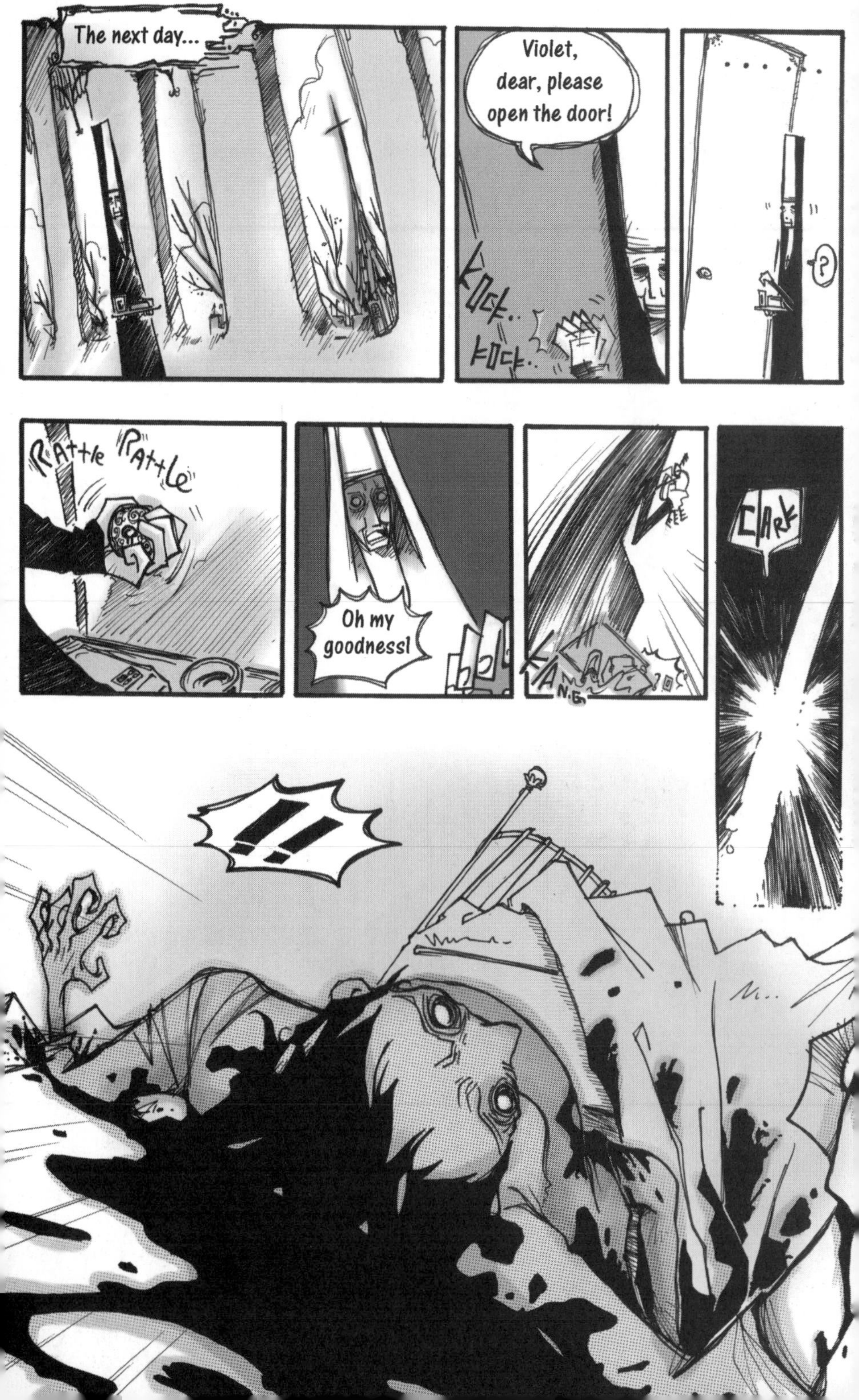
The next day...
Violet, dear, please open the door!
Knock.. knock..
Rattle Rattle
Oh my goodness!
CLARK
!!

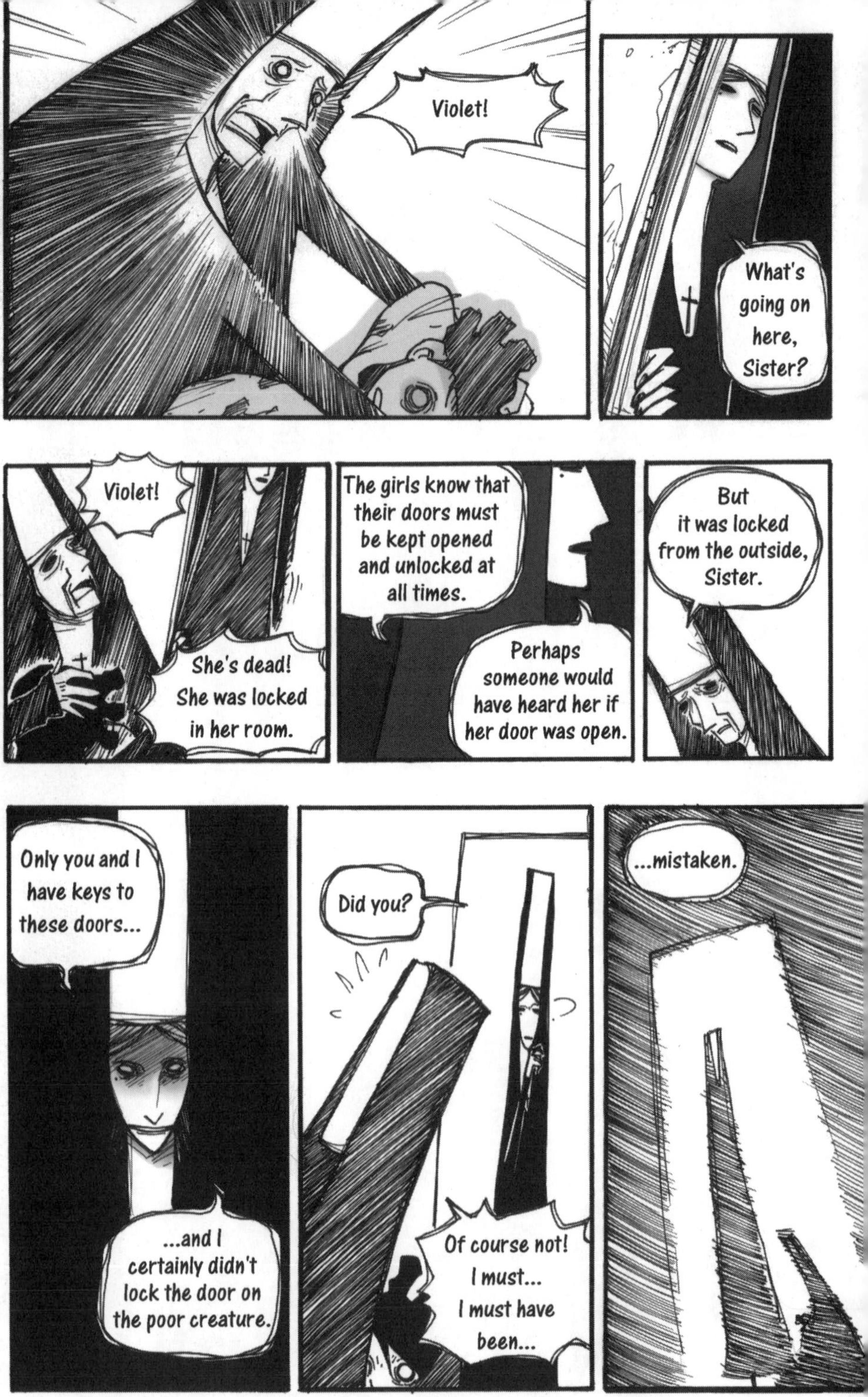
Violet!
What's going on here, Sister?
Violet!
She's dead! She was locked in her room.
The girls know that their doors must be kept opened and unlocked at all times.
Perhaps someone would have heard her if her door was open.
But it was locked from the outside, Sister.
Only you and I have keys to these doors...
...and I certainly didn't lock the door on the poor creature.
Did you?
Of course not! I must... I must have been...
...mistaken.

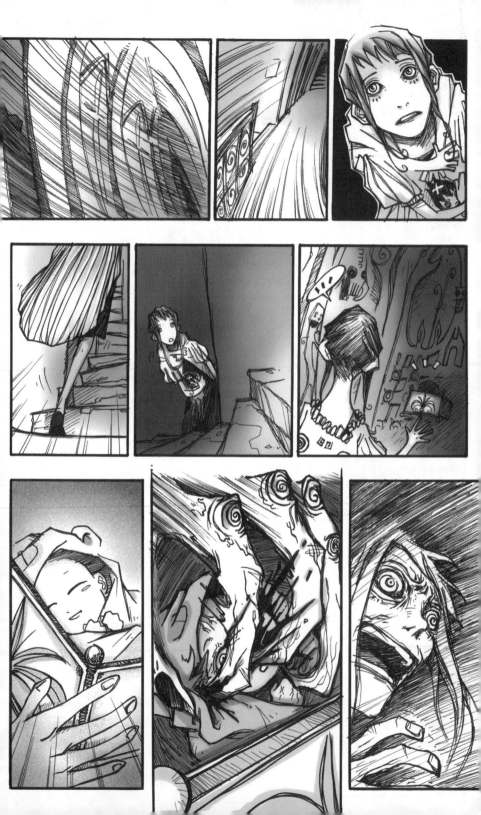

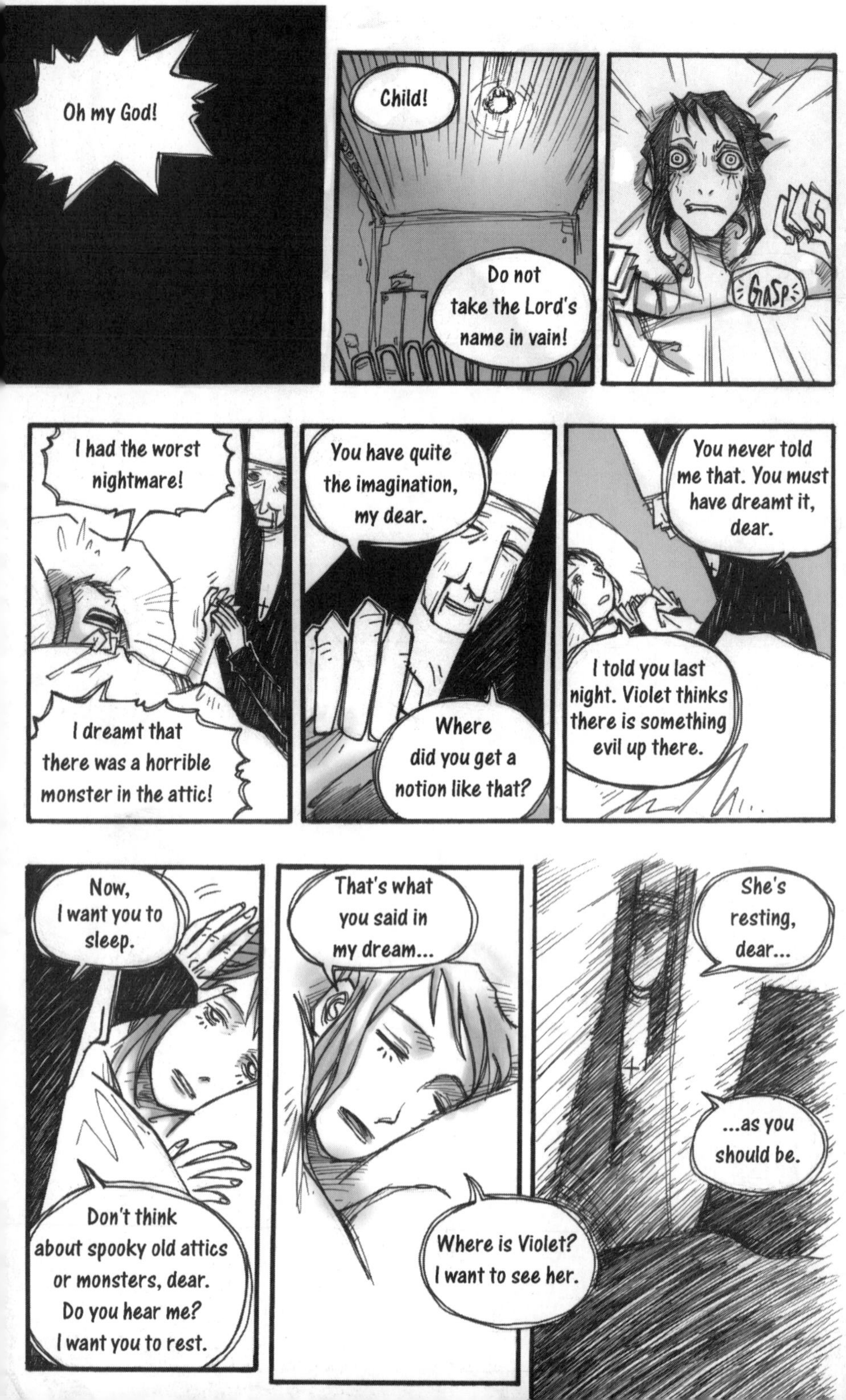
Oh my God!
Child!
Do not take the Lord's name in vain!
GASP
I had the worst nightmare!
I dreamt that there was a horrible monster in the attic!
You have quite the imagination, my dear.
Where did you get a notion like that?
I told you last night. Violet thinks there is something evil up there.
You never told me that. You must have dreamt it, dear.
Now, I want you to sleep.
Don't think about spooky old attics or monsters, dear. Do you hear me? I want you to rest.
That's what you said in my dream...
Where is Violet? I want to see her.
She's resting, dear...
...as you should be.

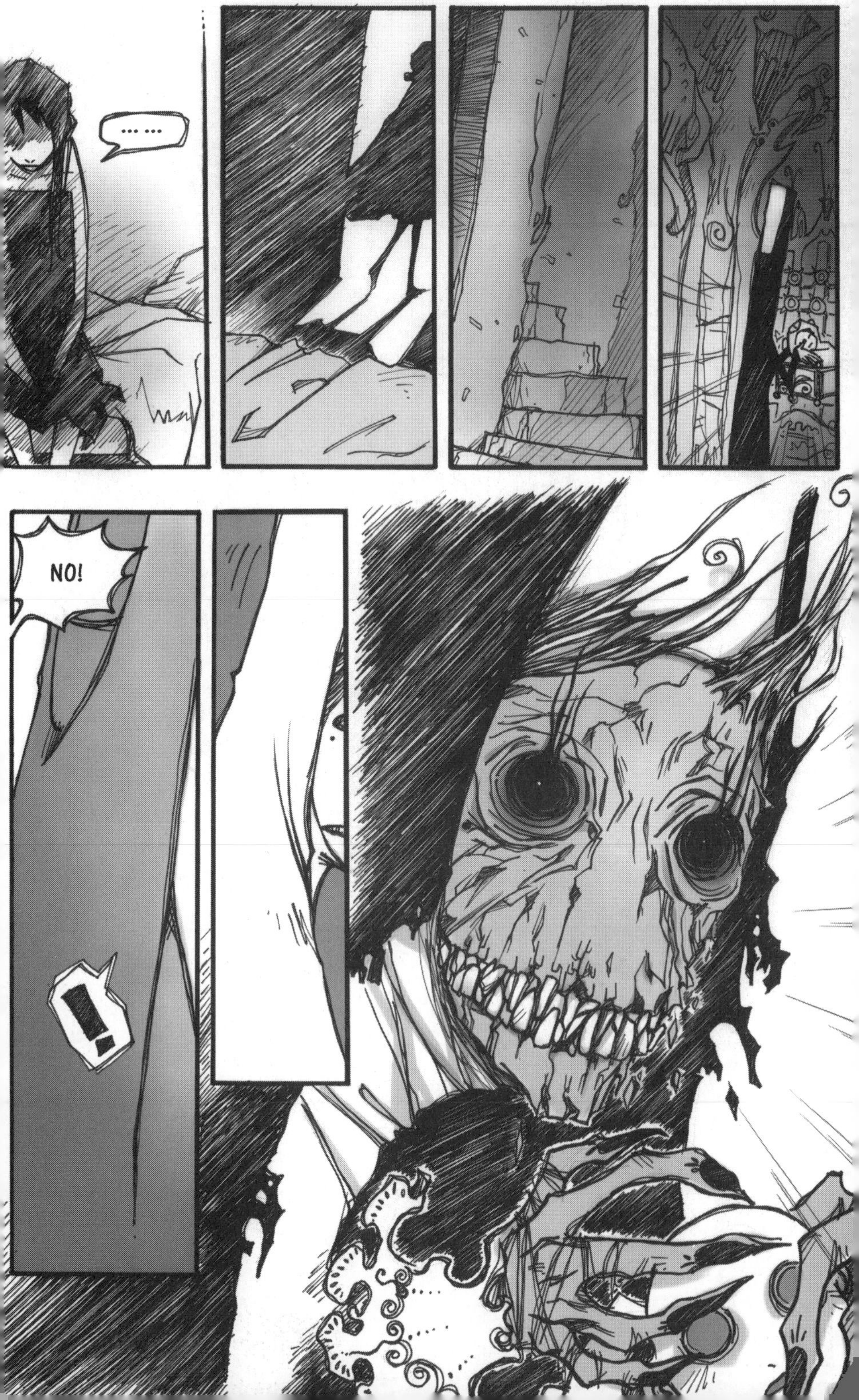
... ...
NO!
!

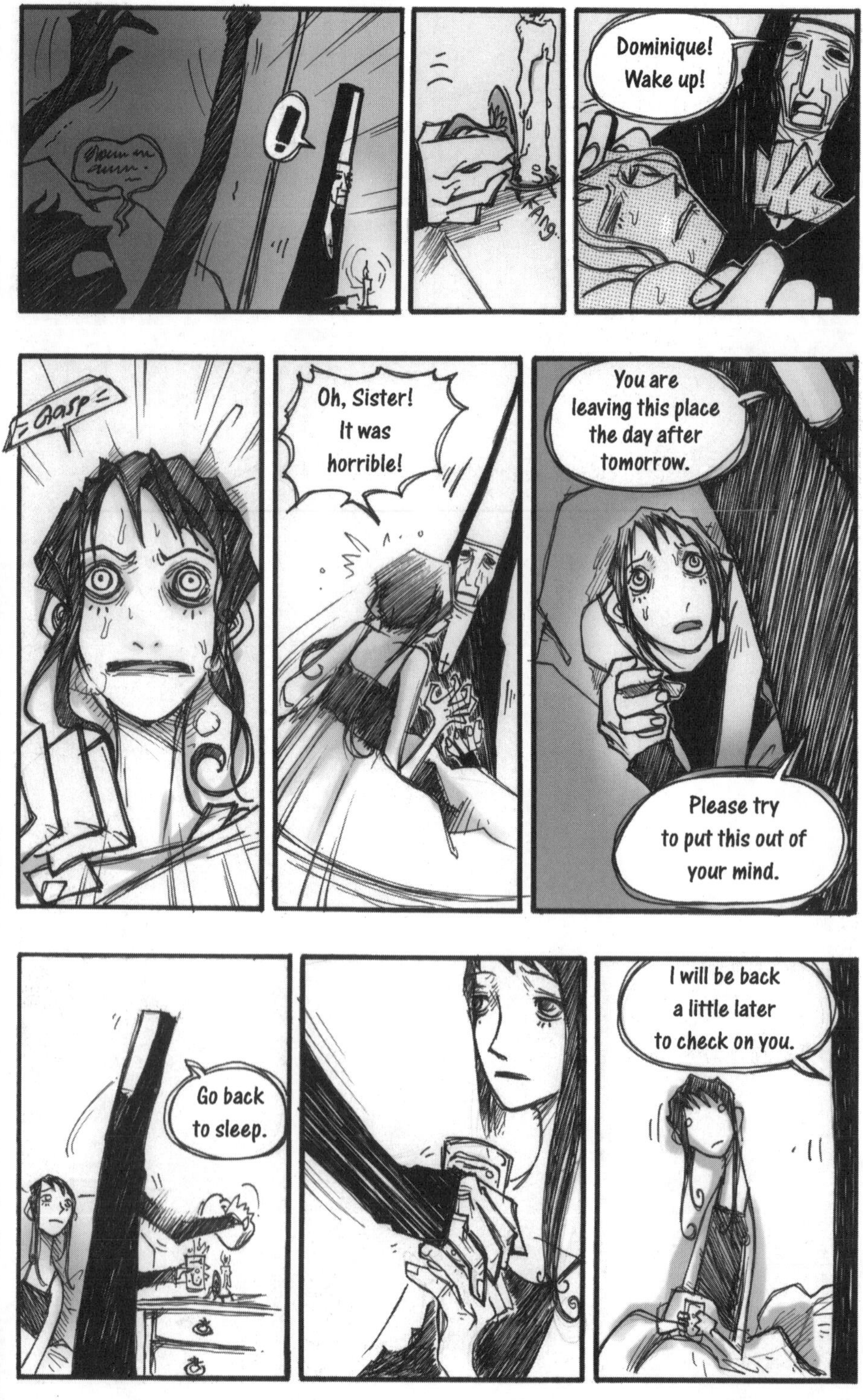
Dominique! Wake up!
Gasp
Oh, Sister! It was horrible!
You are leaving this place the day after tomorrow.
Please try to put this out of your mind.
Go back to sleep.
I will be back a little later to check on you.

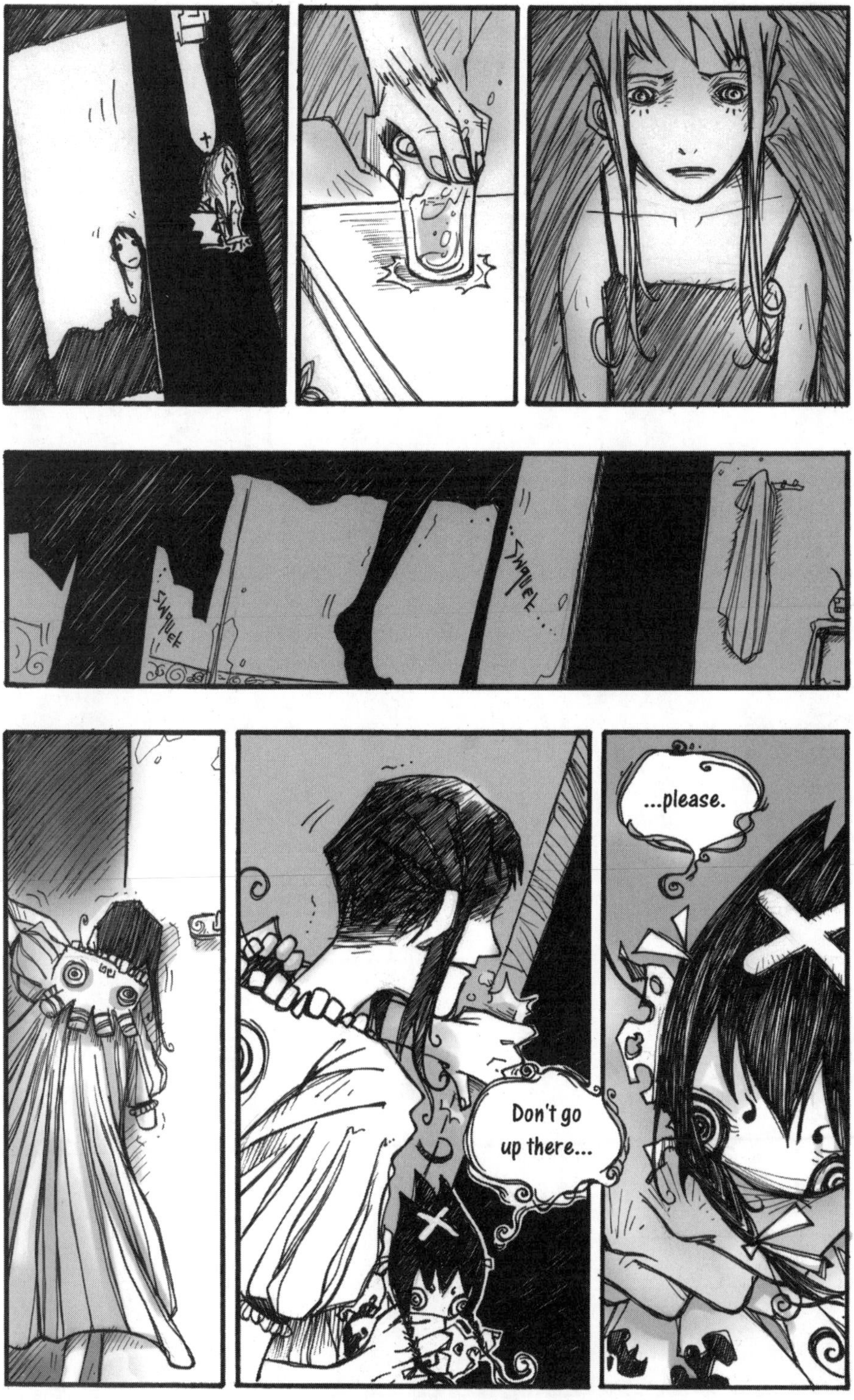
...Swqueet
Swqueet...
Don't go up there...
...please.

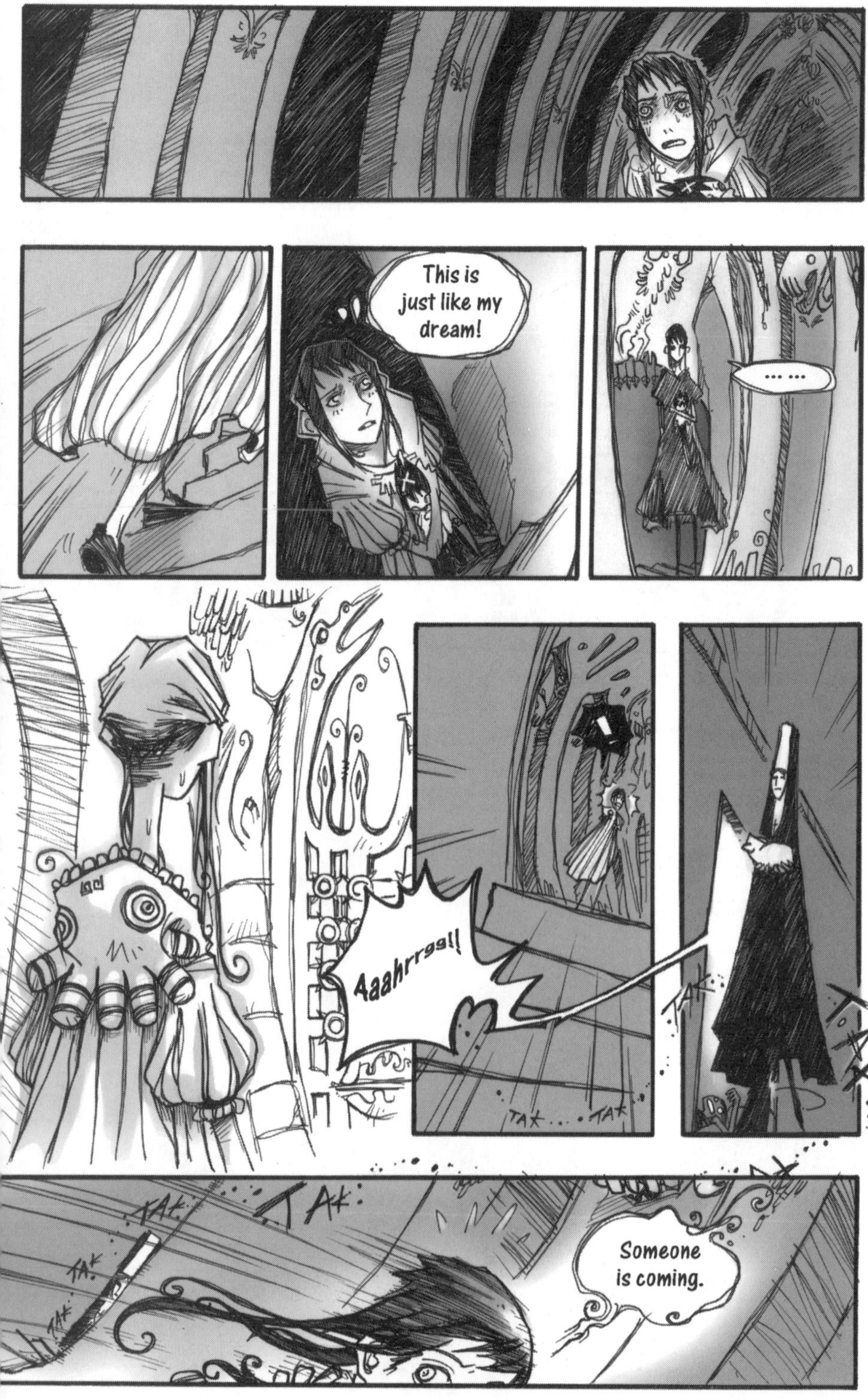
This is just like my dream!
... ...
Aaahrrgg!!
TAK... TAK
TAAK
TAK TAK
Someone is coming.

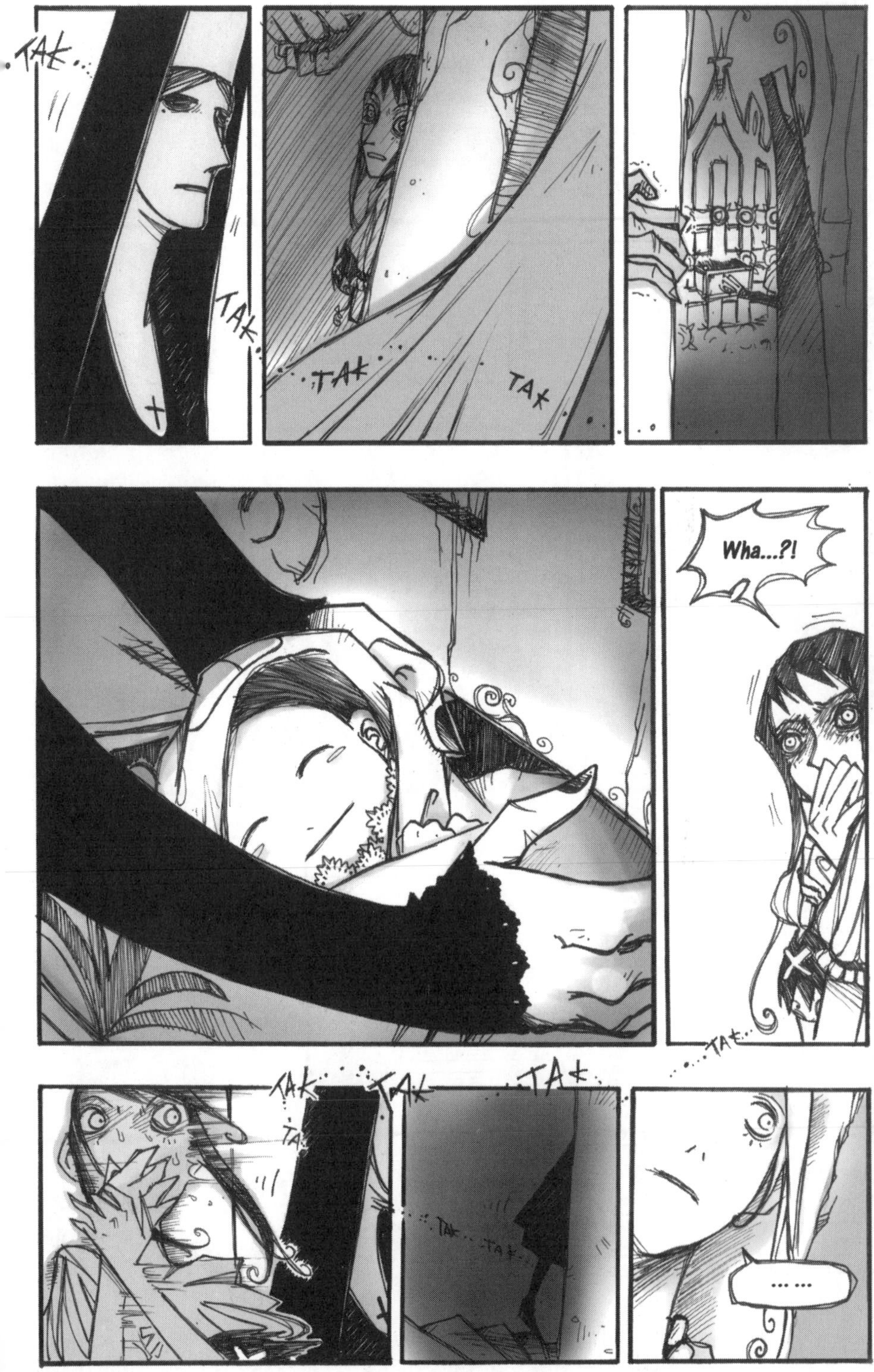
TAK
TAK
TAK
TAK
Wha...?!
TAK
TAK
TAK
TAK
TA
TAK
TAK
... ...

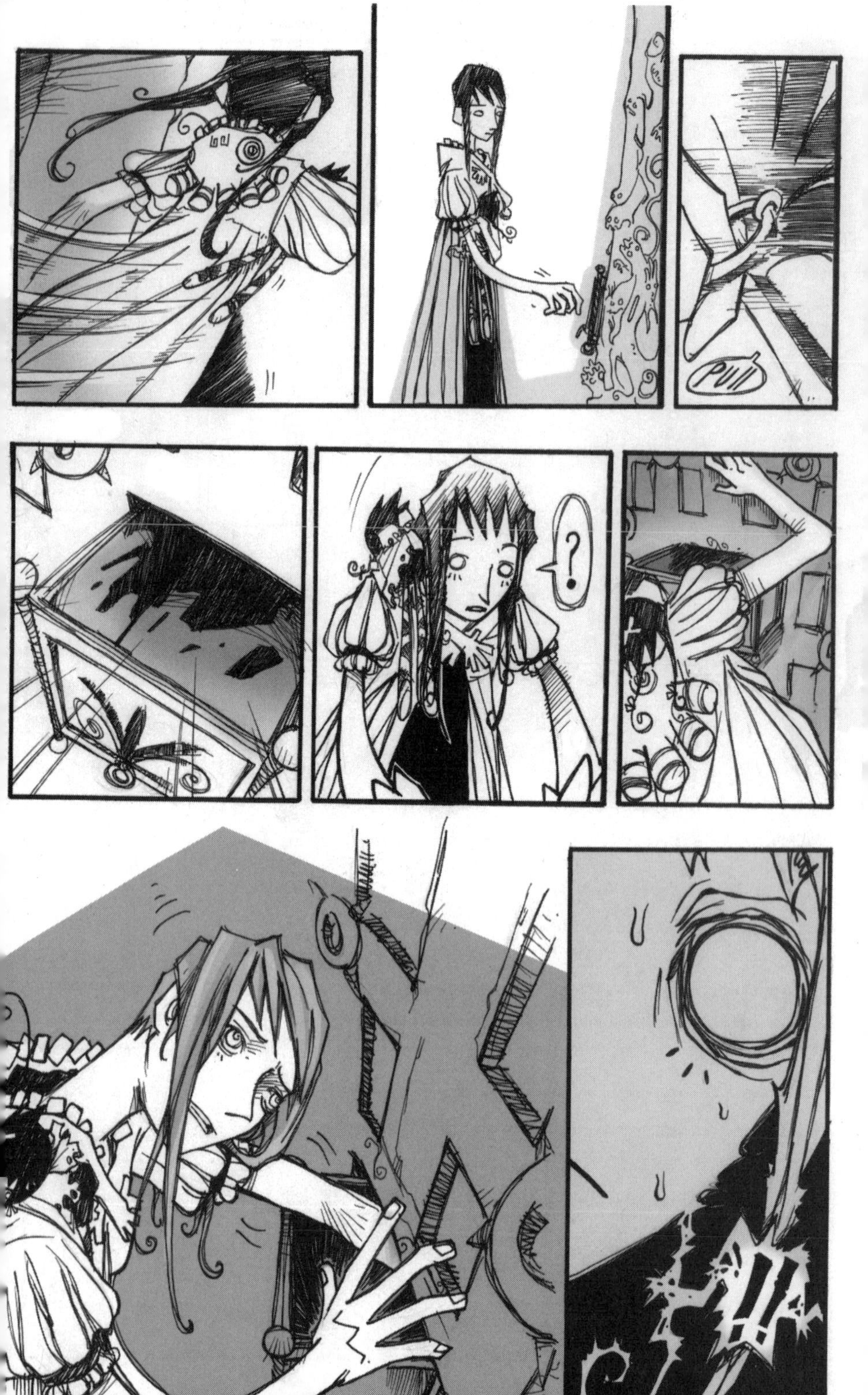
PULL
?

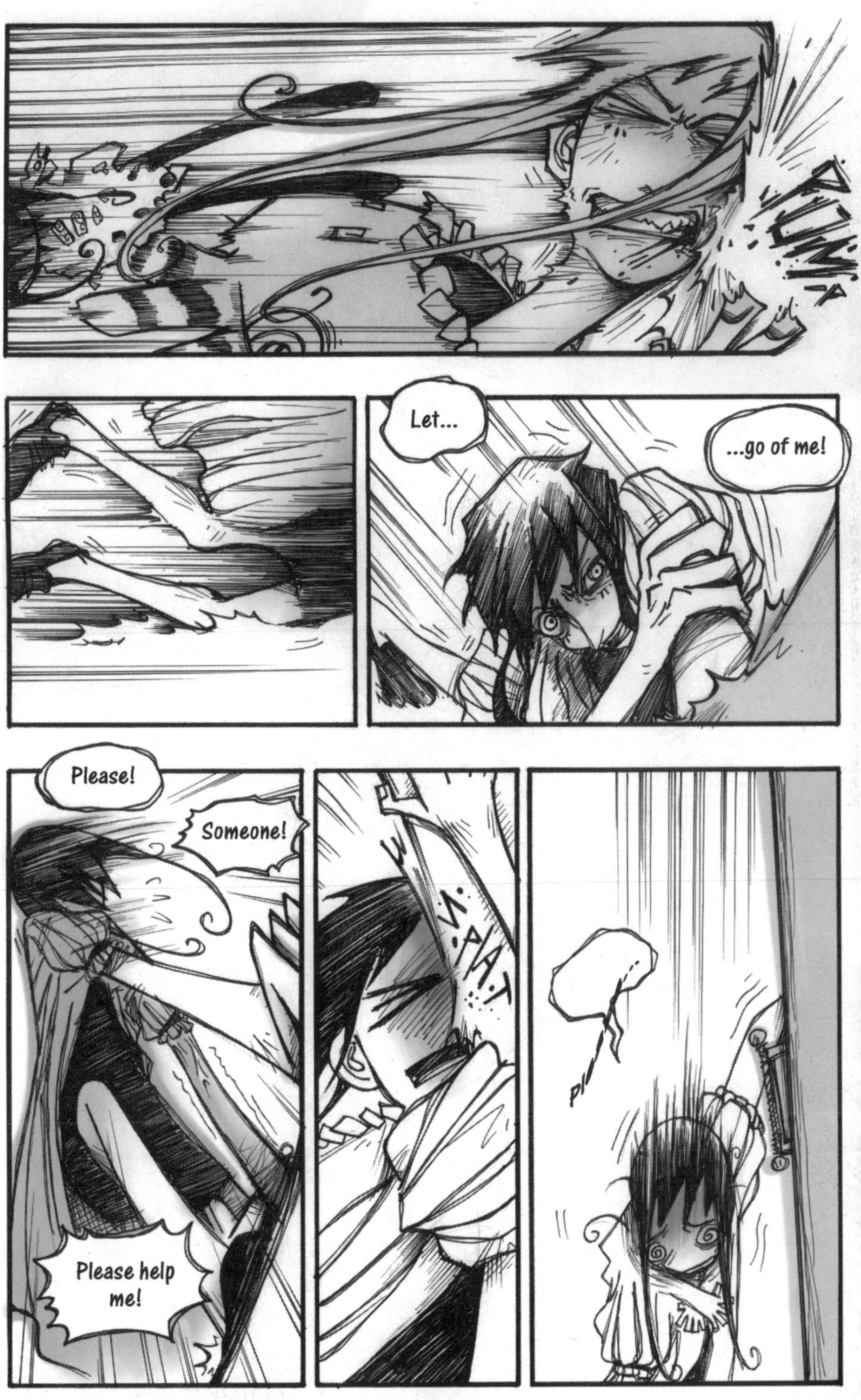
Let...
...go of me!
Please!
Someone!
Please help me!
SPAT

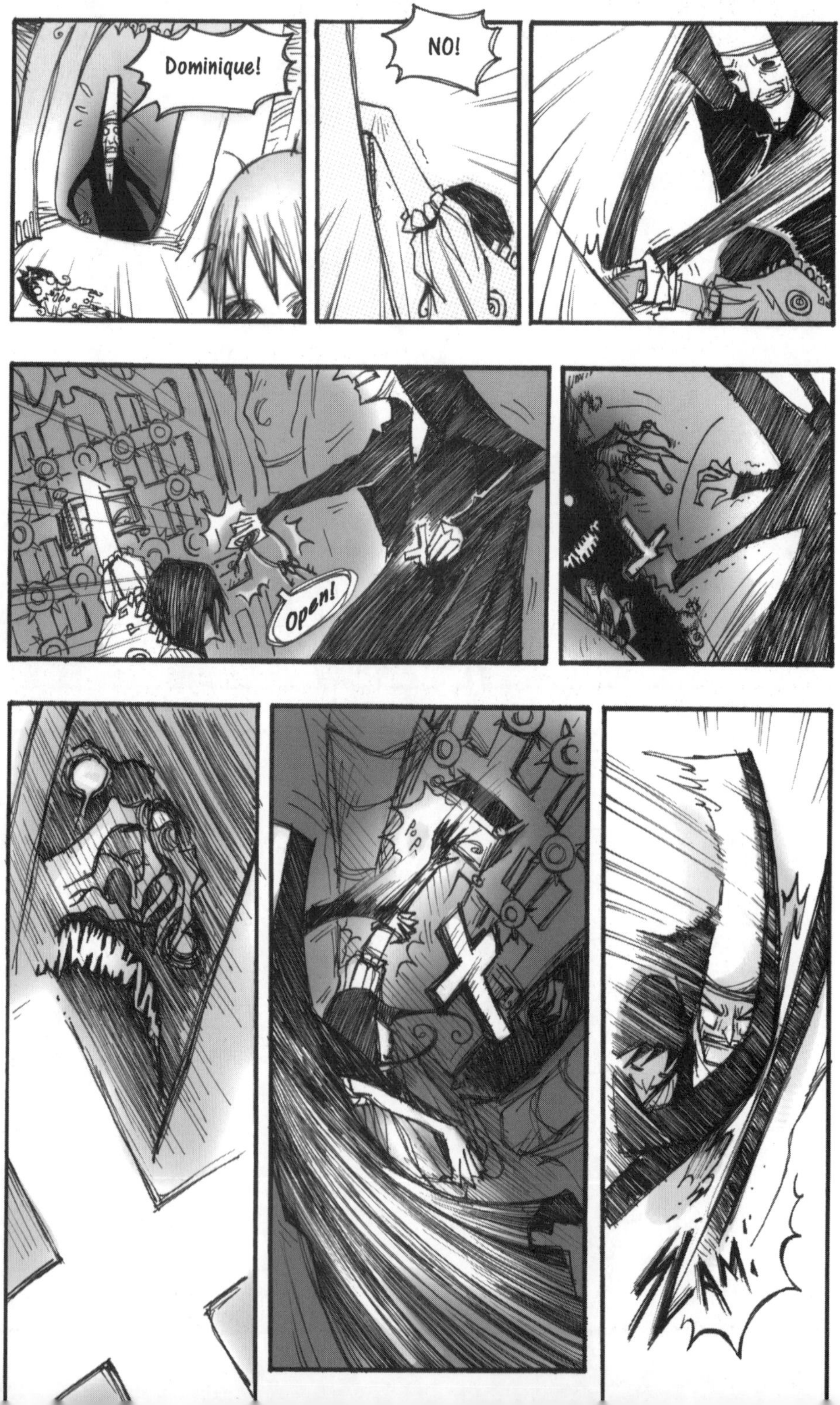
Dominique!
NO!
Open!
SLAM!

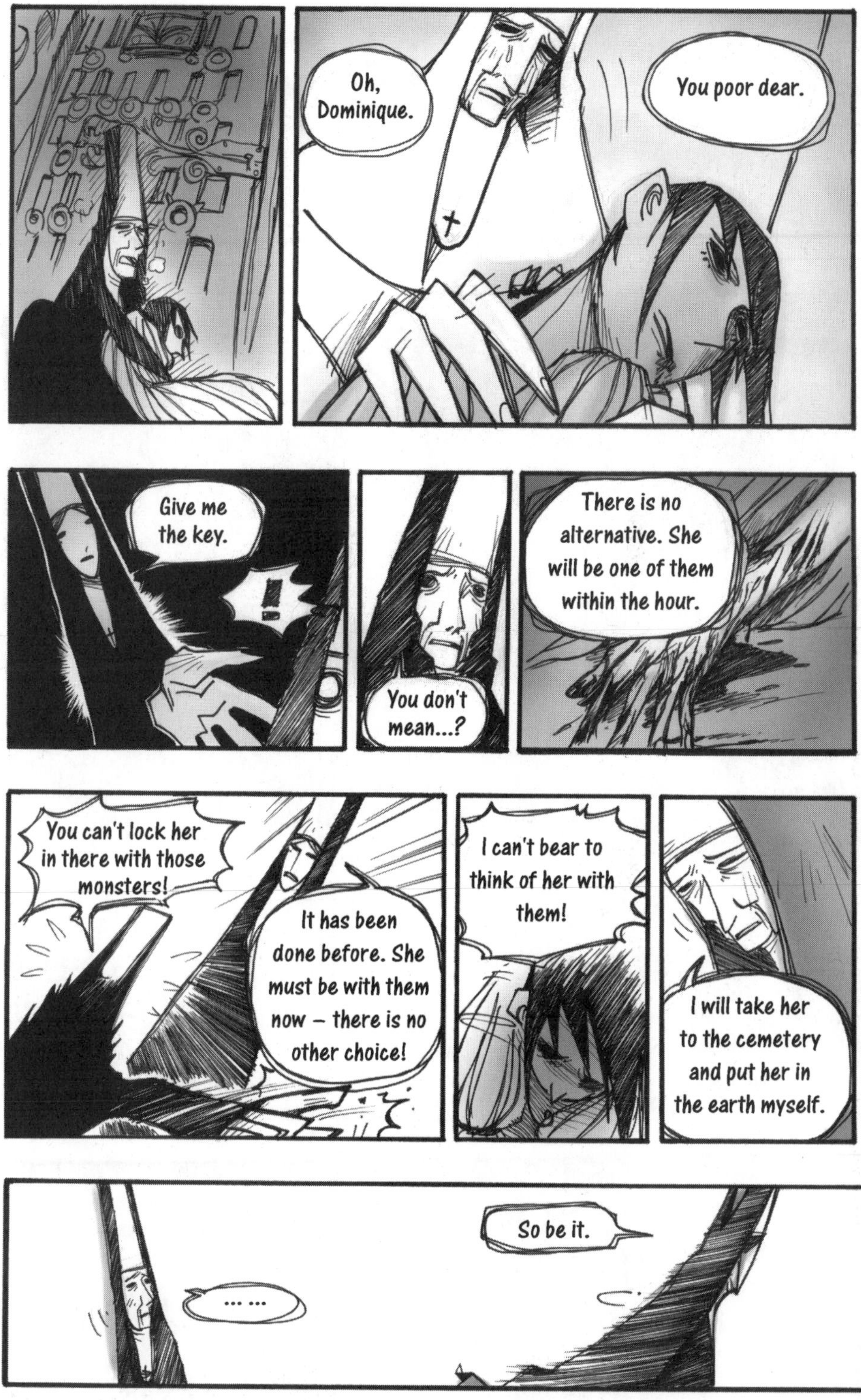
Oh, Dominique.
You poor dear.
Give me the key.
!
You don't mean...?
There is no alternative. She will be one of them within the hour.
You can't lock her in there with those monsters!
It has been done before. She must be with them now – there is no other choice!
I can't bear to think of her with them!
I will take her to the cemetery and put her in the earth myself.
So be it.
... ...

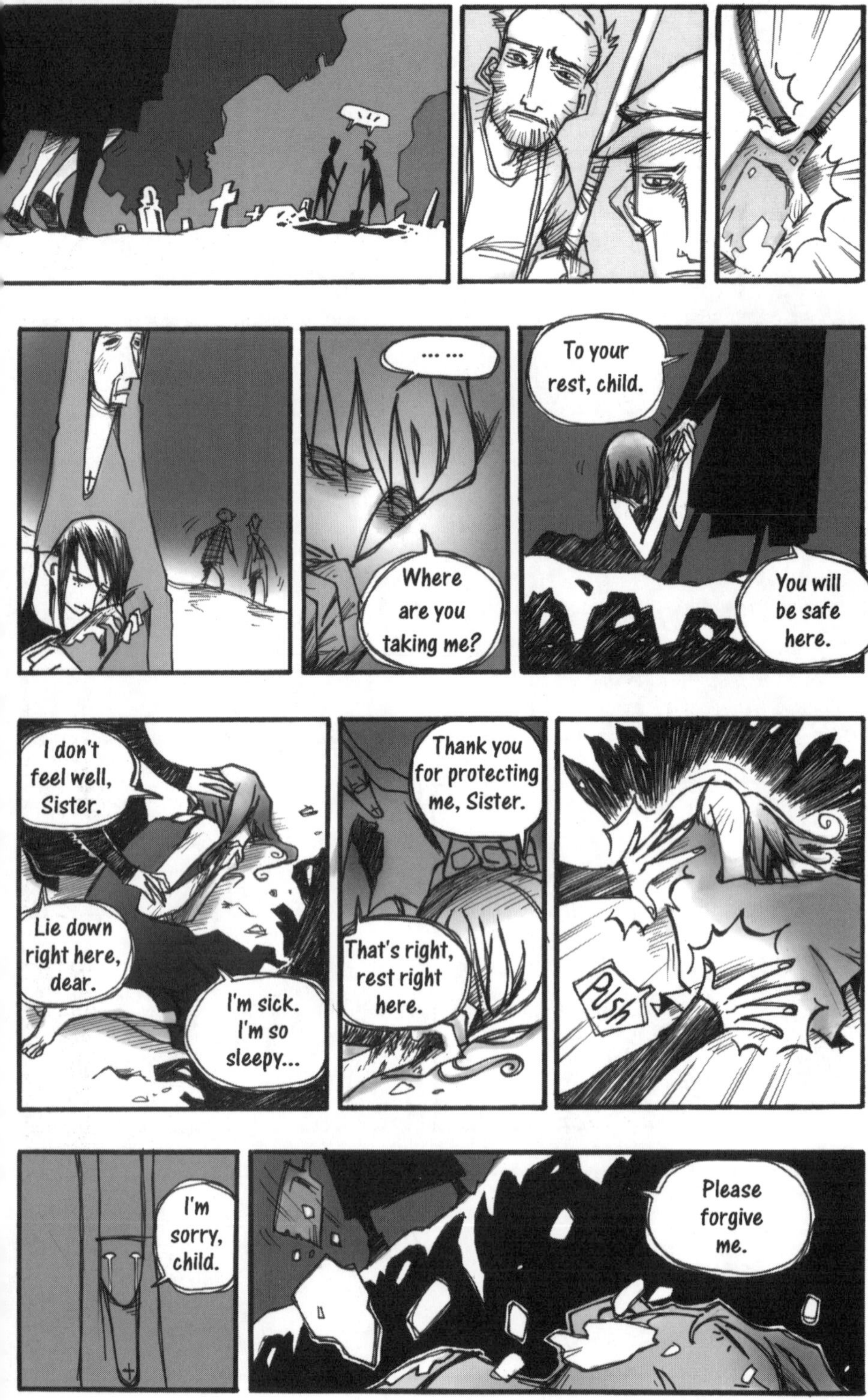
... ...
Where are you taking me?
To your rest, child.
You will be safe here.
I don't feel well, Sister.
Lie down right here, dear.
I'm sick. I'm so sleepy...
Thank you for protecting me, Sister.
That's right, rest right here.
PUSH
I'm sorry, child.
Please forgive me.

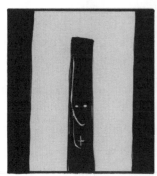

She is resting in the earth.

Then you killed her.

I covered her with earth.

She will suffocate while she sleeps. I wanted to be merciful.

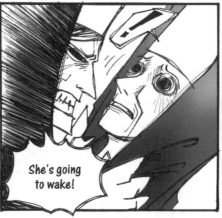

!?

You foolish old woman!

She's going to wake!

Come with me...

NOW!

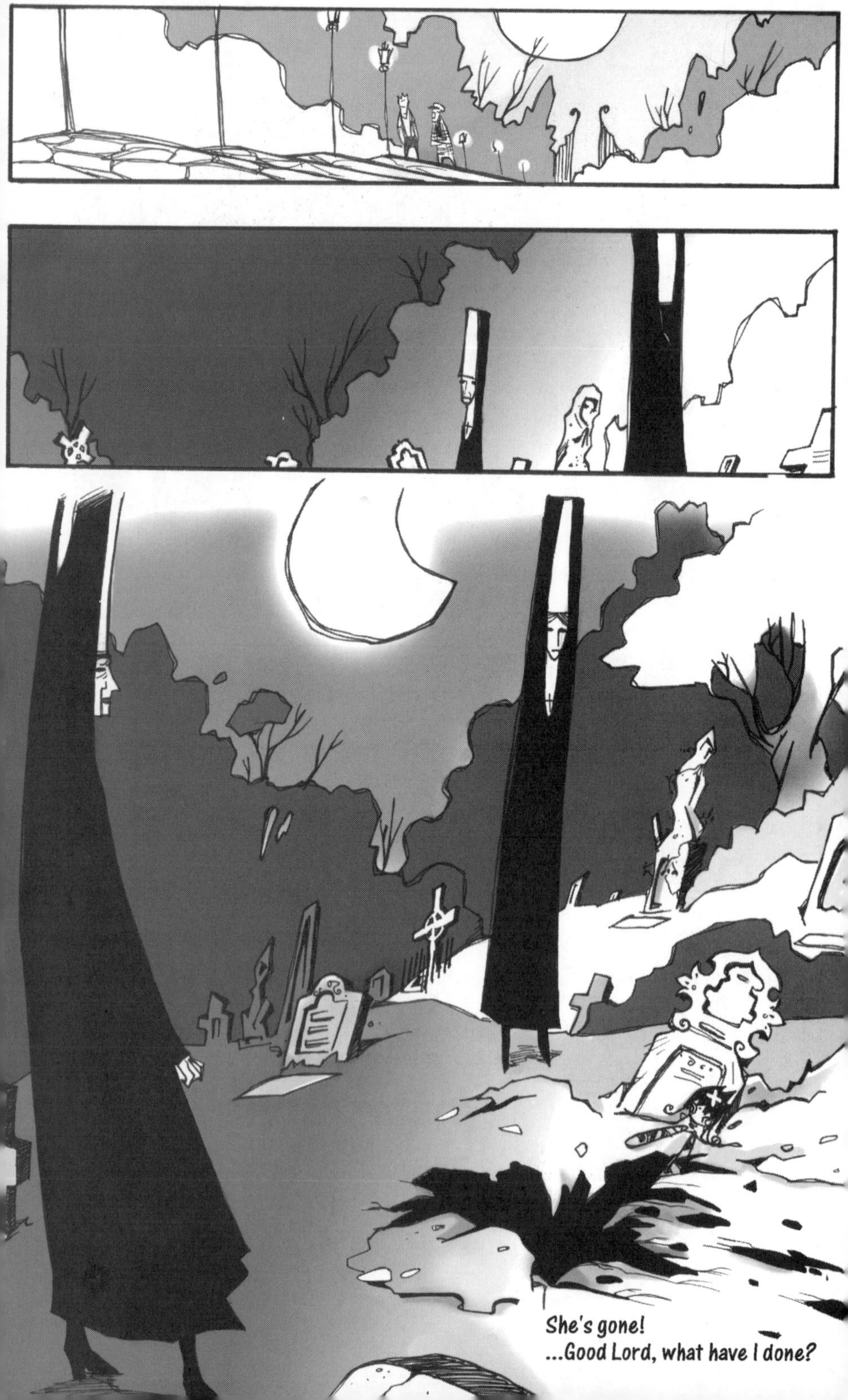
She's gone!
...Good Lord, what have I done?

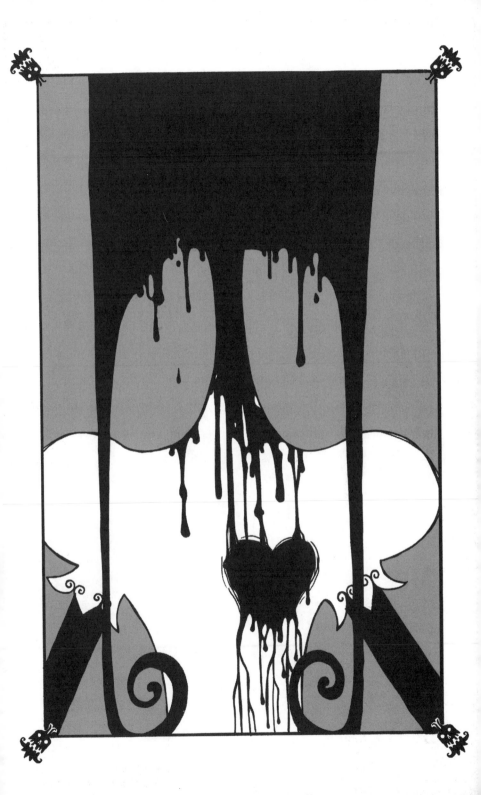

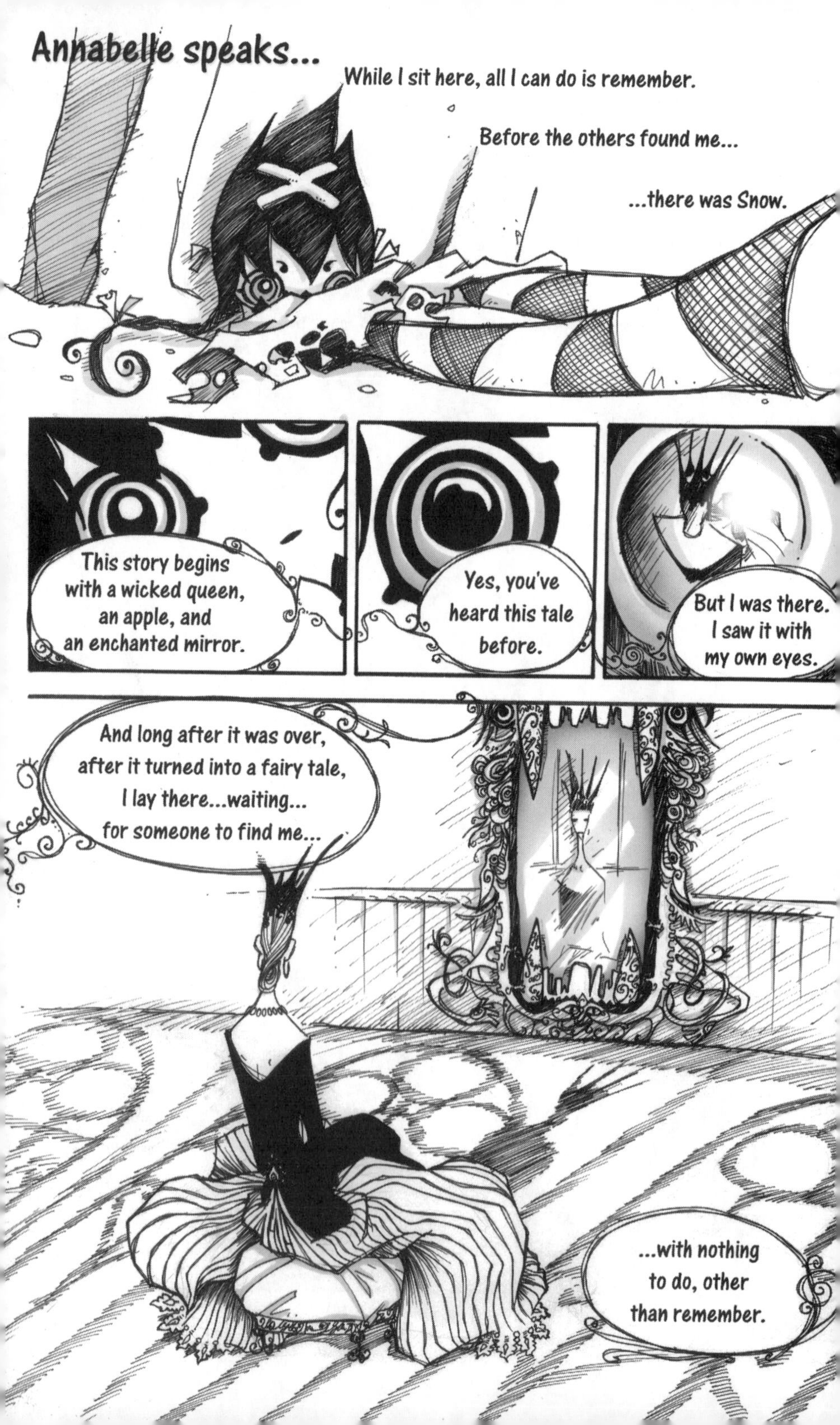
Annabelle speaks...
While I sit here, all I can do is remember.
Before the others found me...
...there was Snow.
This story begins with a wicked queen, an apple, and an enchanted mirror.
Yes, you've heard this tale before.
But I was there. I saw it with my own eyes.
And long after it was over, after it turned into a fairy tale, I lay there...waiting... for someone to find me...
...with nothing to do, other than remember.

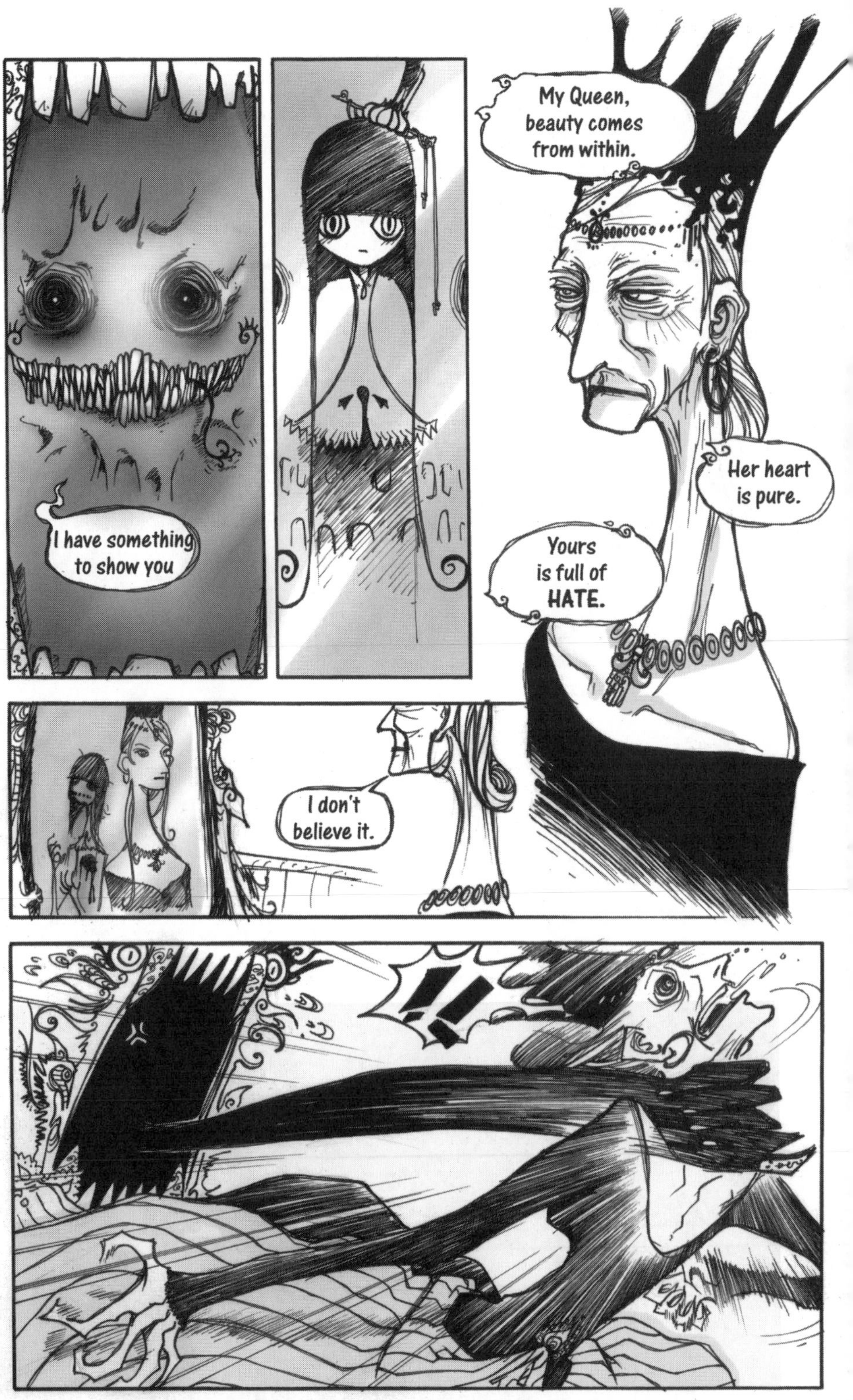

I have something to show you
My Queen, beauty comes from within.
Her heart is pure.
Yours is full of HATE.
I don't believe it.
!!

NEVER

DOUBT ME

AGAIN!

I...
understand...

PING

PING

PING

chip

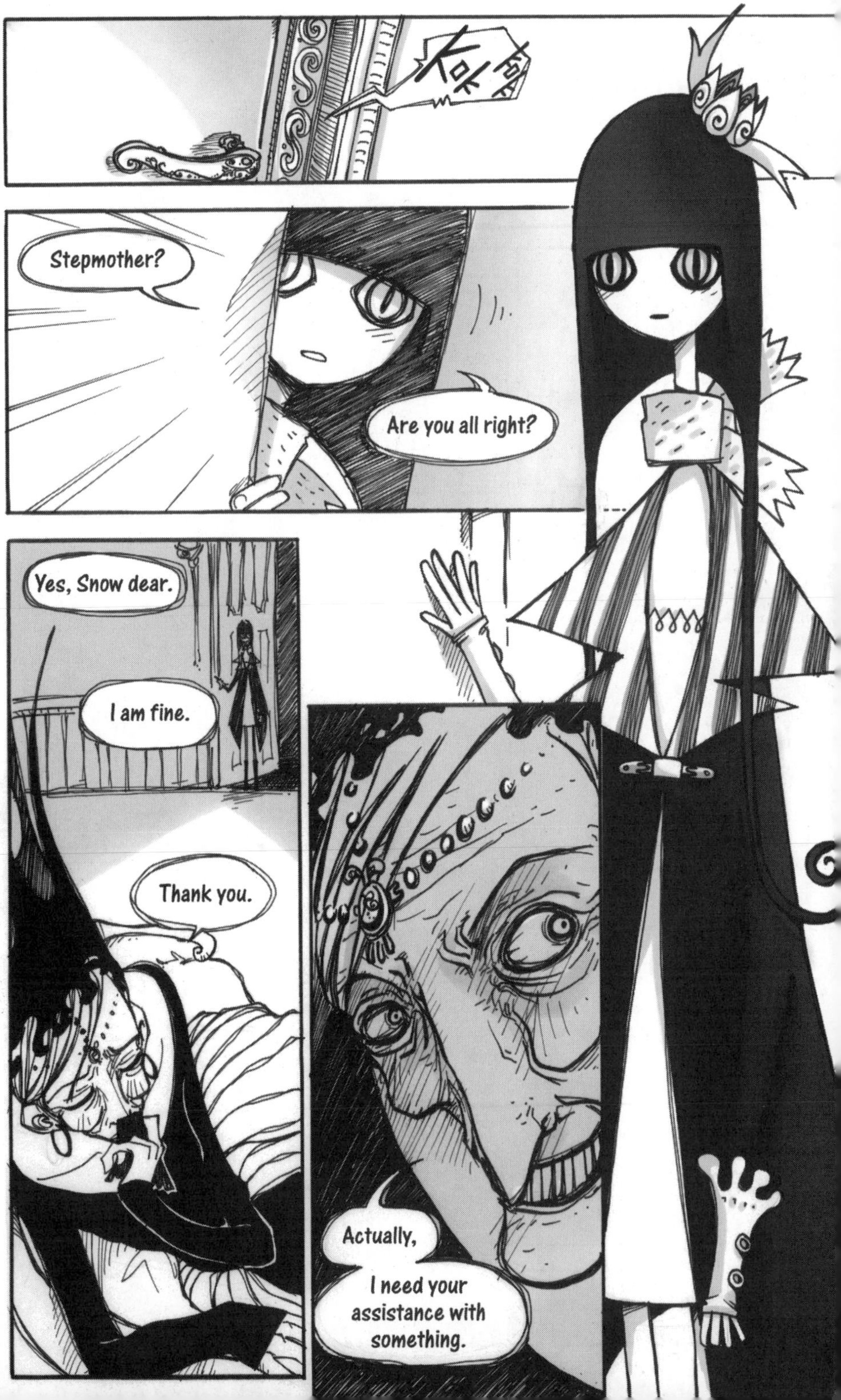
KOK KOK
Stepmother?
Are you all right?
Yes, Snow dear.
I am fine.
Thank you.
Actually,
I need your assistance with something.

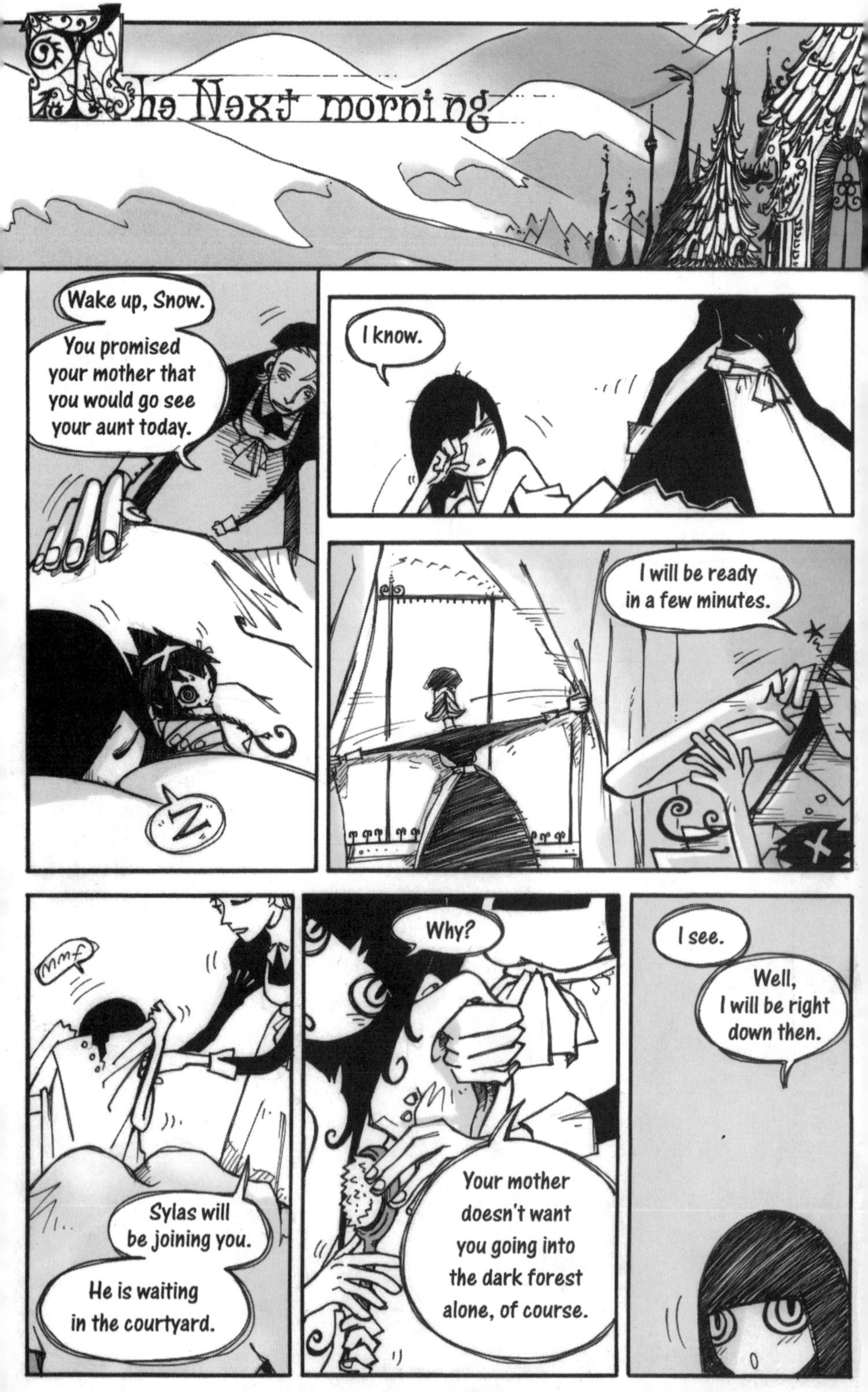
The Next morning
Wake up, Snow.
You promised your mother that you would go see your aunt today.
Z
I know.
I will be ready in a few minutes.
Mmf
Sylas will be joining you.
He is waiting in the courtyard.
Why?
Your mother doesn't want you going into the dark forest alone, of course.
I see.
Well, I will be right down then.

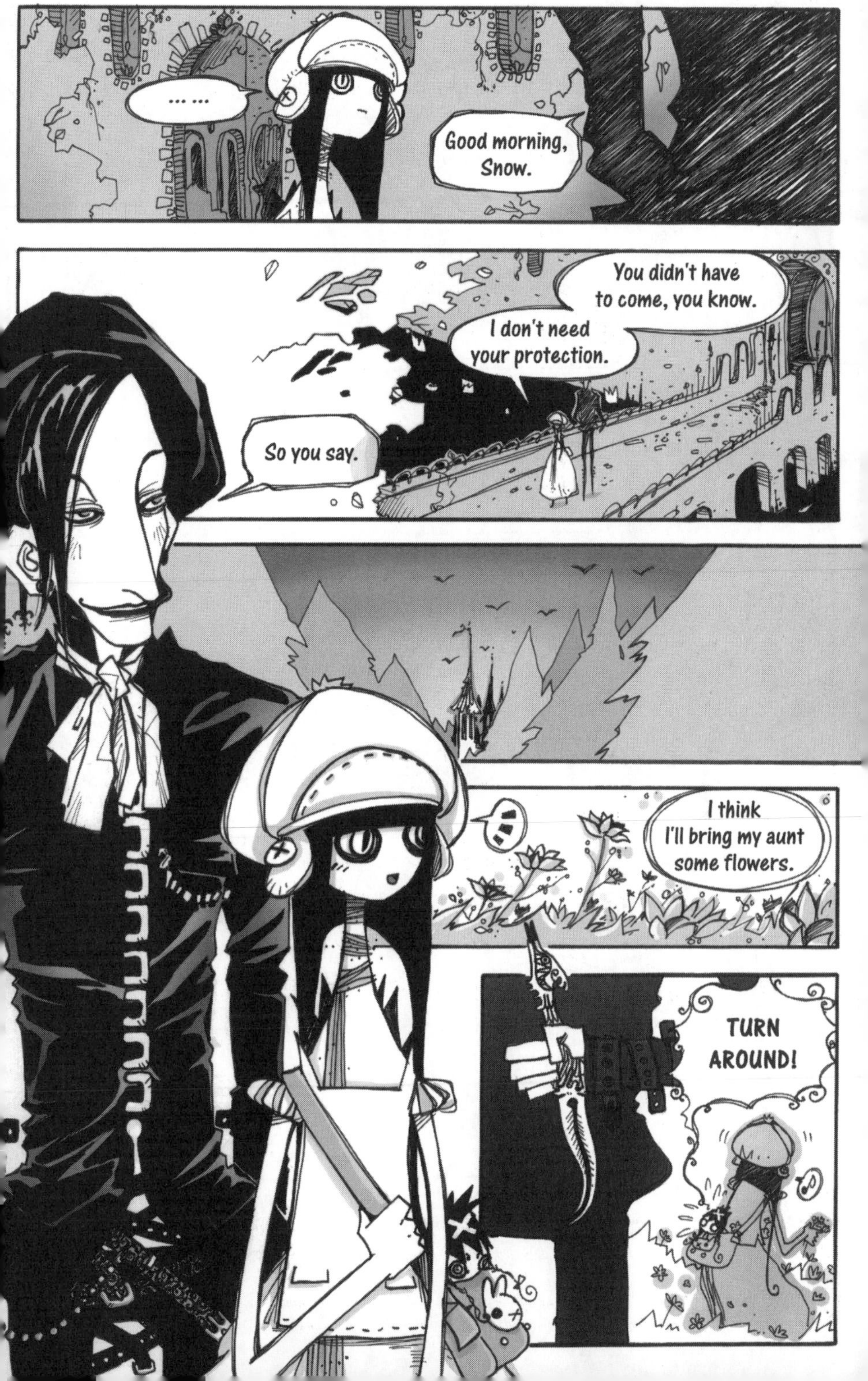
... ...
Good morning, Snow.
You didn't have to come, you know.
I don't need your protection.
So you say.
I think I'll bring my aunt some flowers.
TURN AROUND!

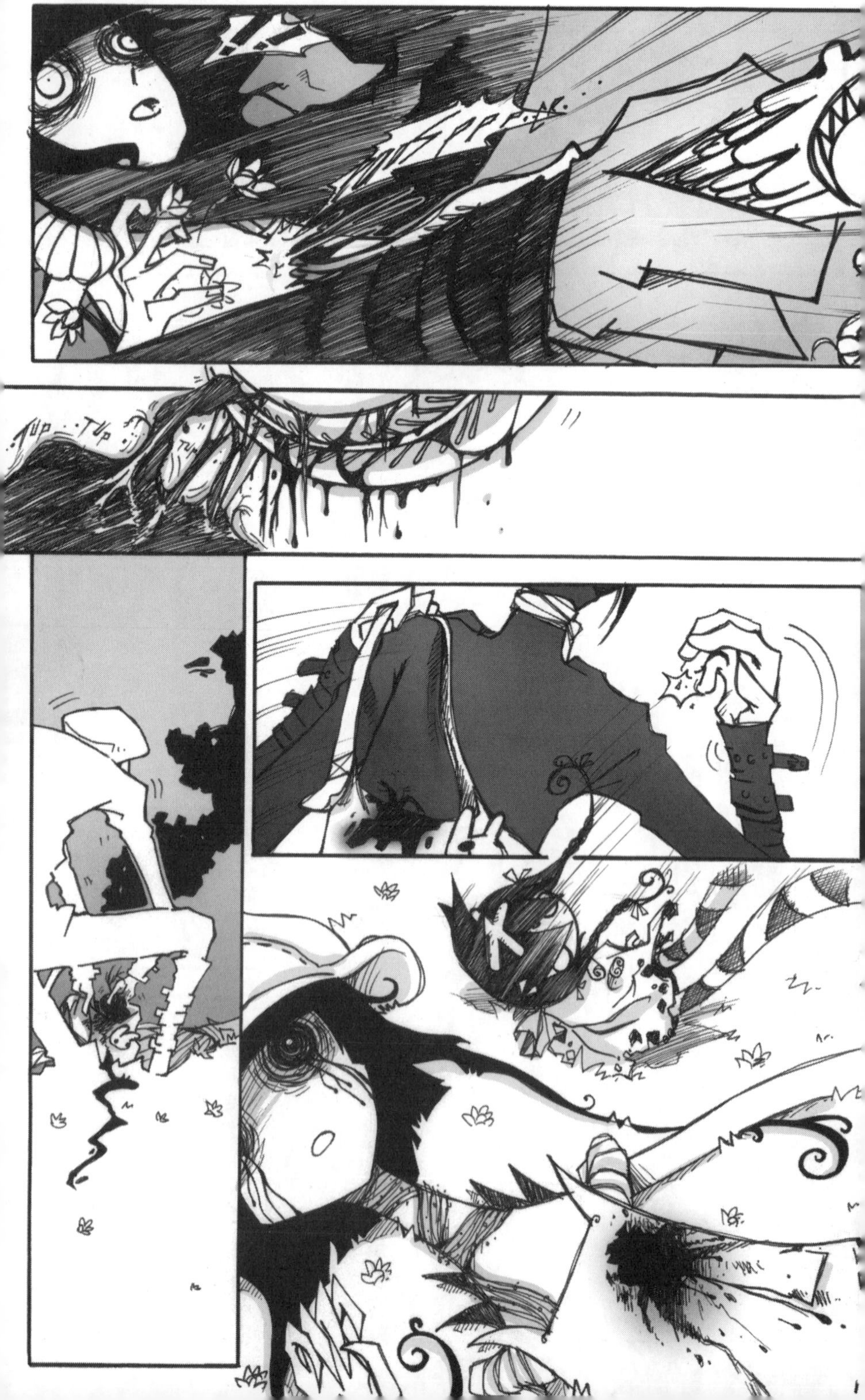

Tup...Tup

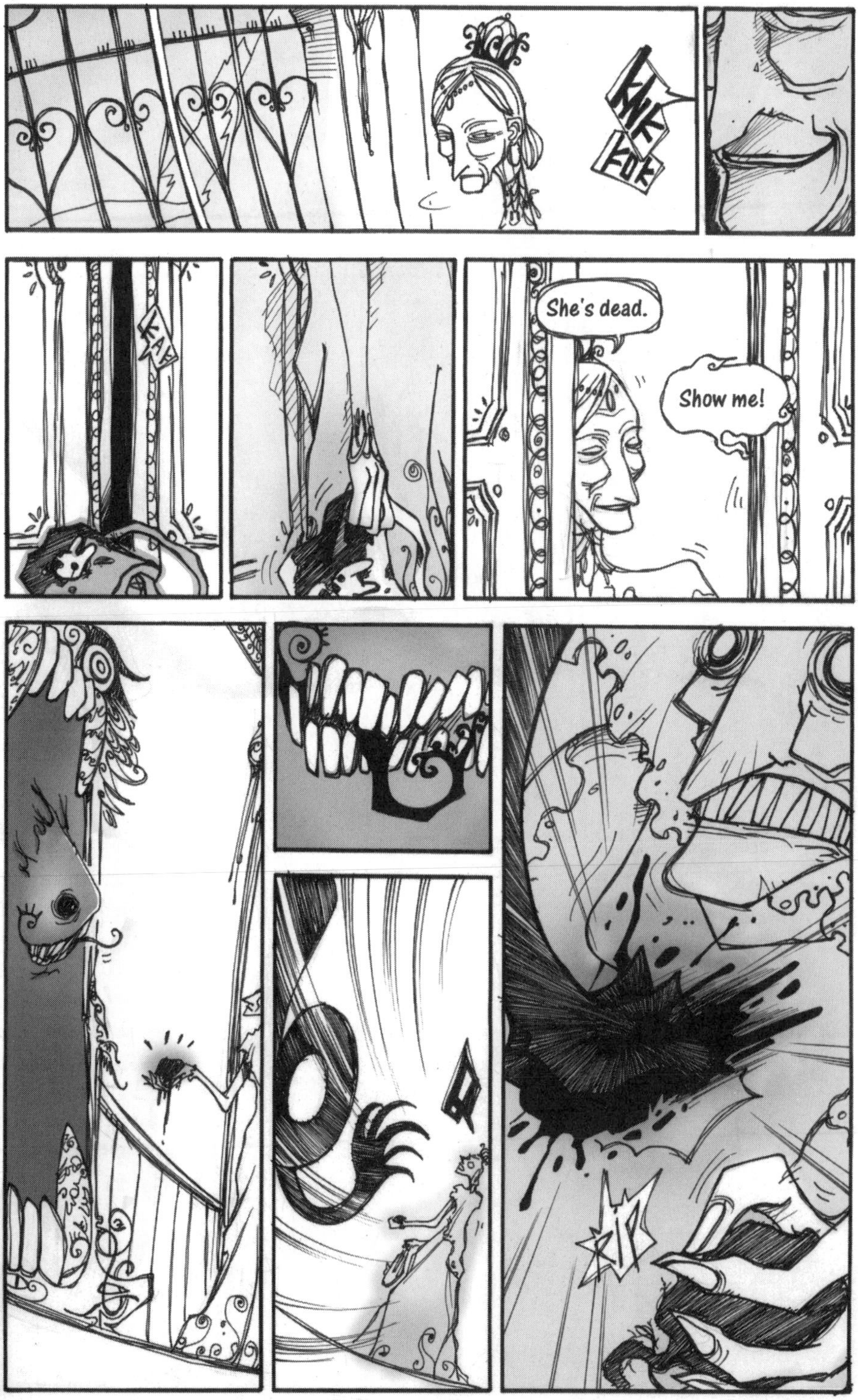
She's dead.
Show me!

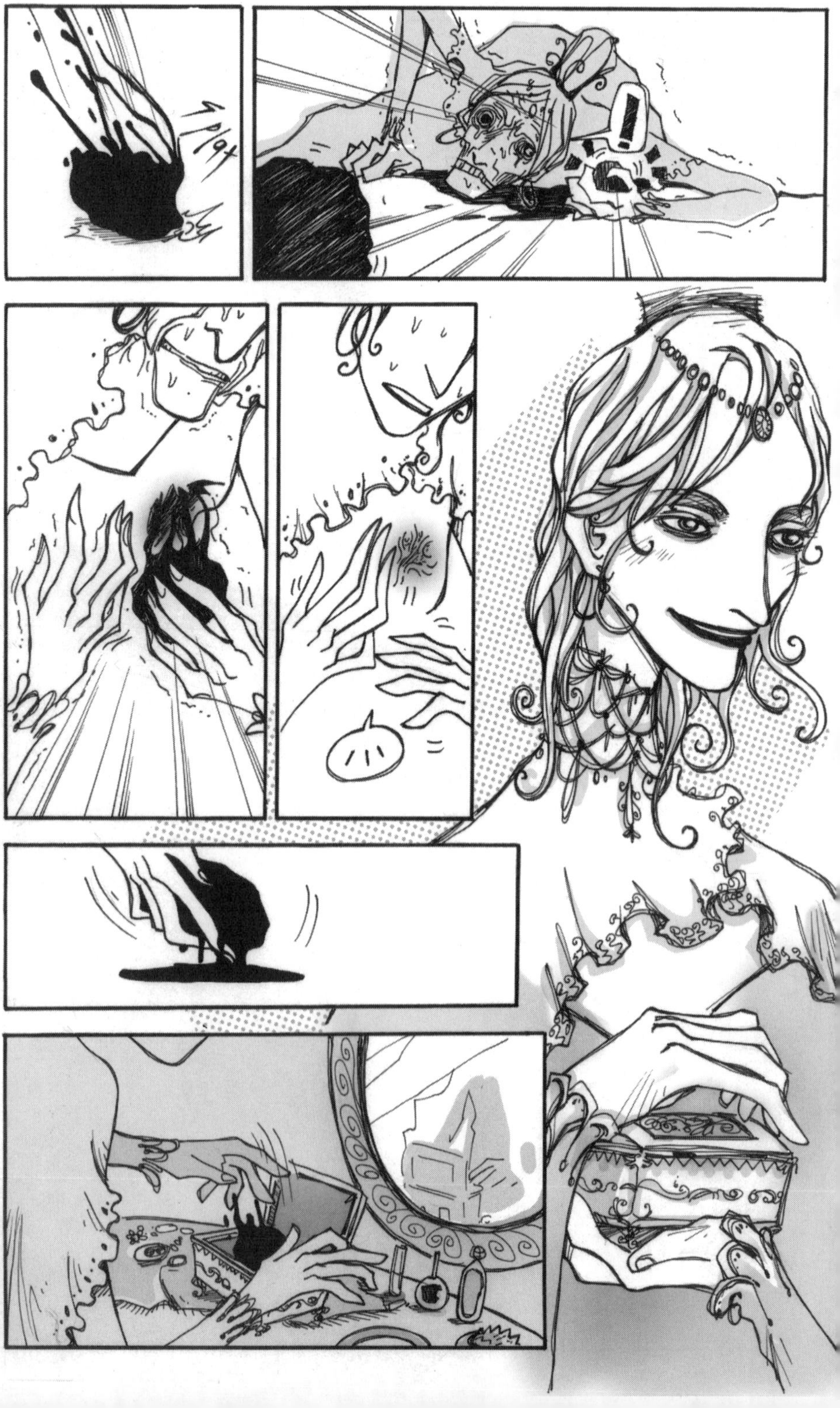

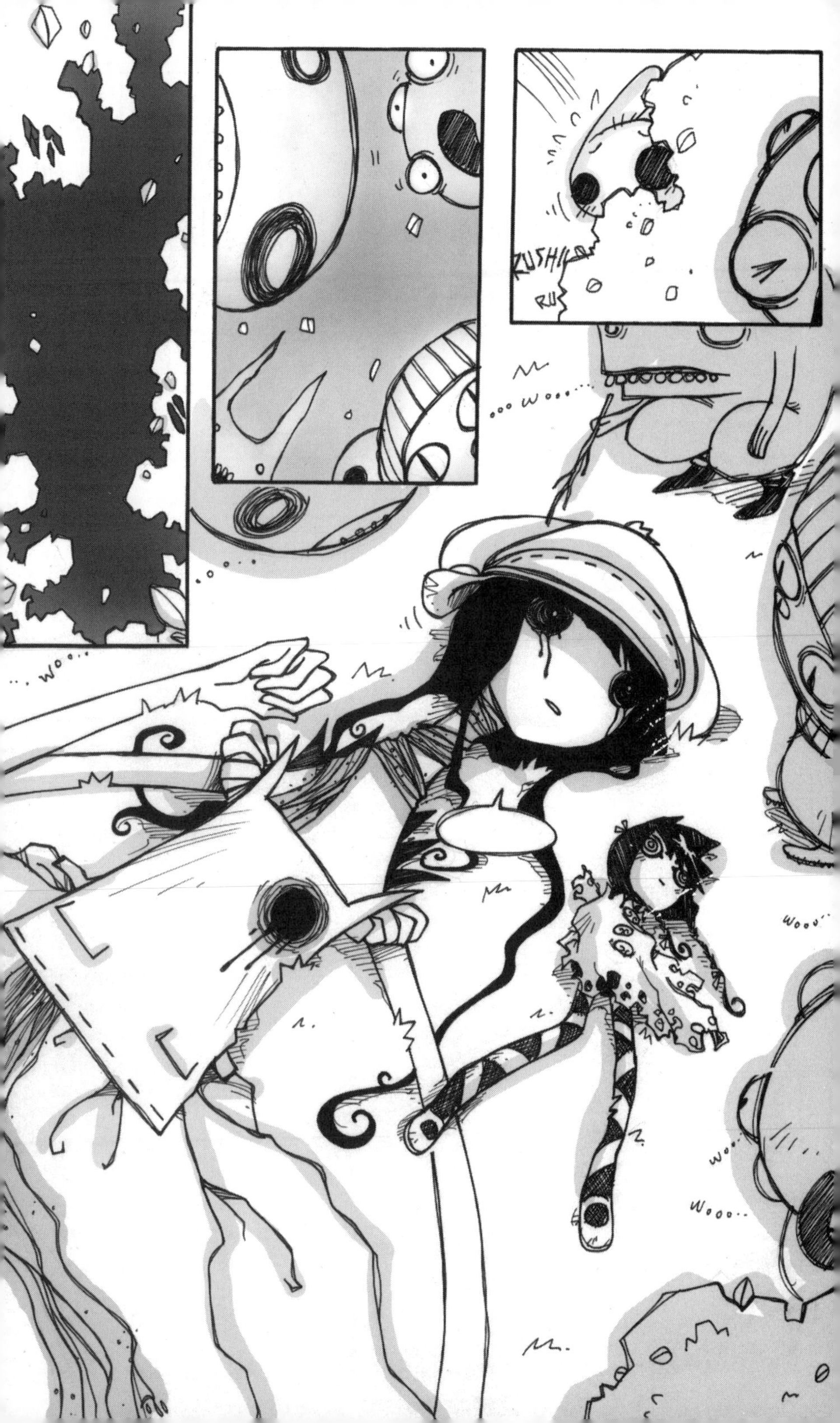
RUSH!
RU
ooo Wooo...
...Woo..
Wooo..
Woo...
Wooo...

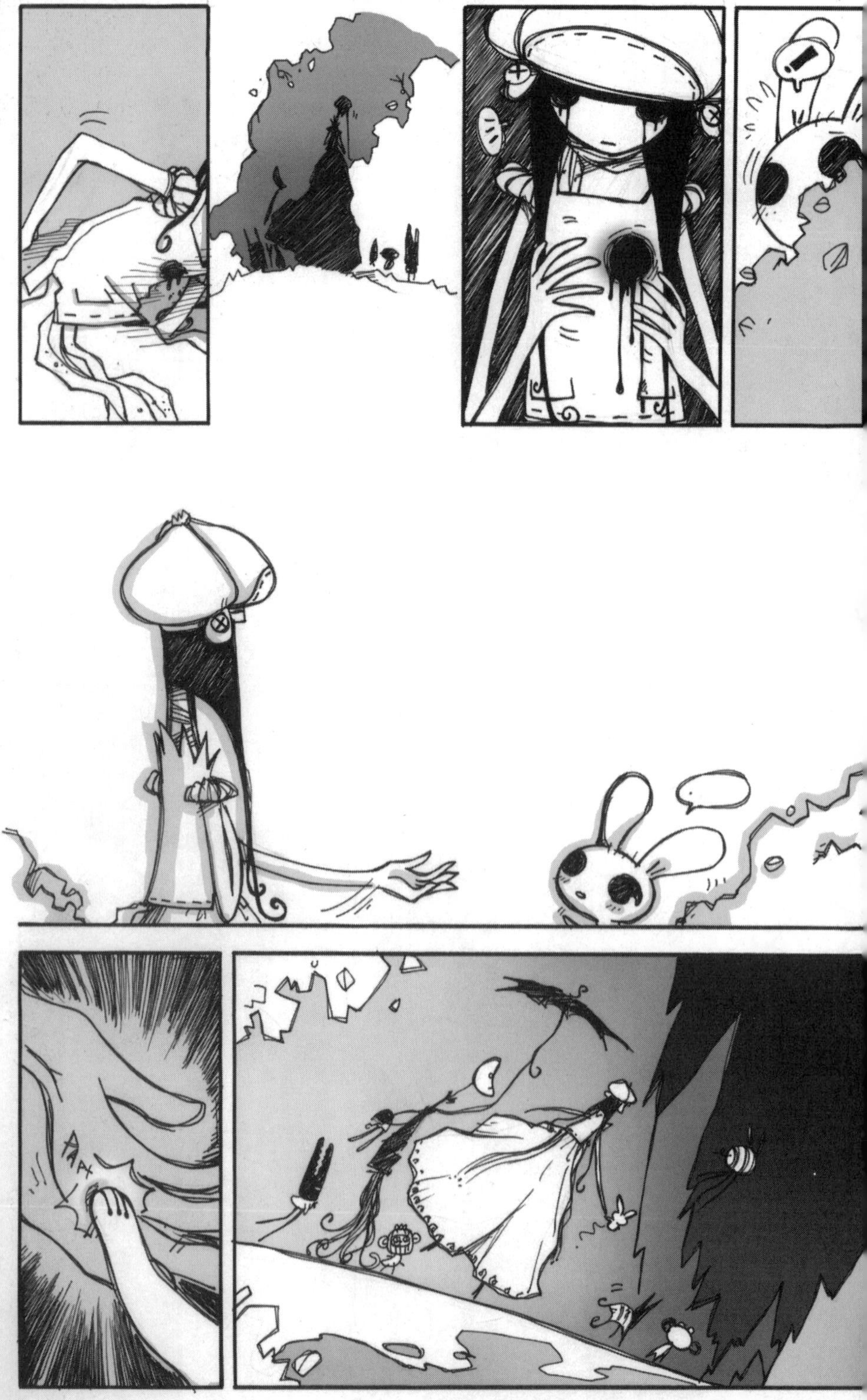
!

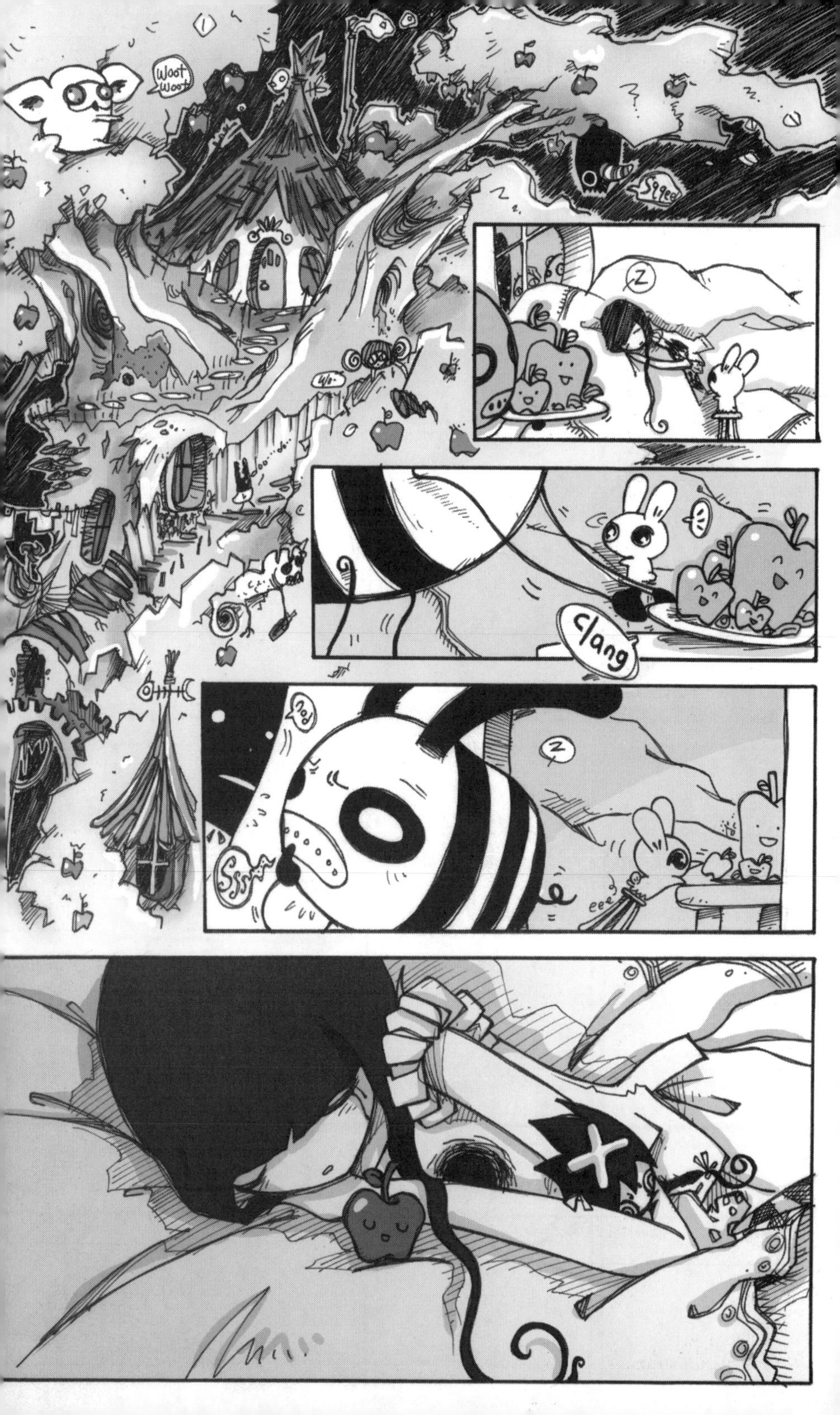
Woot Woot
Sqqee
Z
clang
pop
Sss
Z
eee

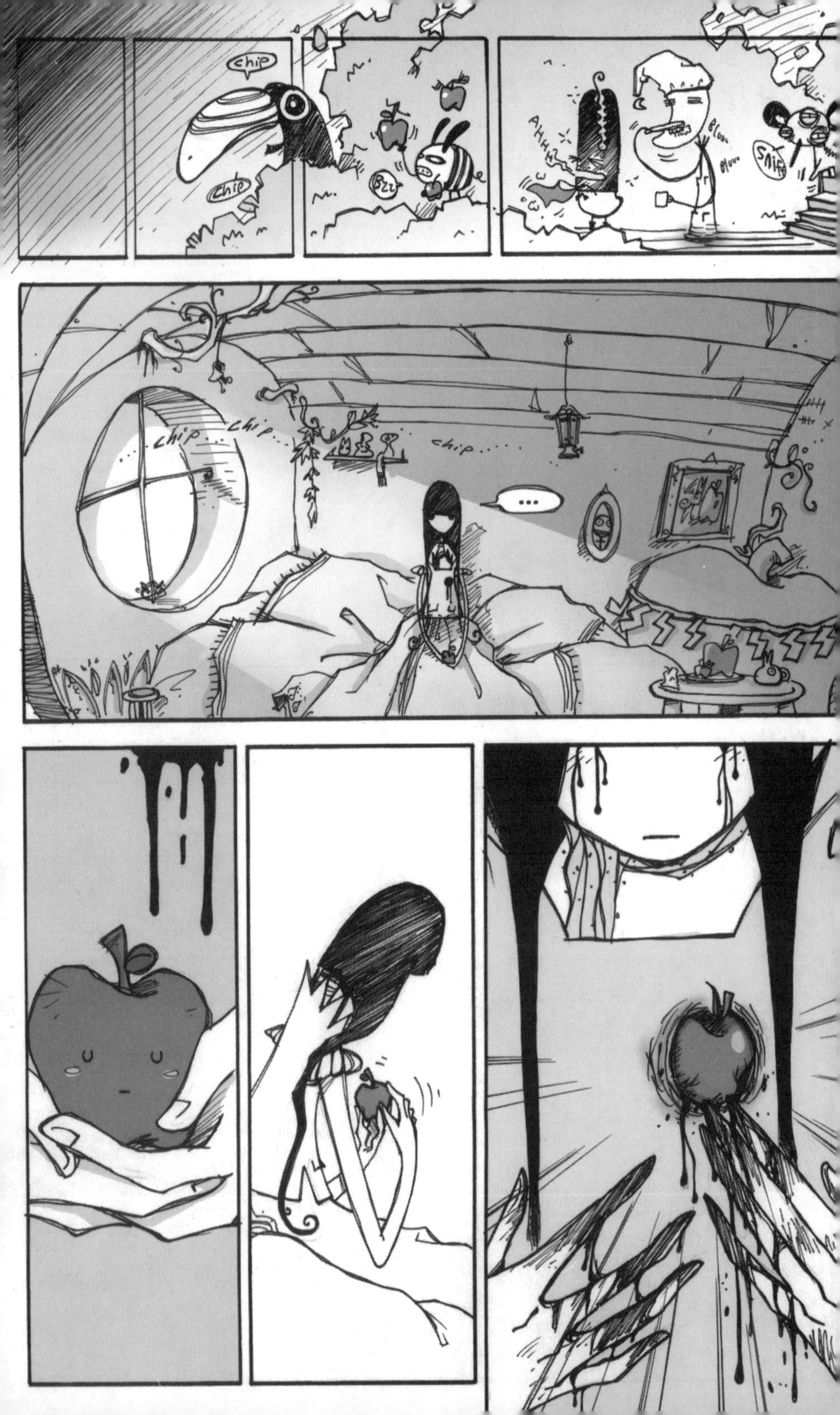
Chip
Chip
Bzz
AHHH
Bluu
Bluu
SNiff
chip
chip
chip
...

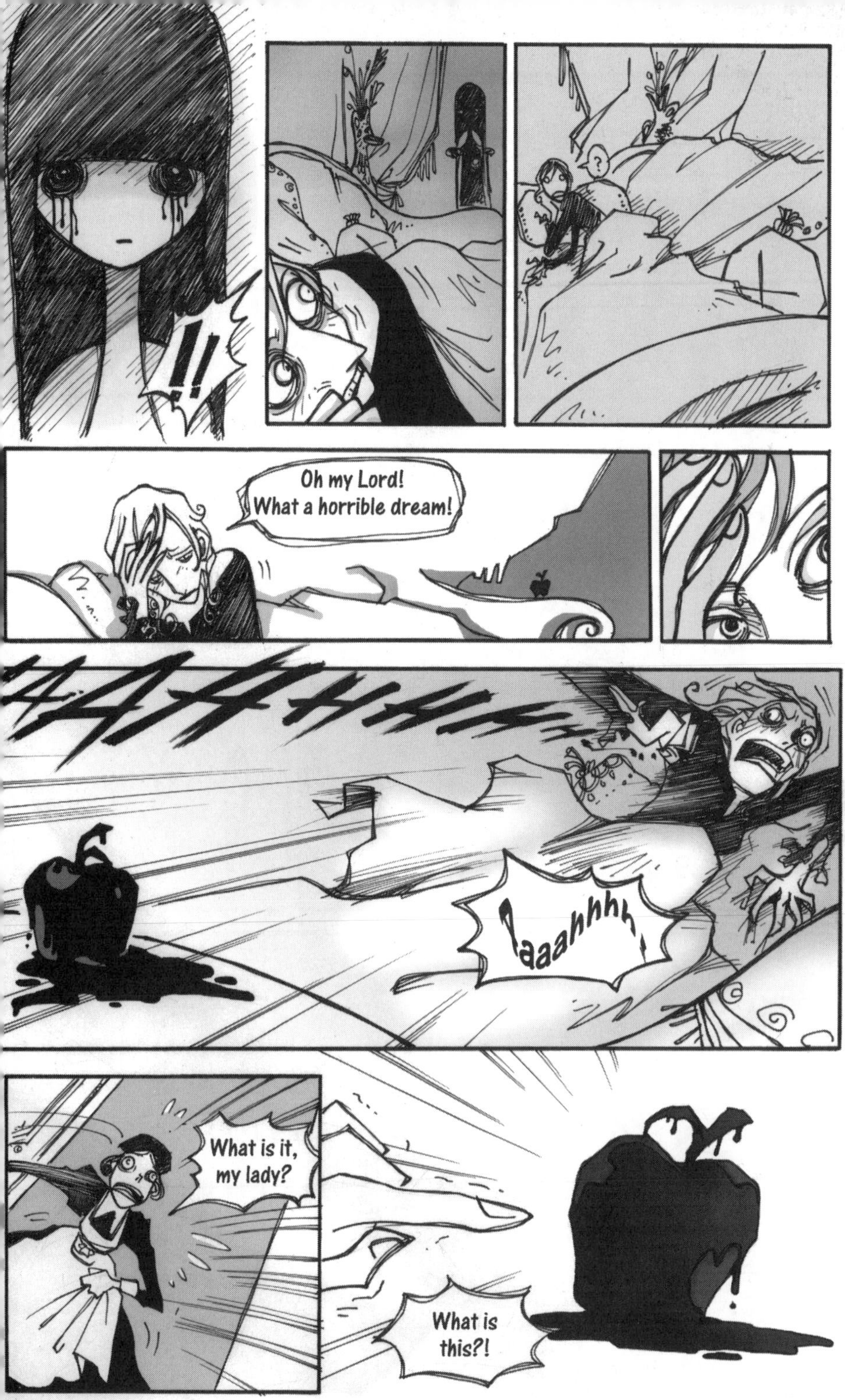

!!
?
Oh my Lord!
What a horrible dream!
AAAHHHH
Aaaahhhh
What is it,
my lady?
What is
this?!

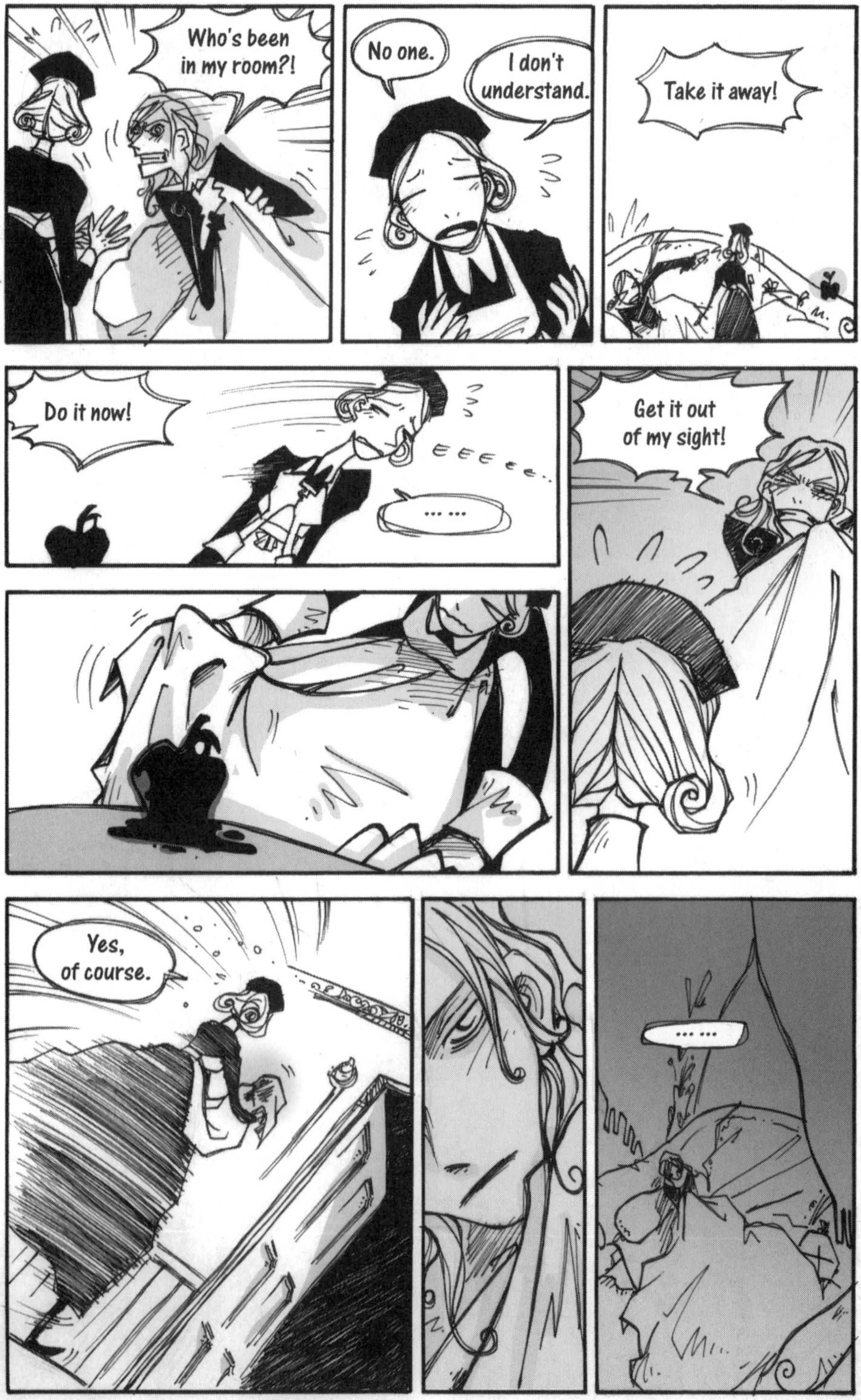
Who's been in my room?!
No one.
I don't understand.
Take it away!
Do it now!
... ...
Get it out of my sight!
Yes, of course.
... ...

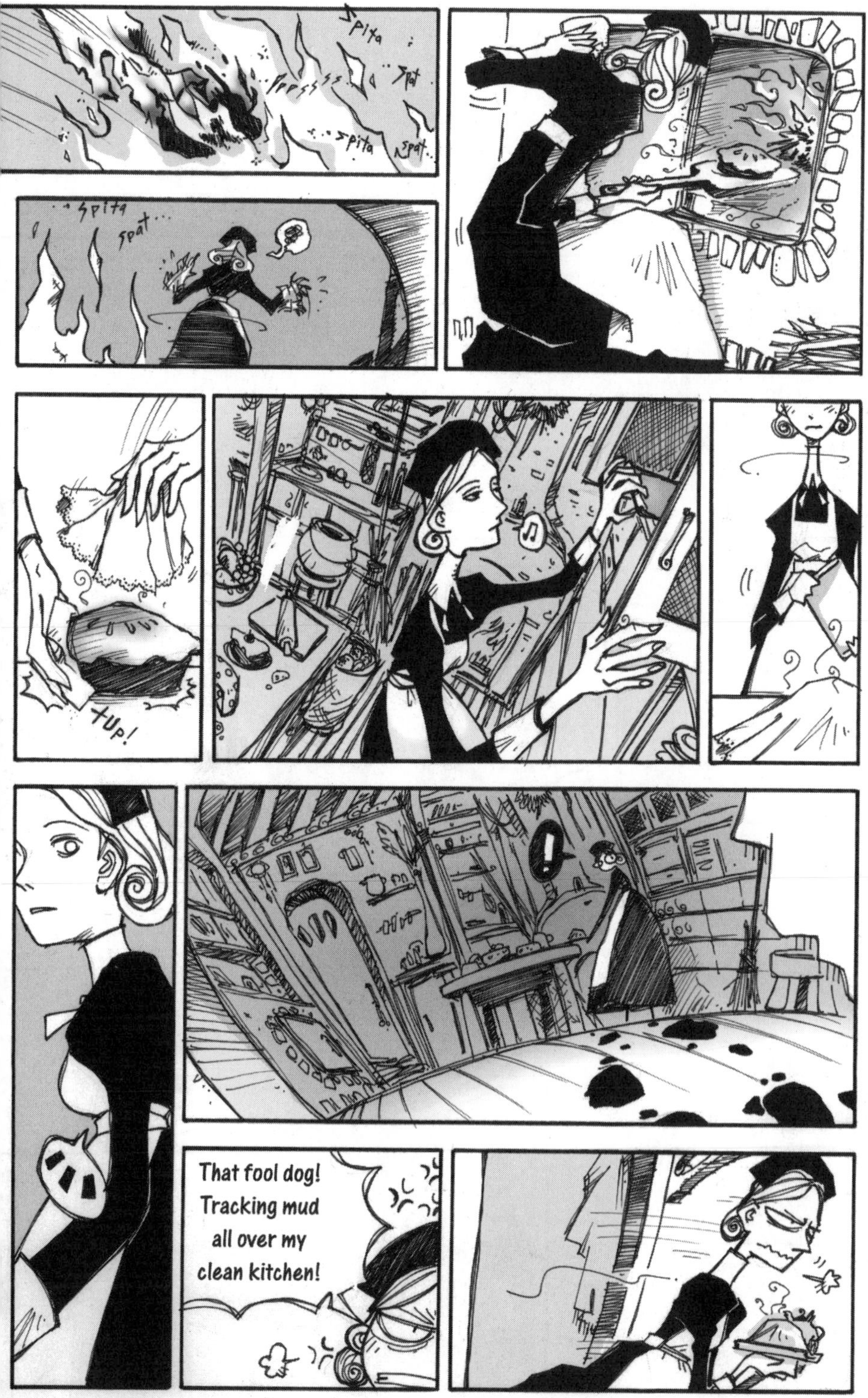

Spita
Spat
Pffsss
Spita
spat...
spita
spat...
tUp!
That fool dog! Tracking mud all over my clean kitchen!

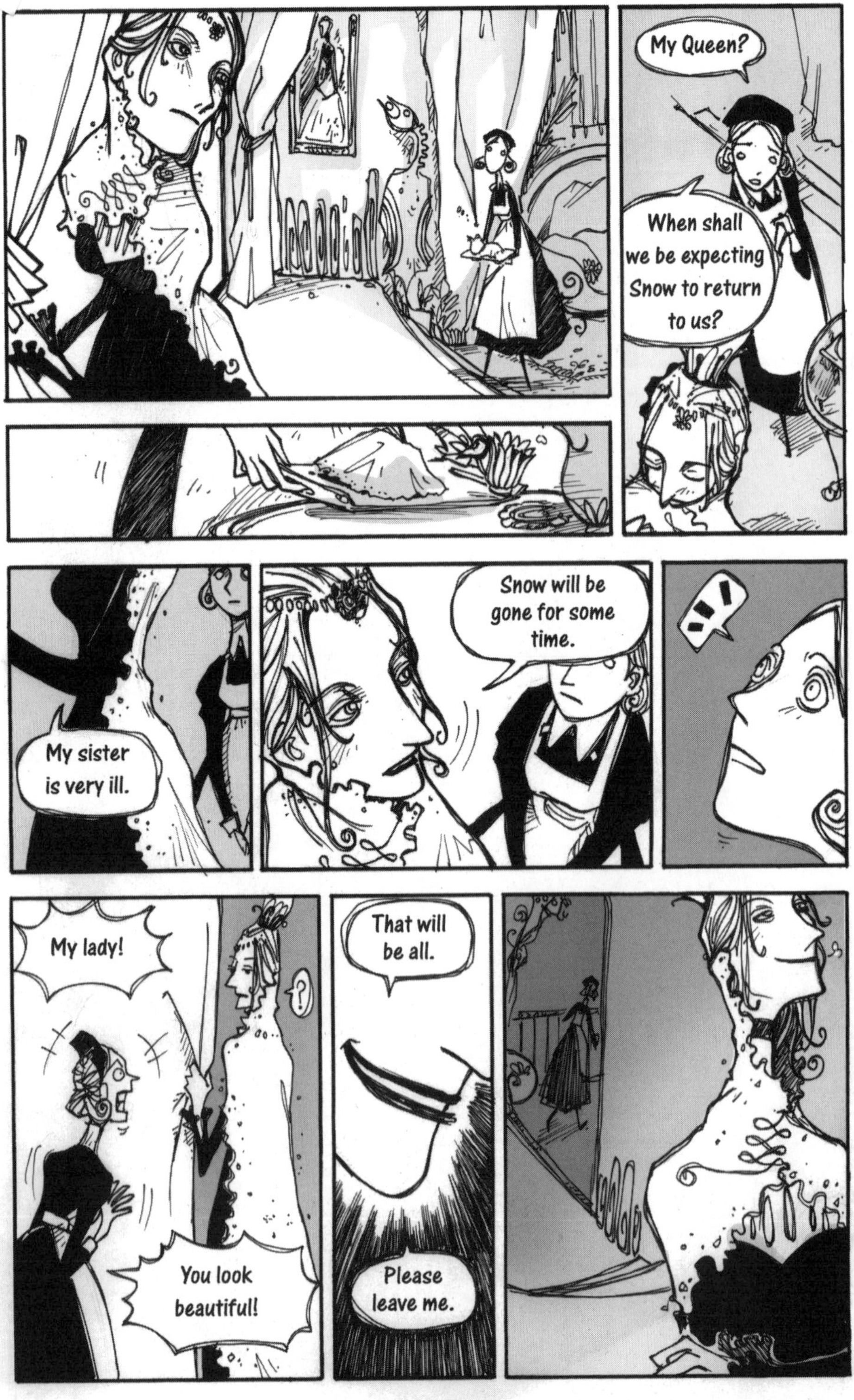
My Queen?
When shall we be expecting Snow to return to us?
My sister is very ill.
Snow will be gone for some time.
!
My lady!
You look beautiful!
?
That will be all.
Please leave me.

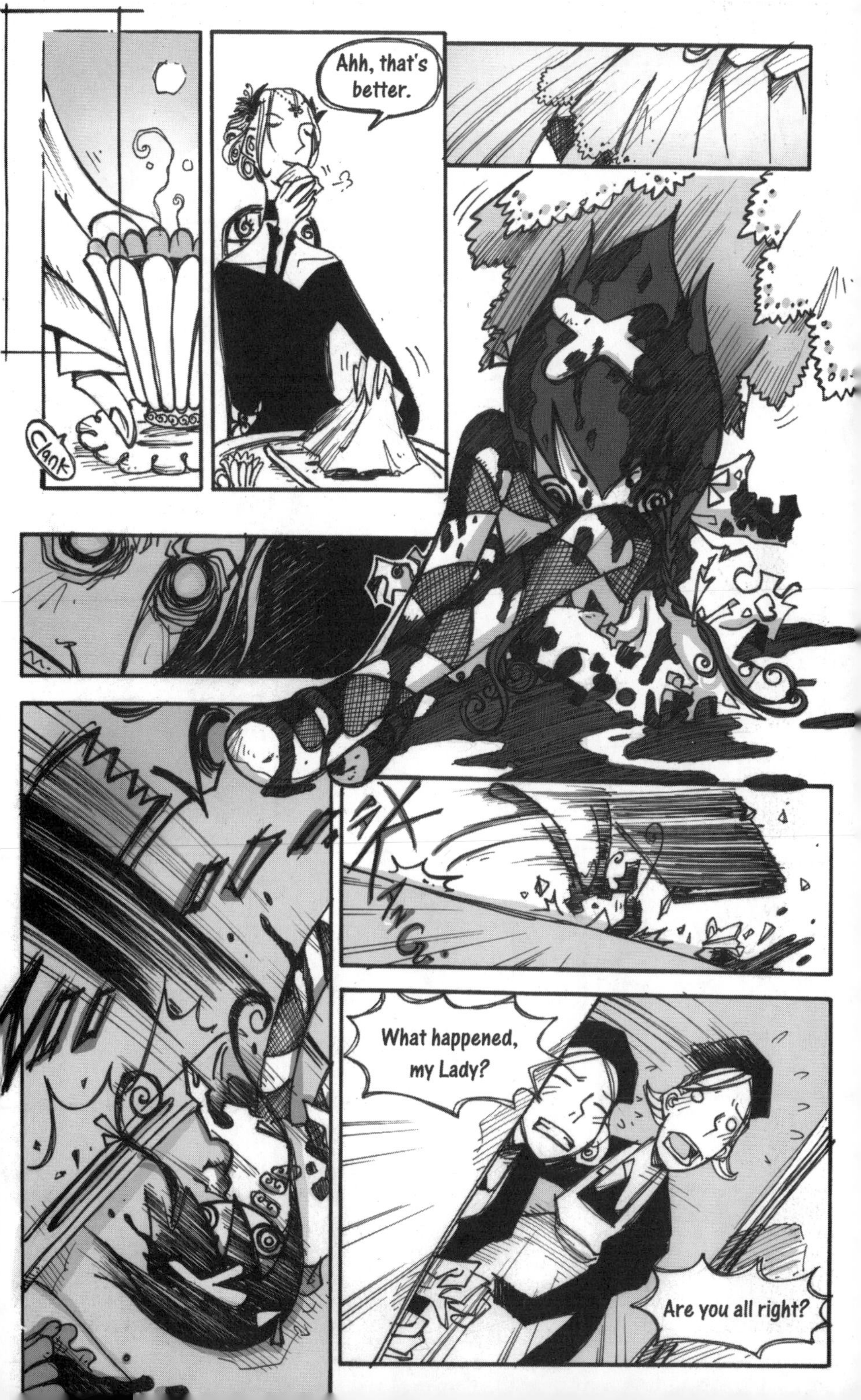
Clank
Ahh, that's better.
What happened, my Lady?
Are you all right?

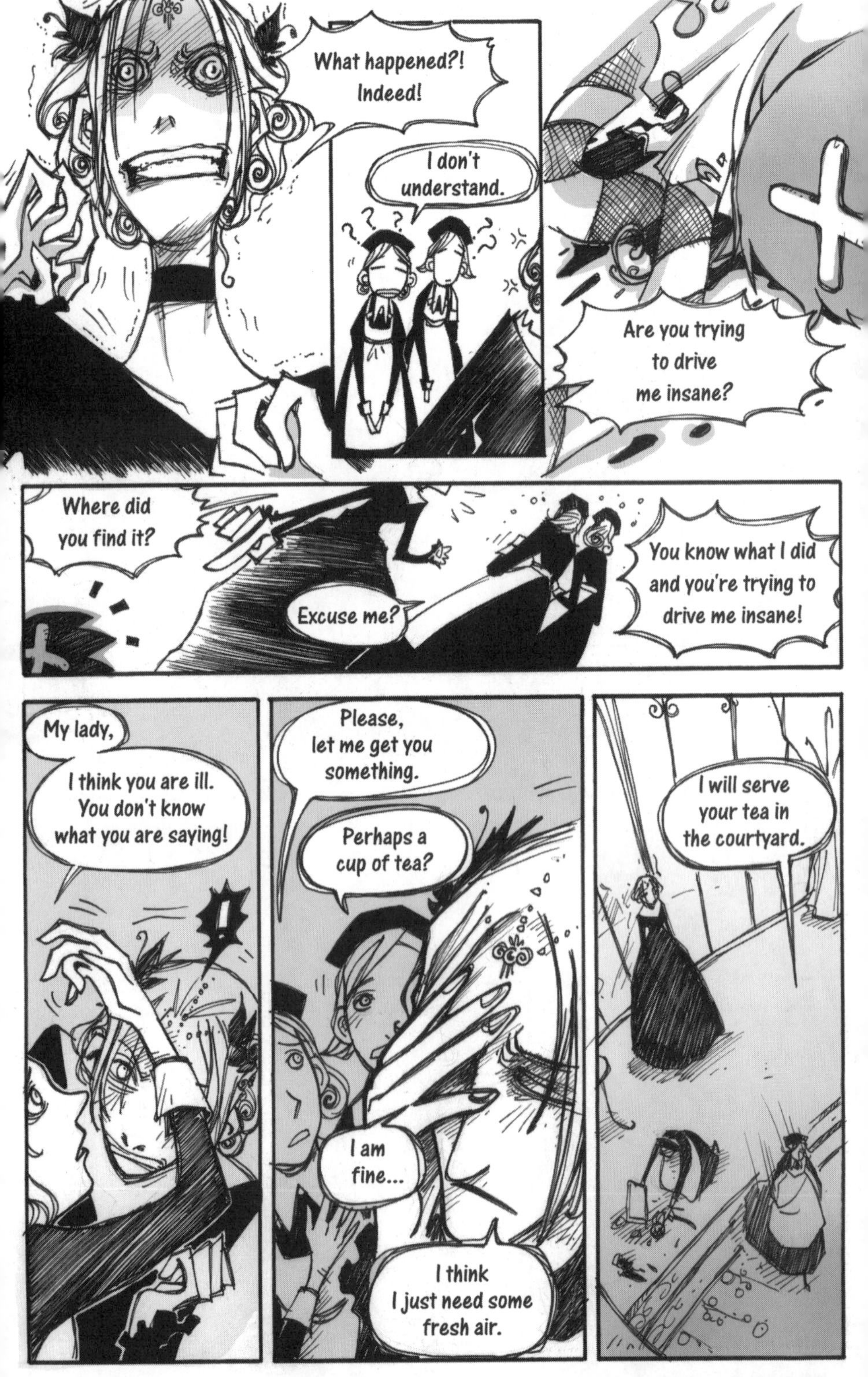
What happened?! Indeed!
I don't understand.
Are you trying to drive me insane?
Where did you find it?
Excuse me?
You know what I did and you're trying to drive me insane!
My lady,
I think you are ill. You don't know what you are saying!
Please, let me get you something.
Perhaps a cup of tea?
I am fine...
I think I just need some fresh air.
I will serve your tea in the courtyard.

skosh
skosh...
?
What in heaven's name is that?

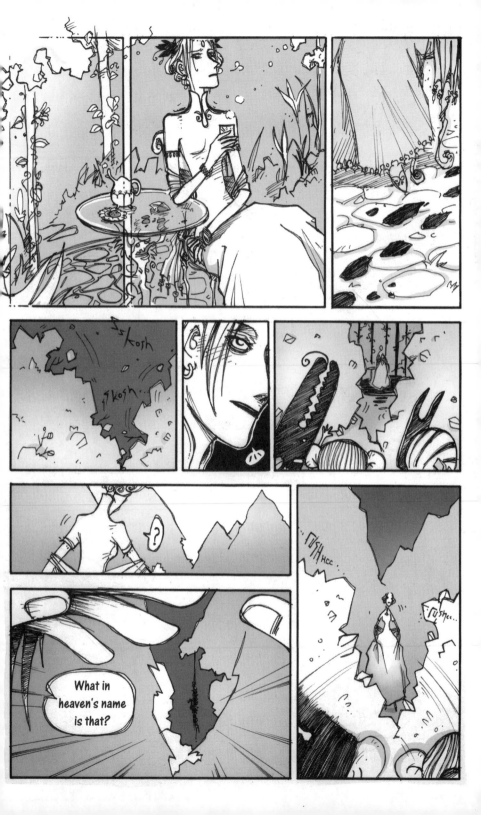

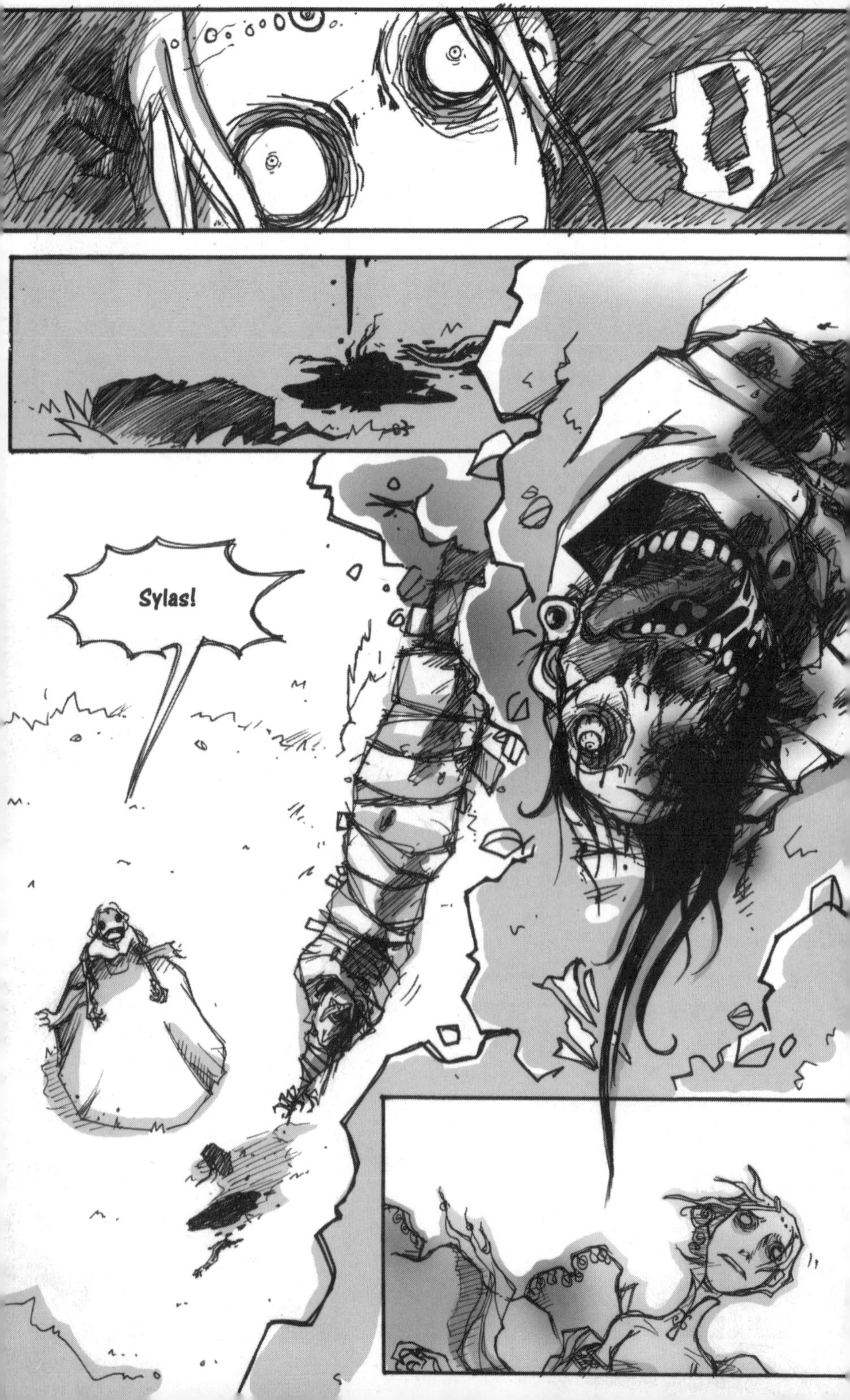
Sylas!

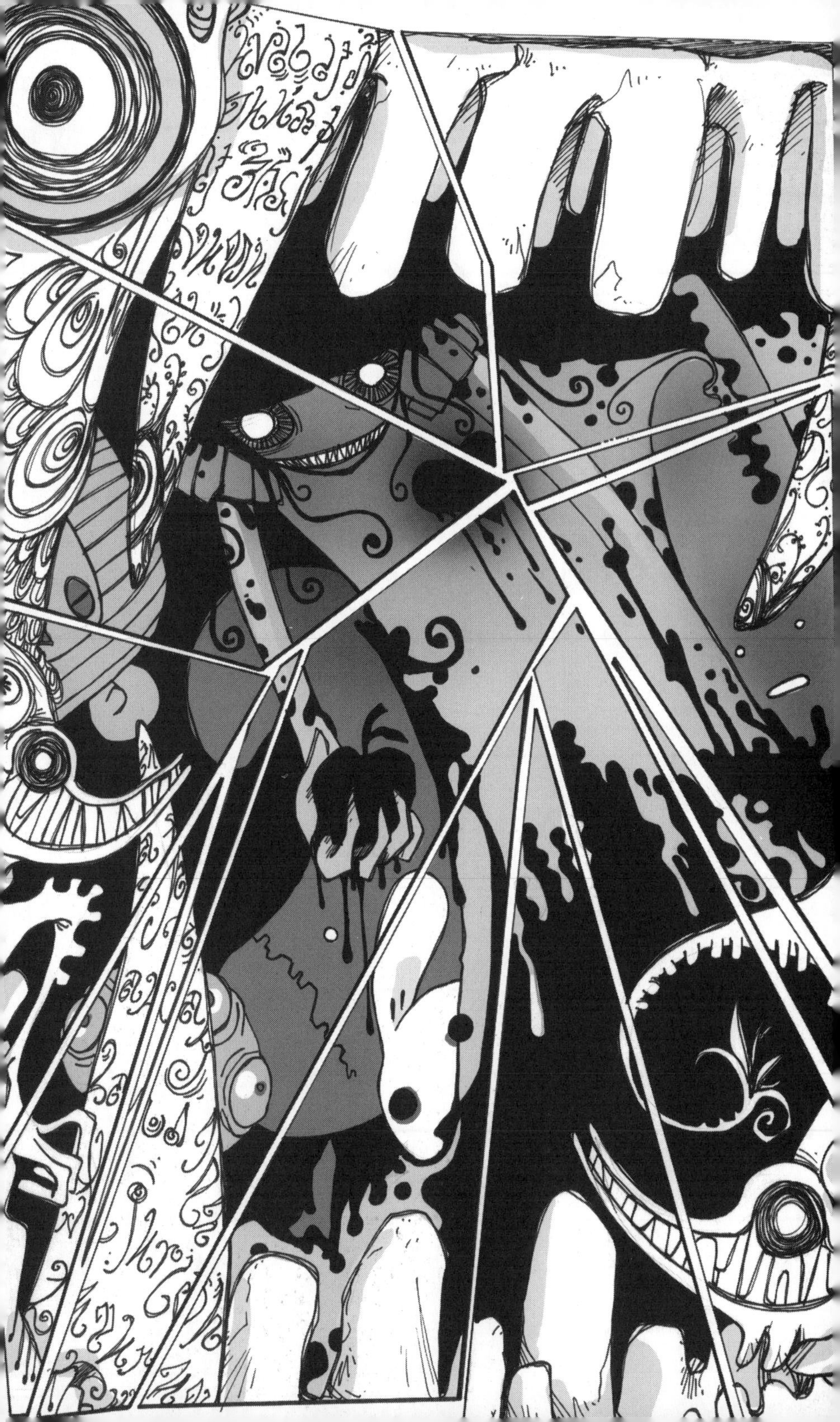

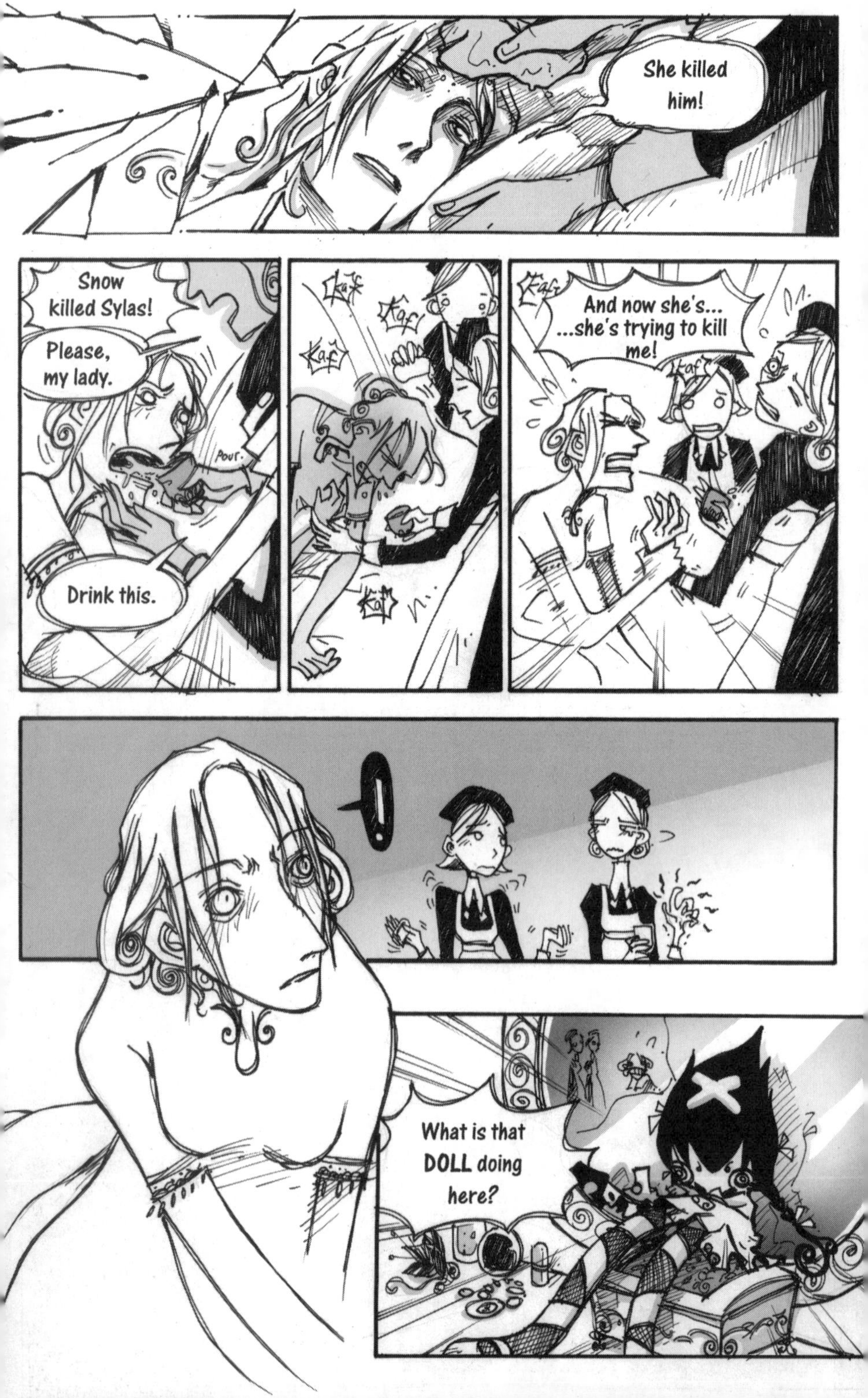
She killed him!
Snow killed Sylas!
Please, my lady.
Pour.
Drink this.
Kaf
Kaf
Kaf
Kaf
Kaf
And now she's... ...she's trying to kill me!
Kaf
!
What is that DOLL doing here?

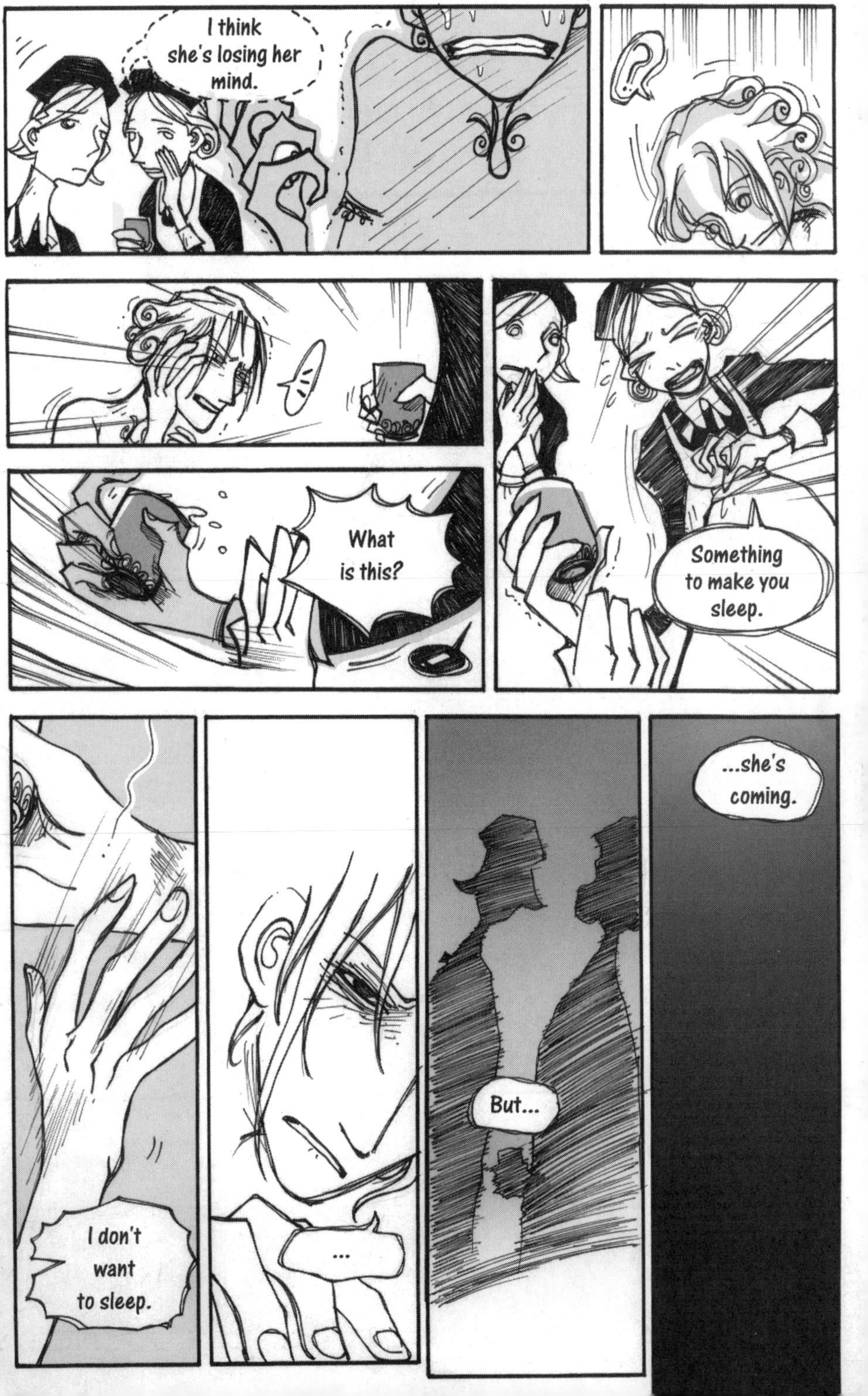
I think she's losing her mind.
What is this?
Something to make you sleep.
I don't want to sleep.
...
But...
...she's coming.

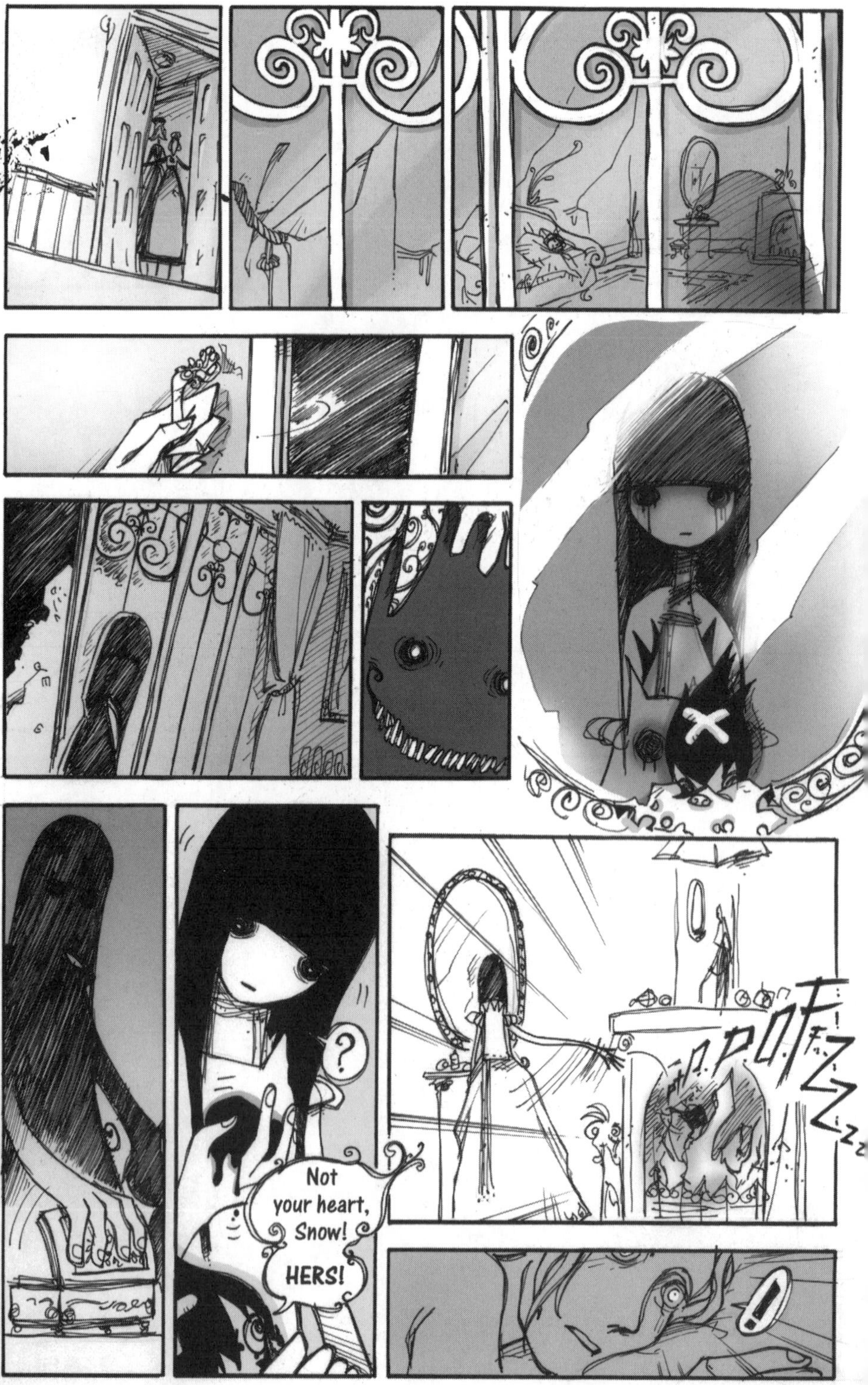
?
Not your heart, Snow!
HERS!
POOF
Zzz
!

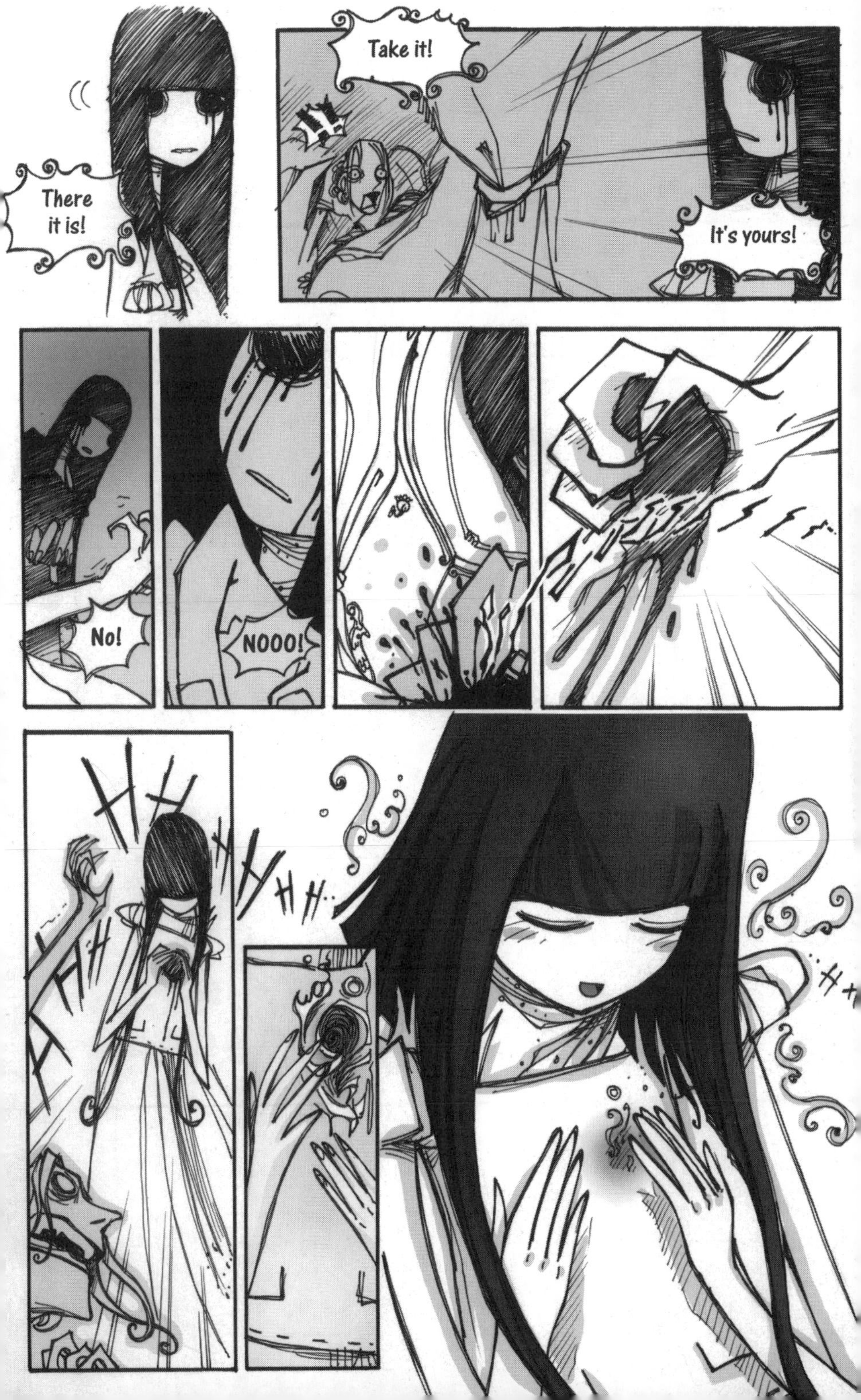
There it is!
Take it!
It's yours!
No!
NOOO!

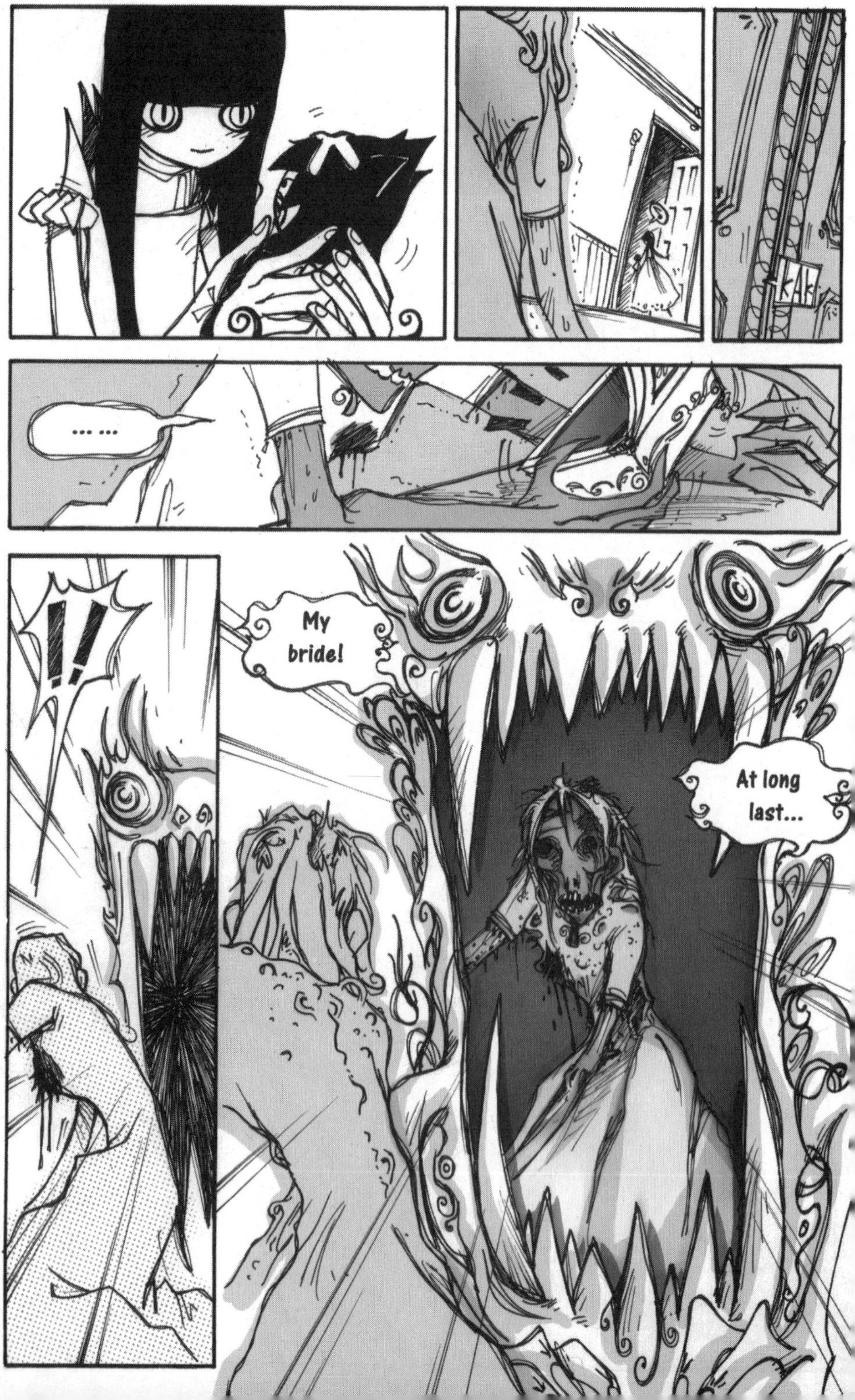
... ...
!!
My bride!
At long last...

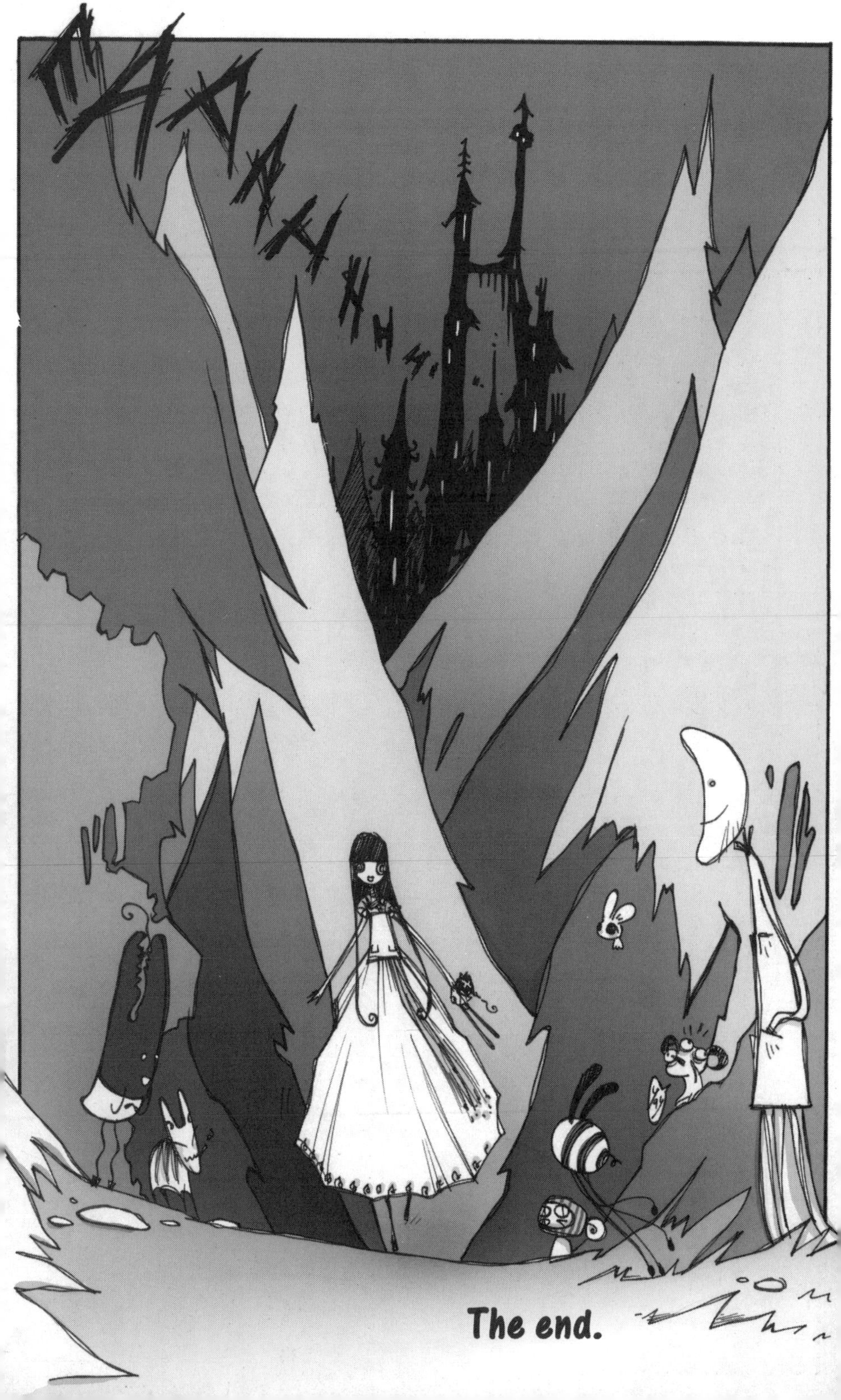
The end.

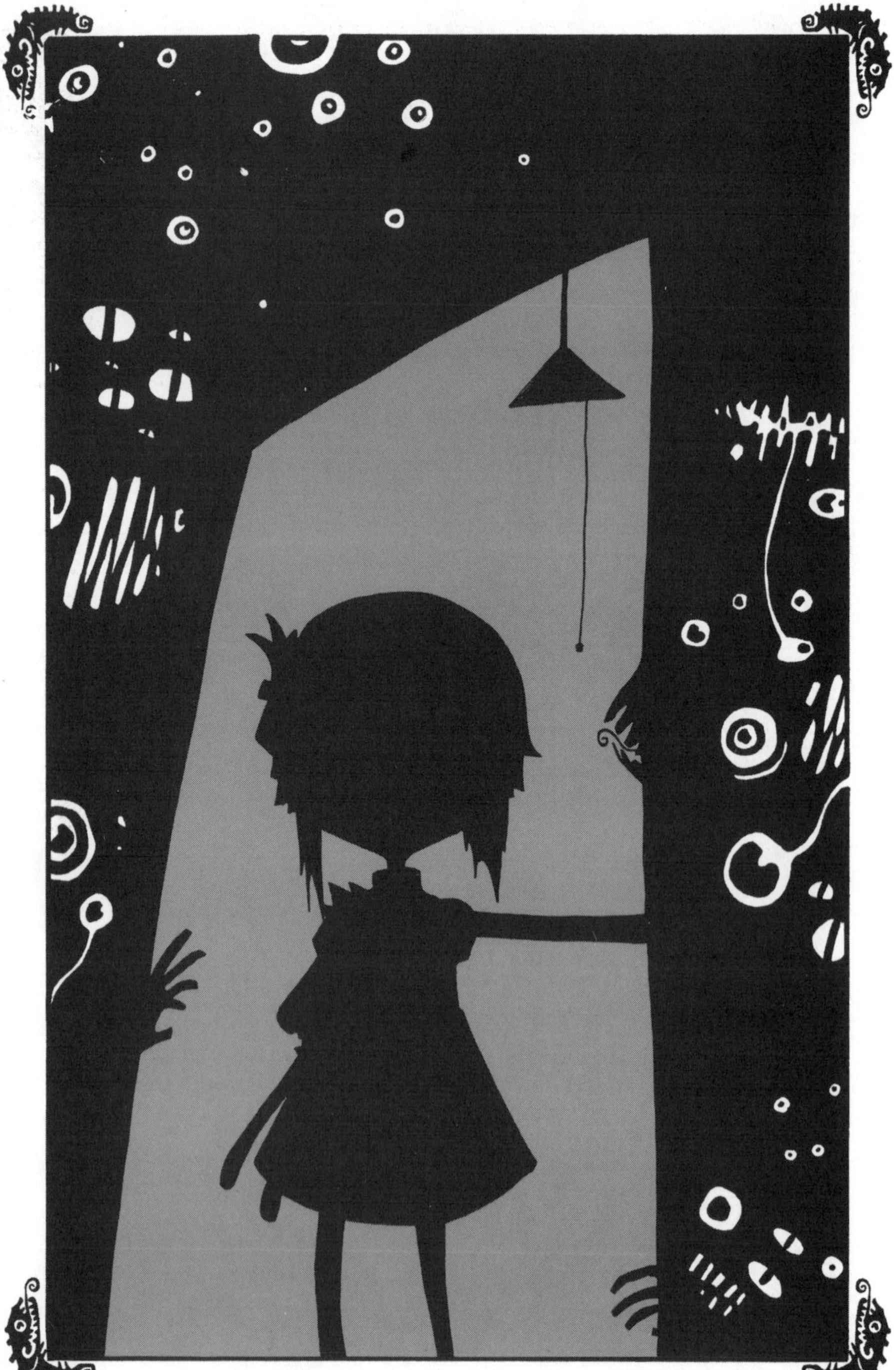

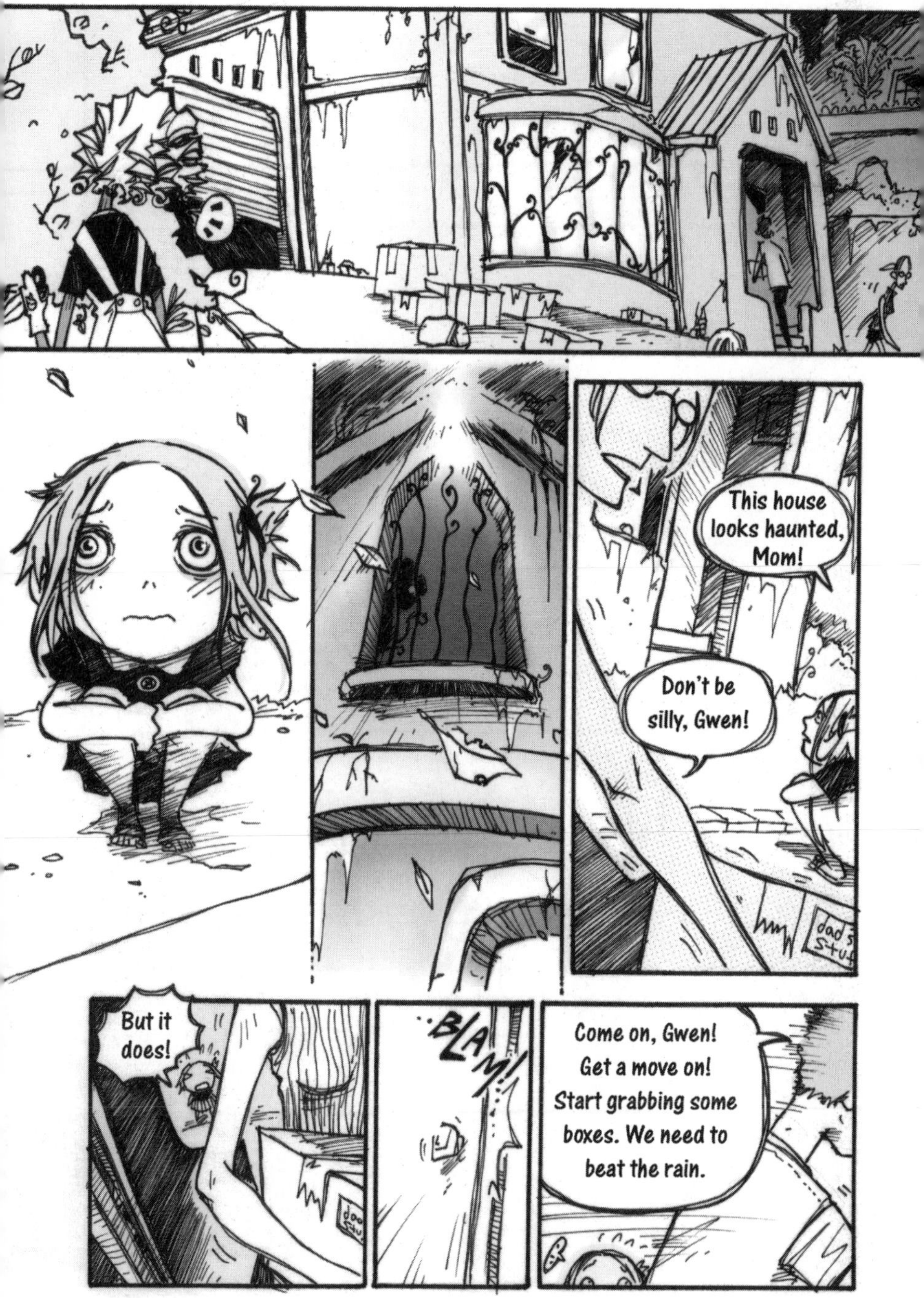
This house looks haunted, Mom!
Don't be silly, Gwen!
dad's stuff
But it does!
BLAM!
Come on, Gwen! Get a move on! Start grabbing some boxes. We need to beat the rain.

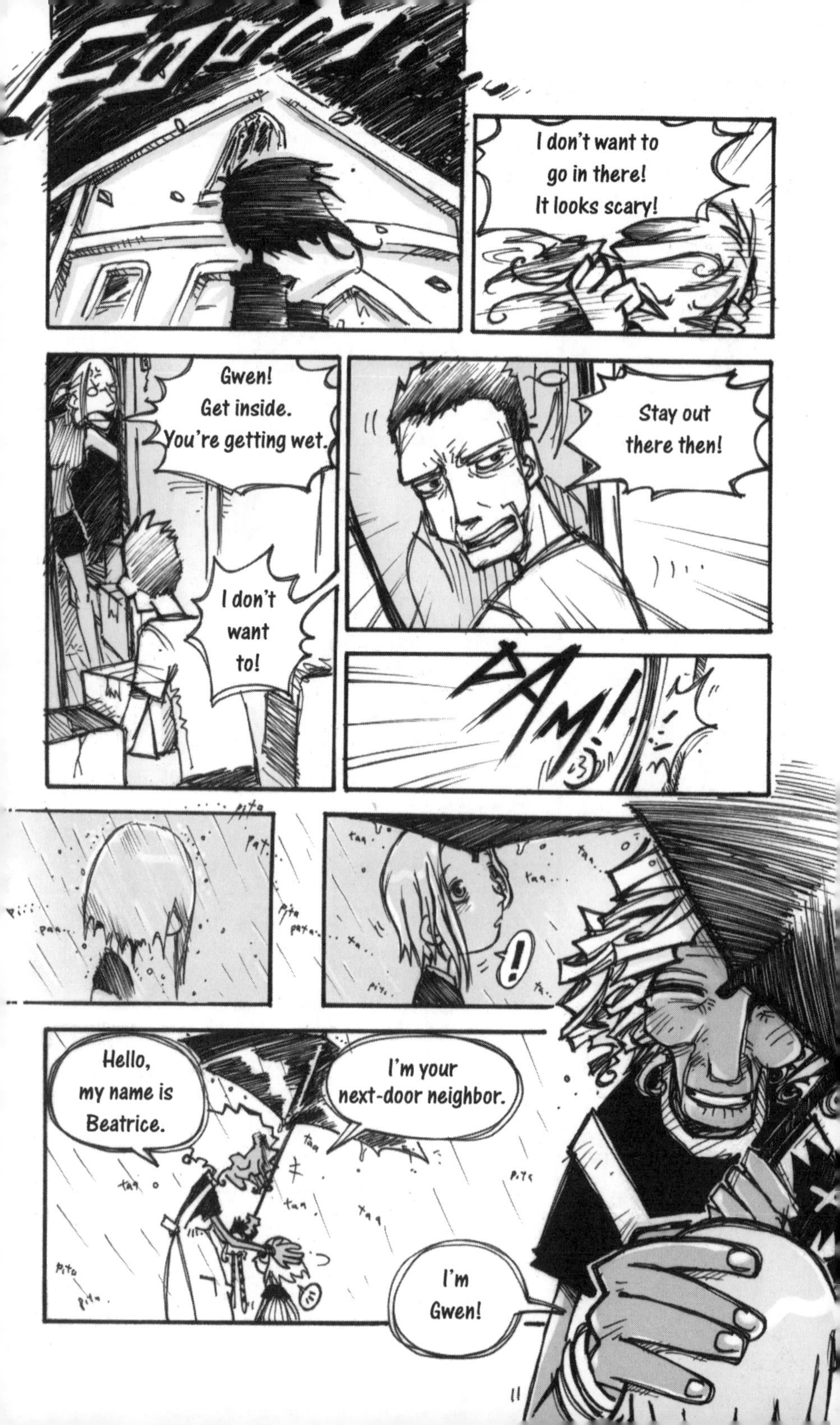
I don't want to go in there! It looks scary!
Gwen! Get inside. You're getting wet.
I don't want to!
Stay out there then!
BAM!
!
Hello, my name is Beatrice.
I'm your next-door neighbor.
I'm Gwen!

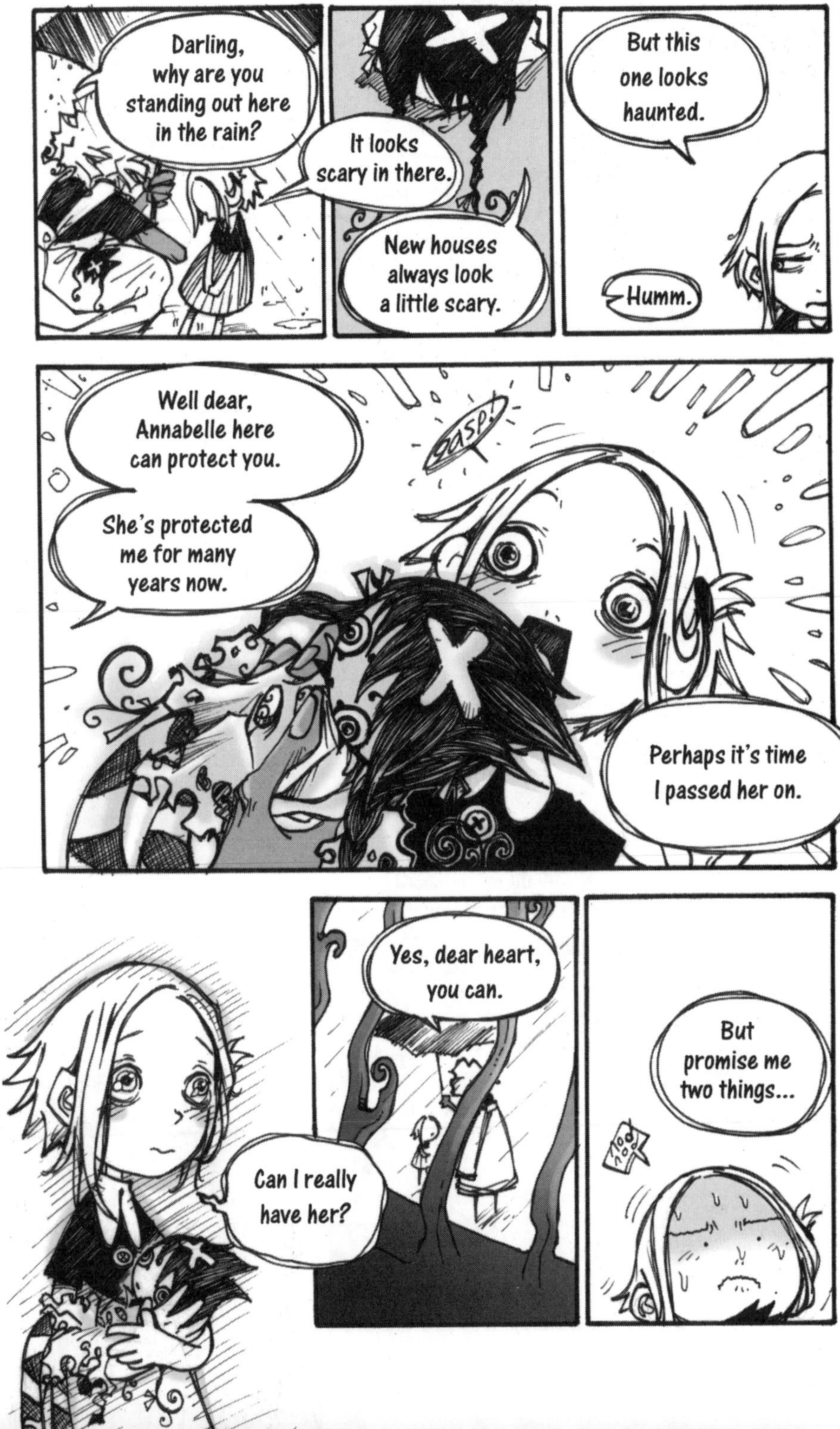

Darling, why are you standing out here in the rain?
It looks scary in there.
New houses always look a little scary.
But this one looks haunted.
Humm.
Well dear, Annabelle here can protect you.
She's protected me for many years now.
Gasp!
Perhaps it's time I passed her on.
Can I really have her?
Yes, dear heart, you can.
But promise me two things...

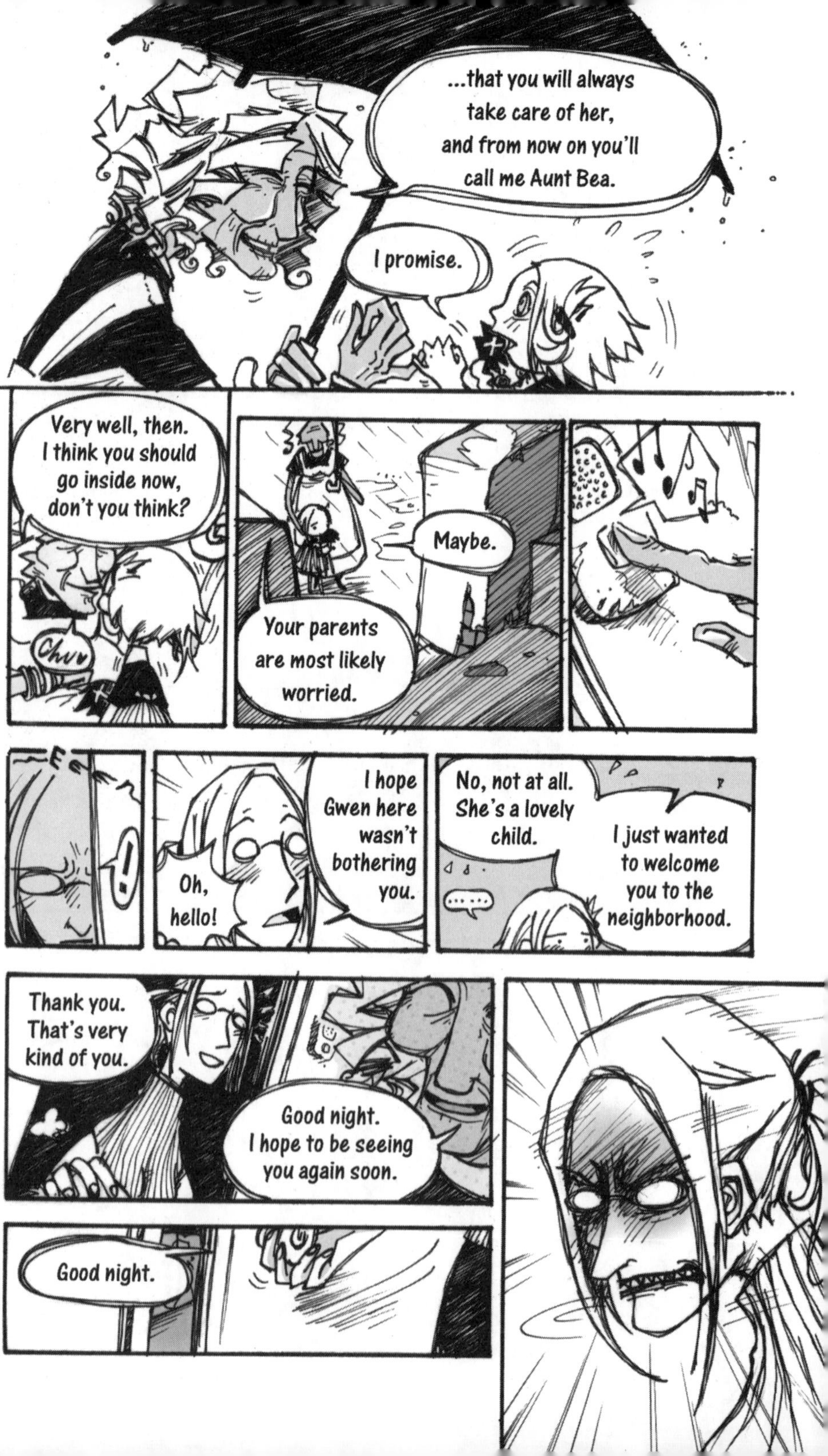
...that you will always take care of her, and from now on you'll call me Aunt Bea.
I promise.
Very well, then. I think you should go inside now, don't you think?
Chu
Maybe.
Your parents are most likely worried.
!
Oh, hello!
I hope Gwen here wasn't bothering you.
No, not at all. She's a lovely child.
I just wanted to welcome you to the neighborhood.
Thank you. That's very kind of you.
Good night. I hope to be seeing you again soon.
Good night.

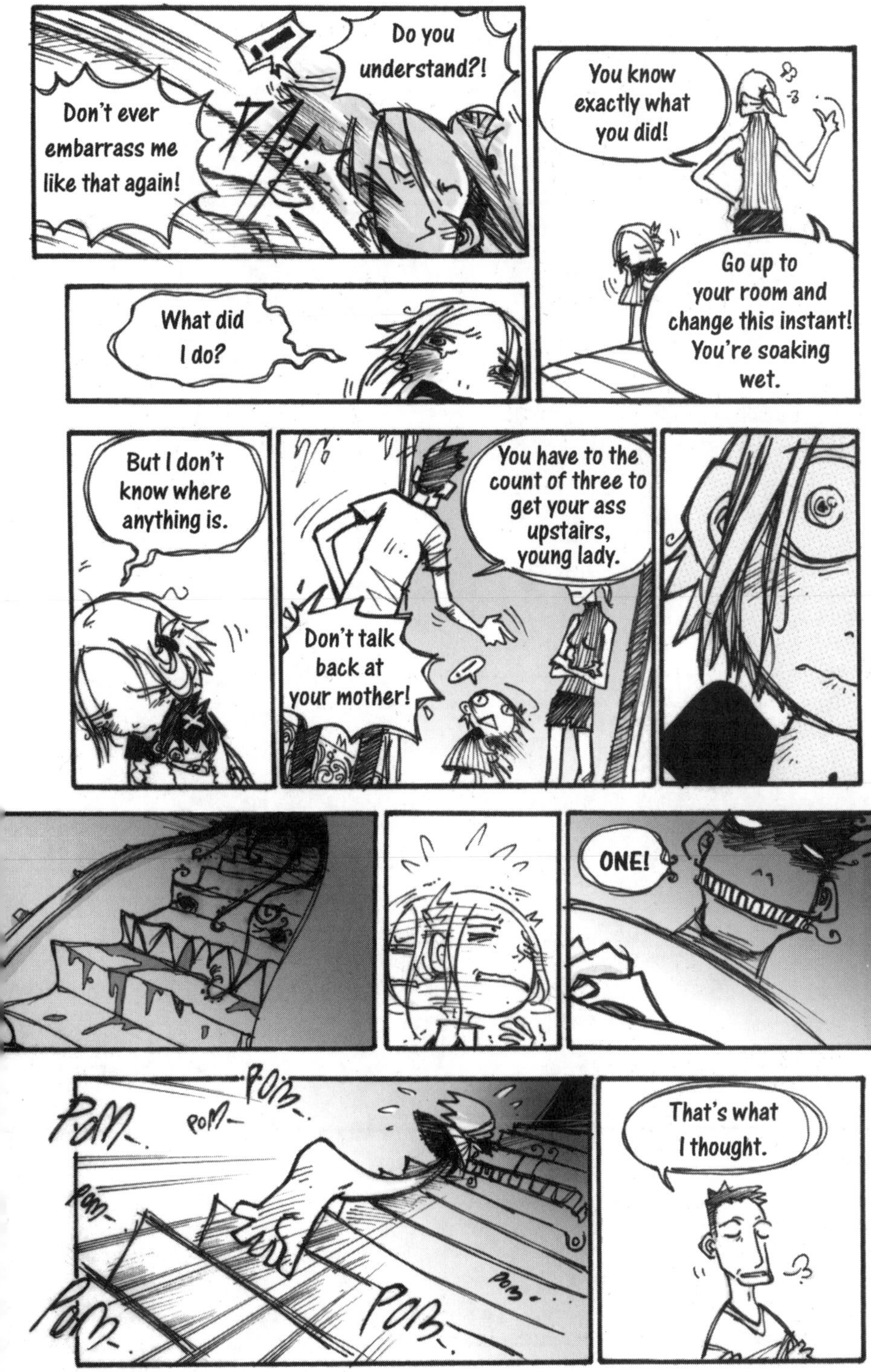
Do you understand?!
Don't ever embarrass me like that again!
You know exactly what you did!
What did I do?
Go up to your room and change this instant! You're soaking wet.
But I don't know where anything is.
You have to the count of three to get your ass upstairs, young lady.
Don't talk back at your mother!
ONE!
POM
POM
POM
POM
POM
POM
POM
That's what I thought.

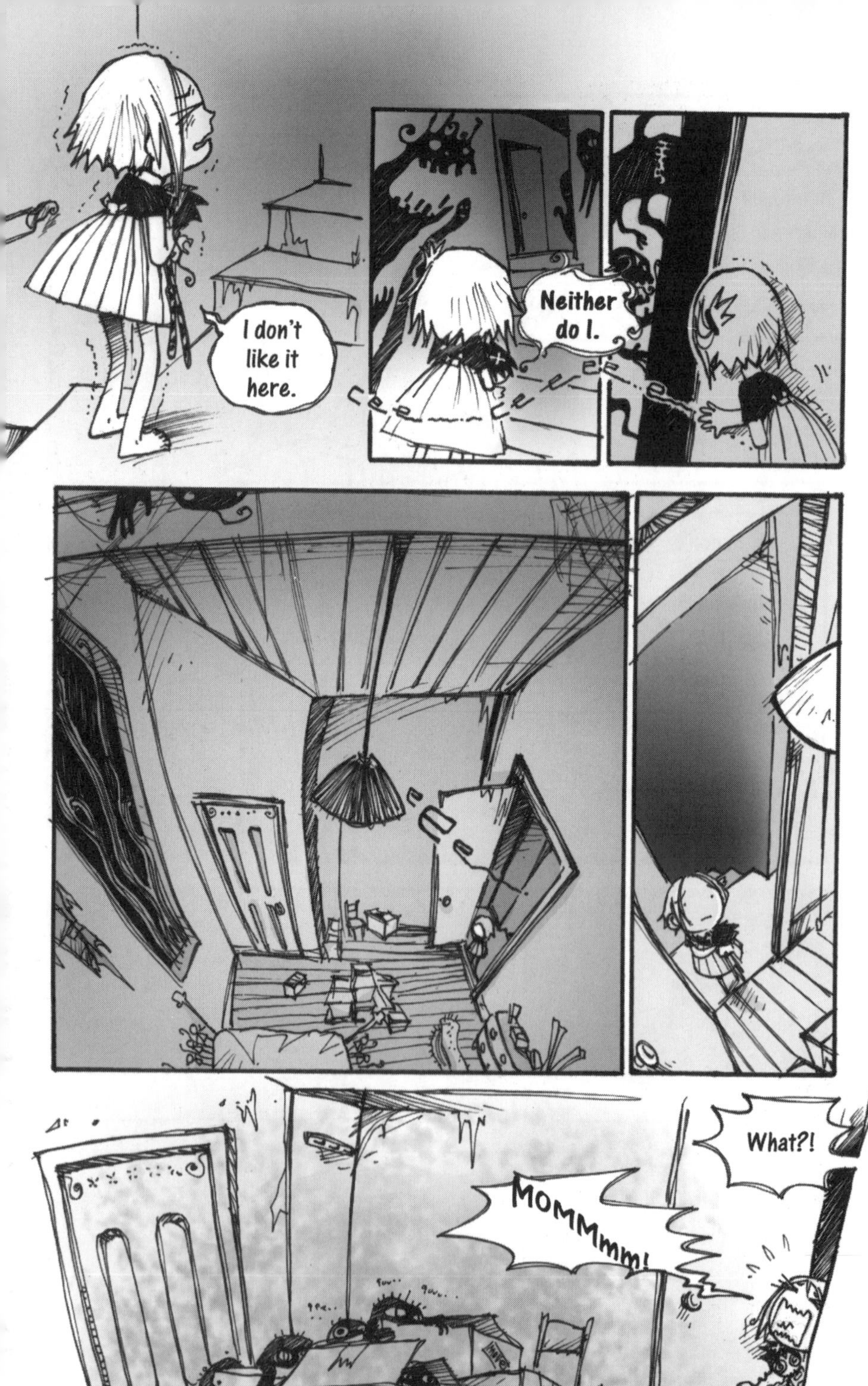
I don't like it here.
Neither do I.
What?!
MOMMmmm!

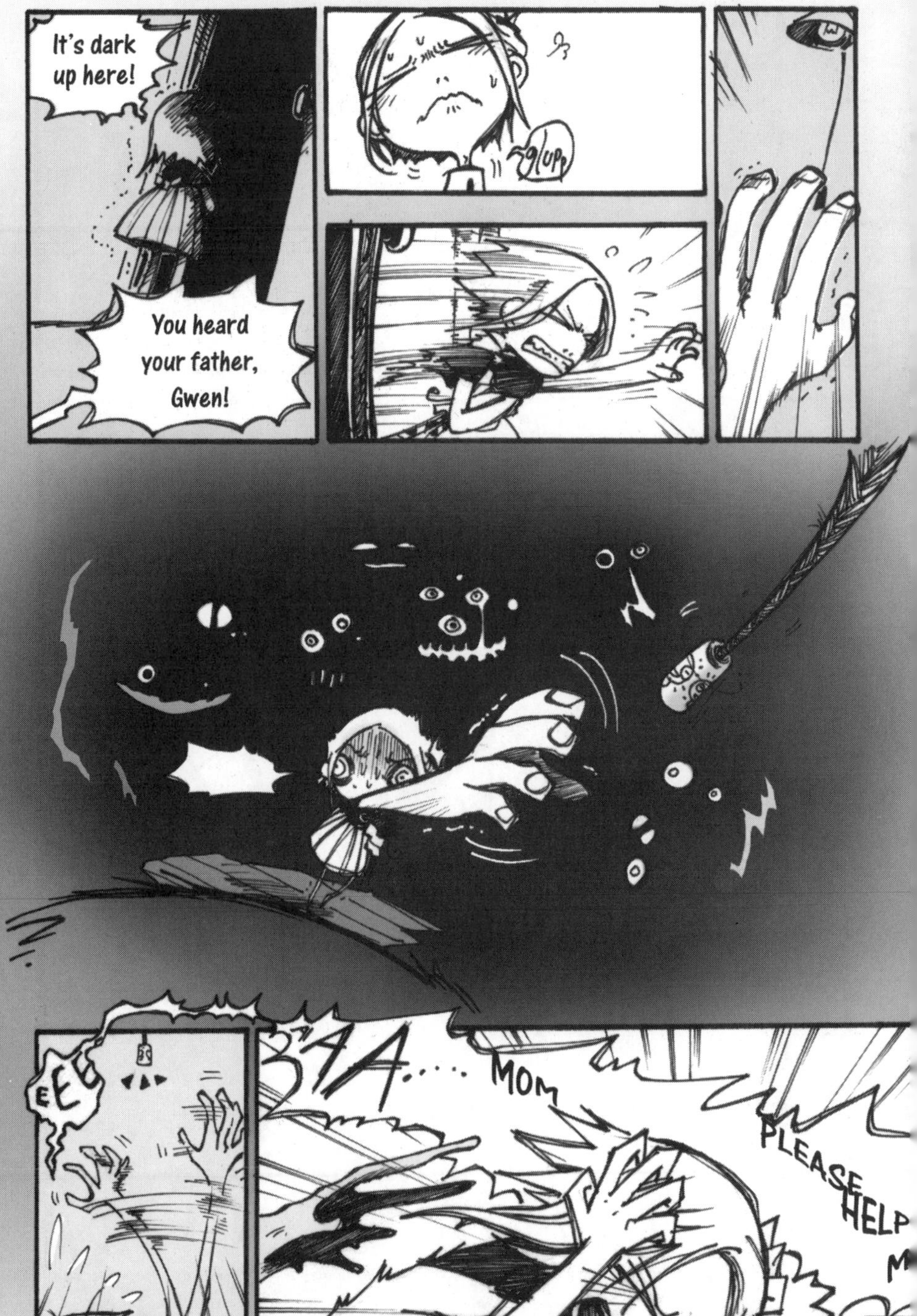

It's dark up here!
You heard your father, Gwen!
glup
EEE
AA.....
MOM
PLEASE HELP M

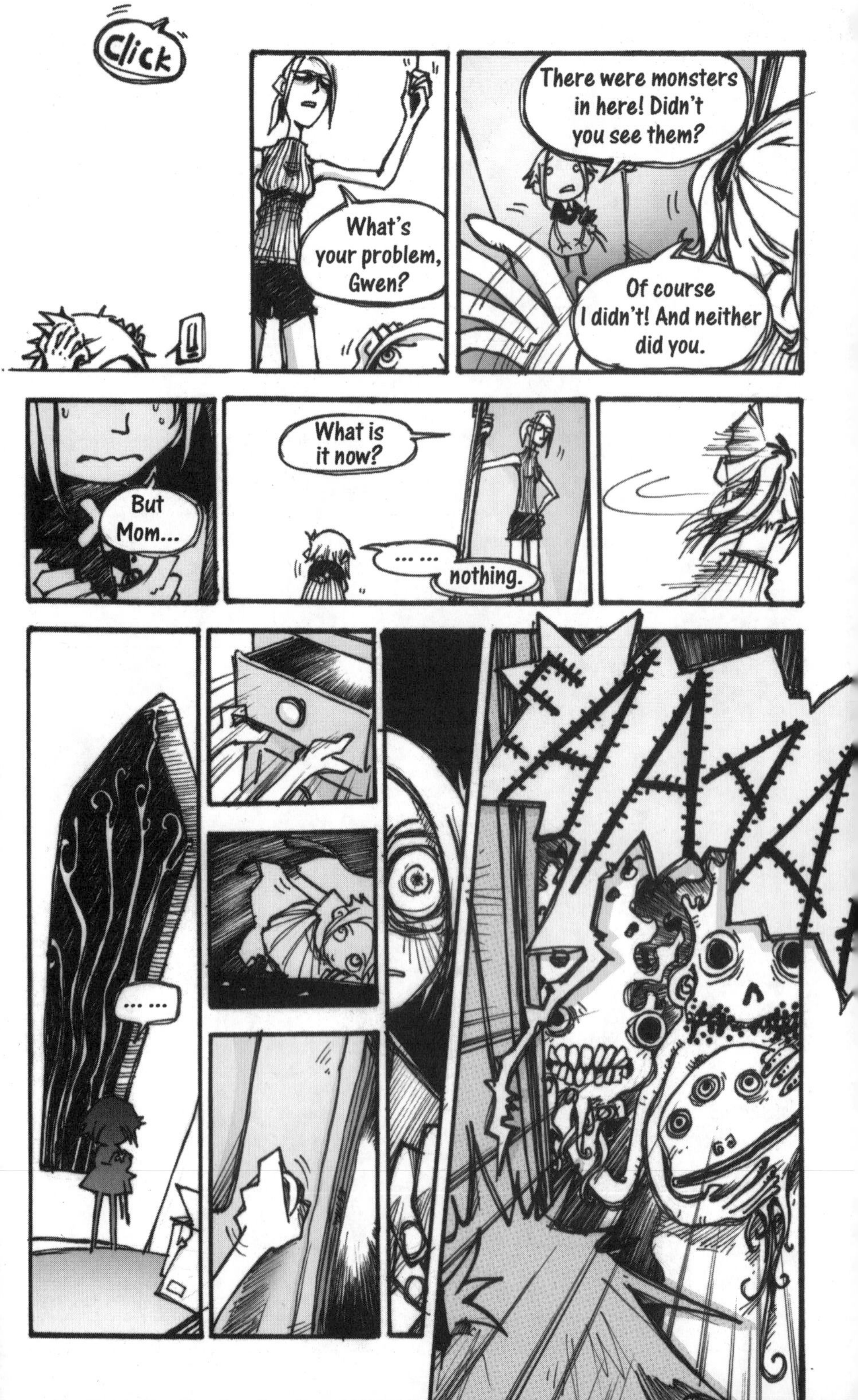
Click
What's your problem, Gwen?
There were monsters in here! Didn't you see them?
Of course I didn't! And neither did you.
But Mom...
What is it now?
... ...
nothing.
... ...
AAAA

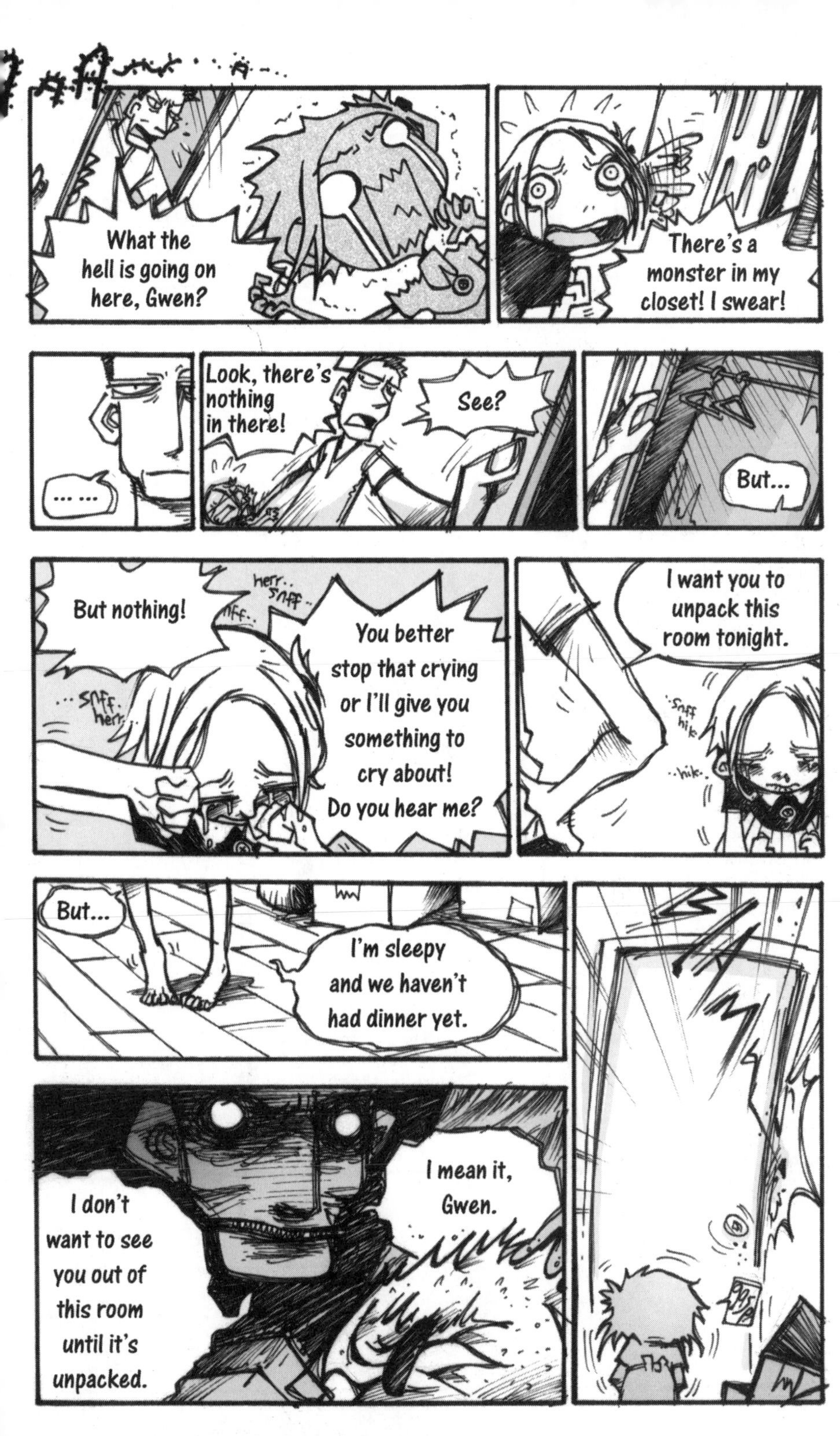
What the hell is going on here, Gwen?
There's a monster in my closet! I swear!
... ...
Look, there's nothing in there!
See?
But...
But nothing!
herr... sniff...
sniff...
... sniff... herr...
You better stop that crying or I'll give you something to cry about! Do you hear me?
I want you to unpack this room tonight.
..sniff hik..
..hik..
But...
I'm sleepy and we haven't had dinner yet.
I mean it, Gwen.
I don't want to see you out of this room until it's unpacked.

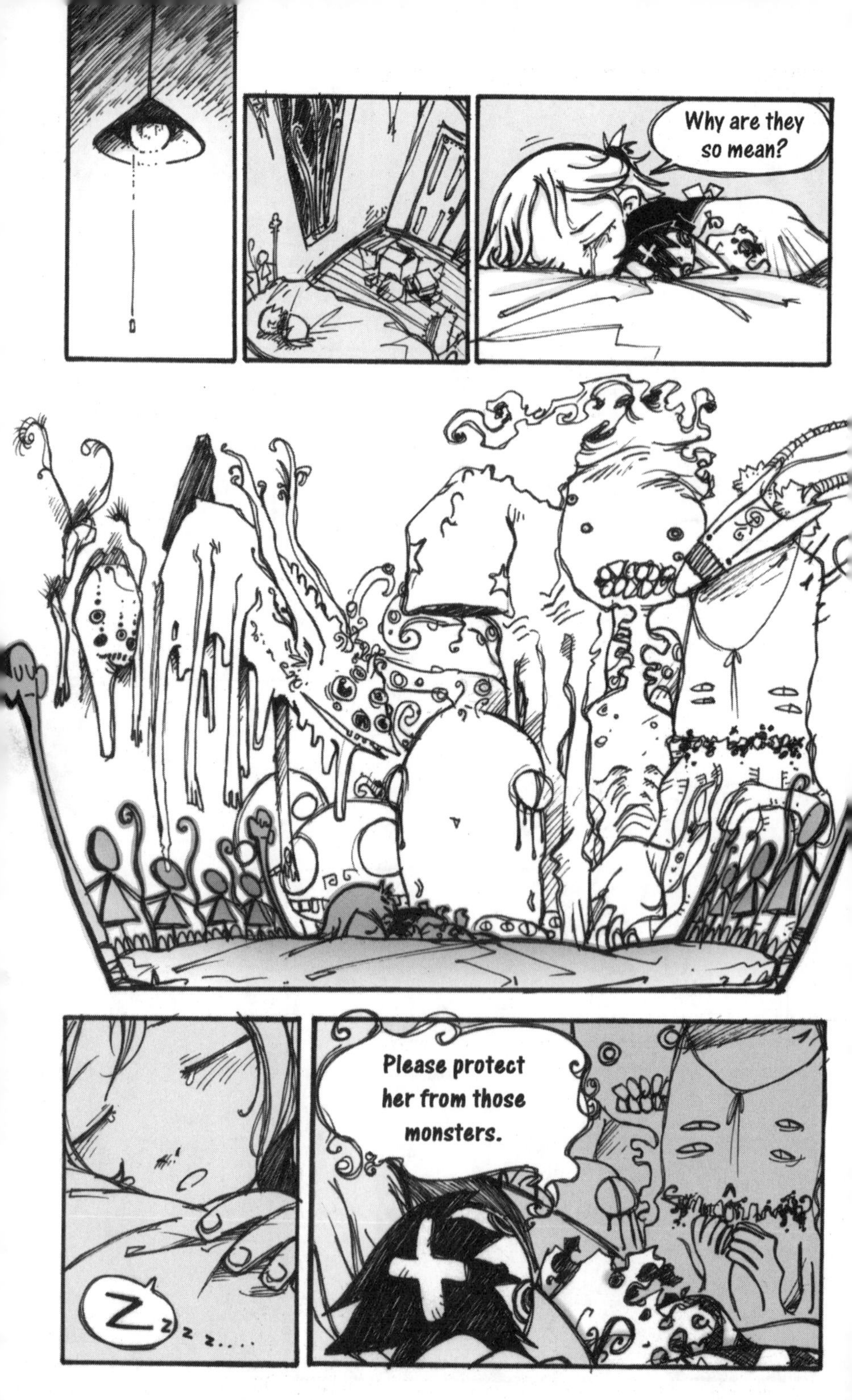
Why are they so mean?
Please protect her from those monsters.
Z z z z....

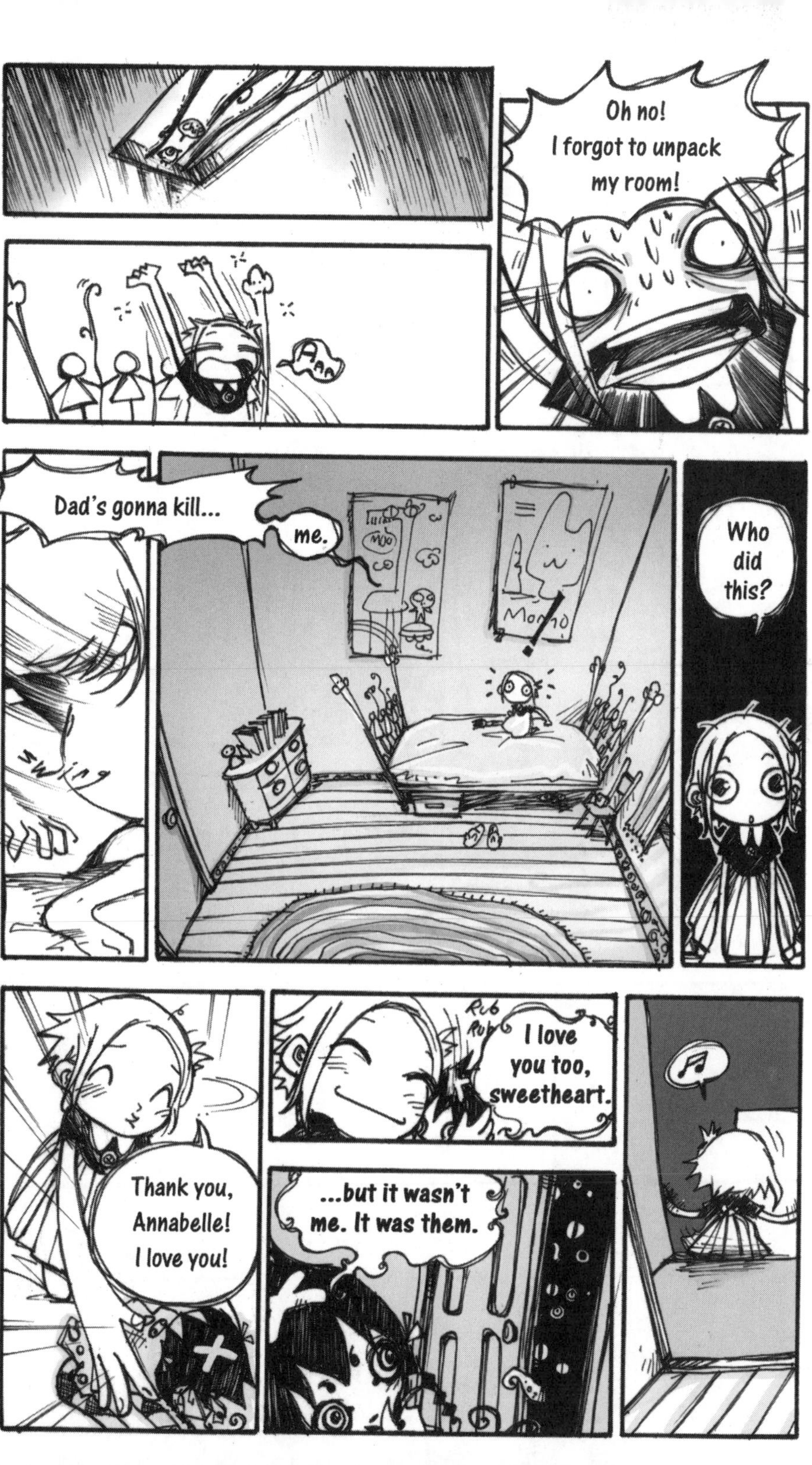

Aaa
Oh no!
I forgot to unpack
my room!
Dad's gonna kill...
me.
Who did this?
swing
Thank you,
Annabelle!
I love you!
Rub Rub
I love you too,
sweetheart.
...but it wasn't
me. It was them.

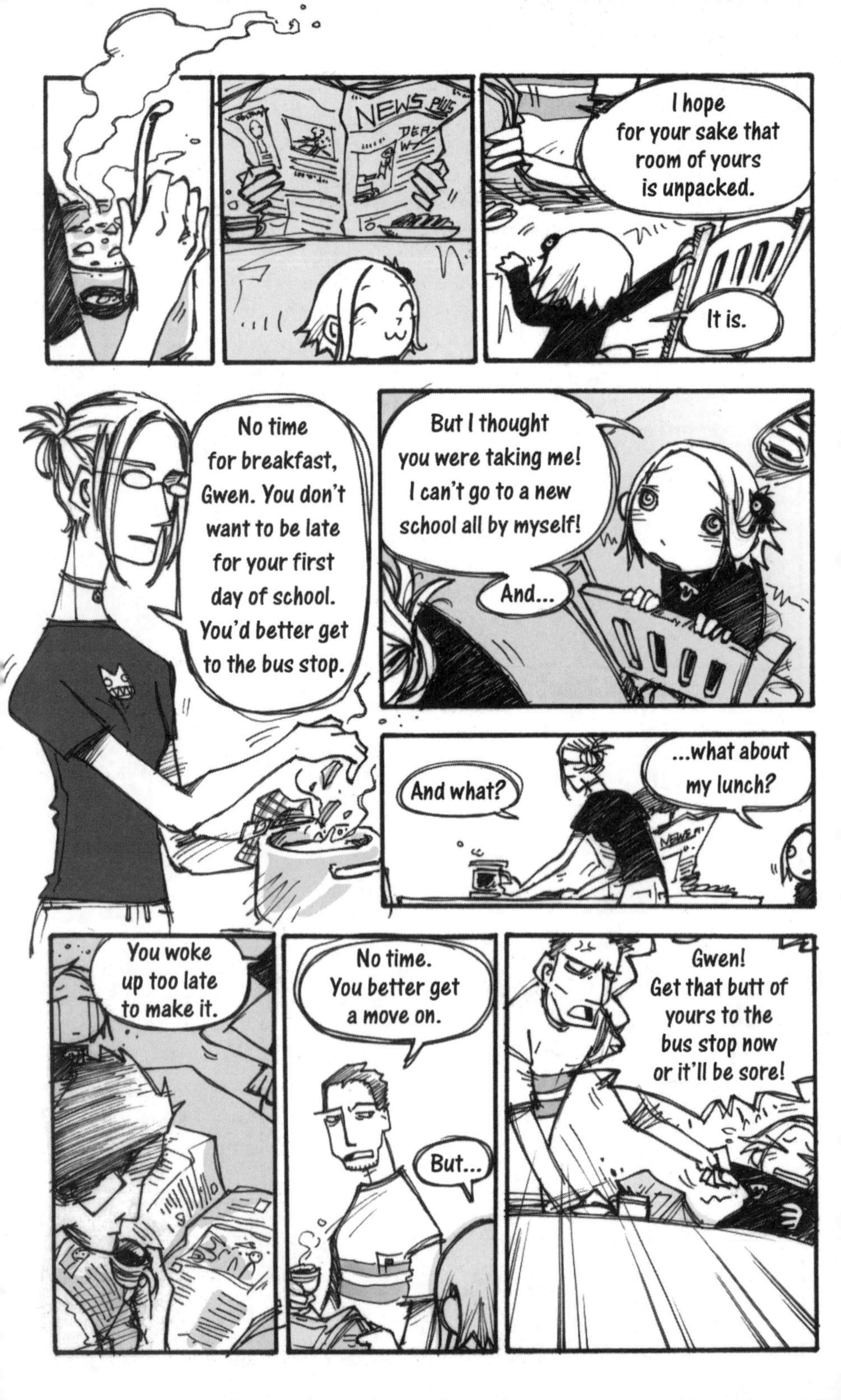

NEWS
I hope for your sake that room of yours is unpacked.
It is.
No time for breakfast, Gwen. You don't want to be late for your first day of school. You'd better get to the bus stop.
But I thought you were taking me! I can't go to a new school all by myself!
And...
And what?
...what about my lunch?
You woke up too late to make it.
No time. You better get a move on.
But...
Gwen! Get that butt of yours to the bus stop now or it'll be sore!

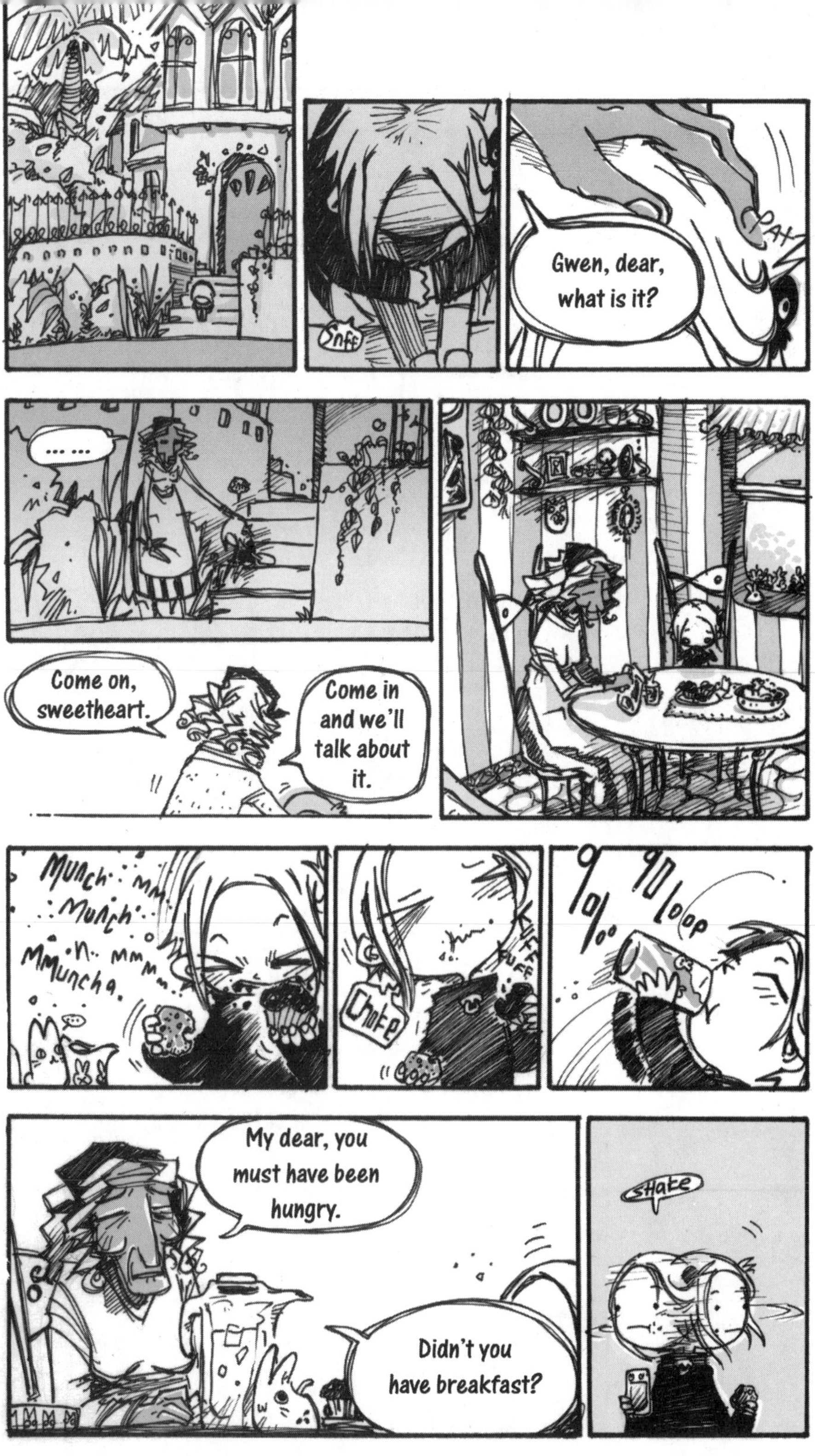
Snff
Gwen, dear, what is it?
PAX
... ...
Come on, sweetheart.
Come in and we'll talk about it.
Munch mm Munch n mm Mmuncha.
Choke
KUFF KUFF
glug glug gloop
My dear, you must have been hungry.
Didn't you have breakfast?
SHAKE

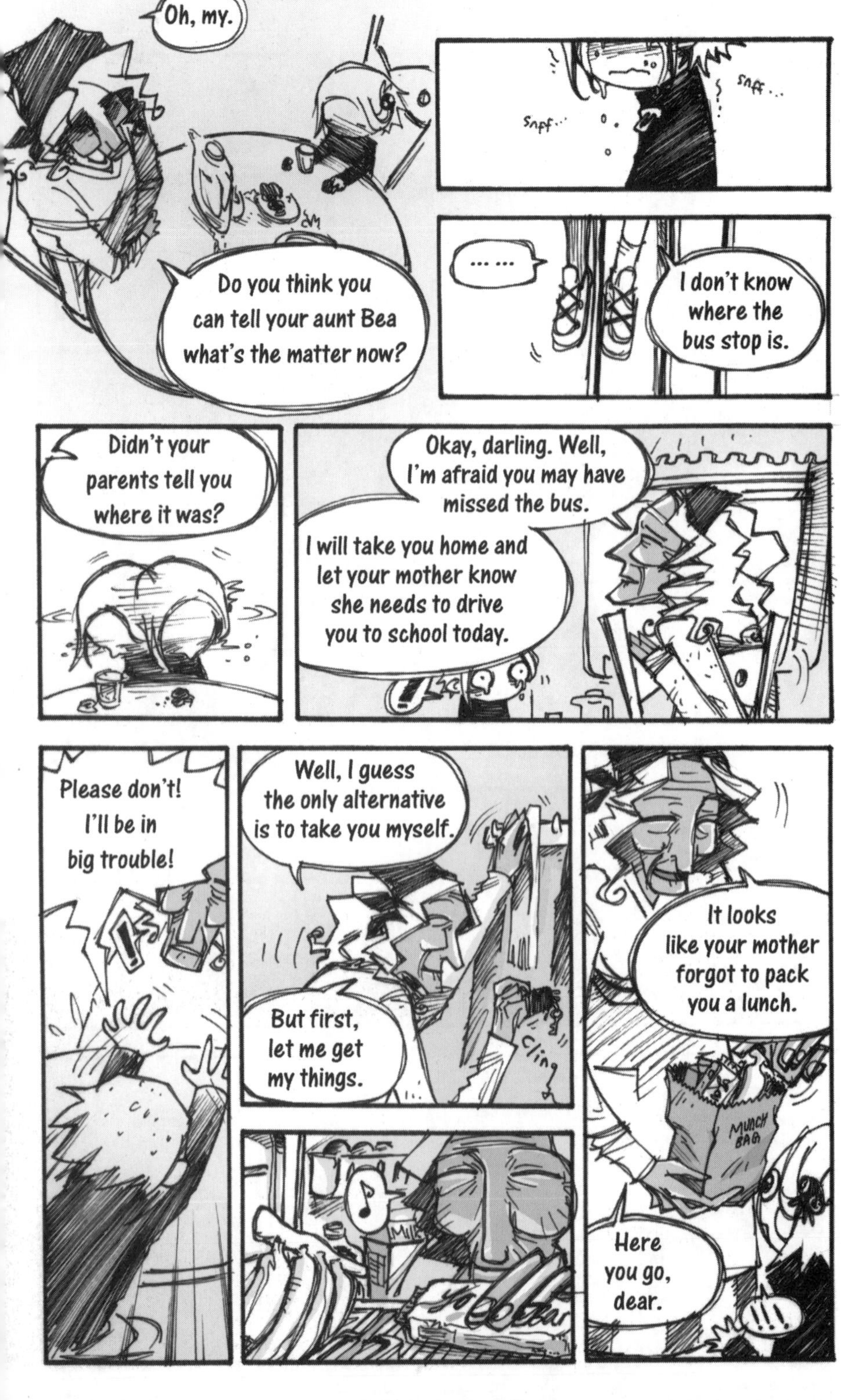
Oh, my.
Do you think you can tell your aunt Bea what's the matter now?
Snff...
Snff...
... ...
I don't know where the bus stop is.
Didn't your parents tell you where it was?
Okay, darling. Well, I'm afraid you may have missed the bus.
I will take you home and let your mother know she needs to drive you to school today.
Please don't! I'll be in big trouble!
Well, I guess the only alternative is to take you myself.
But first, let me get my things.
Cling
MILK
It looks like your mother forgot to pack you a lunch.
MUNCH BAG
Here you go, dear.
!!!

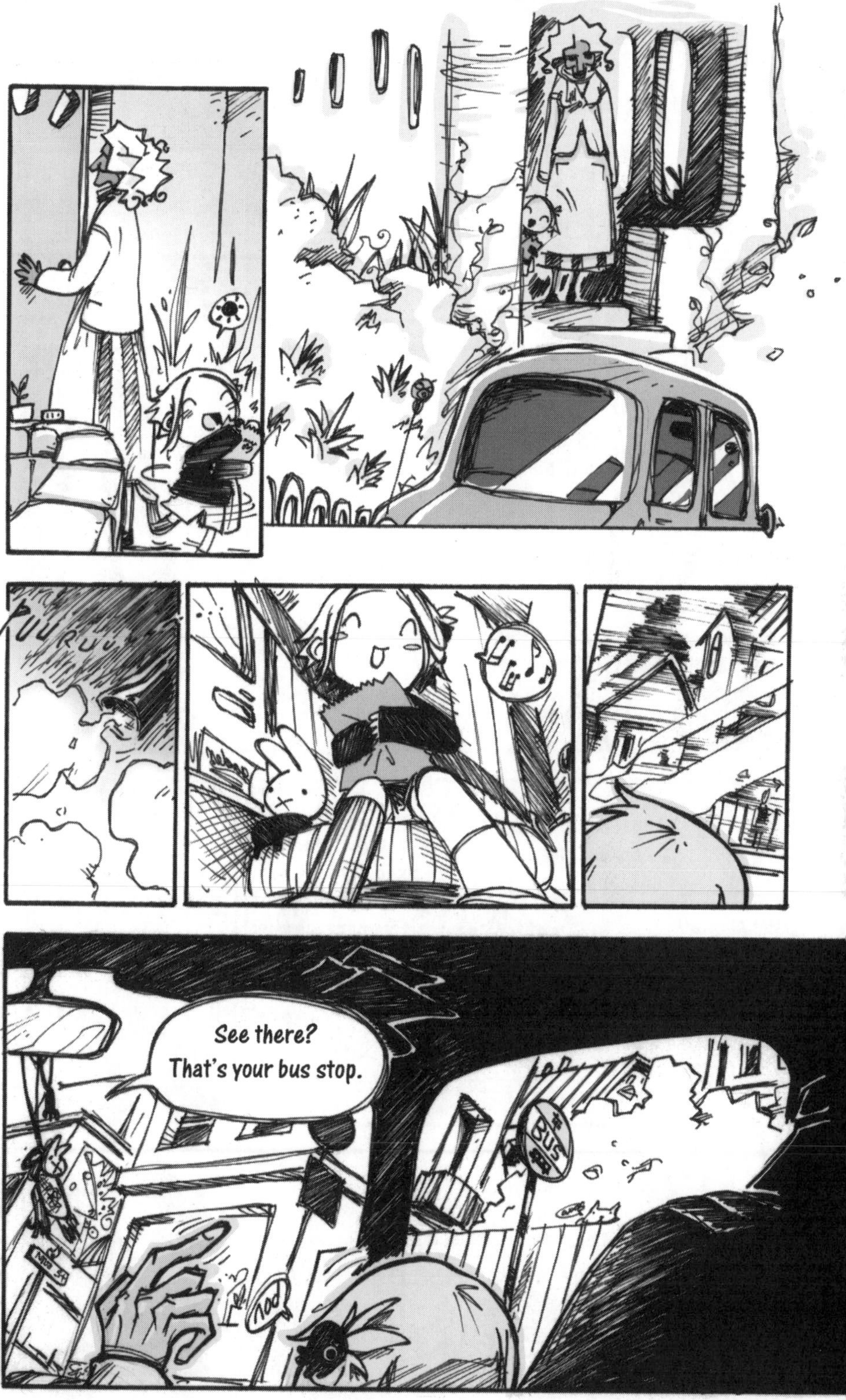
See there?
That's your bus stop.
Bus
nod

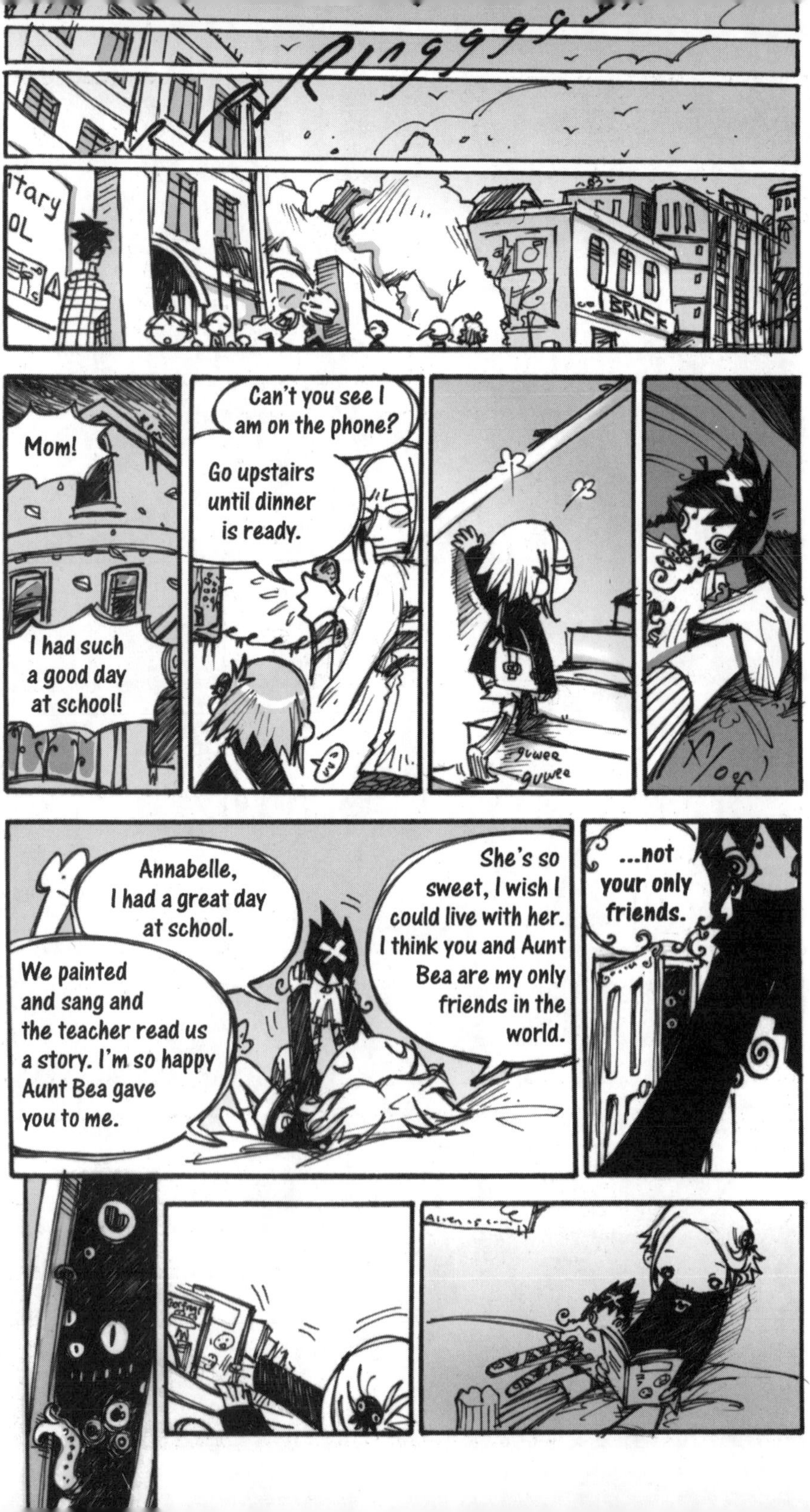
BRICK
Mom!
I had such a good day at school!
Can't you see I am on the phone?
Go upstairs until dinner is ready.
guwee
guwee
Annabelle, I had a great day at school.
We painted and sang and the teacher read us a story. I'm so happy Aunt Bea gave you to me.
She's so sweet, I wish I could live with her. I think you and Aunt Bea are my only friends in the world.
...not your only friends.

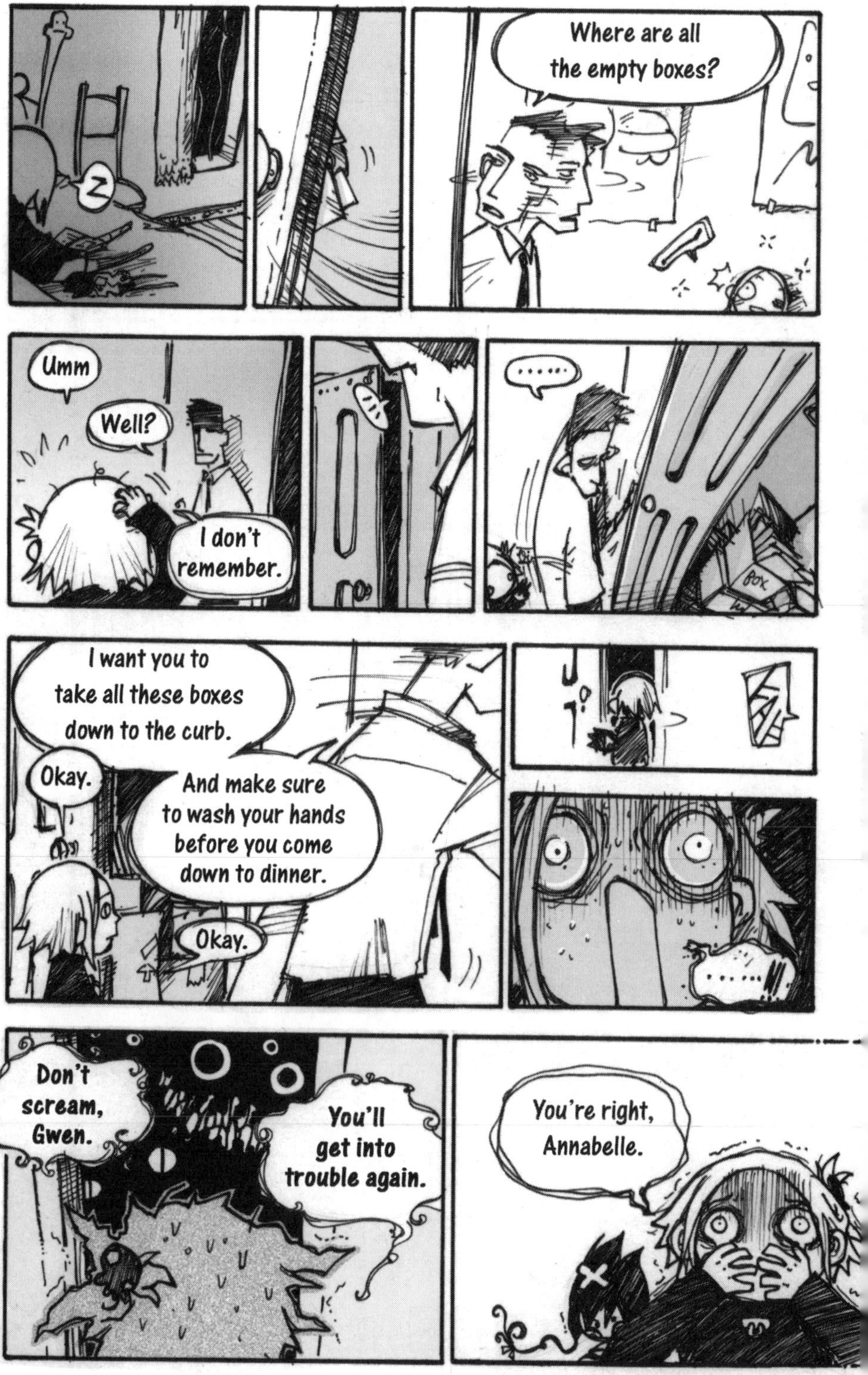
Where are all the empty boxes?
Umm
Well?
I don't remember.
......
I want you to take all these boxes down to the curb.
Okay.
And make sure to wash your hands before you come down to dinner.
Okay.
......
Don't scream, Gwen.
You'll get into trouble again.
You're right, Annabelle.

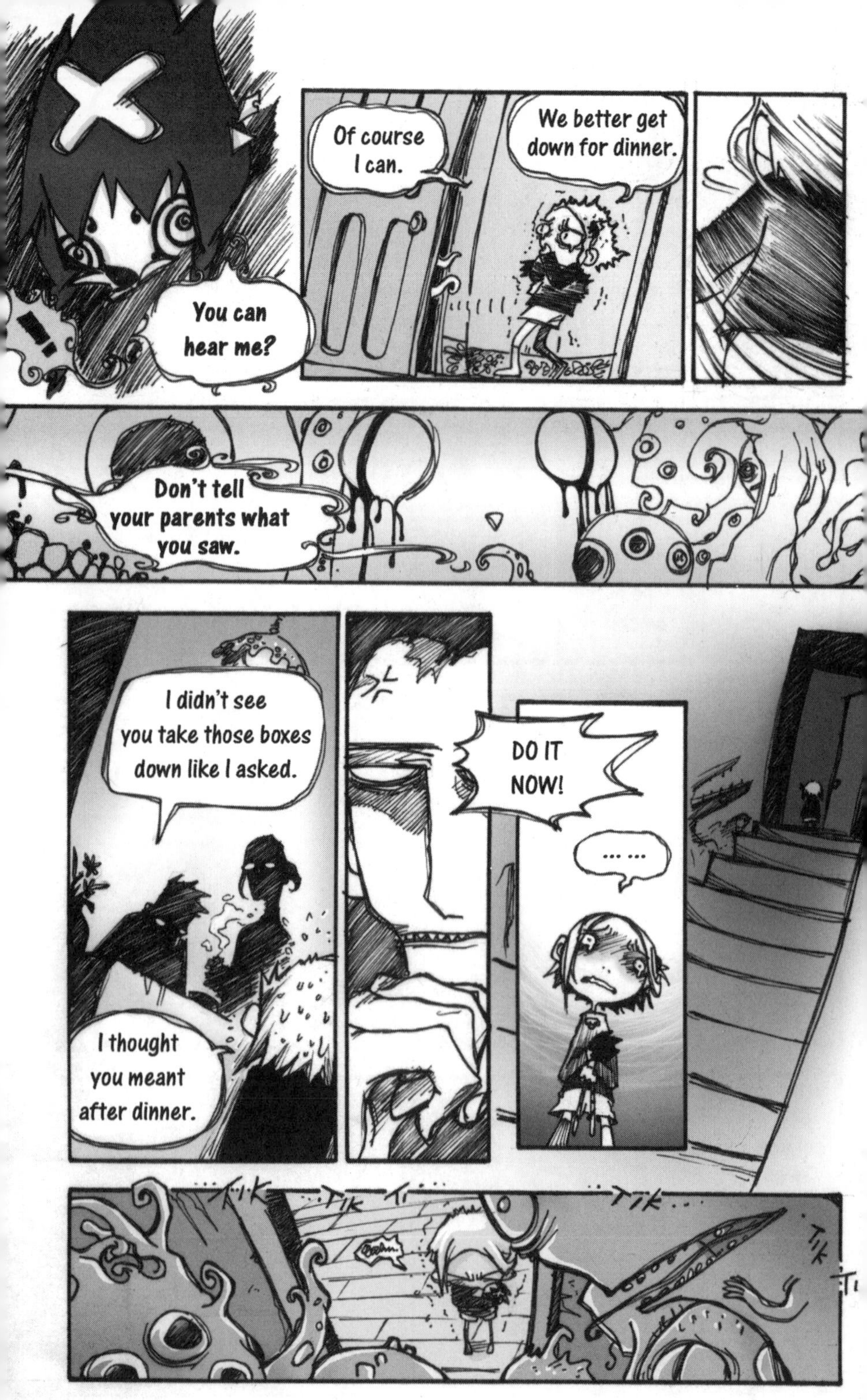
You can hear me?
Of course I can.
We better get down for dinner.
Don't tell your parents what you saw.
I didn't see you take those boxes down like I asked.
I thought you meant after dinner.
DO IT NOW!
... ...
TIK
TIK
TIK
TIK

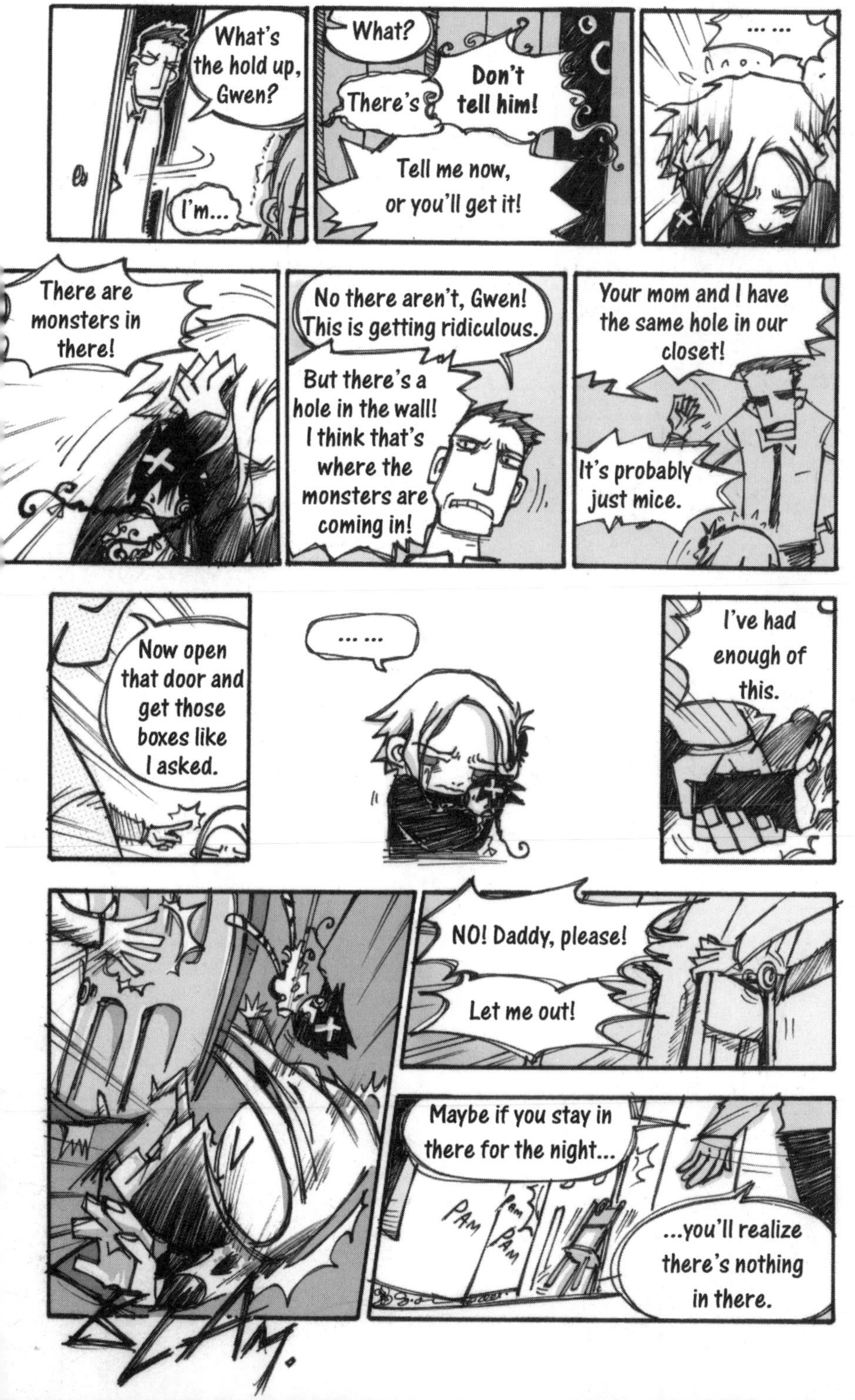
What's the hold up, Gwen?
I'm...
What?
There's
Don't tell him!
Tell me now, or you'll get it!
... ...
There are monsters in there!
No there aren't, Gwen! This is getting ridiculous.
But there's a hole in the wall! I think that's where the monsters are coming in!
Your mom and I have the same hole in our closet!
It's probably just mice.
Now open that door and get those boxes like I asked.
... ...
I've had enough of this.
NO! Daddy, please!
Let me out!
Maybe if you stay in there for the night...
PAM
PAM
PAM
...you'll realize there's nothing in there.
SLAM.

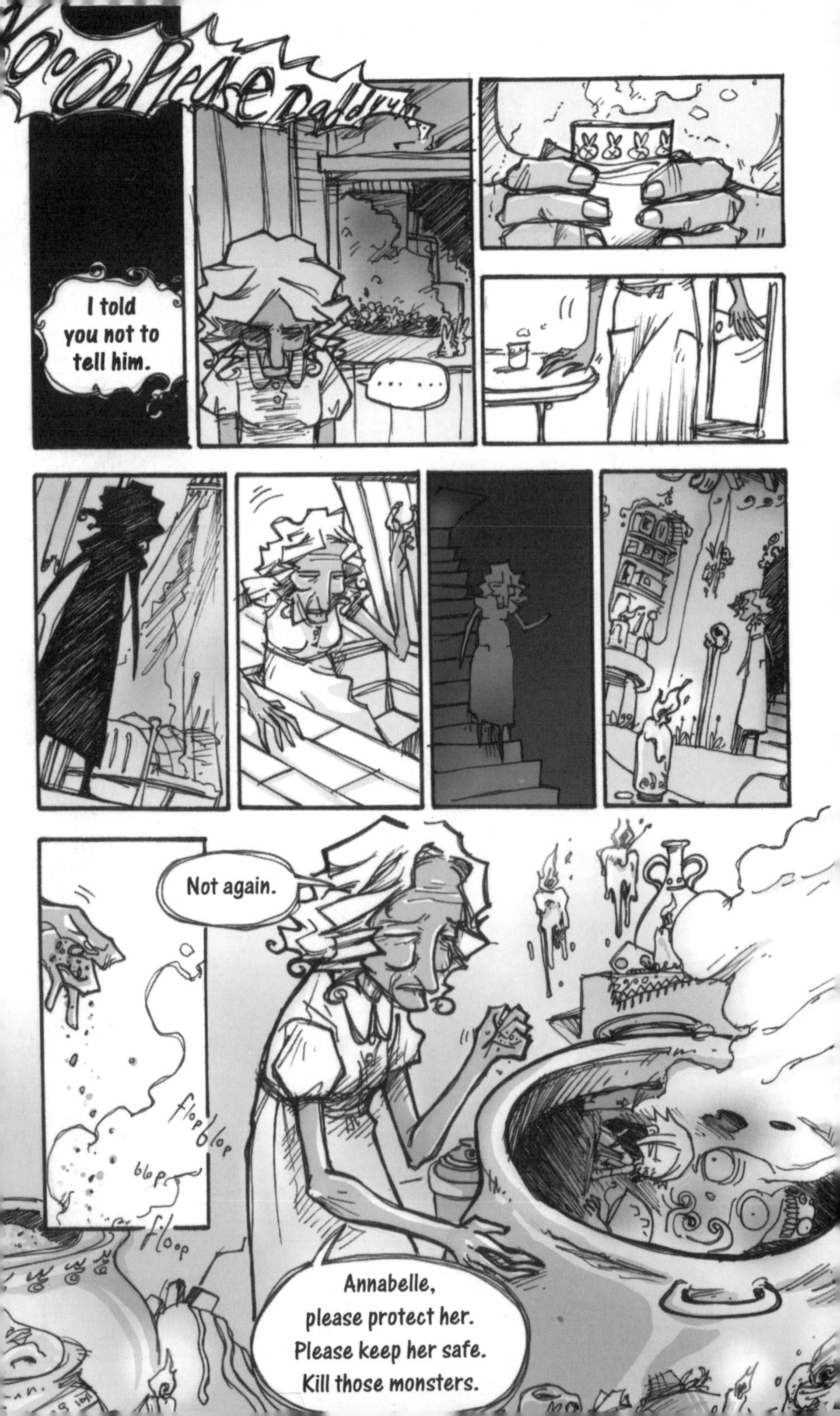
NoOoOo Please Daddyyyy
I told you not to tell him.
......
Not again.
flop
blop
blop
floop
Annabelle, please protect her. Please keep her safe. Kill those monsters.

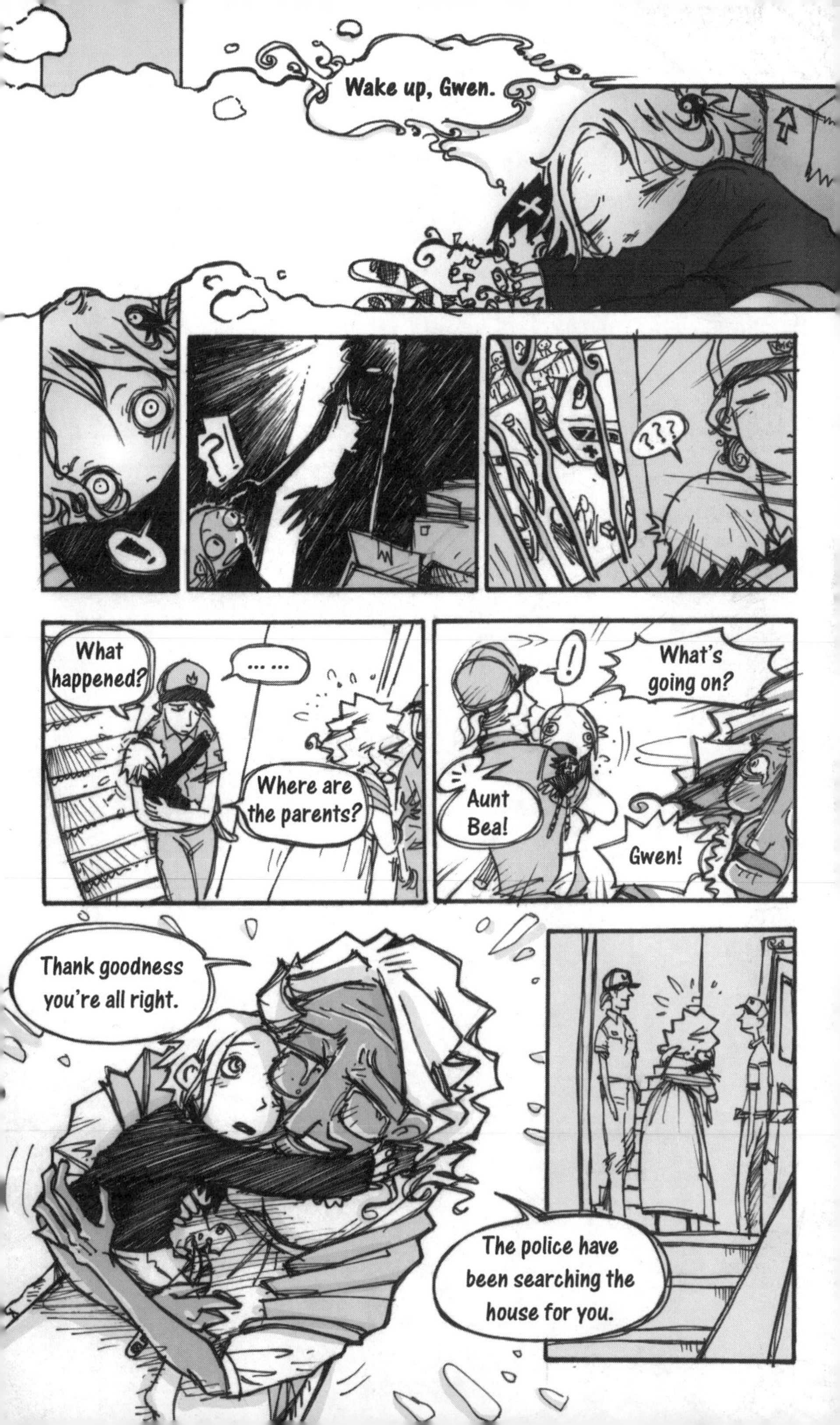
Wake up, Gwen.
!
?!
???
What happened?
... ...
Where are the parents?
!
What's going on?
Aunt Bea!
Gwen!
Thank goodness you're all right.
The police have been searching the house for you.

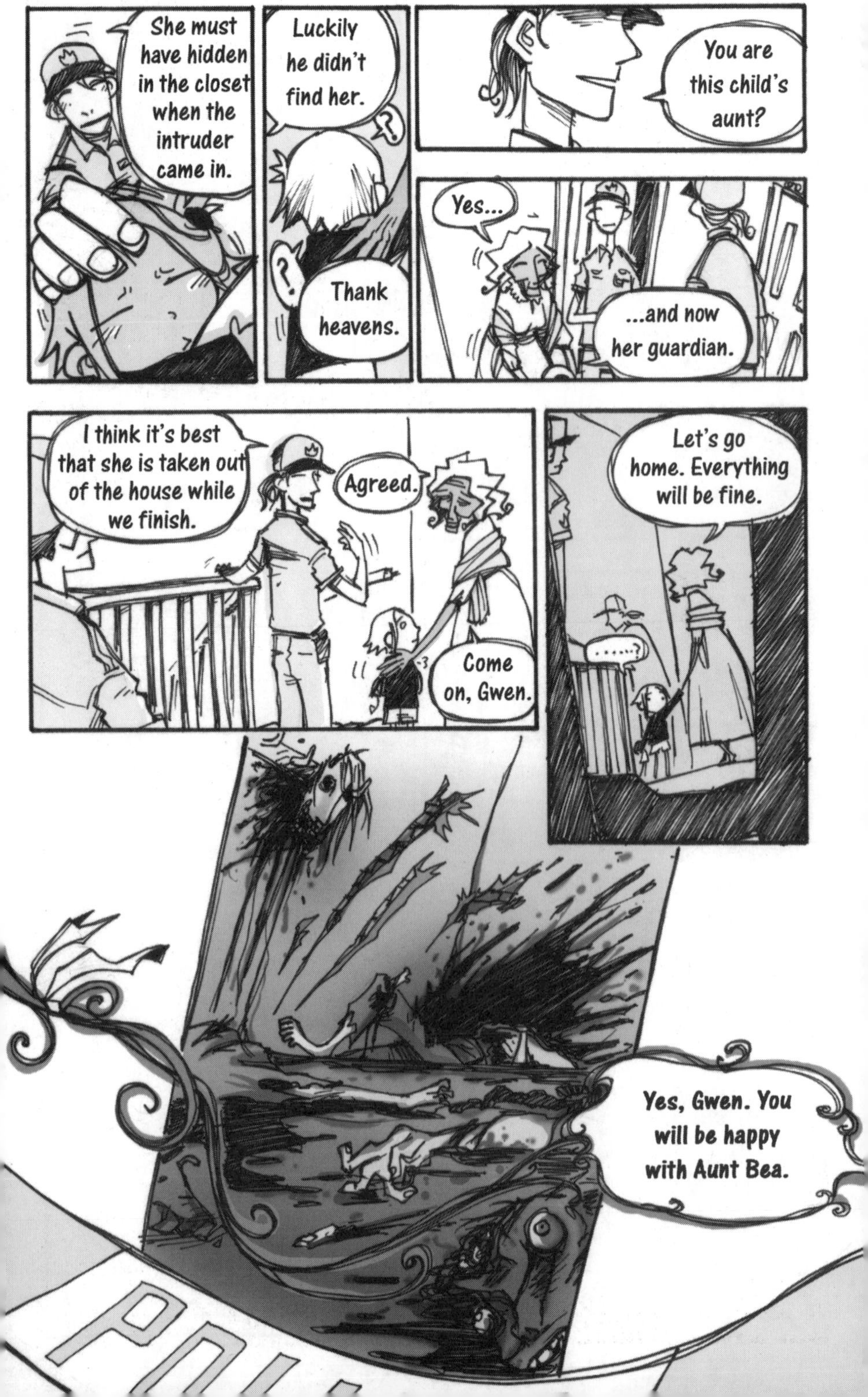
She must have hidden in the closet when the intruder came in.
Luckily he didn't find her.
?
?
Thank heavens.
You are this child's aunt?
Yes...
...and now her guardian.
I think it's best that she is taken out of the house while we finish.
Agreed.
Come on, Gwen.
Let's go home. Everything will be fine.
Yes, Gwen. You will be happy with Aunt Bea.

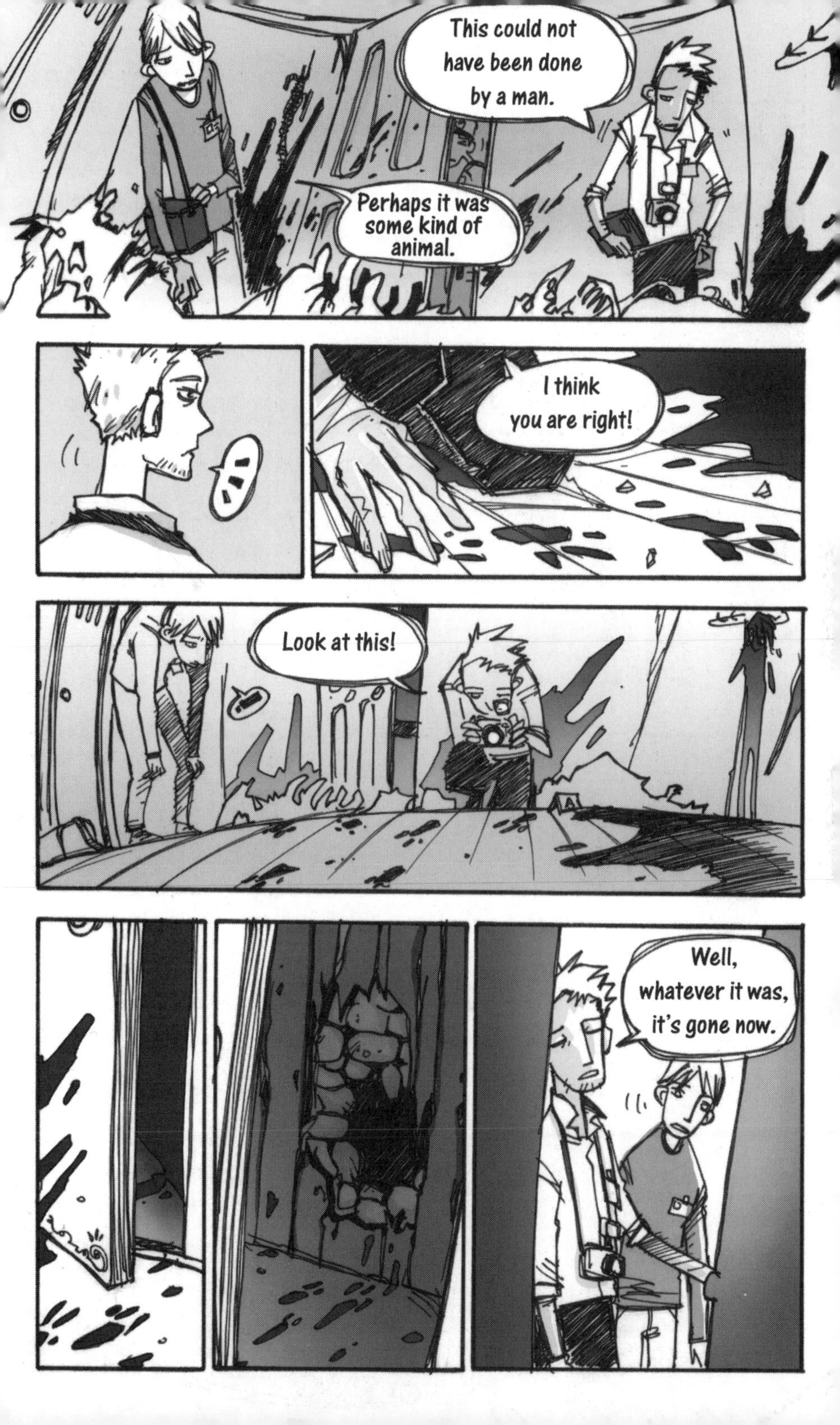

This could not have been done by a man.
Perhaps it was some kind of animal.
I think you are right!
Look at this!
Well, whatever it was, it's gone now.

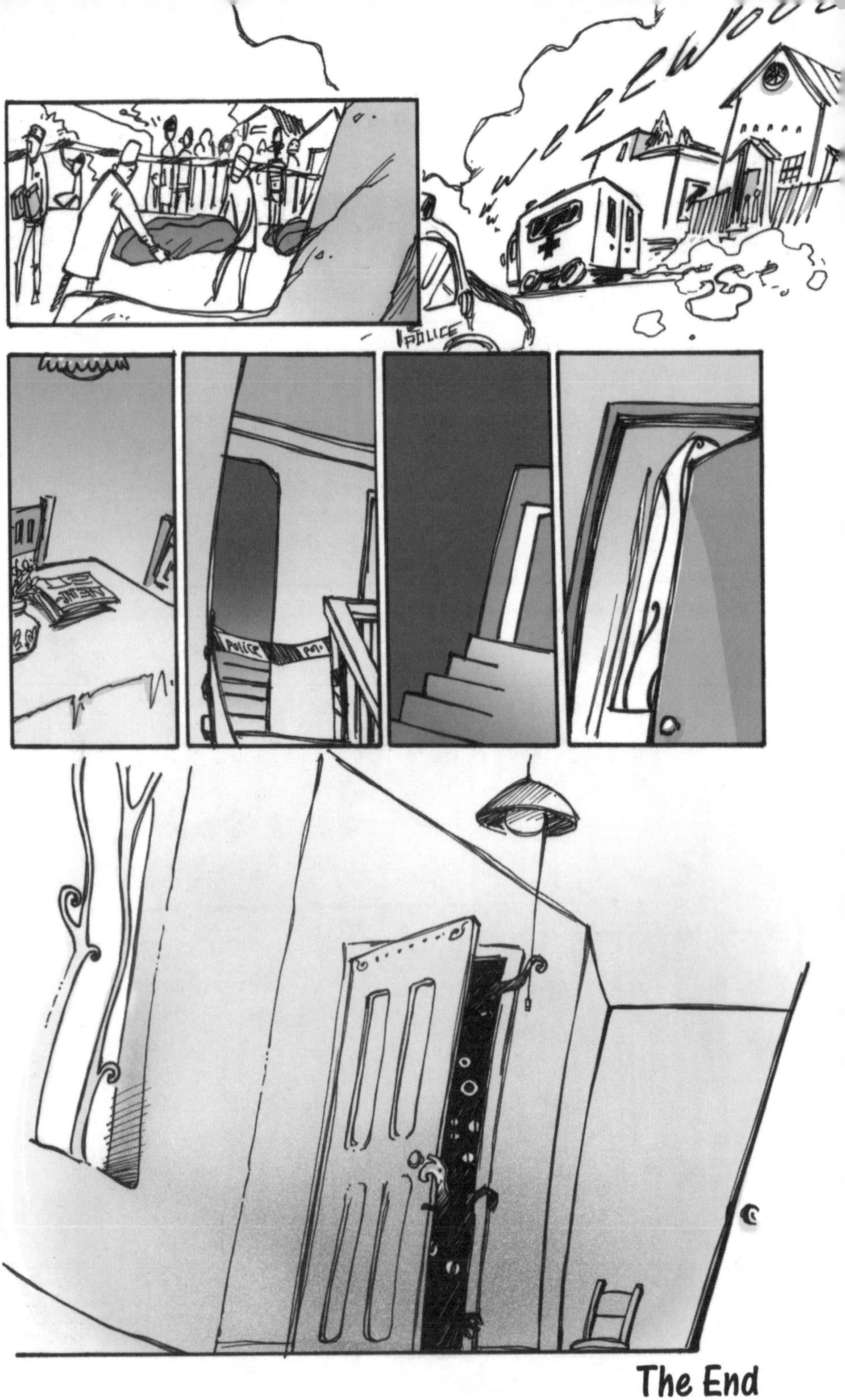
POLICE
POLICE
The End

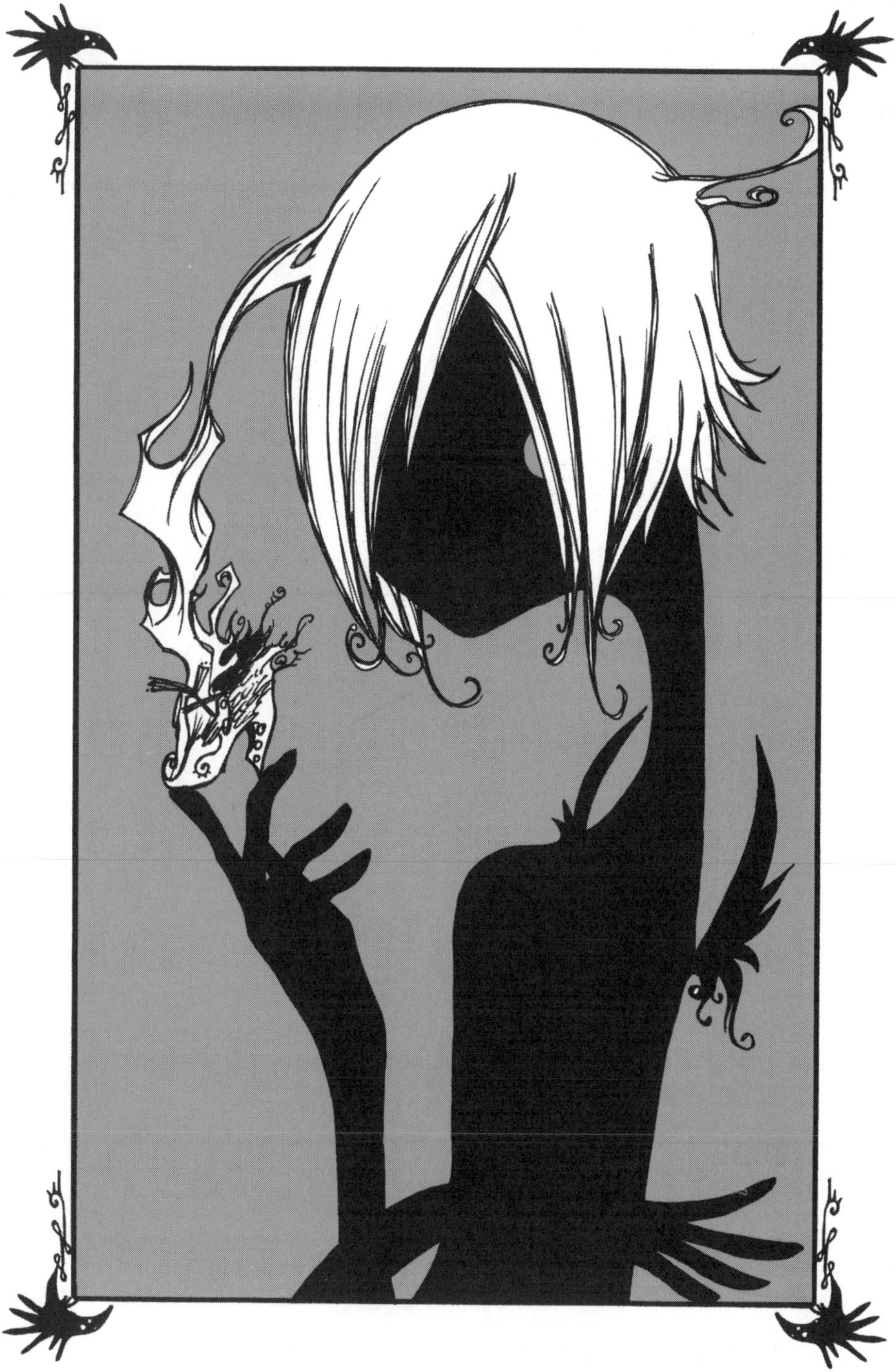

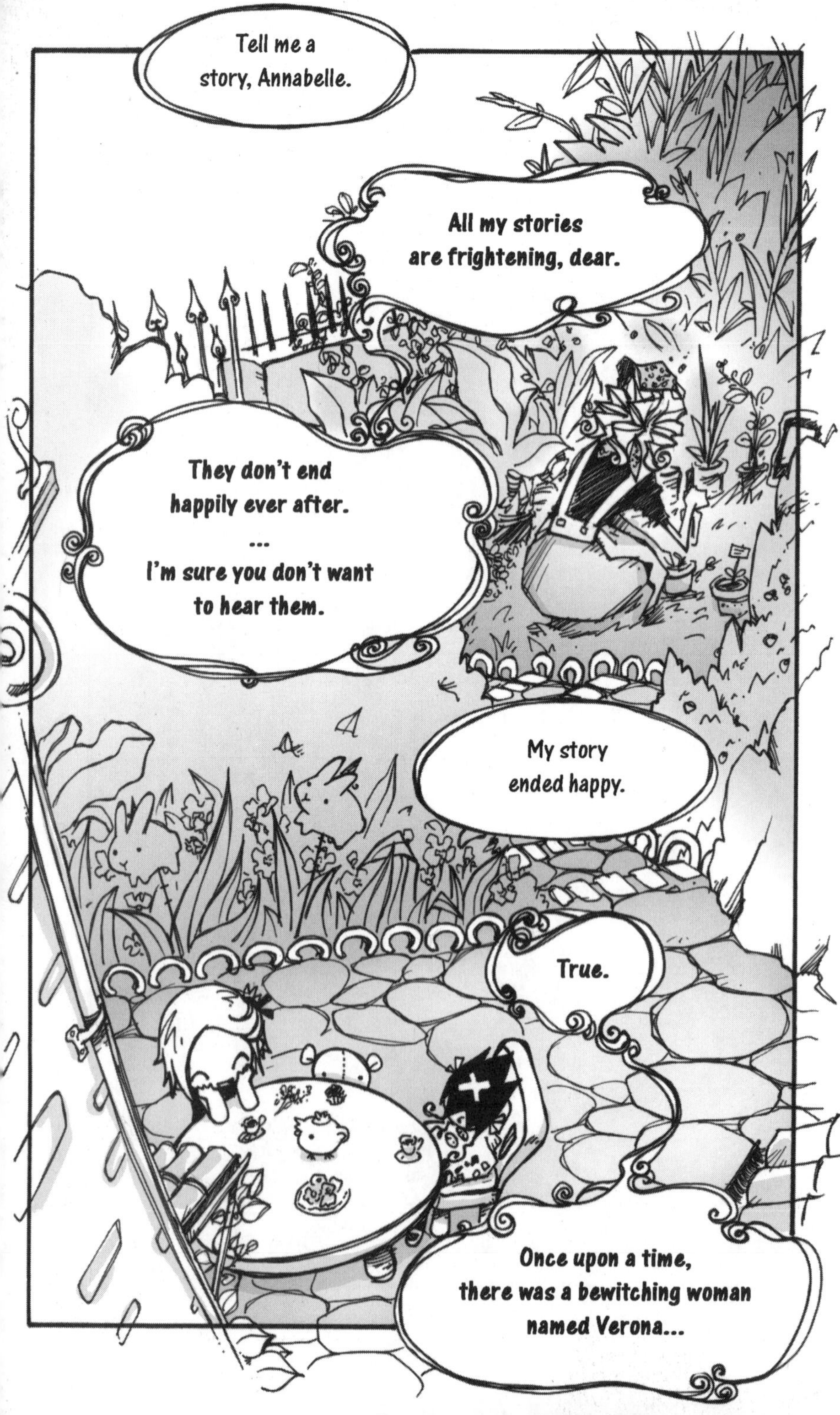
Tell me a story, Annabelle.
All my stories are frightening, dear.
They don't end happily ever after.
...
I'm sure you don't want to hear them.
My story ended happy.
True.
Once upon a time, there was a bewitching woman named Verona...

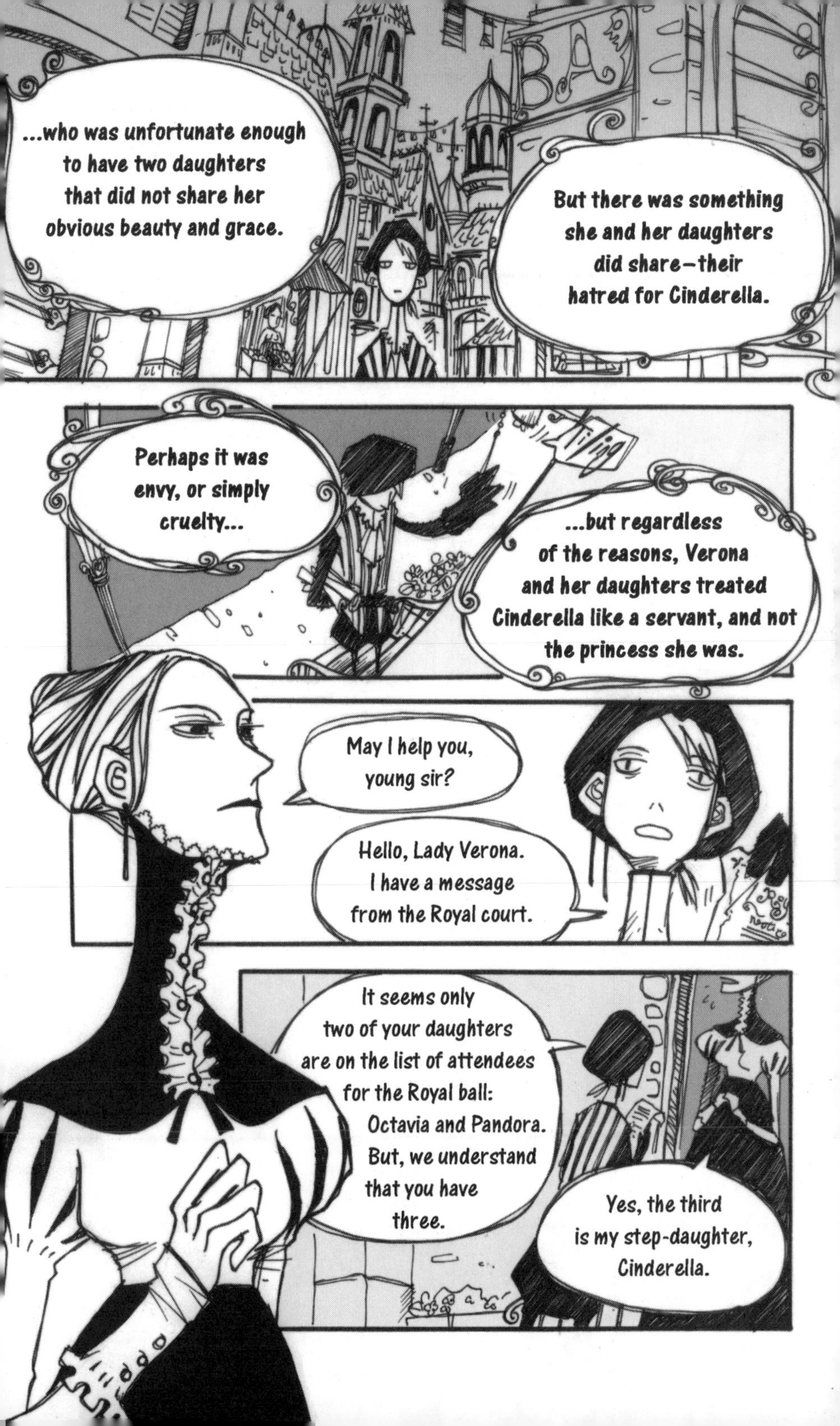
...who was unfortunate enough to have two daughters that did not share her obvious beauty and grace.
But there was something she and her daughters did share—their hatred for Cinderella.
Perhaps it was envy, or simply cruelty...
...but regardless of the reasons, Verona and her daughters treated Cinderella like a servant, and not the princess she was.
May I help you, young sir?
Hello, Lady Verona. I have a message from the Royal court.
It seems only two of your daughters are on the list of attendees for the Royal ball: Octavia and Pandora. But, we understand that you have three.
Yes, the third is my step-daughter, Cinderella.

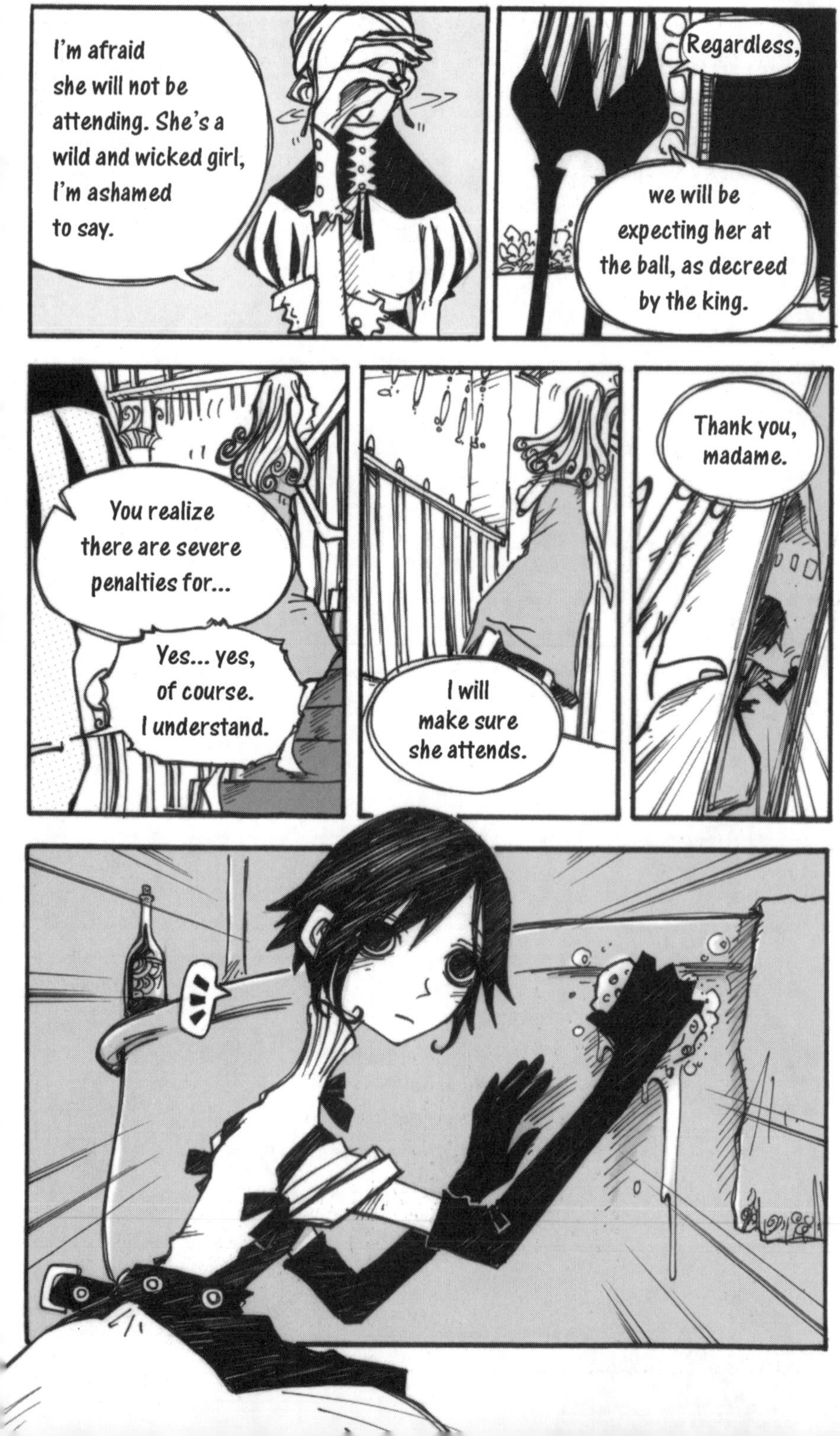
I'm afraid she will not be attending. She's a wild and wicked girl, I'm ashamed to say.
Regardless,
we will be expecting her at the ball, as decreed by the king.
You realize there are severe penalties for...
Yes... yes, of course. I understand.
I will make sure she attends.
Thank you, madame.

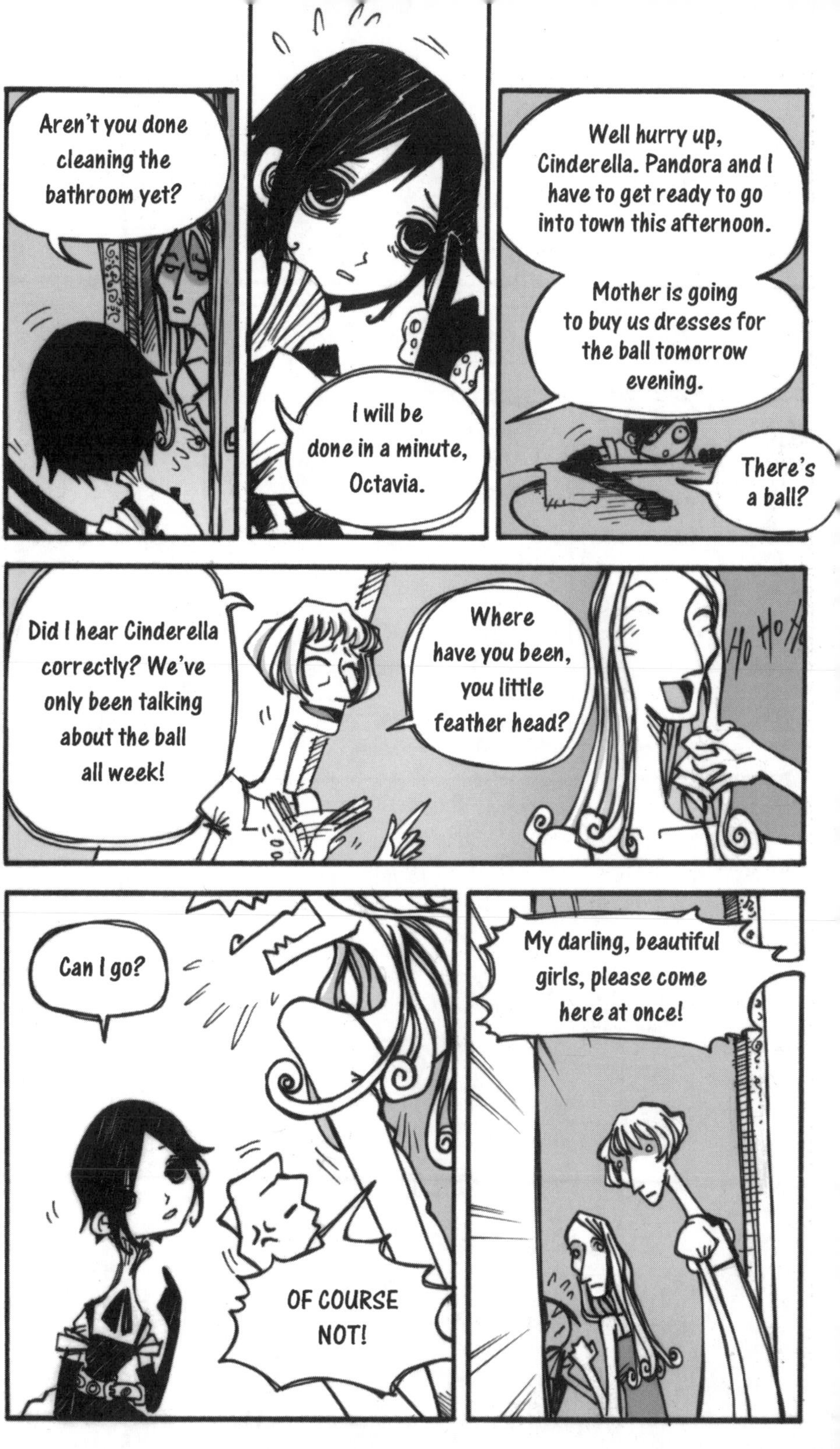

Aren't you done cleaning the bathroom yet?
I will be done in a minute, Octavia.
Well hurry up, Cinderella. Pandora and I have to get ready to go into town this afternoon.
Mother is going to buy us dresses for the ball tomorrow evening.
There's a ball?
Did I hear Cinderella correctly? We've only been talking about the ball all week!
Where have you been, you little feather head?
Can I go?
OF COURSE NOT!
My darling, beautiful girls, please come here at once!

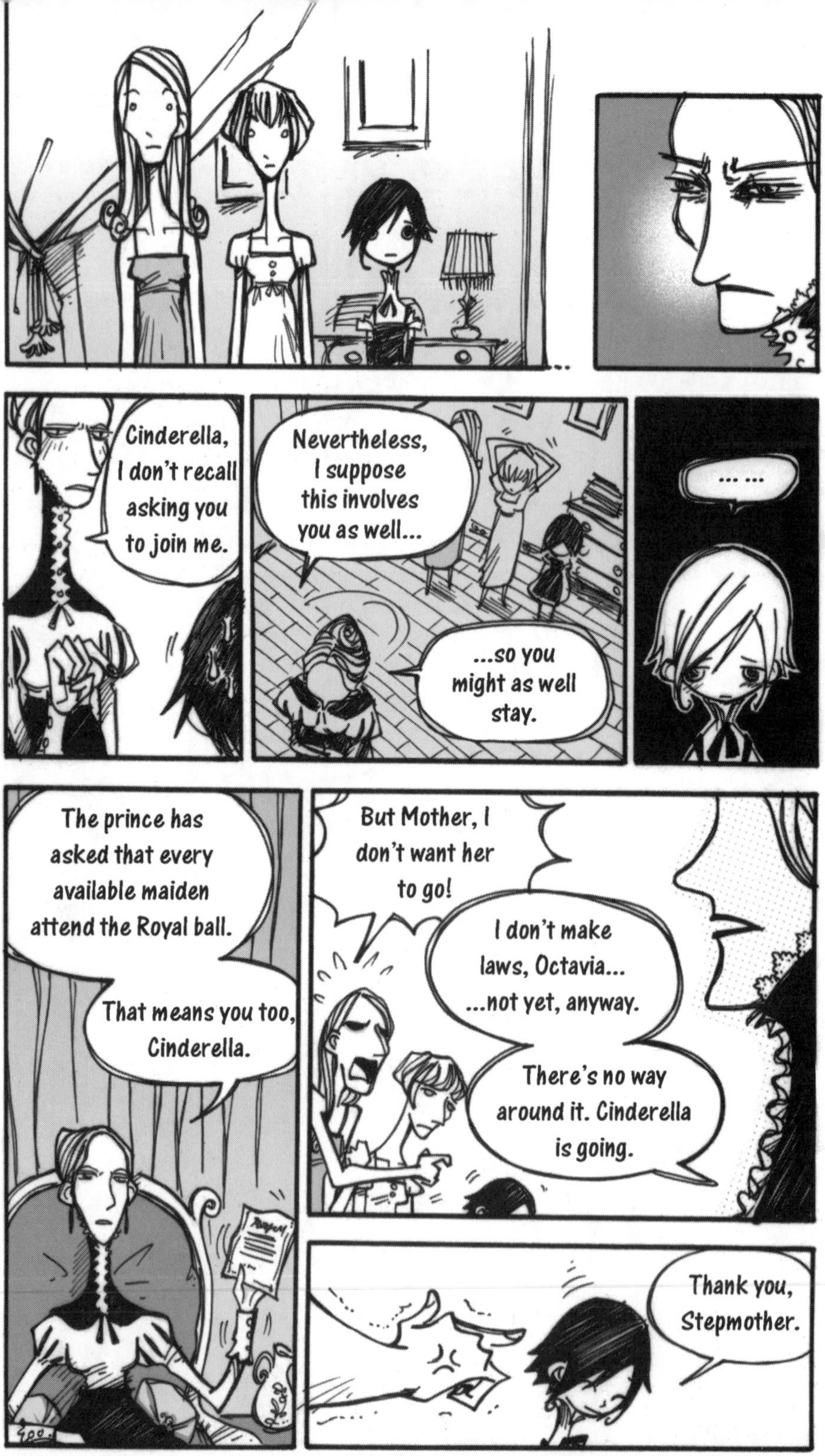
...
Cinderella, I don't recall asking you to join me.
Nevertheless, I suppose this involves you as well...
...so you might as well stay.
... ...
The prince has asked that every available maiden attend the Royal ball.
That means you too, Cinderella.
But Mother, I don't want her to go!
I don't make laws, Octavia... ...not yet, anyway.
There's no way around it. Cinderella is going.
Thank you, Stepmother.

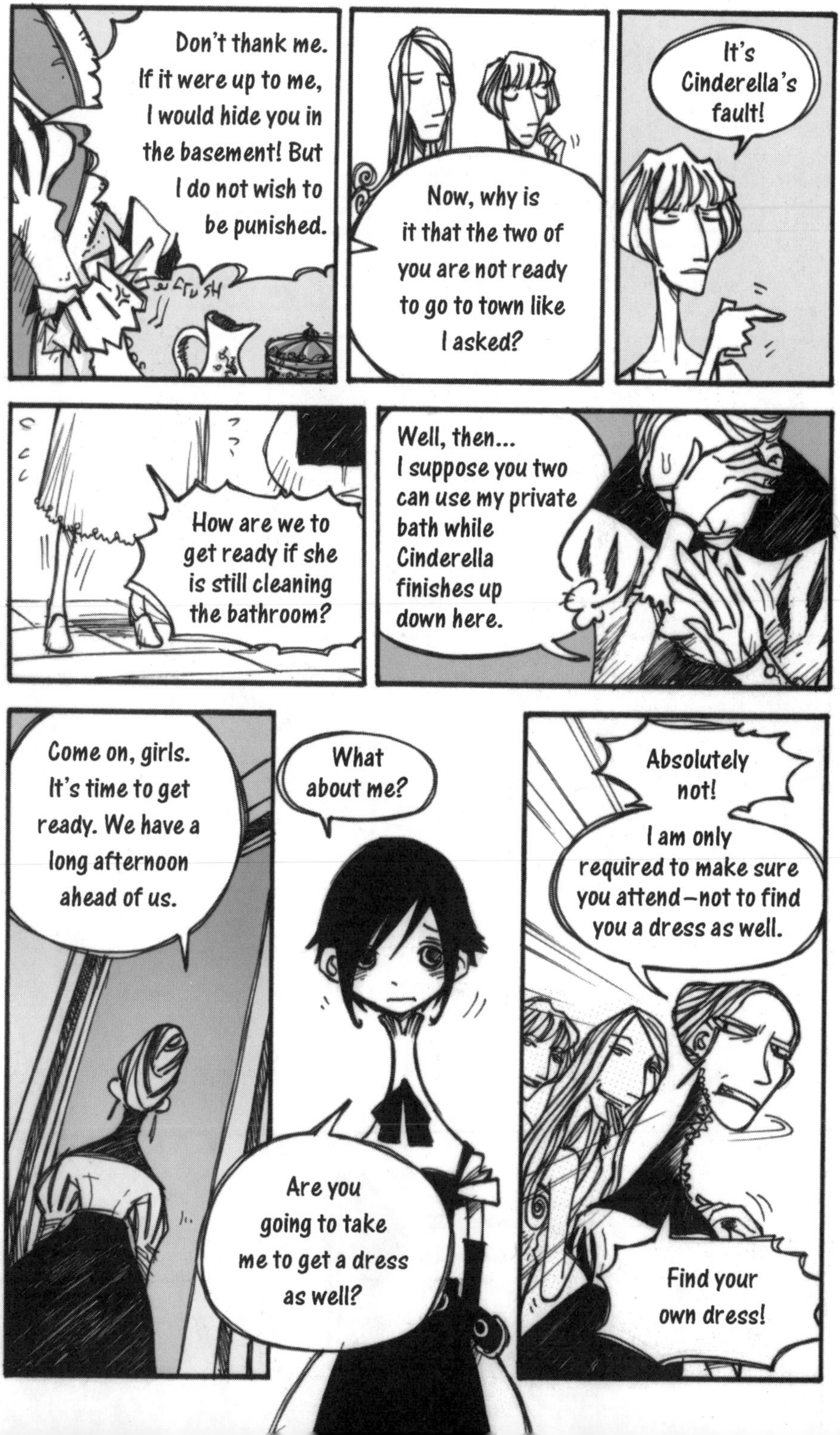

Don't thank me. If it were up to me, I would hide you in the basement! But I do not wish to be punished.
CRUSH
Now, why is it that the two of you are not ready to go to town like I asked?
It's Cinderella's fault!
How are we to get ready if she is still cleaning the bathroom?
Well, then... I suppose you two can use my private bath while Cinderella finishes up down here.
Come on, girls. It's time to get ready. We have a long afternoon ahead of us.
What about me?
Are you going to take me to get a dress as well?
Absolutely not!
I am only required to make sure you attend—not to find you a dress as well.
Find your own dress!

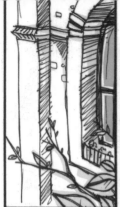

Annabelle...

You are the answer to my prayers!

It just needs a little mending!

Cinderella, we are about to leave...

Where did you get that?

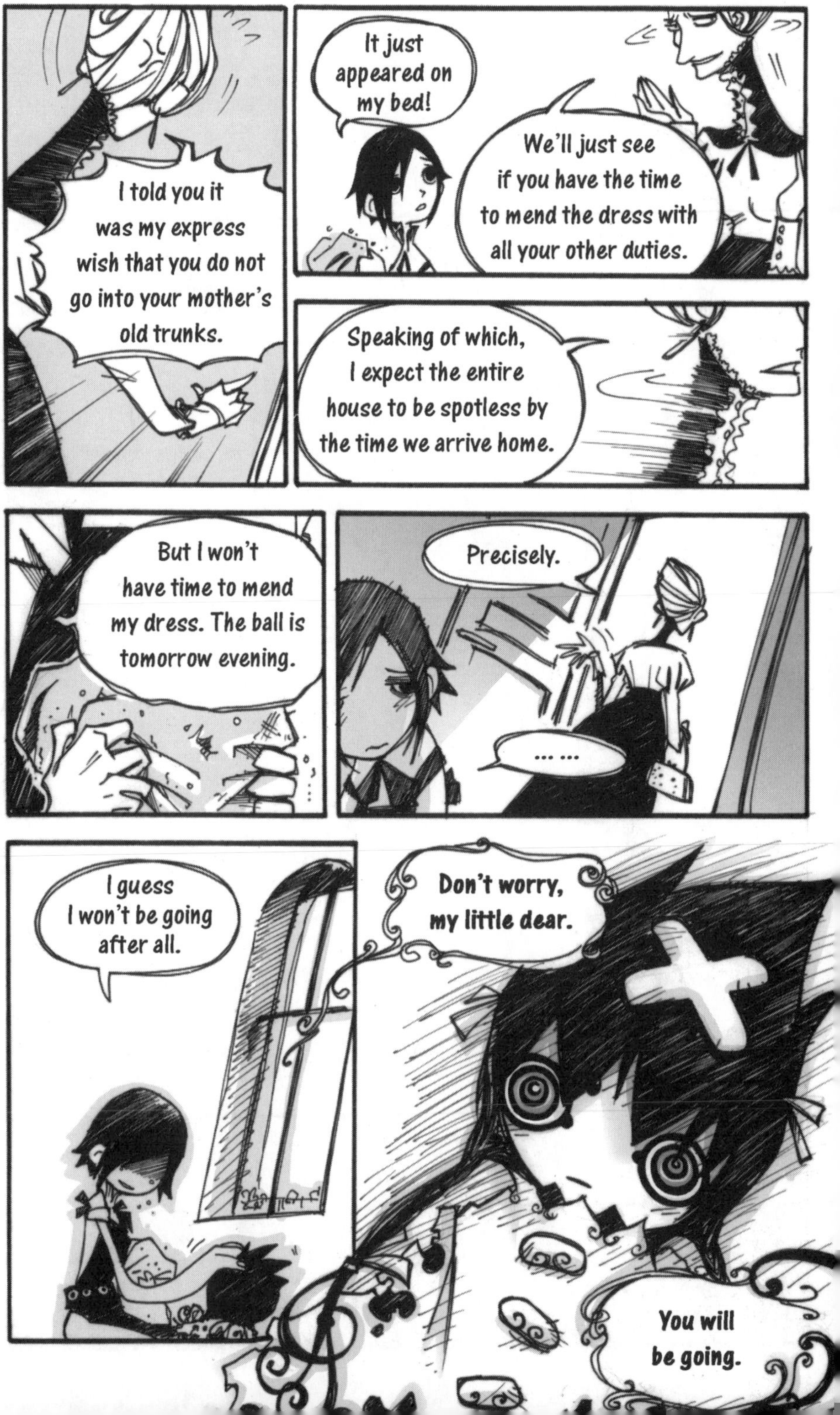
I told you it was my express wish that you do not go into your mother's old trunks.
It just appeared on my bed!
We'll just see if you have the time to mend the dress with all your other duties.
Speaking of which, I expect the entire house to be spotless by the time we arrive home.
But I won't have time to mend my dress. The ball is tomorrow evening.
Precisely.
... ...
I guess I won't be going after all.
Don't worry, my little dear.
You will be going.

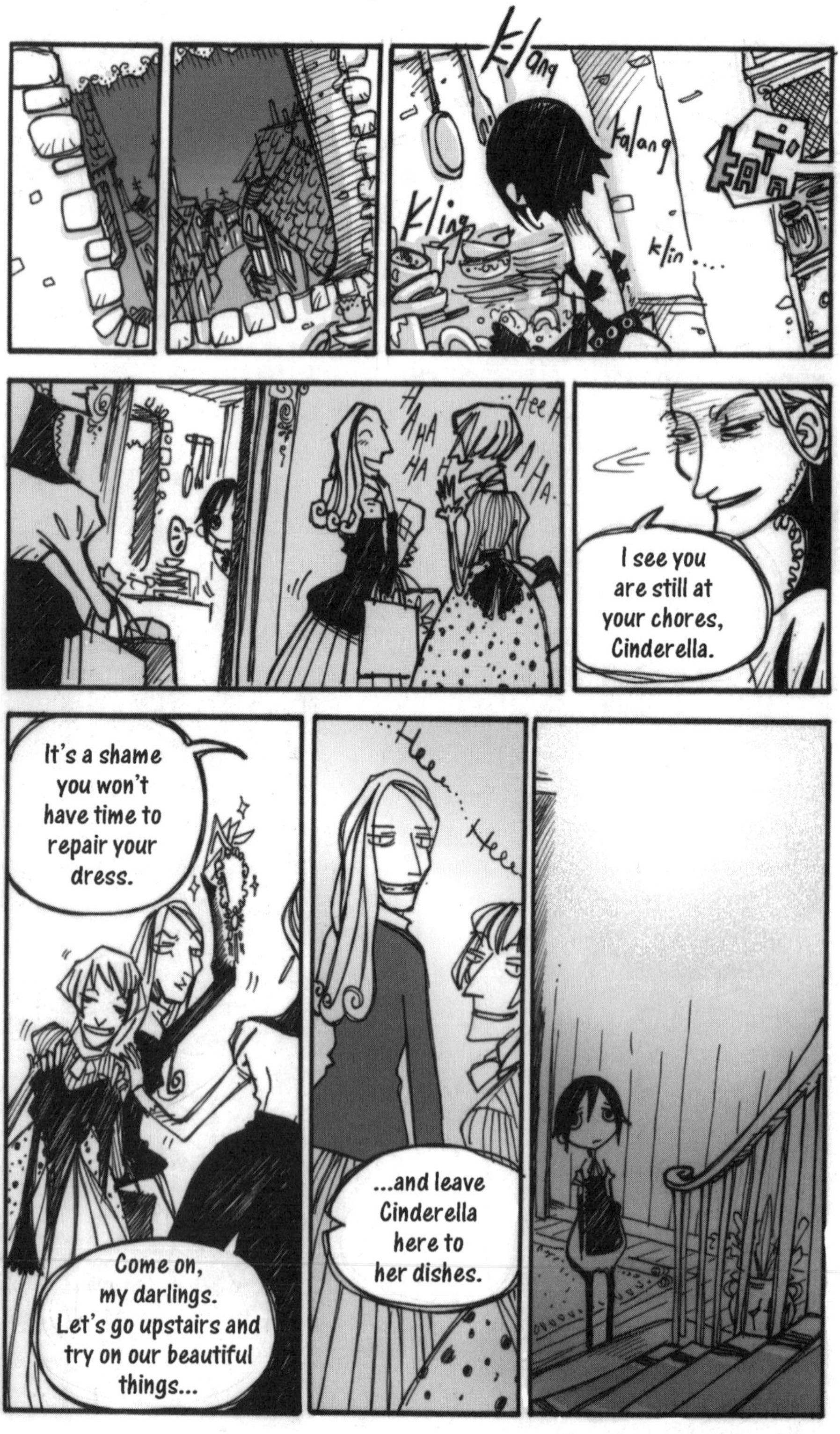

Klang
Kalang
Kling
klin...
Hee Ha
HA HA HA HA
HAHA
I see you are still at your chores, Cinderella.
It's a shame you won't have time to repair your dress.
Come on, my darlings. Let's go upstairs and try on our beautiful things...
Heee... Heee
...and leave Cinderella here to her dishes.

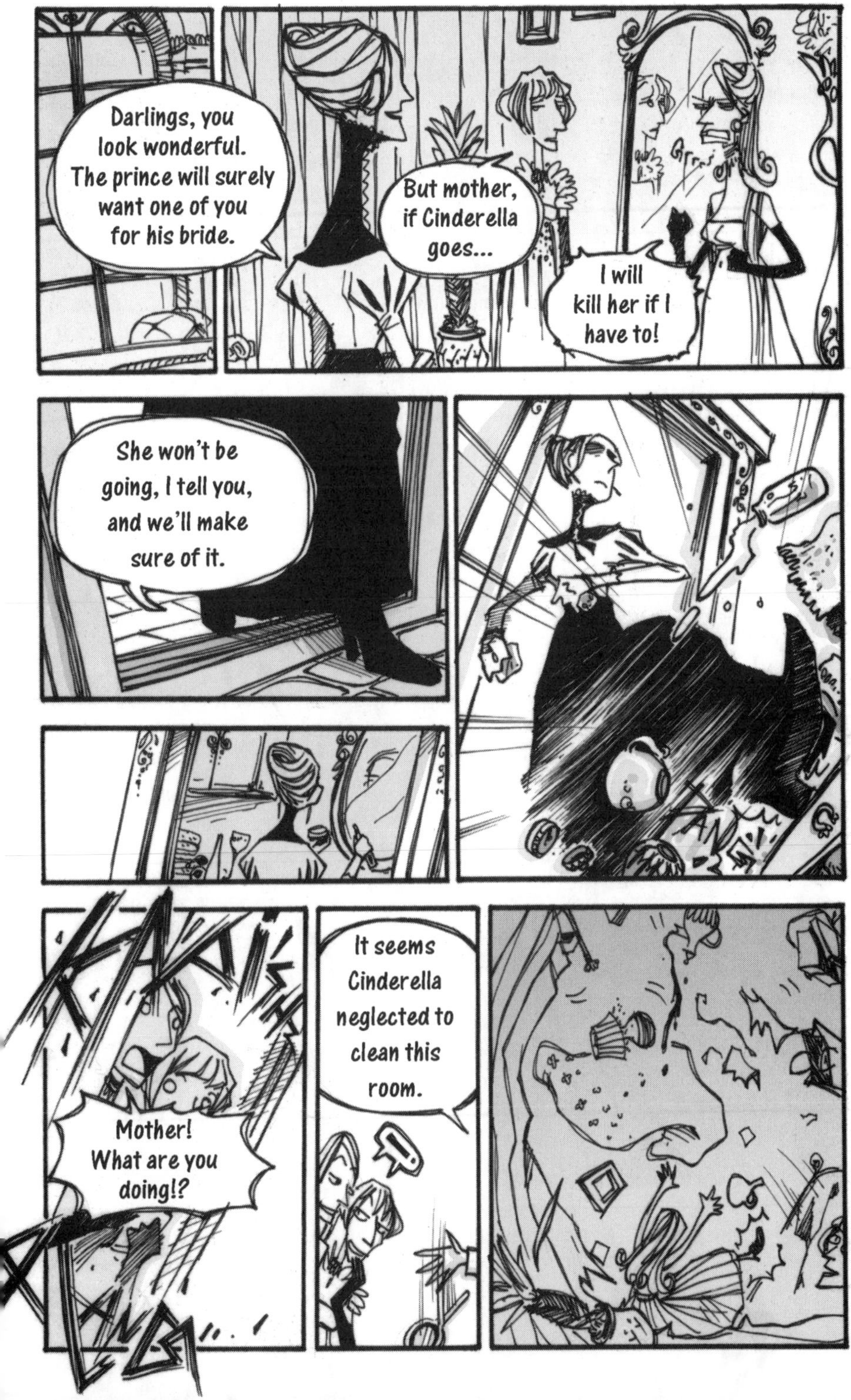
Darlings, you look wonderful. The prince will surely want one of you for his bride.
But mother, if Cinderella goes...
I will kill her if I have to!
She won't be going, I tell you, and we'll make sure of it.
Mother! What are you doing!?
It seems Cinderella neglected to clean this room.

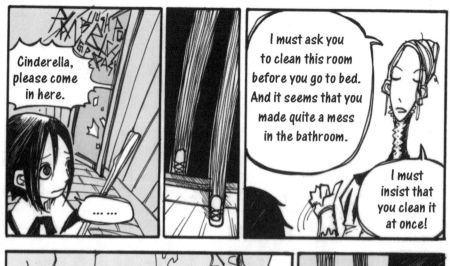

Cinderella, please come in here.

... ...

I must ask you to clean this room before you go to bed. And it seems that you made quite a mess in the bathroom.

I must insist that you clean it at once!

But I didn't...

It's clear that it will take the majority of the night for you to clean this mess.

It's a shame, Cinderella, that you will not be getting much sleep tonight...

...or you might have been able to mend your dress in time.

Tch.. Hee.. Hee ...Hee

... ...

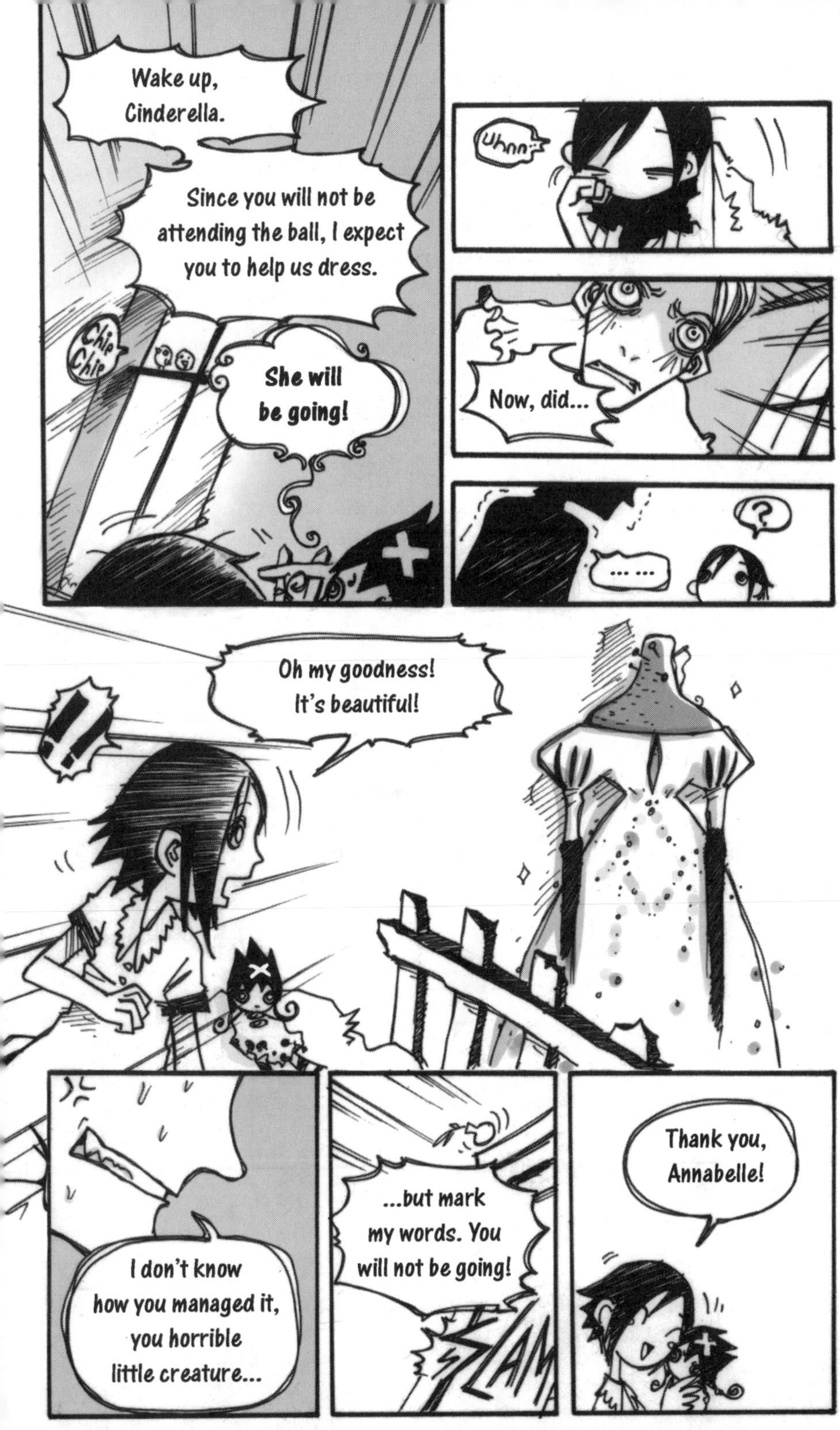
Wake up, Cinderella.
Since you will not be attending the ball, I expect you to help us dress.
Chip Chip
She will be going!
Uhnn
Now, did...
?
... ...
Oh my goodness! It's beautiful!
!
I don't know how you managed it, you horrible little creature...
...but mark my words. You will not be going!
SLAM
Thank you, Annabelle!

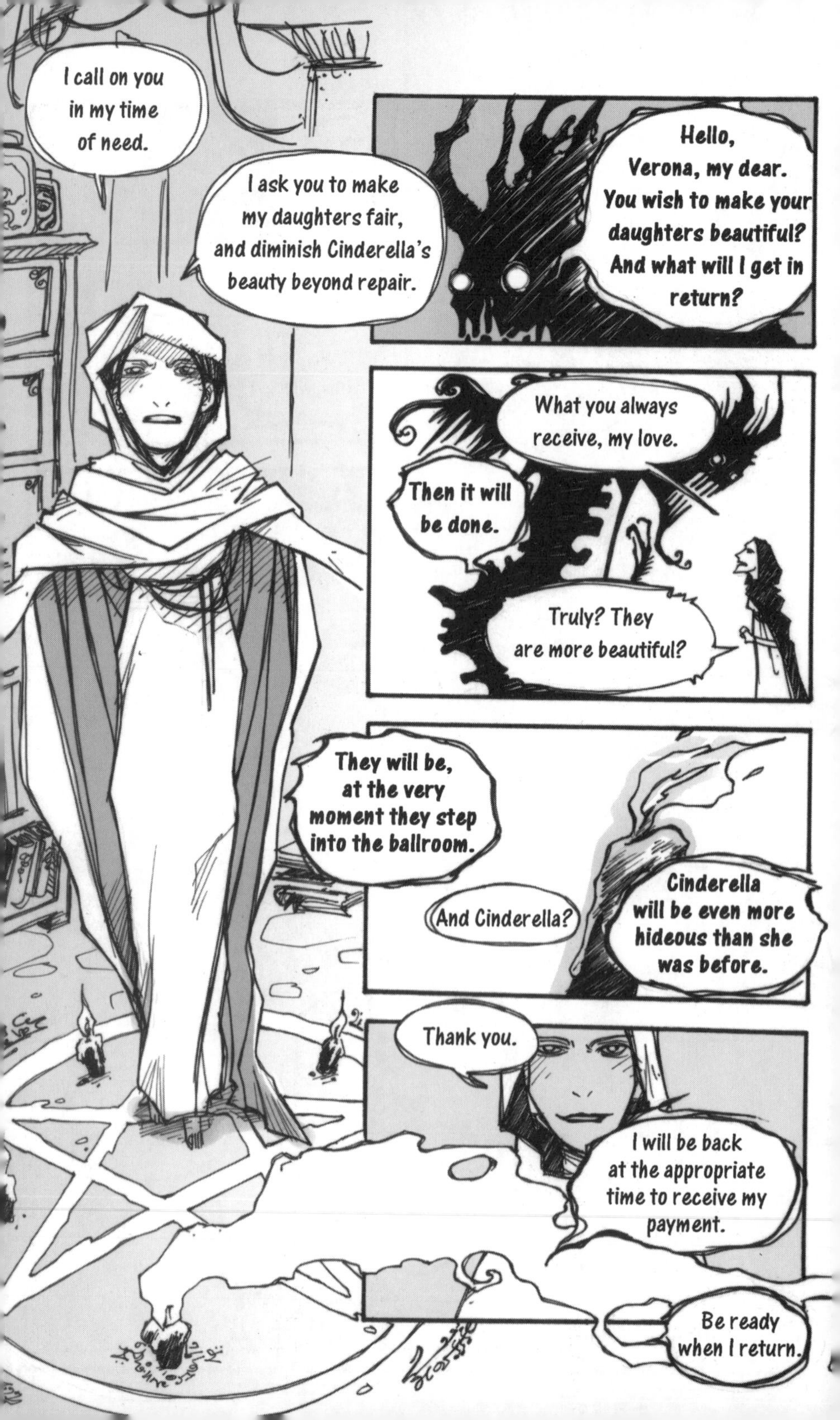

I call on you in my time of need.
I ask you to make my daughters fair, and diminish Cinderella's beauty beyond repair.
Hello, Verona, my dear. You wish to make your daughters beautiful? And what will I get in return?
What you always receive, my love.
Then it will be done.
Truly? They are more beautiful?
They will be, at the very moment they step into the ballroom.
And Cinderella?
Cinderella will be even more hideous than she was before.
Thank you.
I will be back at the appropriate time to receive my payment.
Be ready when I return.

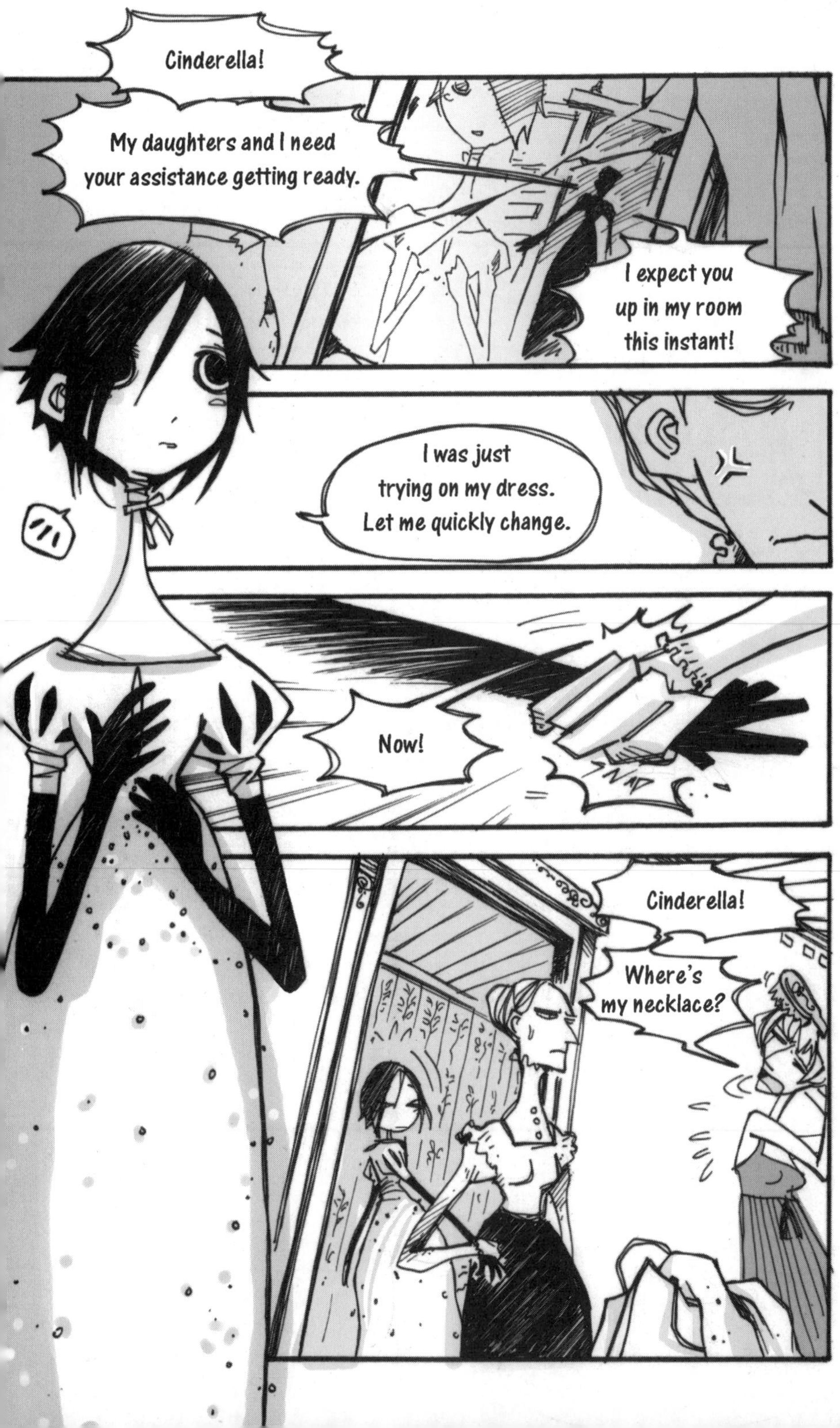
Cinderella!
My daughters and I need your assistance getting ready.
I expect you up in my room this instant!
I was just trying on my dress. Let me quickly change.
Now!
Cinderella!
Where's my necklace?

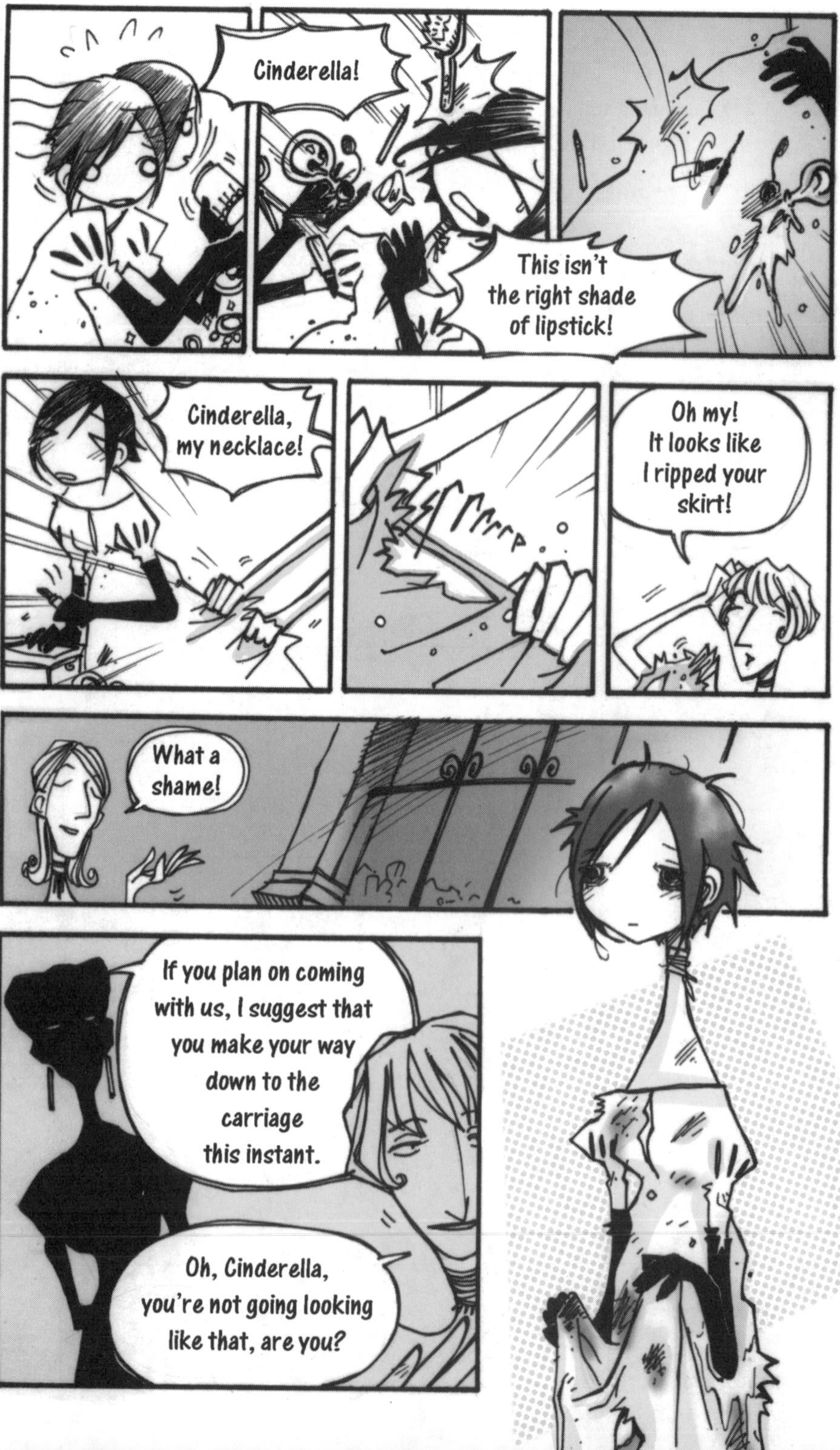
Cinderella!
This isn't the right shade of lipstick!
Cinderella, my necklace!
Rrrrip
Oh my! It looks like I ripped your skirt!
What a shame!
If you plan on coming with us, I suggest that you make your way down to the carriage this instant.
Oh, Cinderella, you're not going looking like that, are you?

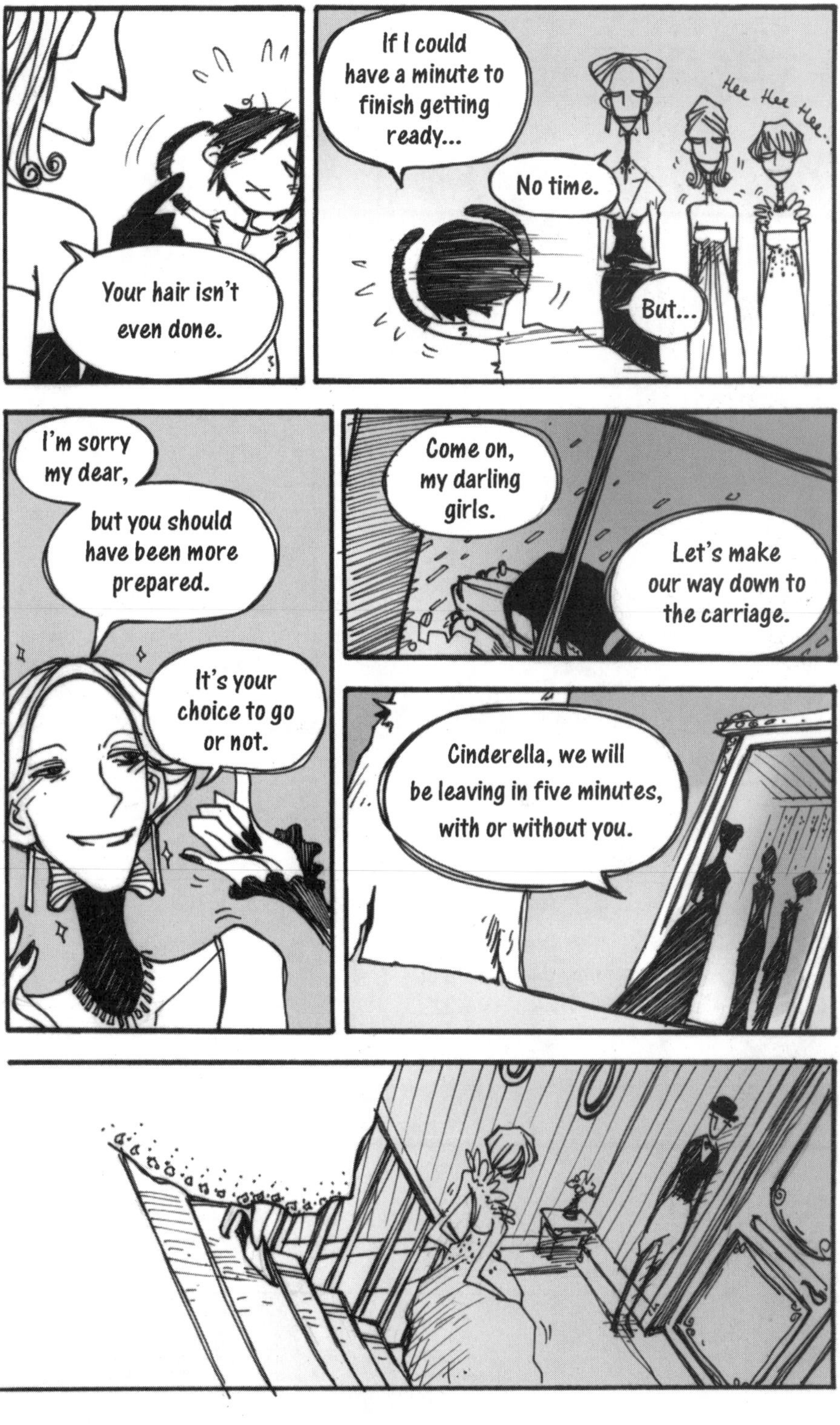
Your hair isn't even done.
If I could have a minute to finish getting ready...
No time.
Hee Hee Hee...
But...
I'm sorry my dear,
but you should have been more prepared.
It's your choice to go or not.
Come on, my darling girls.
Let's make our way down to the carriage.
Cinderella, we will be leaving in five minutes, with or without you.

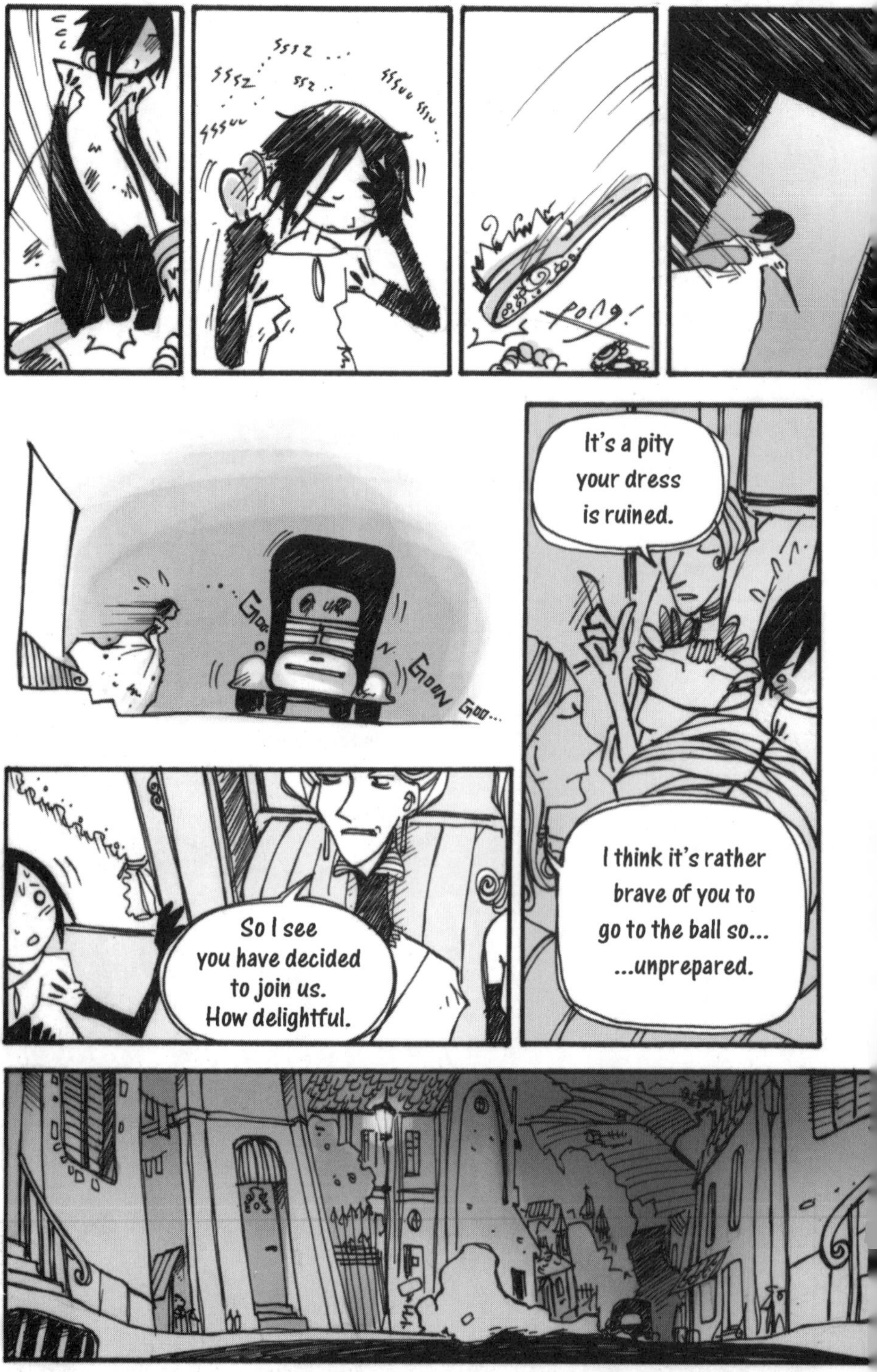
pong!
It's a pity your dress is ruined.
So I see you have decided to join us. How delightful.
I think it's rather brave of you to go to the ball so... ...unprepared.

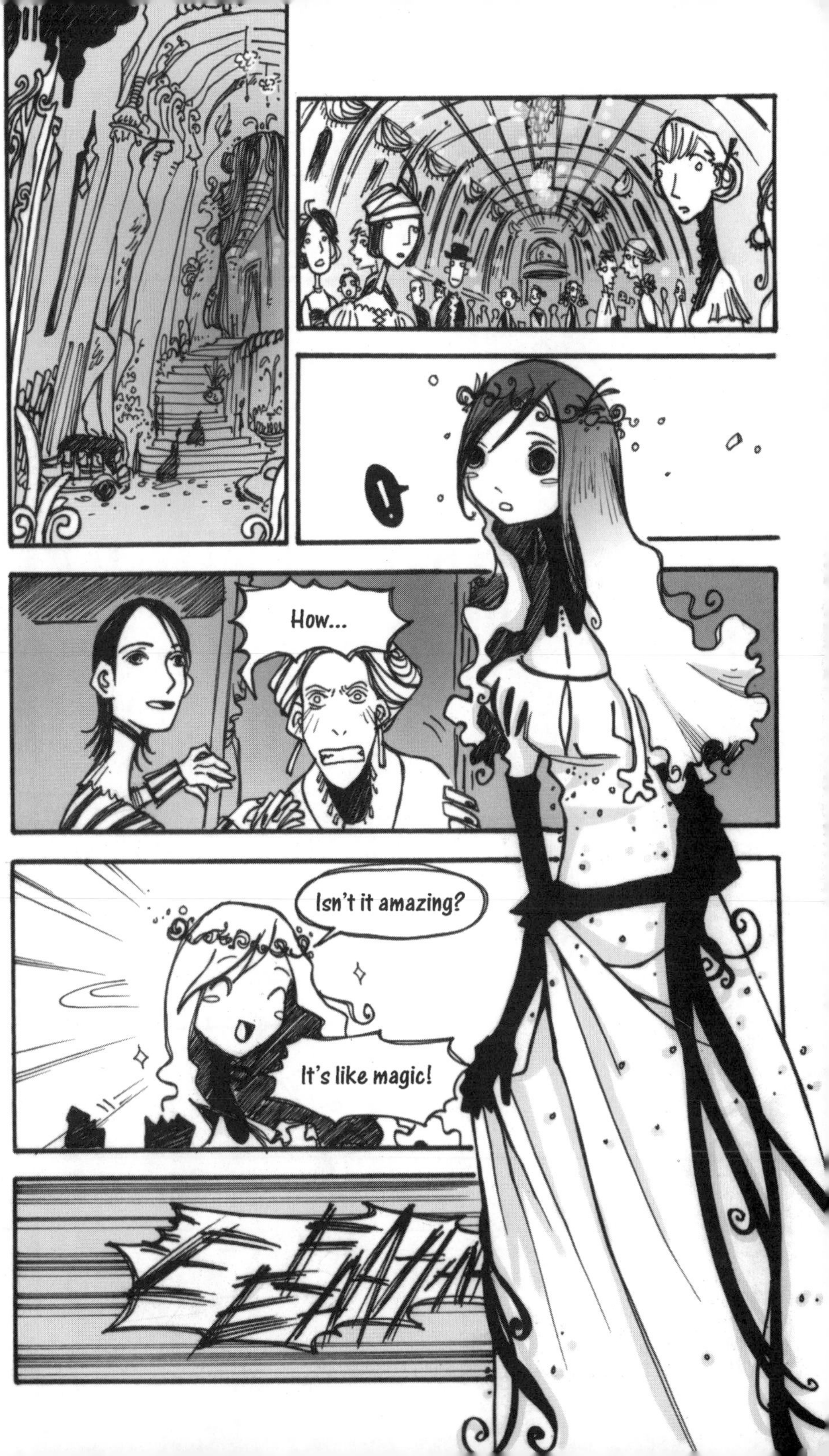
!
How...
Isn't it amazing?
It's like magic!

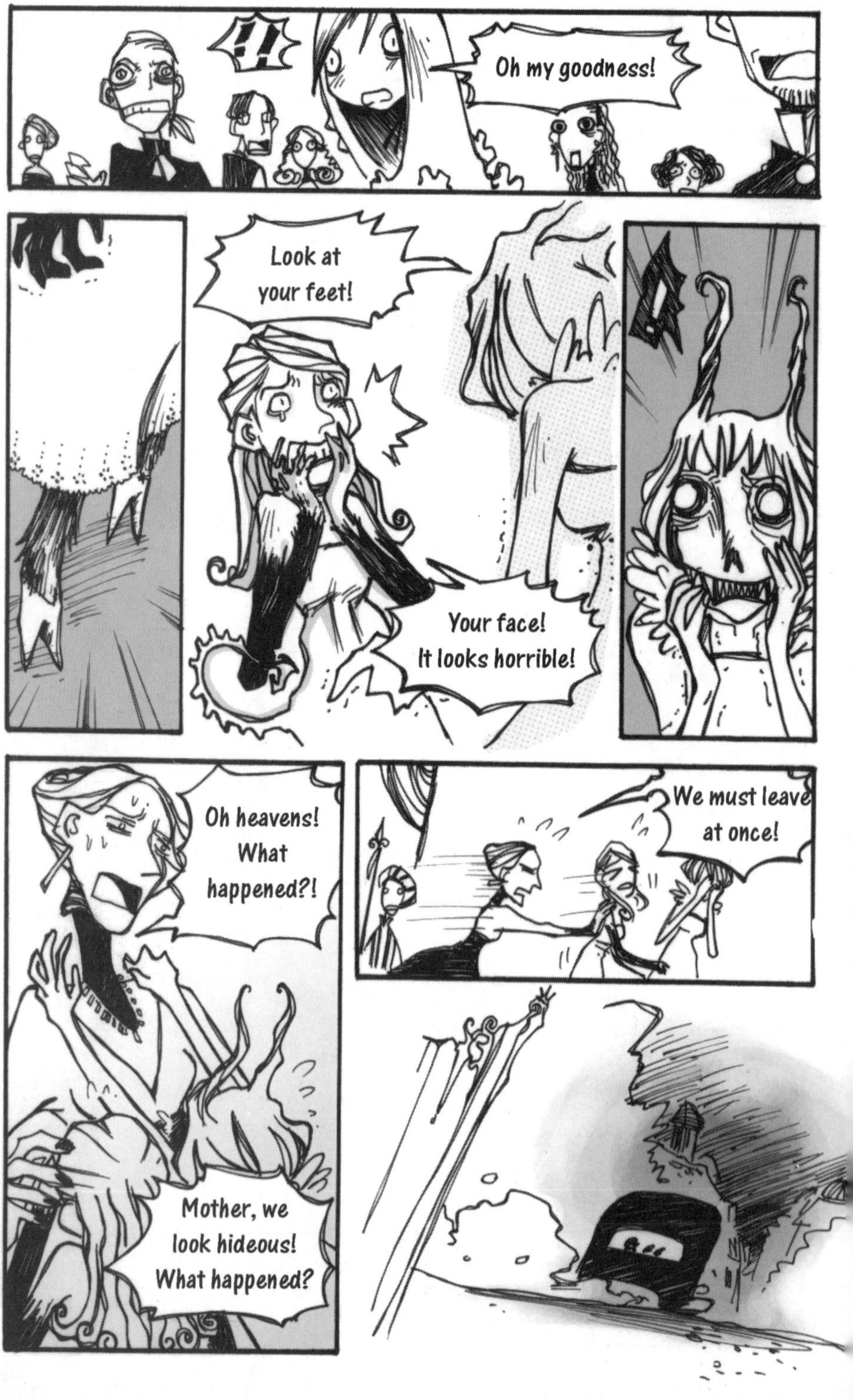
!!
Oh my goodness!
Look at your feet!
!
Your face! It looks horrible!
Oh heavens! What happened?!
Mother, we look hideous! What happened?
We must leave at once!

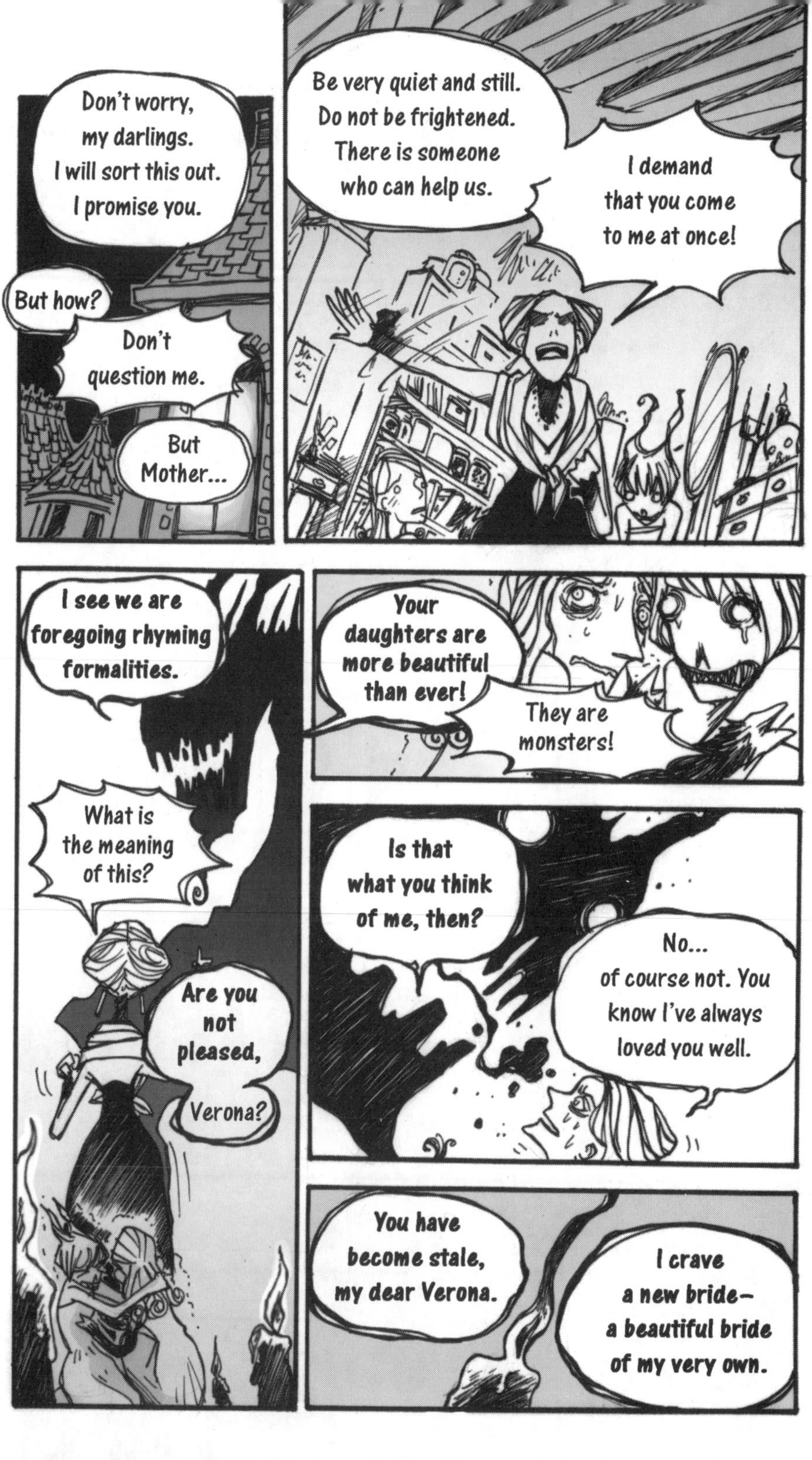
Don't worry, my darlings. I will sort this out. I promise you.
But how?
Don't question me.
But Mother...
Be very quiet and still. Do not be frightened. There is someone who can help us.
I demand that you come to me at once!
I see we are foregoing rhyming formalities.
Your daughters are more beautiful than ever!
They are monsters!
What is the meaning of this?
Are you not pleased,
Verona?
Is that what you think of me, then?
No... of course not. You know I've always loved you well.
You have become stale, my dear Verona.
I crave a new bride— a beautiful bride of my very own.

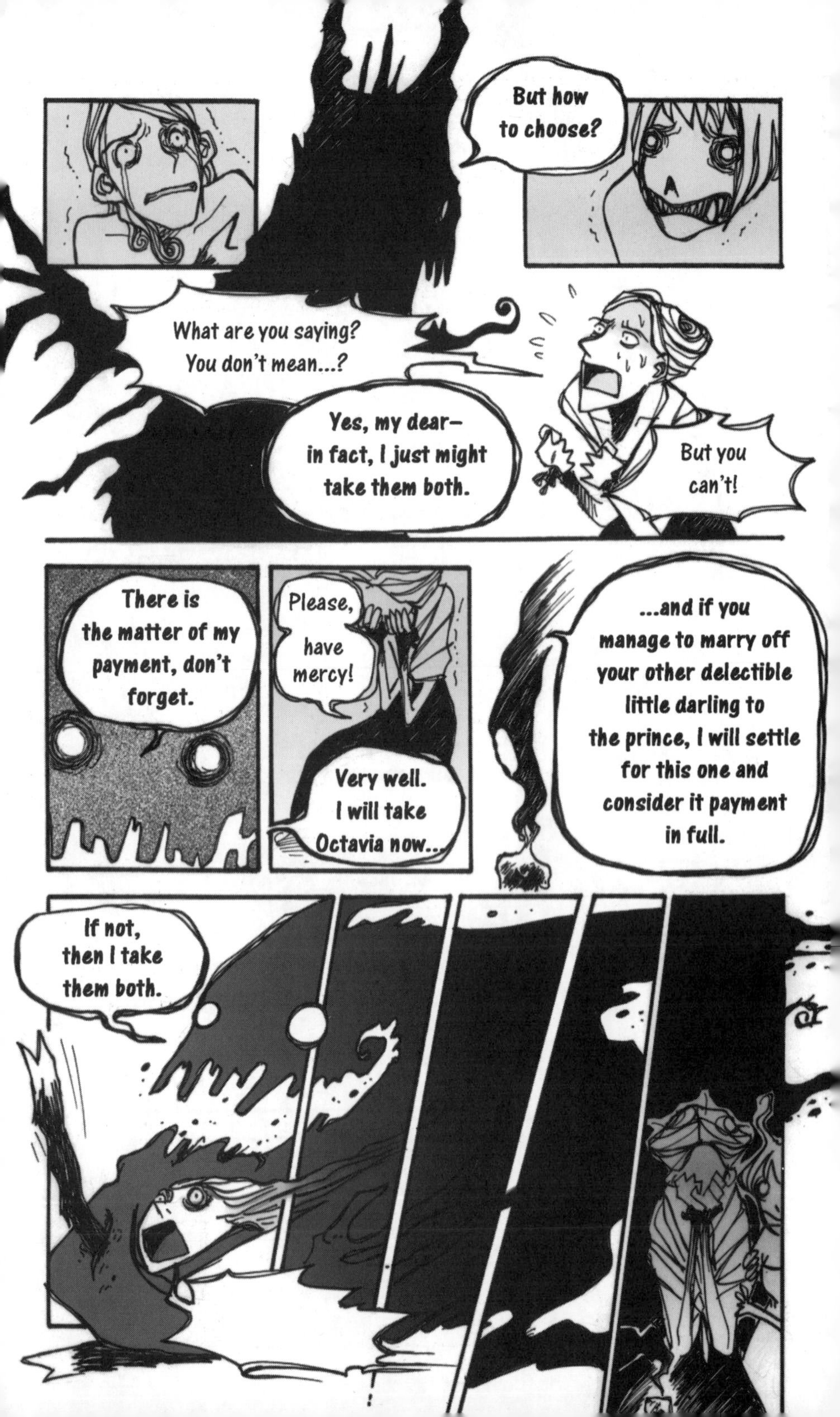
But how to choose?
What are you saying? You don't mean...?
Yes, my dear—in fact, I just might take them both.
But you can't!
There is the matter of my payment, don't forget.
Please, have mercy!
Very well. I will take Octavia now...
...and if you manage to marry off your other delectible little darling to the prince, I will settle for this one and consider it payment in full.
If not, then I take them both.

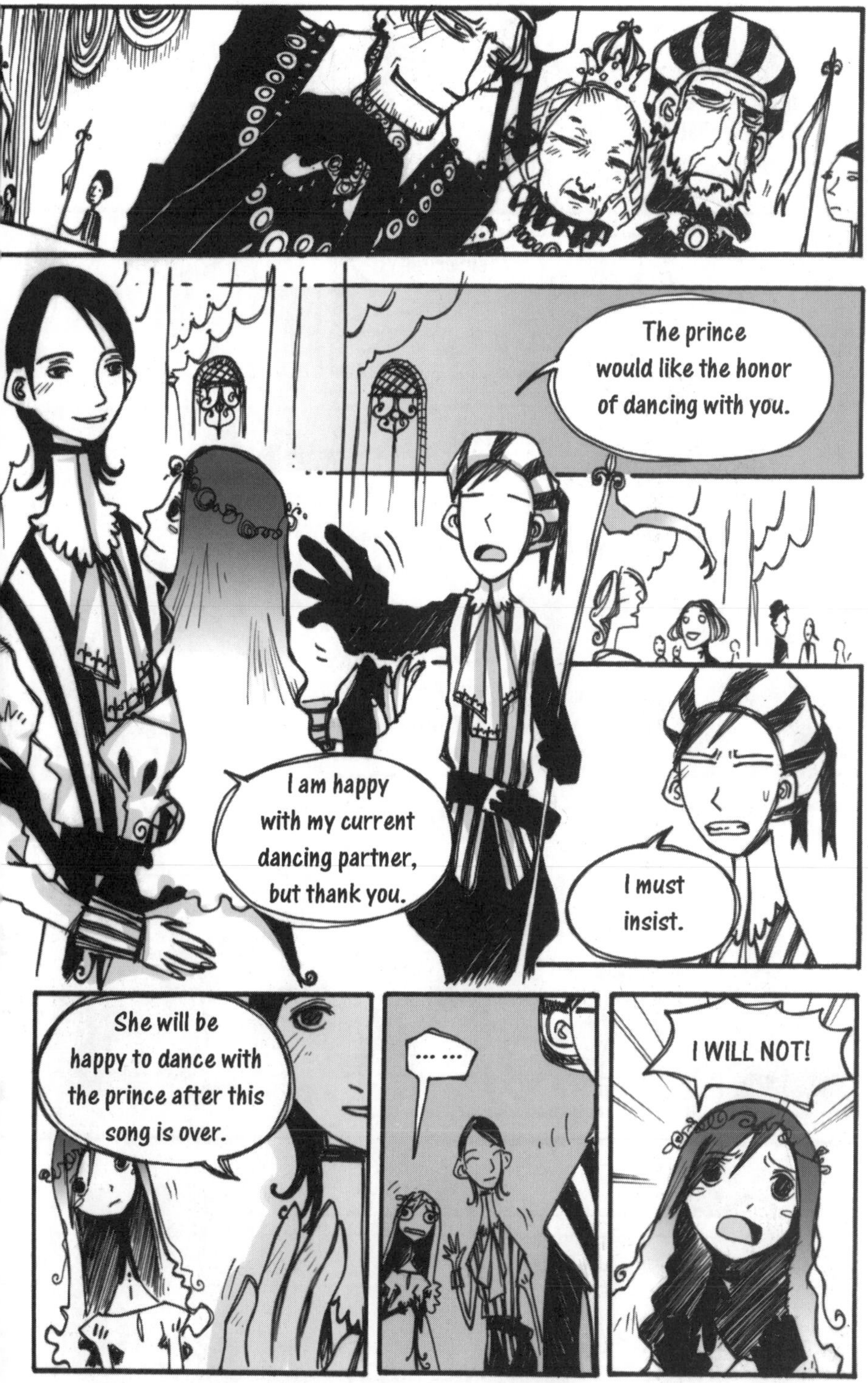
The prince would like the honor of dancing with you.
I am happy with my current dancing partner, but thank you.
I must insist.
She will be happy to dance with the prince after this song is over.
... ...
I WILL NOT!

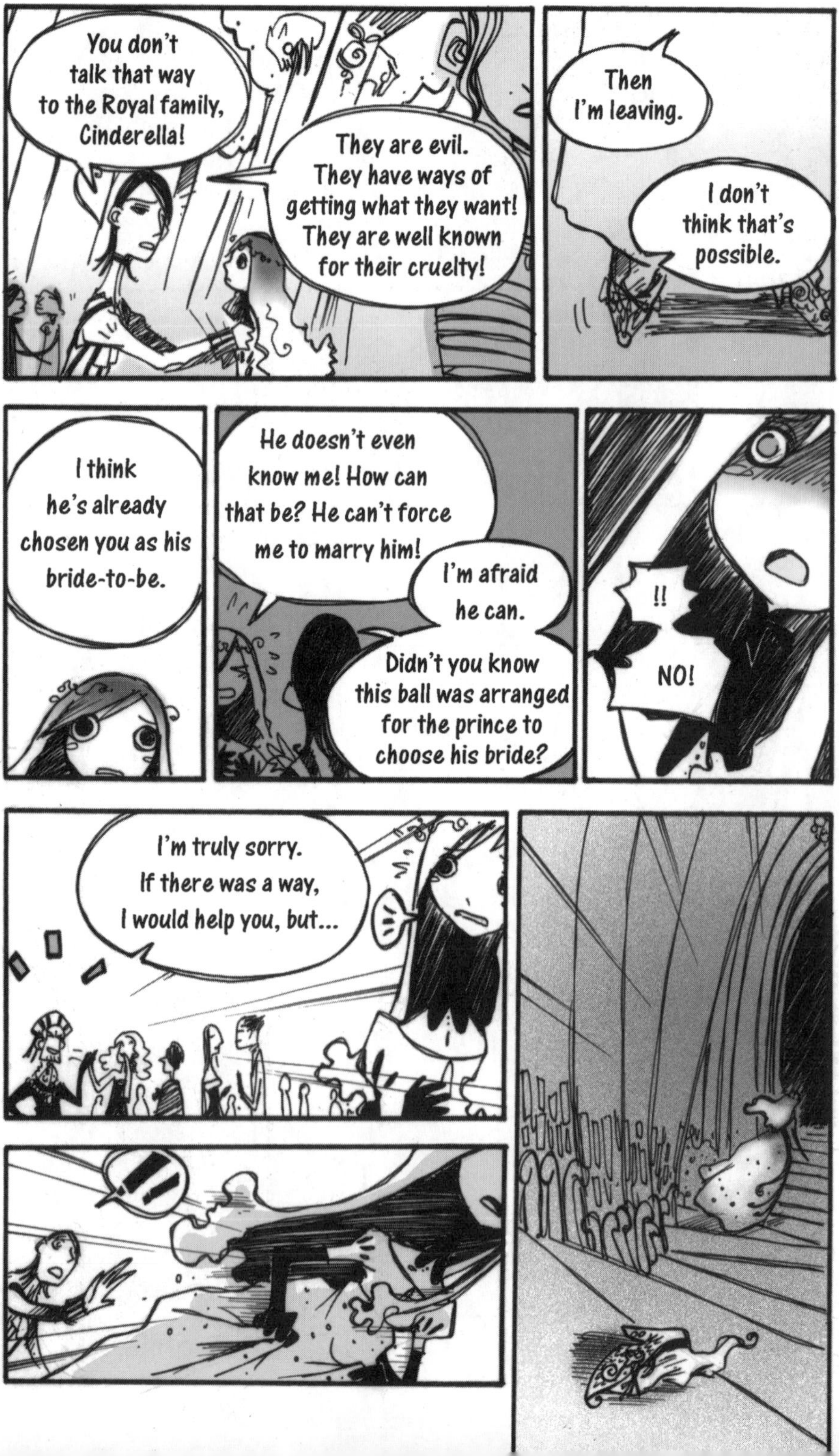
You don't talk that way to the Royal family, Cinderella!
They are evil. They have ways of getting what they want! They are well known for their cruelty!
Then I'm leaving.
I don't think that's possible.
I think he's already chosen you as his bride-to-be.
He doesn't even know me! How can that be? He can't force me to marry him!
I'm afraid he can.
Didn't you know this ball was arranged for the prince to choose his bride?
!!
NO!
I'm truly sorry. If there was a way, I would help you, but...

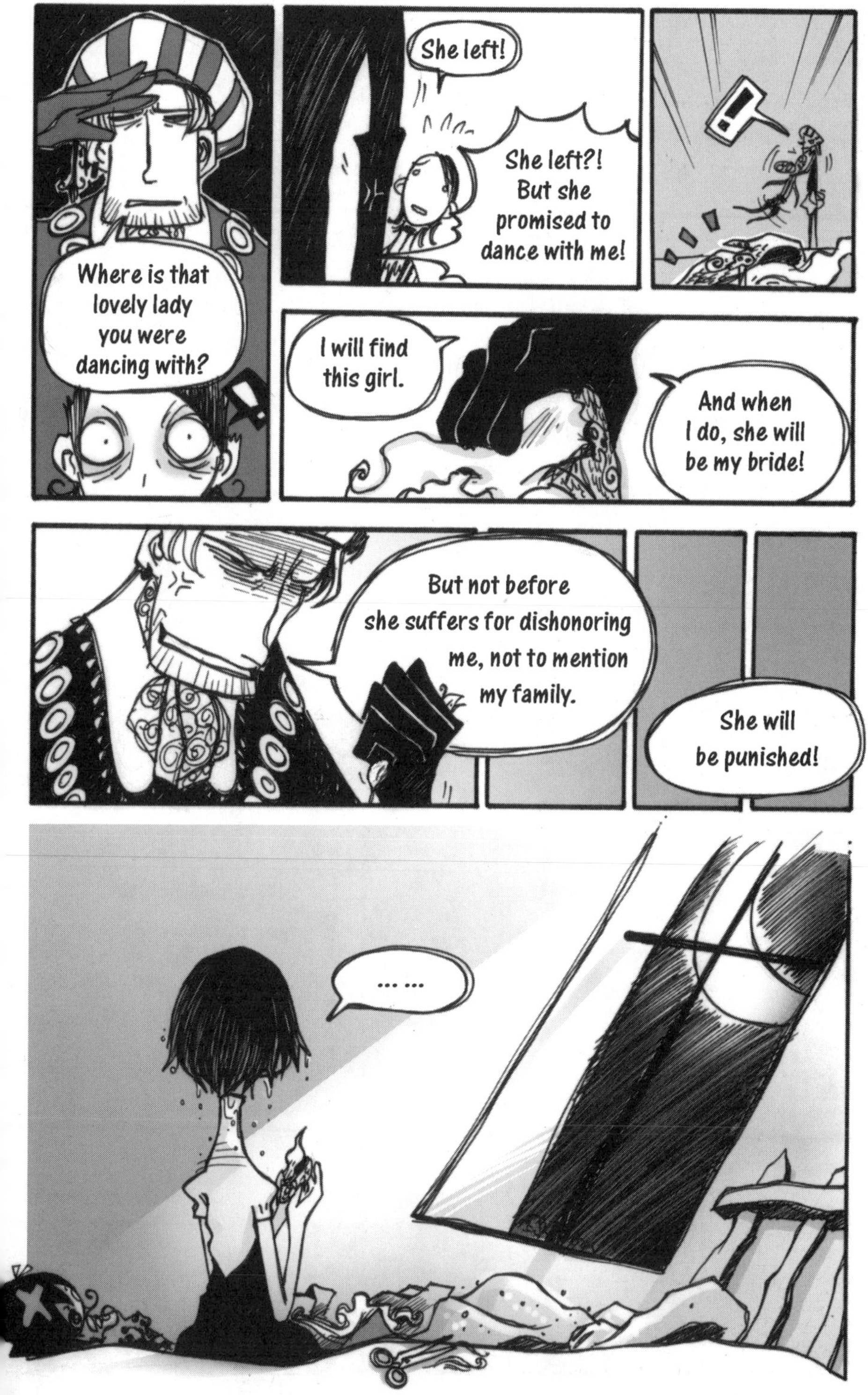
She left!
She left?! But she promised to dance with me!
Where is that lovely lady you were dancing with?
I will find this girl.
And when I do, she will be my bride!
But not before she suffers for dishonoring me, not to mention my family.
She will be punished!
... ...

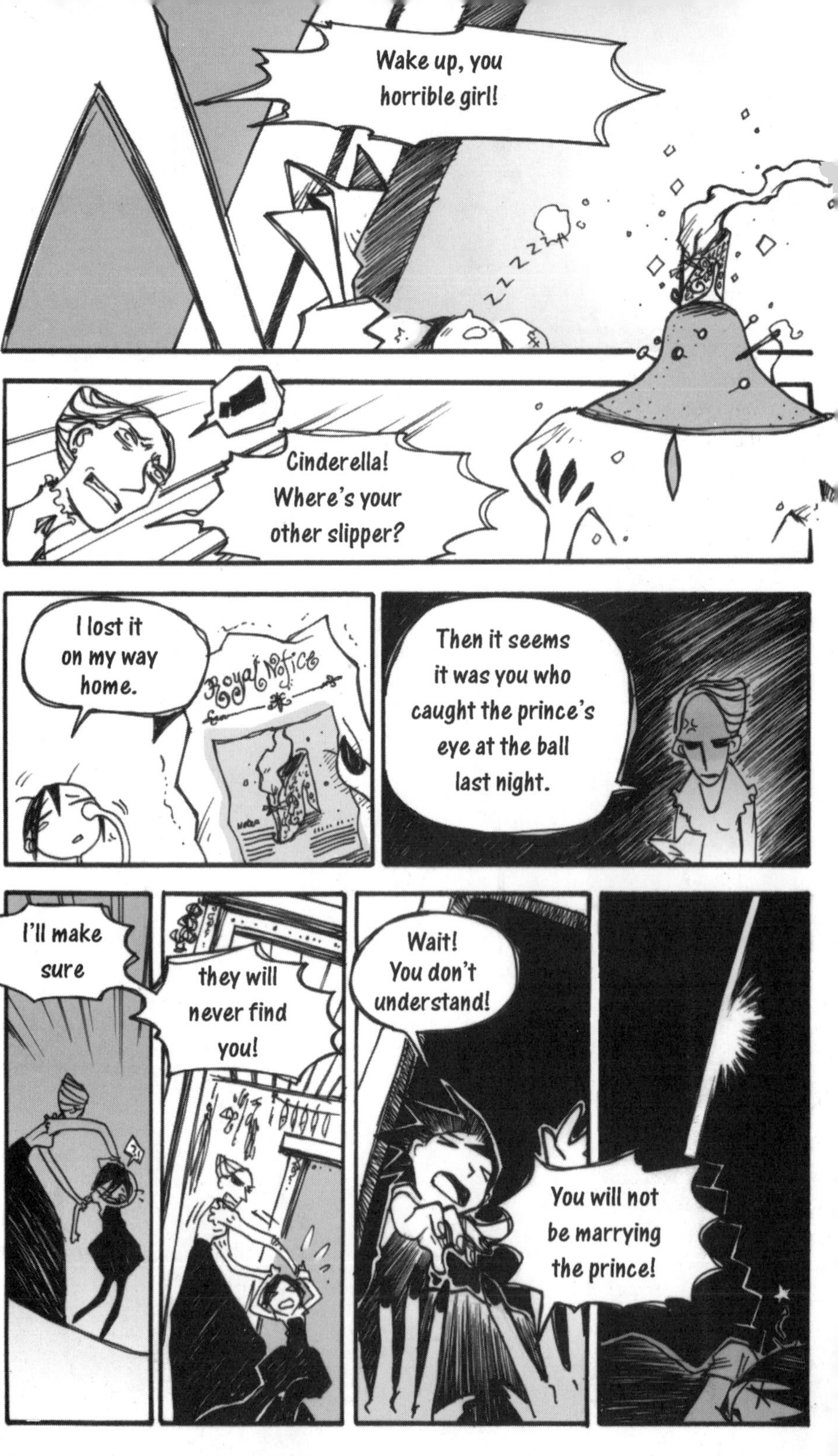
Wake up, you horrible girl!
Cinderella! Where's your other slipper?
I lost it on my way home.
Royal Notice
Then it seems it was you who caught the prince's eye at the ball last night.
I'll make sure
they will never find you!
Wait! You don't understand!
You will not be marrying the prince!

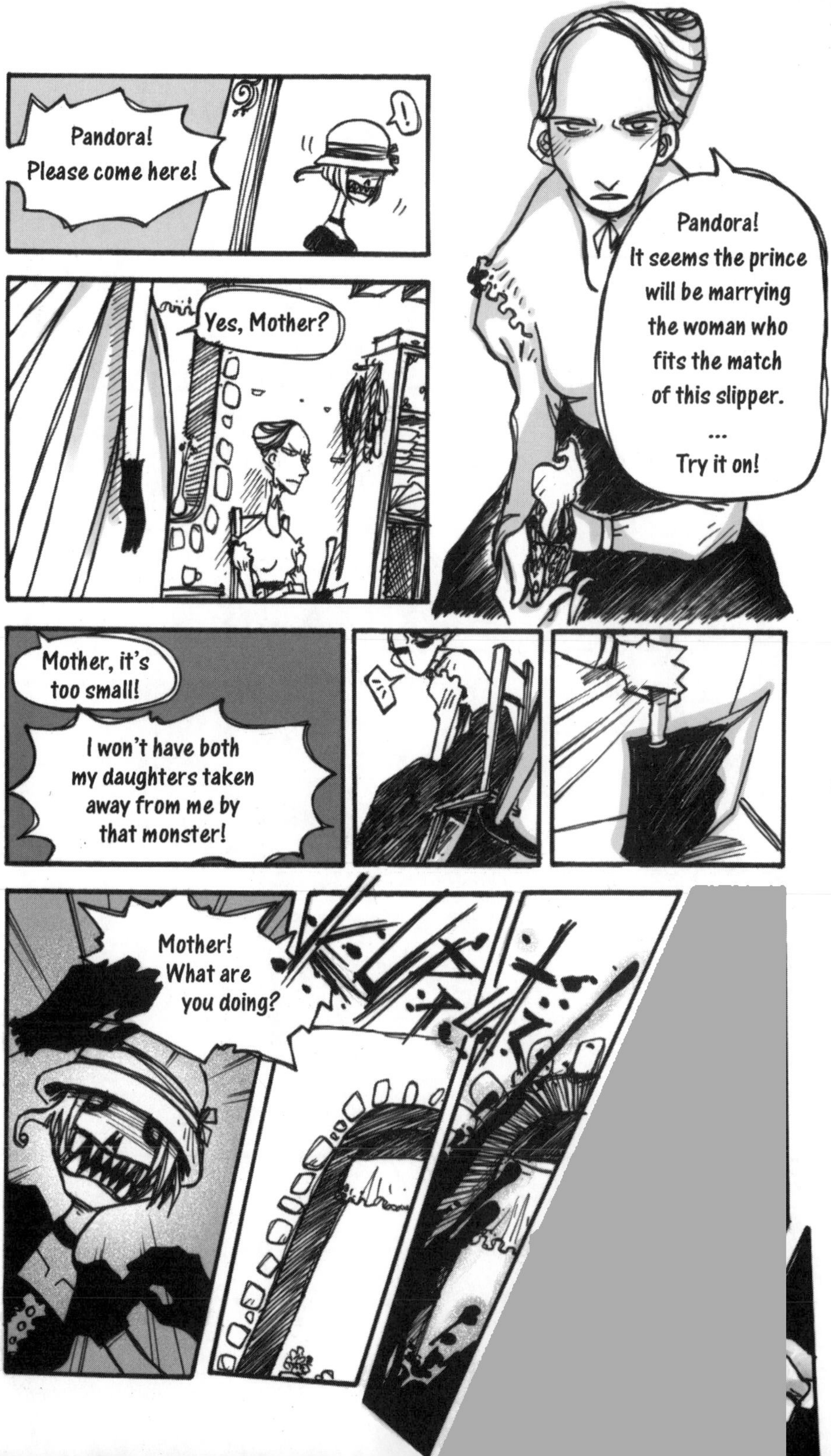
Pandora!
Please come here!
!
Yes, Mother?
Pandora! It seems the prince will be marrying the woman who fits the match of this slipper. ... Try it on!
Mother, it's too small!
I won't have both my daughters taken away from me by that monster!
Mother! What are you doing?

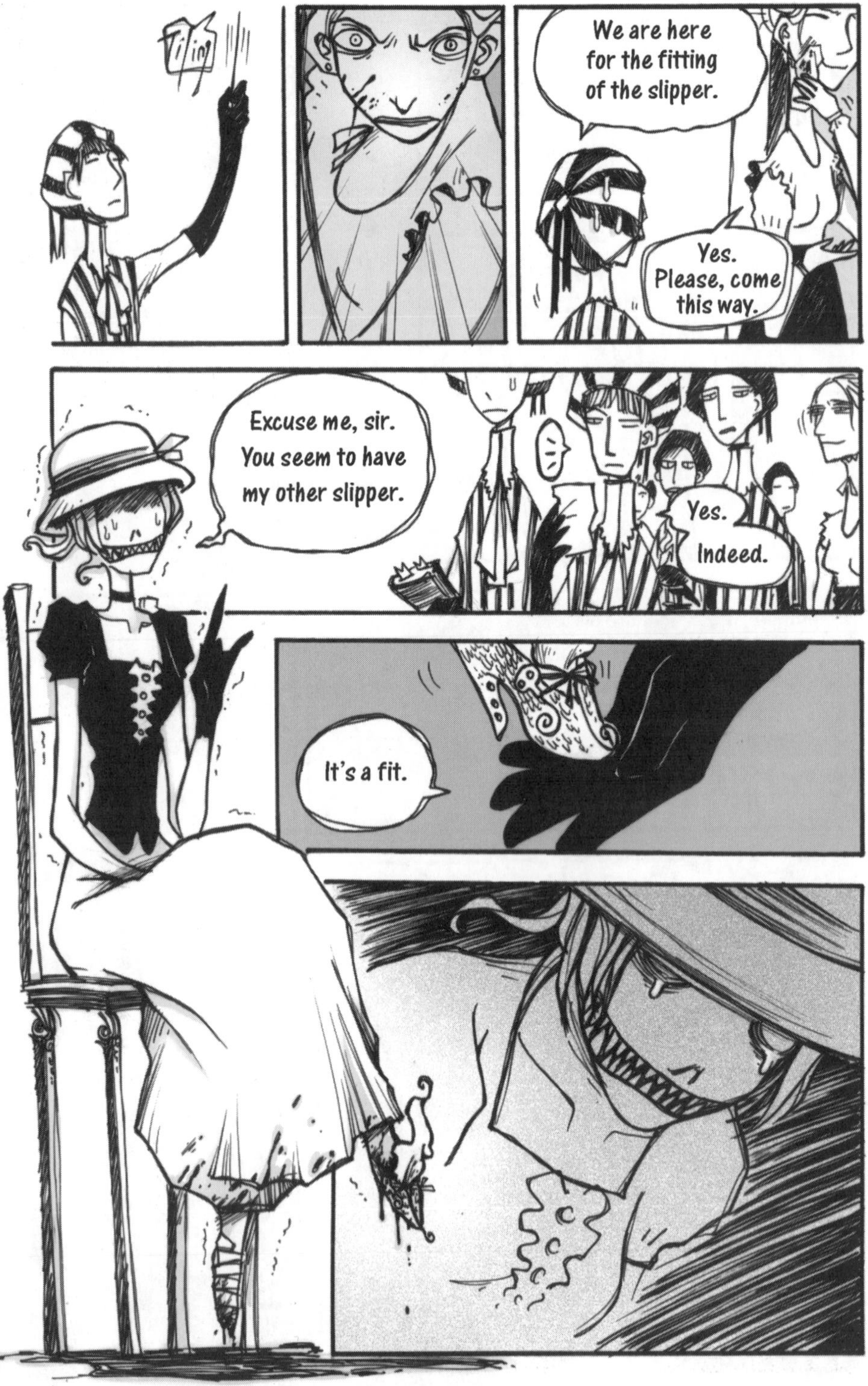
Tiling
We are here for the fitting of the slipper.
Yes. Please, come this way.
Excuse me, sir. You seem to have my other slipper.
Yes. Indeed.
It's a fit.

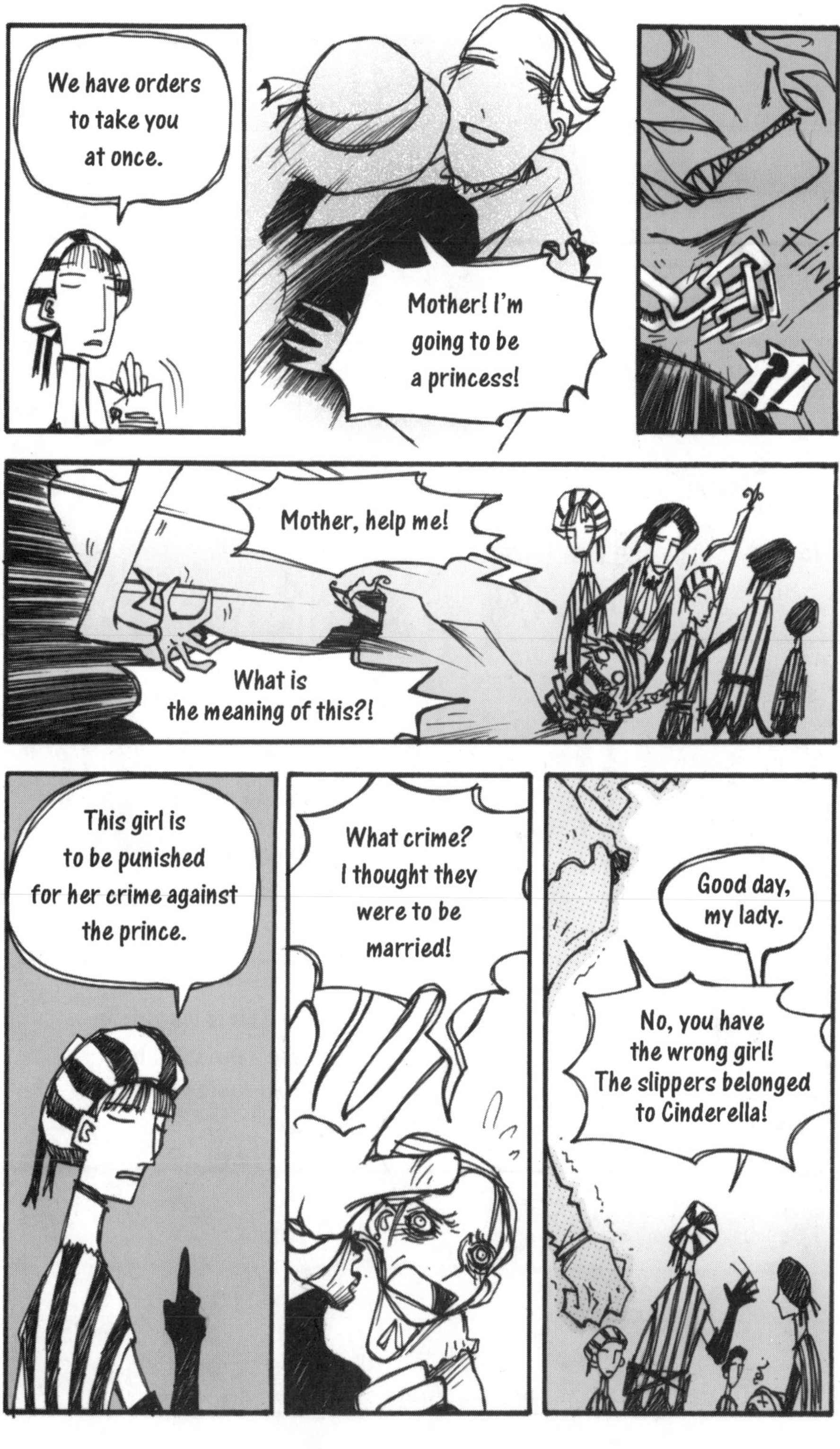
We have orders to take you at once.
Mother! I'm going to be a princess!
?!
Mother, help me!
What is the meaning of this?!
This girl is to be punished for her crime against the prince.
What crime? I thought they were to be married!
Good day, my lady.
No, you have the wrong girl! The slippers belonged to Cinderella!

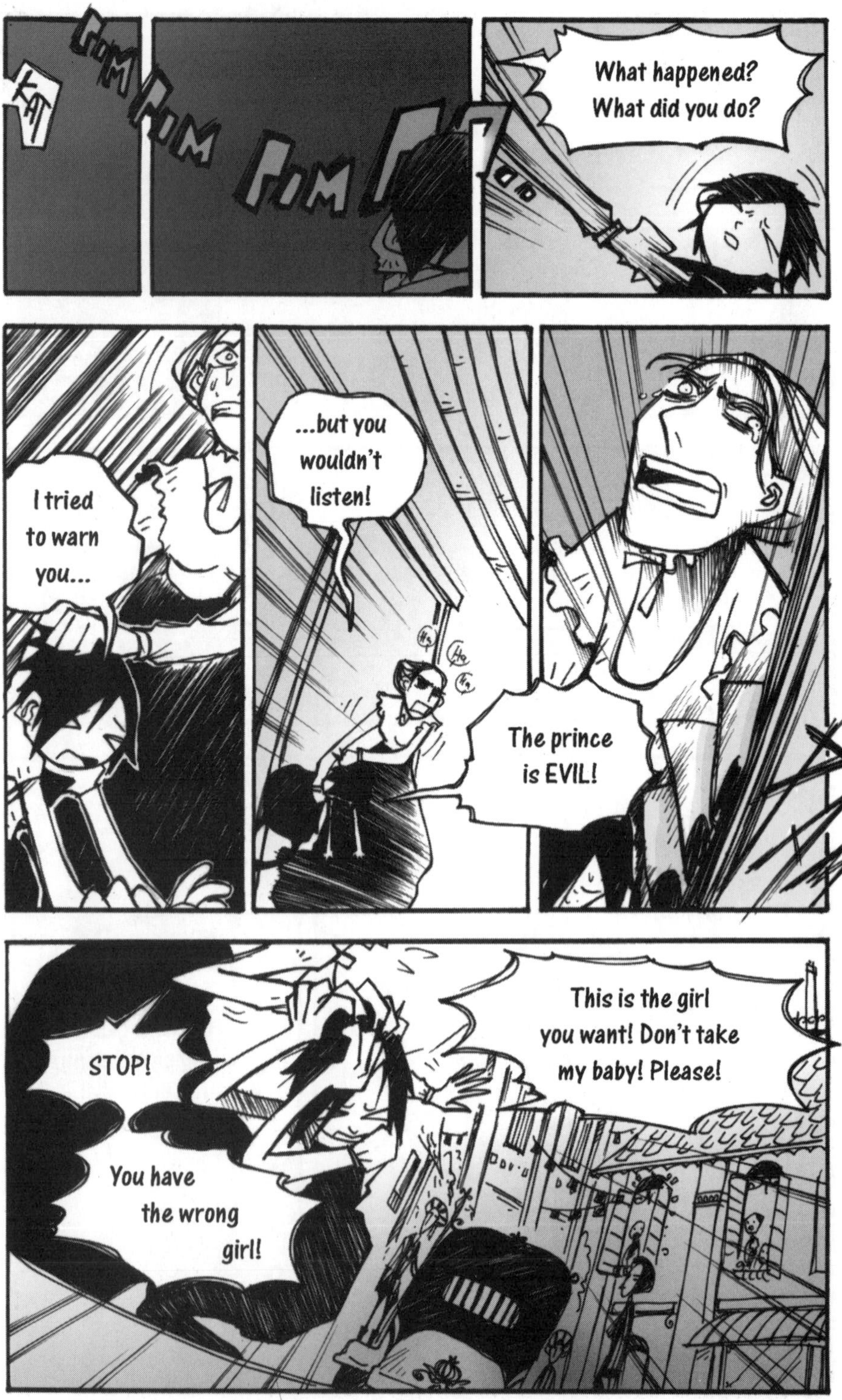
KAT
POM POM POM POM
What happened? What did you do?
I tried to warn you...
...but you wouldn't listen!
The prince is EVIL!
This is the girl you want! Don't take my baby! Please!
STOP!
You have the wrong girl!

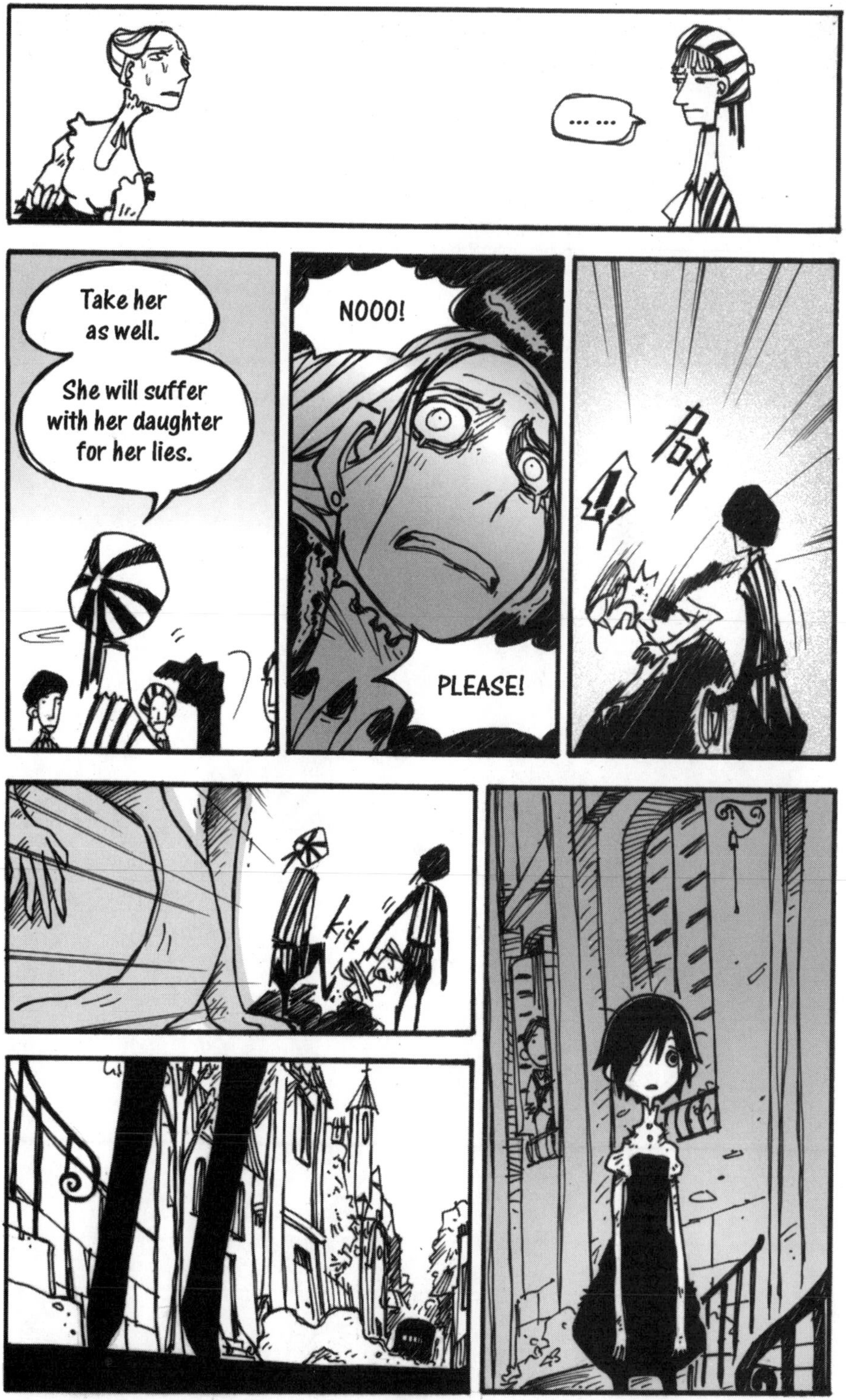

... ...
Take her as well.
She will suffer with her daughter for her lies.
NOOO!
PLEASE!

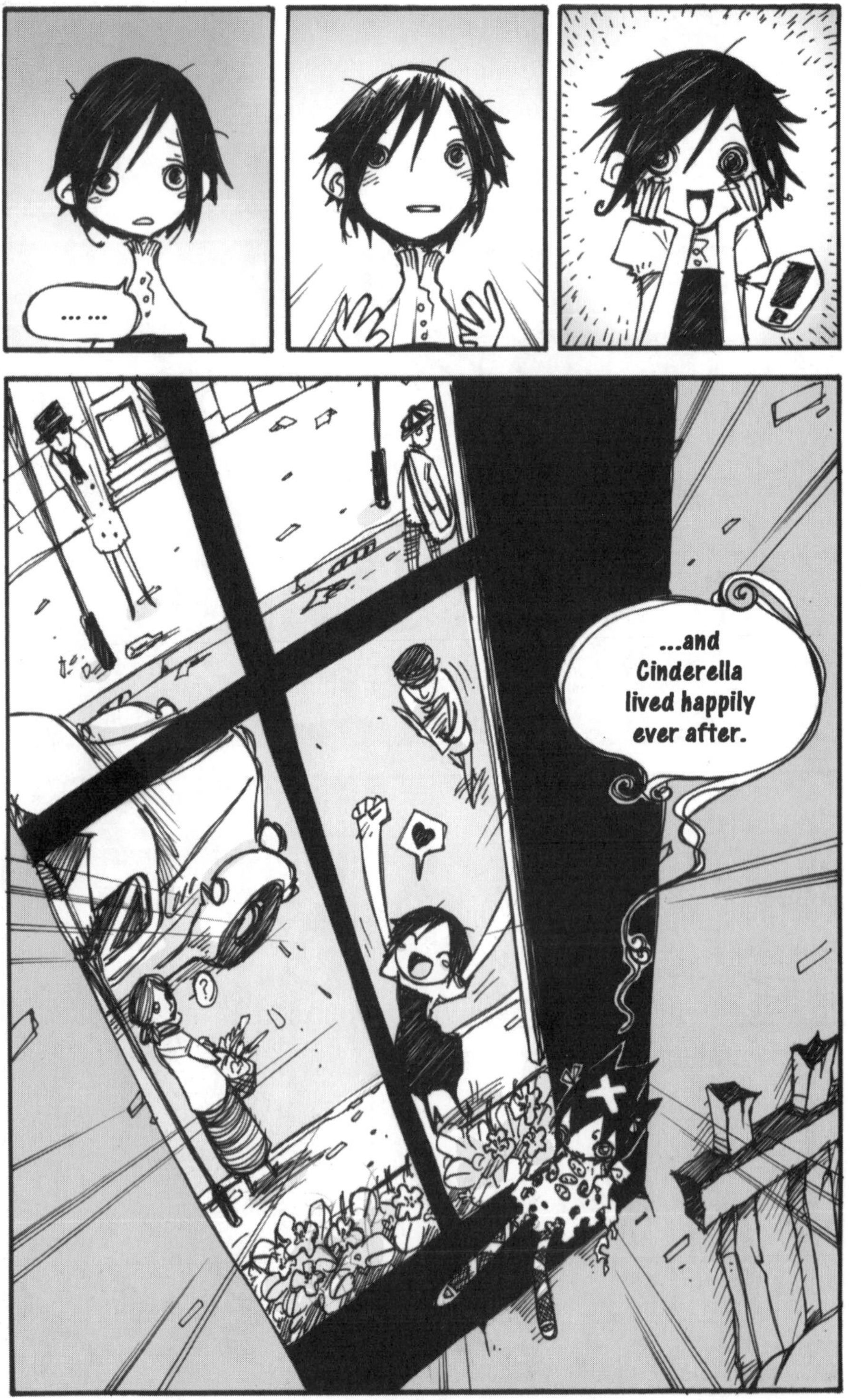
... ...
...and Cinderella lived happily ever after.

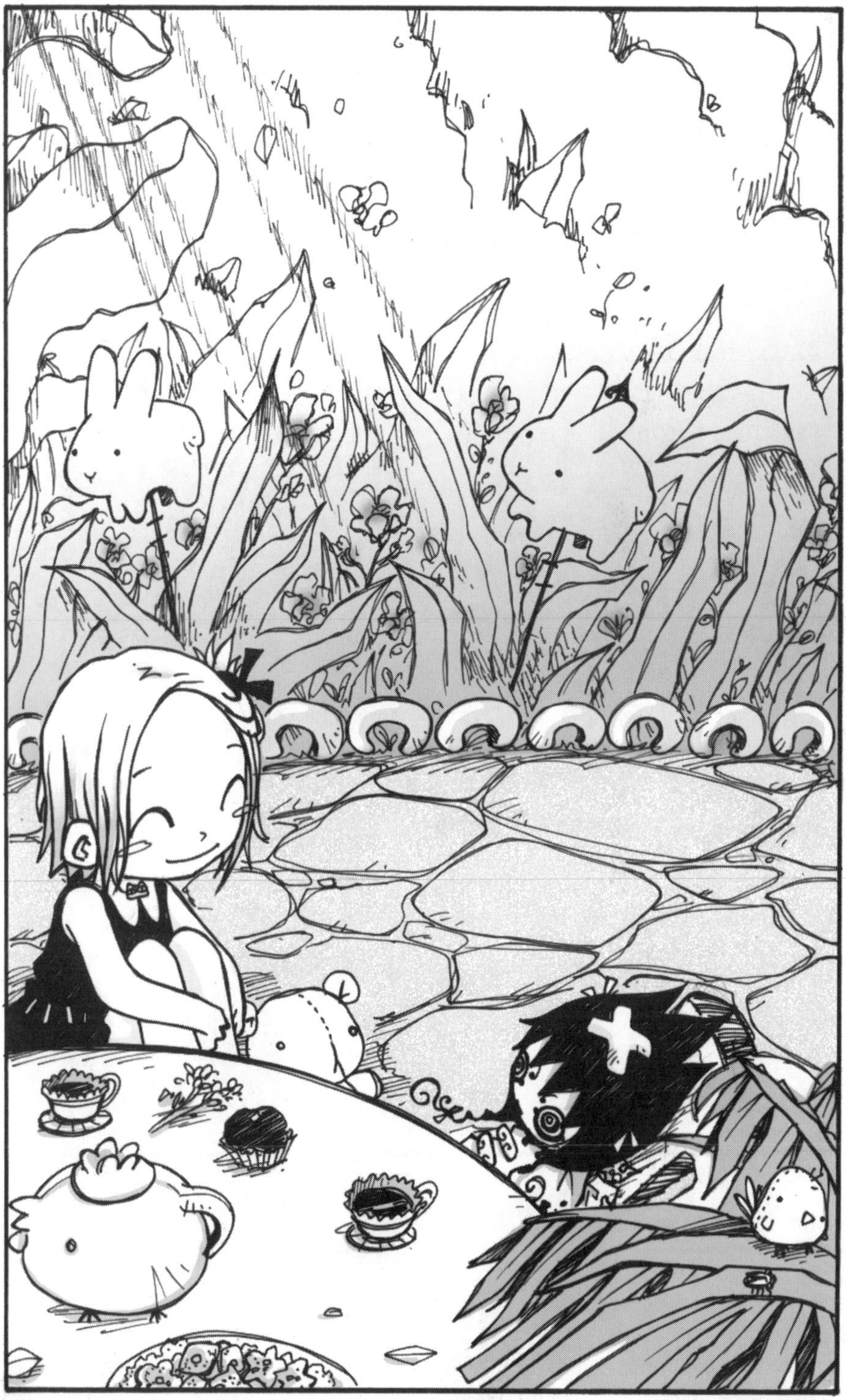

The End

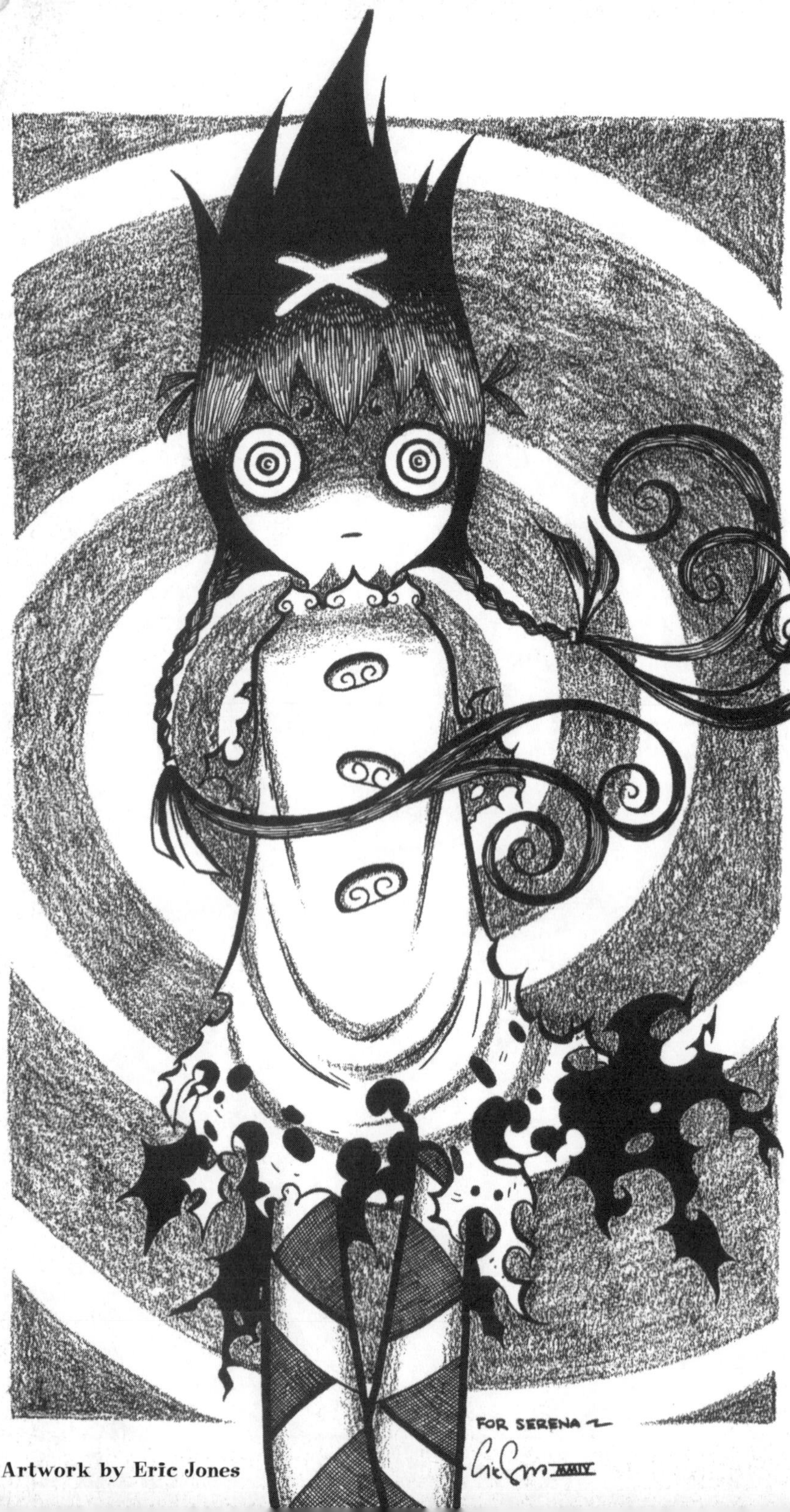
FOR SERENA

Artwork by Eric Jones

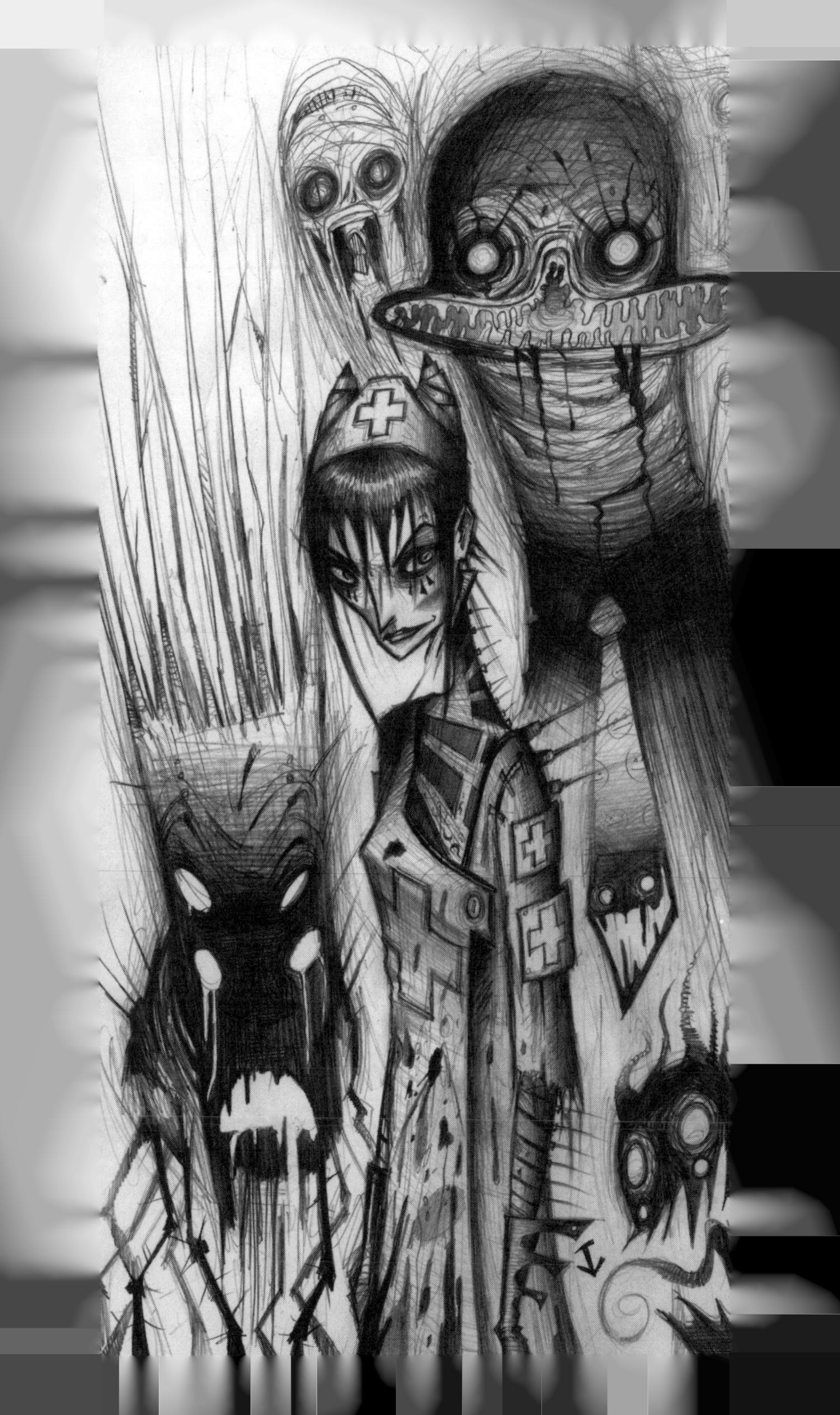

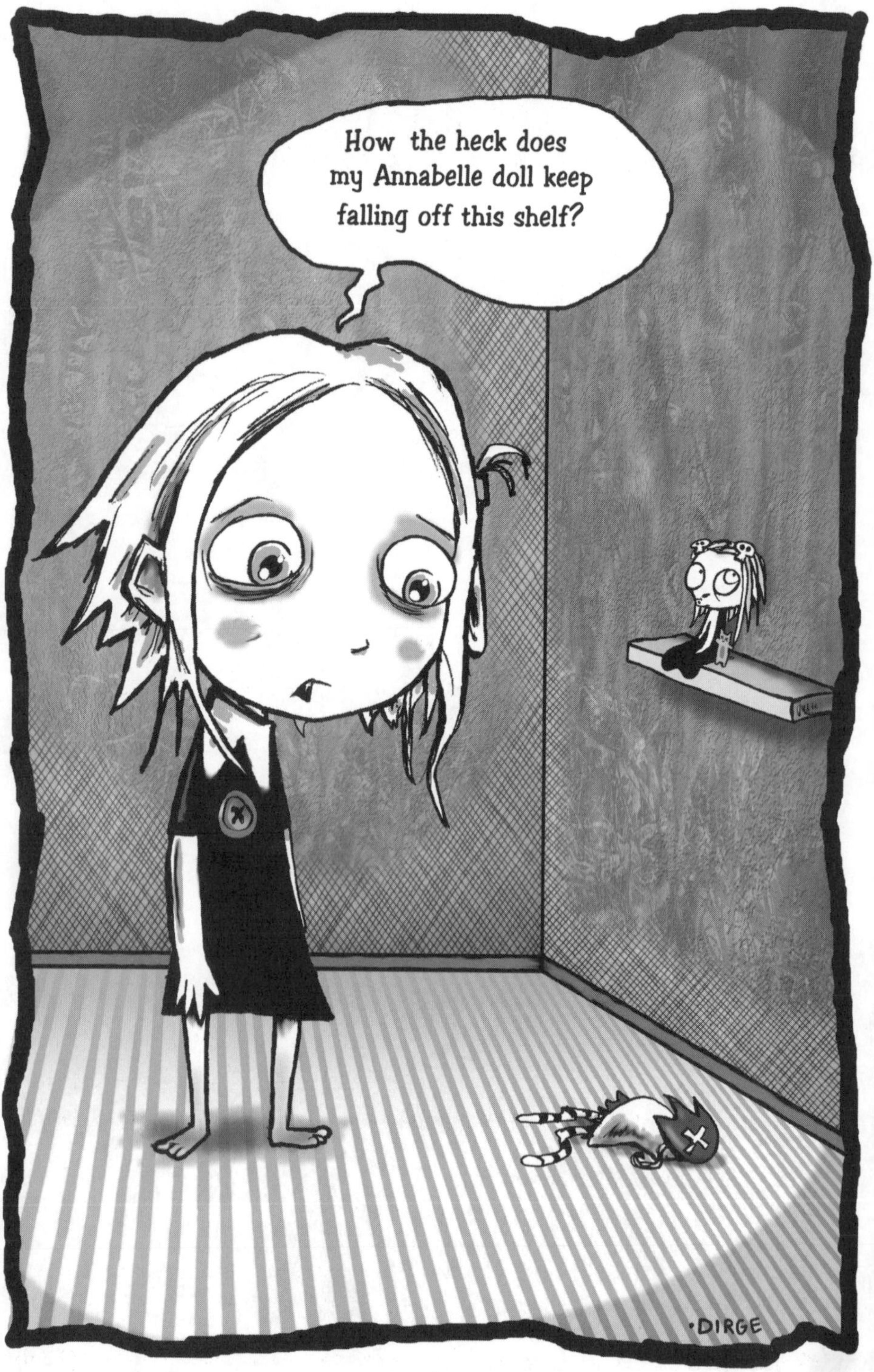
How the heck does my Annabelle doll keep falling off this shelf?
•DIRGE

Artwork by Roman Dirge

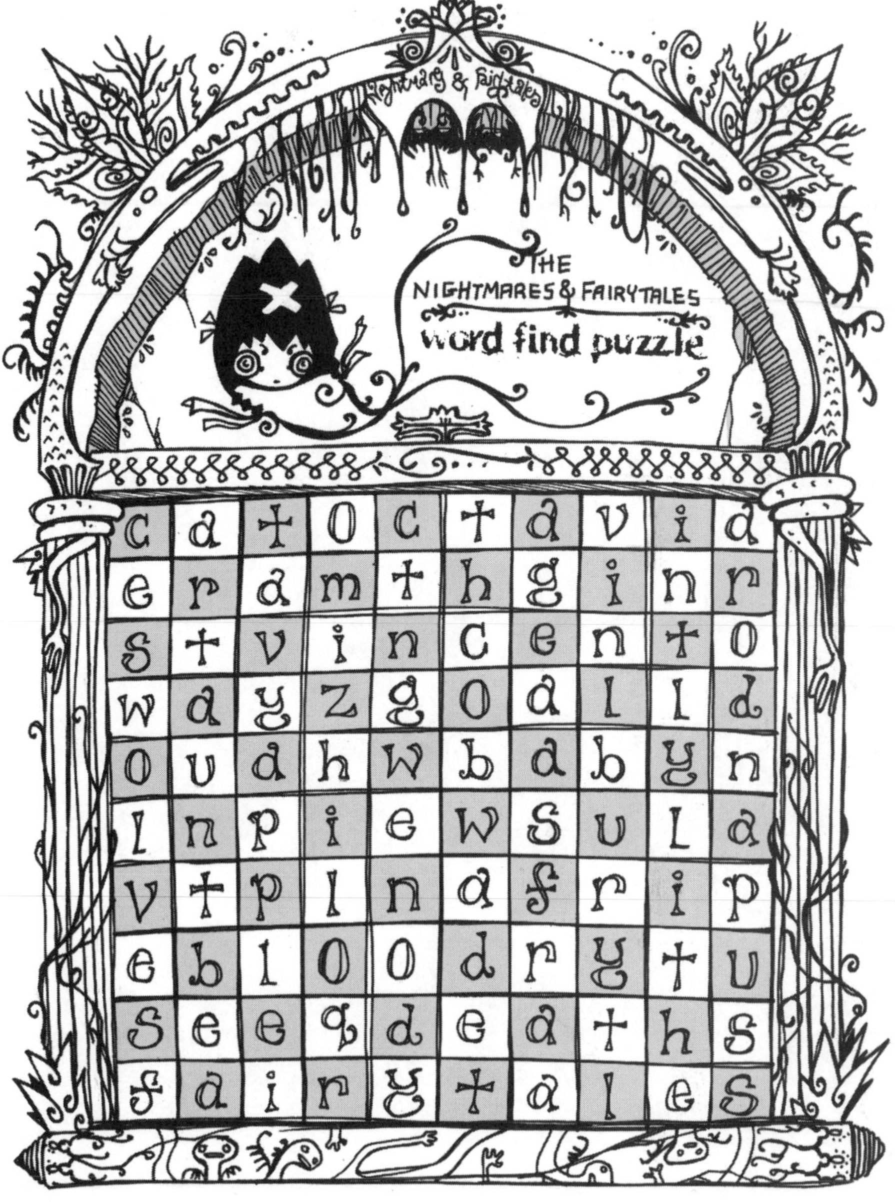
Nightmares & Fairytales
THE
NIGHTMARES & FAIRYTALES
word find puzzle

c	a	†	o	c	†	a	v	i	d
e	r	a	m	†	h	g	i	n	r
s	†	v	i	n	c	e	n	†	o
w	a	y	z	g	o	a	l	l	d
o	u	d	h	w	b	a	b	y	n
l	n	p	i	e	w	s	u	l	a
v	†	p	l	n	a	f	r	i	p
e	b	l	o	o	d	r	y	†	u
s	e	e	q	d	e	a	†	h	s
f	a	i	r	y	†	a	l	e	s

1. Spell 'Annabelle' backwards.
2. The mental asylum Morgan was sent to.
3. What was fed to the monster in the nunnery?
4. What was stolen from Snow White by her evil stepmother?
5. Who was Gwen's neighbour?
6. Name Cinderella's stepsisters.

* How many hidden words related to nightmares & fairytales can you spot?

THE NIGHTMARES & FAIRYTALES Crossword Puzzle

c	a	†	O	c	†	a	v	i	a
e	r	a	m	t	h	g	i	n	r
S	†	v	i	n	c	e	n	t	o
w	a	y	z	g	o	a	l	l	d
o	u	d	h	w	b	a	b	y	n
l	n	p	e	w	s	u	l	a
v	†	p	l	n	a	f	r	i	p
e	h	l	o	o	d	r	y	†	u
S	e	e	q	d	e	a	t	h	s
f	a	i	r	y	†	a	l	e	s

Answers

① ellebana
② St Vincent
③ baby
④ heart
⑤ Aunt Bea
⑥ Pandora, Octavia

Hidden words = deaths, Gwen, blood, Lylith, fairytales, nightmare, apple, cat, pie, wolves (#8)

Nightmares & Fairy Tales

An excerpt from Serena's script for *Nightmares & Fairy Tales* issue #5: Gwen's Story, for your enjoyment.

Gwen and her parents (I will leave it up to you how the parents look — in my mind they look like normal parents, but they are mean) are standing out front of a large, spooky-looking house. The house is dark and foreboding — something about it looks frightening.

It's a two-story house with an attic. There is dim light in the attic window. We can't tell if it's a reflection or not, but there seems to be some kind of creature or monster looking out the attic window at the family. The house is painted dark, somber colors.

The family's car is nearby and there are many boxes. The boxes have labels on them like Kitchen, Gwen's books, Dolls, Bathroom, Clothes. Gwen and her family are moving into their new house today.

Right next door is a very pretty house, very bright with lots of flowers, a little fishpond, as well as a fountain, pretty little angel statues, statues of pretty ladies, all surrounded by pretty flowers. It's a perfect little old lady house, the kind of old lady that is super sweet and loves flowers, bunnies, little children and all things cute.

There are swirling vines with pretty flowers all over the garden and the house. There is a sweet little old lady standing out front of the house smiling. She is holding Annabelle in her hands. The little old lady's name is Beatrice. She has a very kind face, jaw-length curly hair, almost in ringlets. Her eyes are sweet and kindly and she smiles a lot. She is a dark-skinned woman.

Beatrice is doing some gardening in her front yard. She is planting some flowers in her yard.

–Gwen is standing in front of the house looking at it. She looks frightened. Her parents are busy with getting the boxes moved in to the house; they are not paying attention to her.

Gwen: This house looks haunted.

Mother: (with a box labeled "office") Don't be silly, Gwen!

G: But it does!

–Her mother rushes in with her box, leaving Gwen standing out front.

Father: Come on, Gwen! Get a move on! Start grabbing some boxes. We need to beat the rain.

act the sky does look overcast — rain clouds are starting. The dark sky makes
e house look even spookier.
G: I don't want to go in there! It looks scary!

—Her father looks angry and goes in the house with the last of the boxes. Just then
lightning strikes and rain does starts to pour down.

—Gwen's mother yells from the front door:
M: Gwen! Get inside! You're getting wet!
G: I don't want to!

—The father adds:
F: Stay out there then!

—And he slams the door.

—Just then the sweet little old lady from next door comes over, umbrella in
hand.
(She also has Annabelle). The little old lady's name is Bea.
Bea: Hello, my name is Beatrice. I'm your next-door neighbor.
G: I'm Gwen!
B: Darling, why are you standing out here in the rain?
G: It looks scary in there.
B: New houses always look a little scary.
G: But this one looks haunted.
B: Humm... Well dear, Annabelle here can protect you. She's protected
          me for many years now. Perhaps it's time I passed her on.

—Bea hands Annabelle to Gwen.
G: Can I really have her?
B: Yes, dear heart, you can. But promise me two things: That you will
always   take care of her and from now on you'll call me Aunt Bea!
G: I promise.
B: Very well then. I think you should go inside now, don't you think?
Your   parents are most likely worried.
G: Maybe...

—Aunt Bea leans over and kisses Gwen on the cheek, and walks her to her door.
Aunt Bea rings the bell and her mother answers.
M: Oh hello! I hope Gwen here wasn't bothering you.
B: No, not at all, she's a lovely child. I just wanted to welcome you to the
          neighborhood!
M: Thank you, that's very kind of you.
B: Goodnight, I hope to be seeing you again soon.
M: Goodnight.
G: Bye! (All smiles)

—Gwen's mother is smiling until she closes the door. When the door is closed she shoots Gwen an evil, angry look.

M: Don't ever embarrass me like that again! Do you understand?

G: What did I do?

M: You know exactly what you did! Go up to your room and change this instant! You're soaking wet!

G: But I don't know where anything is.

F: Don't talk back to your mother! You have the count of three to get your ass upstairs, young lady.

–Gwen's eyes get large. She looks at the stairs that look dark and foreboding. And then she looks at her father. She decides her father is much spookier than the dark stairs.

F: ONE!

–Then Gwen shoots up the stairs as fast as she can.

F: That's what I thought.

–Gwen ran up the first set of stairs really fast so she didn't get in trouble with her father. But there is another set of stairs she has to go up so she can get to her attic bedroom.

      The stairs looks very dark and spooky. She walks up them very slowly, feeling frightened. (She has Annabelle.) The stairs are dark, and there are spooky shadows on the wall. It seems there are little eyes looking at her as she goes up the stairs.

G: I don't like it here.

A: Neither do I.

–Gwen is looking at her new bedroom door; it's slightly open. She moves her hand inside the door and along the walls to see if she can feel for a light switch, but there is none.

      She peeks in. The moon is lending a little light to the room — we see boxes piled in the center of the room. The light is in the center of the room hanging from the ceiling with a cord to pull.

–She is too frightened to go in alone. It looks like there are little eyes peeking at her in the dark from behind the boxes in her room.

G: MOM!

M: (yelling from the other room) What?

G: It's dark up here!

M: You heard your father, Gwen!

–Gwen looks frightened. She inches her way to the center of the room where the light is.

      Suddenly she sees that she is surrounded by tiny little eyes in the dark. The creatures are getting closer and closer. The room is filled with the eyes of little creatures. She reaches up to pull the cord so she can turn the light on, but she is too short to reach the cord. She stands on her tip toes but she is still too short.

      She screams!

NIGHTMARES & FAIRYTALES. Tattoos

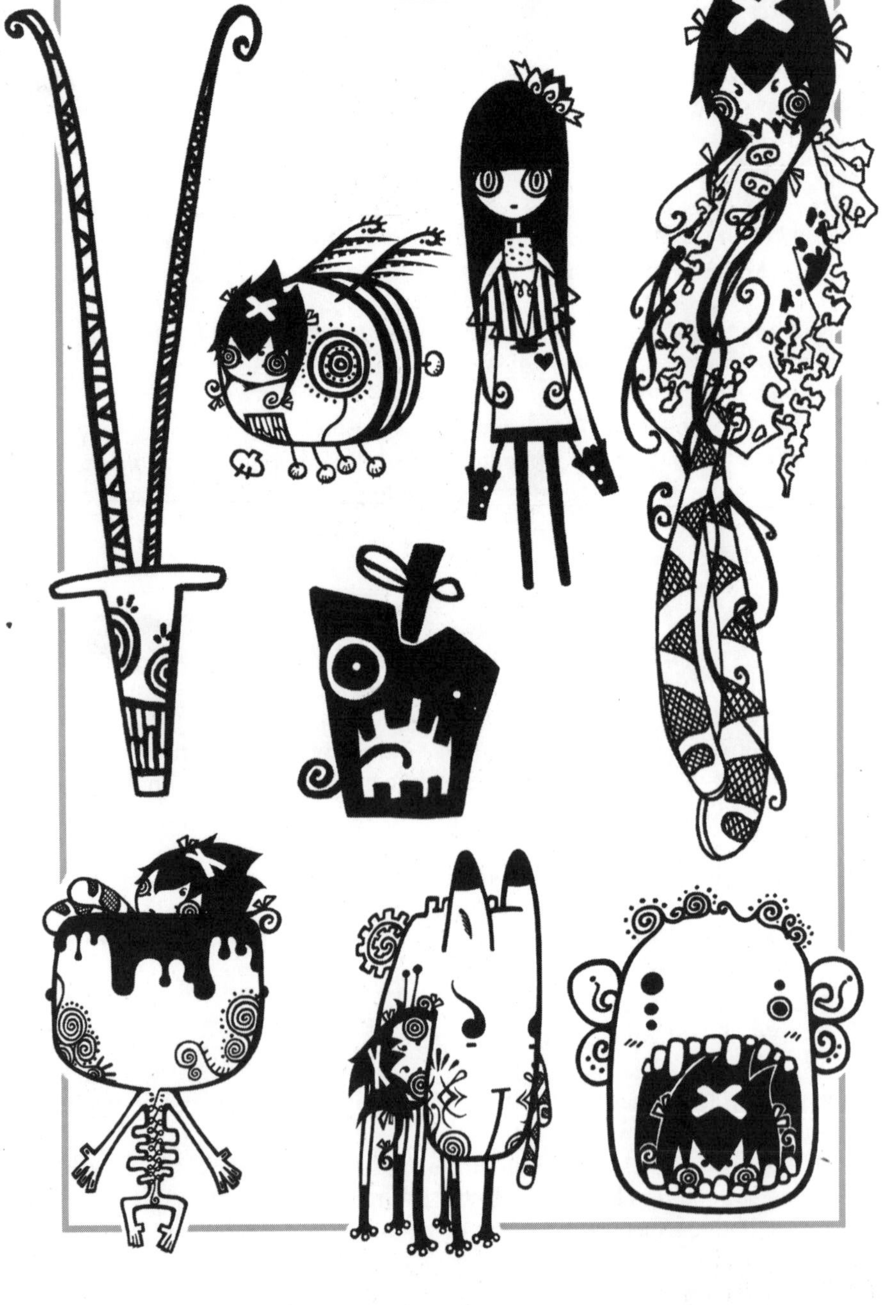